CONFISCATED POWER

By the Same Author

Decline of an Empire: *The Soviet Socialist Republics in Revolt*

CONFISCATED

POWER ☭

How Soviet Russia Really Works

Hélène Carrère d'Encausse

Translated from the French by George Holoch

A Cornelia and Michael Bessie Book

HARPER & ROW, PUBLISHERS, New York
Cambridge, Philadelphia, San Francisco, London
Mexico City, São Paulo, Sydney

This work was first published in France under the title *Le Pouvoir Confisqué*.
© Flammarion, 1980.

FIRST EDITION

Designer: Sidney Feinberg

Library of Congress Cataloging in Publication Data

Carrère d'Encausse, Hélène.
  Confiscated power.
  Translation of: Le pouvoir confisqué.
  Bibliography: p.
  Includes index.
  1. Soviet Union—Politics and government—1953-
2. Elite (Social sciences)—Soviet Union. 3. Social
classes—Soviet Union. 4. Political participation—
Soviet Union. I. Holoch, George. II. Title.
SN6531.C3713   306'.2'0947   82-47521
ISBN 0-06-039009-3   AACR2

---

82 83 84 85 86 10 9 8 7 6 5 4 3 2 1

CONTENTS

Peoples in revolt work only for a few tyrants
and for their own ruin, with as blind an instinct
as silk-worms who die while spinning magnificent
clothing for the elect of a superior nature.

—JONATHAN SWIFT

INTRODUCTION

"The rulers of Russia owe no explanations to anyone. They can reward or punish their subjects as they wish."

This definition of power in Russia comes from Peter the Great. But it has a strangely contemporary ring. It sums up in a few words the nature of Soviet power and the troubled history of its relationship with society.

In October 1917, the Bolsheviks seized the power that the revolutionary masses had taken and were attempting to organize. They transformed popular power into a "dictatorship of the proletariat"—that is, a dictatorship of the party over the proletariat, as over the rest of society. The political system born from this substitution of the party for the masses is based on several principles. The party claims a monopoly of power and a monopoly of ideology. It legitimates this claim by identifying the interests of society with its program and by invoking "historical necessity," the imperatives of class struggle, the support of "Marxist science." This legitimacy owes nothing to society. The party *is* the consciousness of society, and it can therefore find no limits to its power in society.

The condition of Russia in 1917 explains in part how the Communist Party was able to impose this unlimited authority. Its field of action was a country ravaged by war and defeat, a country whose imperial unity had exploded and all of whose social structures had collapsed. The society was ill educated, without political experience, and bewildered by the modernization begun at the end of the nineteenth century, which had been carried out rapidly and had shaken the foundations of the traditional way of life and the values of the past without replacing them with anything else. Moreover, Russia had an old tradition of authoritarian power. If this situation does not suffice to explain the dictatorship that was established, it nevertheless facilitated the Bolsheviks' task and paralyzed any possibility of effective social resistance.

For all that, the Communist dictatorship was not an isolated phenomenon in interwar Europe. One-party states flourished—in Germany, in Italy, and elsewhere. Even if the legitimacy invoked differed from one dictatorial regime to another, they all had common features. A group held substantial power and left no room for any legal protest by any element of society. It ruled through the intermediary of a single party and legitimated its authority by a widely propagated official ideology. It completely controlled the means of communication. Finally, the armed forces and the police were at its complete disposal. Born in Europe, for the most part out of the First World War, one-party dictatorships came to an end after the Second. Defeat or the death of the dictator everywhere tolled the knell for tyranny and allowed the various peoples to resume the path of democracy. At this point the Soviet Union became an exception. Neither the war nor Stalin's death put an end to the one-party dictatorship. The only countries where this continued, on the continent of Europe, were those that draped the dictatorship with the Communist flag. The extraordinary capacity for survival of authoritarian Communist power, while other dictatorships have disappeared, raises several questions.

First of all, is this apparently immutable system identical to the one Lenin and Stalin bequeathed to their successors? It is clear that its forms have not changed. The Communist Party, the only party, still dominates society and justifies its power by repeating the Marxist-Leninist vulgate. But is this party of the same nature as the party of past decades? Are the present leaders in real harmony with the Party and with the elite layers of society? And does the manner in which the system is now organized, and its rules of operation, correspond to those forged by the past?

A second question concerns the relationships between government and society. Although the government has not changed, society has been in a state of constant transformation. Change has come from education, of which the Soviet government is justly proud, from new social demands, and especially because widespread terror has disappeared. Can all this have no effect on relations between this society, which has emerged from the inertia into which it had been plunged by frightful poverty and constant fear, and the government? No doubt the ruling group maintains its power of decision undisturbed. But to what extent can it ignore the needs and wishes of society and escape from social pressures?

A third question is that of the degree and nature of the changes that have taken place, and are still taking place, in the U.S.S.R. during the last quarter century. No doubt the changes carried out in the political system have on the whole been minor, scattered, and sometimes short-lived. But by weighing too carefully the value and scope of each change that has occurred, one eliminates the possibility that minor changes, of little significance considered in isolation, achieve a different impact by their accumulation and represent a qualitatively new factor in political life, capable of deeply modifying it. This leads to a consideration of the conflicts that exist in the U.S.S.R., as in any other society. It is generally accepted that, in the Soviet system, these inevitable conflicts—within or outside the sphere of government—remain completely under the control of the Communist Party, which has surrendered none of its authority. Is it certain that all existing conflicts in the U.S.S.R. remain within this perfect and perfectly effective system of control? Is it not true that certain profound social movements escape from the category of ordinary conflicts and become destabilizing forces that might, at any given moment, weigh on the future of the entire system?

Although it is dangerous to make predictions in this area, it is at least possible to examine the political system, the society, and the relations between them and attempt to understand what contributes to the perpetuation of an anachronistic form of power and what may lead to its transformation. For if we refuse to accept with our eyes closed the idea that the Soviet system survives because it is not an authoritarian system but a manifestation of the "progress of history," there is no more reason to accept without examination the contrary idea that this system alone can escape from the constraints that weigh on all the others, from the necessity of adapting to changes in society and the surrounding world. To attribute the extraordinary survival of Soviet power to its harmony with the laws and the "meaning of history," or to attribute that survival to an exceptional ability to overcome the constraints and burdens of history, amounts to a similar technique of denying the place of man and of human will in the development of human destiny. That is why this book seeks to understand the U.S.S.R. and its political system—through its institutions and their operation, to be sure, but especially through the men who embody those institutions and who submit to or challenge them.

CHAPTER 1

THE POWER OF THE PEOPLE:
MYTH AND REALITY

"All power in the U.S.S.R. belongs to the people," affirms Article Two of the Soviet Constitution of 1977. This postulate dominates more than sixty years of Soviet history and is at the core of the four constitutions which have punctuated that history: 1918, 1924, 1936, and finally 1977. Beyond the documents establishing the Soviet state, the idea of popular power is deeply rooted in the revolution, which was, as the basic texts also assert, the accomplishment of the workers. The idea goes back even further, to the old Russian dream of social justice and to the Marxist utopia. But from dream and utopia to reality, the path followed by those who forged Soviet power is not as straight as might appear. Thus, before examining the present reality of Soviet power, it is important to consider its evolution in fact, not simply as it is reflected in the documents.

Marx's Legacy: State or Freedom?

Heirs of Marx, the Bolsheviks found in their legacy no clear indications about the nature of power in a society that had completed the proletarian revolution.[1] No doubt Marx had discussed the state at length, had described its alienating power and the necessity for people to confront this problem in order to assure their emancipation. But at that point Marx's thought gives rise, if not to a clear contradiction, at least to a perpetual tension between two conceptions of power, a tension that the Bolsheviks have not resolved. First of all, it is striking to note Marx's insistence on the state as the privileged framework for social relations. Even though Marx's political thought cannot be restricted to his reflections on the state—in his eyes, the economy is the principal historical location of the political relations of human societies—by linking the state and class interests, Marx constantly reintroduces the state into his conception of power. Moreover, he saw in the state both "an organization of the property-owning class designed to protect it against the propertyless class"[2] and the concentration, the incarnation in a specialized body of leaders—politicians, bureaucrats, soldiers, police—of the powers of society. The state is thus, at one and the same time, a monster created by society that has turned against its creator to dominate it, and an apparatus for the domination by the property owners over the rest of society. From this dual vision of the state flow two opposed certainties: There is permanent opposition between state and society; or else, on the contrary, the state is always an instrument of society, of a particular class in society—the economically dominant class before the revolution, the proletariat thereafter.

The "dictatorship of the proletariat," proposed by Marx as a form of organization of society immediately after the revolution, does not resolve the tension we have noted in his thought. Although he ardently called for this dictatorship of the proletariat and considered it a decisive stage on the road to human emancipation, he nevertheless did not say that it was a *just* political order. If we follow Marx's thought closely, we find in the end a dual aspiration. There is the fundamental anarchism of the thinker, the philosopher, who places human freedom at the summit of his system of values and who thinks that *freedom* and *state* are antithetical. This conviction shows through in the *Critique of the Gotha Program,* in which he challenged the

German Workers' Party's ambition to create a "free state." Moreover, Engels demonstrated the same skepticism with respect to the compatibility of the state with freedom when he suggested that the concept of the state ought to be replaced with that of community *(gemeinwesen)* which the French of 1870 called the Commune.[3] Anarchist in his philosophical views, in the political arena Marx became an enemy of anarchism. He maintained that the anarchists' revolutionary strategy—the immediate and definitive destruction of the state—was a serious mistake, for he believed that the proletariat could gain prominence precisely by conquering the state. Furthermore, he disagreed with the anarchists about the basic problem of the cause of the oppression humanity had suffered through the centuries. For the anarchists, the state was the cause of all oppression; it was an absolute evil, evil incarnate, and therefore the revolution must take the state as its target. Without in any way justifying the state, Marx and Engels considered it a consequence of the oppression of which economic relations were the basis. If the suppression of the state was to be considered, that would occur at the end of a long revolution, in the course of which the proletariat would as a first step take charge of the state.

The Russian Legacy: State or Anarchy?

Among Marx's heirs, those who were most sensitive to this debate and most directly concerned were the Russian socialists. For them, the choice between the philosophical-anarchist and political-statist variants of Marxism presented itself in an urgent manner. This was true first of all because they encountered the two tendencies—statism and anarchism—in their own country. As Nikolai Berdyaev said, "The Russian people has been a statist people, it has agreed to serve as raw material for the construction of a great state. And at the same time it is inclined toward revolt and disorder."[4]

Here we enter the domain of the peculiar and difficult legacy of the Russian past. The state, its power, and its disproportionate authority over a society which could not succeed in organizing itself were brought to Russia by the Mongol invaders. The state survived by borrowing many characteristics from them, and it justified its continued existence by the need to protect an immense territory which was constantly threatened and invaded. Society accepted the omnipotence of the state and its intervention in every domain for various reasons: because, following the insecurity of the age of invasions, it was the only hope for safety; because, further, the Russian people had been totally cut off from the external world, ignorant of it, and frightened by it; because, finally, the government transmitted a self-justifying ideology which combined an appeal to a quasi-mystical nationalism with the idea that Russian society was a fraternal, egalitarian, and just community.[5]

Until the turn of the twentieth century, Russia was thus organized according to a patriarchal model in which the state and the sovereign were identified with one another, and where their authority, supported by the Orthodox Church, made the sovereign head of state the earthly representative and the double of a paternal God, equally concerned with all his children. The people's adhesion to this model can be understood if we remember that this was a peasant society, whose life was enveloped in a religious cloak mingling the notions of Russia, of power, and of common life. The entire political and social vocabulary of the pre-revolutionary period refers to this communitarian and patriarchal system of values. Society was united in the Orthodox Church by the central notion of *sobornost*— that is, by the feeling of belonging to a living and fraternal community, the community of believers. No other Christian church had developed the sense of community to such an extent. Power always had a paternal connotation, since the sovereign was first of all the father of his people, *batushka*. In the same way, authority in the villages lay with the elders, *starosta*, and the master of the house, *khoziain* (a term which refers principally to his authority over things), was the *starchyi*—that is, the elder, in relation to his family. Berdyaev has emphasized that the idea most familiar to this people dominated by the state was the idea of "social justice"; the idea of freedom which stirred Western and Central Europe throughout the nineteenth century found few echoes in Russia.[6] This desire for social justice, rooted in the consciousness of the Russian people, the center of its political culture, had as a consequence another deep tendency of the people: latent anarchism.

Russian history is made up of long periods of submission to domination, by the Mongols and by the state. But it is made in equal measure of sporadic popular uprisings that suddenly and violently rejected all domination. The men who channeled and led these uprisings, like Stenka Razin and E.I. Pugachev,[7] took on legendary status and have always occupied a considerable space in the Russian collective consciousness. Mikhail Bakunin understood this anarchism latent in Russian society and concluded that, beneath the obedient postures imposed on society by the government, anarchism impregnated social consciousness and made up its real basis. For Bakunin, society's adhesion to the state was only an appearance. The Russian, a perpetual rebel, submitted to the state but never developed a statist consciousness. The state was alien. The Russian state of the nineteenth century—an amalgam produced by Mongol influence combined with the Western—more precisely, German—interests of the enlightened rulers Peter the Great and Catherine II —owed nothing, according to Bakunin, to popular culture and its traditions. Thus Bakunin distinguished the innate insurrectional force he detected in the Russian people from the statism that he saw as a purely foreign contribution to which that force was opposed. Indeed, the development of Russian revolutionary thought in the nineteenth century essentially followed this anarchist direction and justified Bakunin's analysis. The Russian intelligentsia, distant from power, set itself up more and more strongly as a force that challenged the existing system and saw an opposition between state and change, state and society.[8] The populists who, in the 1860s, wanted to "go to the people" felt, like Bakunin, a deep revulsion for any form of state and saw the future without any state at all.

At the turn of the century, when the Russian revolutionary movement was organized and moved from philosophical to political debate about the forms and aims of action, the question of power and its organization became central for each group or party. The Socialist Revolutionary Party, the offspring of Marx and the populists, moved away from populist anarchism and admitted that revolutionary power could take on state forms.[9] No doubt the Socialist Revolutionaries, who saw the revolution as a movement from below that was to sweep away hierarchical authority, were aware of the need to permanently weaken the state, to place it under popular control in order to prevent a return to the old dichotomy between state and society. Nevertheless, even before the revolution, they participated in the statist direction undertaken by Russian revolutionary thought. As for the Social Democrats, who proclaimed themselves the only authentic disciples of Marx, they carried on interminable discussions about the directions Russian development should follow. Did Russia have to travel the hard road of capitalism? In this debate, the question of the nature of revolutionary power was relegated to secondary status. In fact, this omission was logical. For one faction of the Social Democrats, the Mensheviks, convinced that a long historical process had to be gone through before a revolution would be possible, the problem of power remained out of reach. As for their adversaries, the Bolsheviks, their position was that of Lenin, who concentrated his attention on the technical problem of the *seizure* of power, its ways and means. This explains why Lenin did not really raise the question of the *nature* of revolutionary power until the moment when he was about to establish it, when the revolution was already in full cry.

From Theory to Action: Power Snatched from the Kitchen Maid

State and Revolution, the only work by Lenin that deals thoroughly with the problems of power and the state, was written in the feverish atmosphere of the summer of 1917. The work reveals above all Lenin's haste, the ambiguities of the Marxist debate, and the complexity of the Russian situation. The mixture of all these incompatible elements explains the difficulty of interpreting *State and Revolution.* [10] Lenin clearly proclaims that the post-revolutionary state belongs to all, that it requires no special competence, that a simple "kitchen maid" could take care of its management. But at the same time he describes the dictatorship of the proletariat as a perfectly organized and disciplined state system, in which the attribution of tasks, the allocation of skills and responsibilities, is not at all improvised. This book, which is simultaneously anarchist and statist, mirrors the tension in Marx's thought and the debates that had divided the revolutionaries since Marx. But when Lenin wrote it, the problem of power had emerged from the intellectual framework within which it had until then been confined into the difficult domain of practice.

The imperial state collapsed in February 1917; the provisional government was unable to reconstruct a viable state system, and the Bolshevik revolution had as its function less the seizure of power than the channeling, harnessing, and organization of growing anarchy.[11] In October 1917 there was no longer any single organized power in Russia, but rather a proliferation and juxtaposition of particular powers that had risen from below and were embodied in innumerable committees in the cities and the countryside.[12] The "kitchen maid's power" existed and was spontaneously exercised. The problem the Bolsheviks confronted was that of their attitude toward these spontaneous powers. Should they ratify them and encourage this spontaneity, this dispersal of power through society? Should they reconstruct a political framework outside the rank-and-file power centers? Or should they establish a system to organize and integrate those centers?

Lenin's personal response was immediately devoid of ambiguity, even if the terms he used still fostered ambiguity and concealed his choice. From his return to Russia in April 1917, at the moment when the slippage of power from the provisional government to the soviets was accelerating, Lenin proclaimed "all power to the soviets" and seemed to encourage by that very statement the anarchist orientation of the revolution. But everything indicates that his analysis of the evolution of Russia had already led him in fact to counter growing anarchism with a coherent political order. His appeal was not an act of faith in the power of the soviets but a recognition of the situation he had found in Russia. The revolution was going forward and developing in the soviets, which were, in the spring of 1917, the expression of authentic popular power. Because he had become aware of this, Lenin decided to use the soviets as an instrument for the seizure of power, and to infiltrate them with Bolsheviks in order to do this. His party, conceived of as a revolutionary apparatus, in no way put itself at the service of the soviets; quite the contrary, the party would "penetrate" the soviets and turn them into an instrument for the triumph of bolshevism.[13]

As soon as he had taken power with his party and in its name, on October 25, 1917, all Lenin's decisions pointed in the same direction: They confirmed a government that had its own logic and techniques, that imposed itself on society and refused to bend to the whims of society. This choice by Lenin in favor of a real government breaking with the surrounding anarchism is indicated by three decisions he made in the weeks following the revolution. These decisions, badly understood at the time, had a critical effect on Soviet power in the succeeding decades. The first was the creation, at the very moment when the revolution was unfolding, of an embryo of repressive power over which society had no control. Marx had always emphasized that popular power depended on one essential condition: that the instruments of repression (police and army) be under popular control.[14] A government which holds in its hands one of these organisms of authority is already no longer a popular government. At the very moment when he was about to take power, Lenin created, within the small cell that was carrying out his plan, the Revolutionary Military Committee (the Cheka), a police power. He gave his old comrade-in-arms Feliks Dzerzhinski the responsibility of setting up this instrument of repression. In Lenin's mind, this was no doubt merely a matter of struggling against the adversaries of the revolution. It is nevertheless significant that he did not assign this task of revolutionary protection to the people who had risen in revolt with him, but created a specialized repressive instrument removed from the outset from popular initiative and supervision. From this still embryonic police cell emerged the most formidable repressive apparatus of the twentieth century, Stalin's GPU and the KGB of today. The bond that unites these institutions through their various stages is logical and inevitable. By considering that a specialized body, outside society, was needed to defend the revolution, Lenin implicitly chose to consolidate the revolution in a state that would be distinct from society.

Lenin's second choice was no less decisive. What kind of government was to be drawn from a revolution in which many tendencies and political groups participated? The masses, when they expressed themselves (through the powerful railroad workers' union, for example), were in favor of a broad coalition of opposing parties. It seemed normal to them that all existing revolutionary parties be represented in the government that was in the process of formation. Within his own party, Lenin found numerous supporters of this position. However, with a tenacity that was all the more remarkable because he was practically isolated, Lenin rejected the idea of establishing a coalition socialist government and managed to impose his will.[15]

Finally and above all, his attitude toward the Constituent Assembly indicated the nature of his choice. The elections for the Constituent Assembly, organized immediately after the October revolution, were a repudiation of Lenin. Popular suffrage favored the Socialist Revolutionary Party, which peasant society considered its surest representative. Out of 707 seats filled, the Socialist Revolutionaries won 410, Lenin's party only 175. To be sure, a split developed within the Socialist Revolutionary Party, and the left (forty seats) quit and joined the Bolsheviks; but this did not make them into the majority. From this popular vote which ratified a pluralistic politics, Lenin drew an authoritarian lesson. Society, he said, had not taken into account the changes that had taken place; the vote which expressed this backward consciousness therefore had no value. And, following a consistent logic, he dissolved the Constituent Assembly, thereby placing above popular suffrage the interests of his party and his interpretation of events and of the general interest.

From the beginning of 1918, relations between Bolshevik power and society were thus clarified. For Lenin, the Bolshevik Party (and the government based on it, in which the element of coalition was reduced to the presence of a few left-wing Socialist Revolutionaries alongside the Bolsheviks) was not only the vanguard of society and its consciousness but the guardian of social interests and desires that society does not always see clearly. Popular power, which manifested itself between February and October 1917, disappeared from that moment on, to be replaced by Bolshevik power. By excluding from government the parties the society had voted for, by suppressing the Constituent Assembly that had emerged from general elections, by placing the entire press under Bolshevik control, by establishing a police organization (which incidentally had to be rapidly developed in order to impose these various decisions and prevent the organization of opposition parties or committees), Lenin created, in a very brief space of time, a perfectly coherent system of power, one which escaped from society and dominated it.[16] A final stage had yet to be reached: depriving the soviets (a survival of rank-and-file power) of all substance and transferring their functions to the center and to the Party. This stage was completed by 1919.

Lenin justified this confiscation of power, from society and from the insurrectionary workers of 1917, by the exigencies of a revolution which had to be saved from internal and external threats.[17] But in considering the sequence of events, the historian notes that the choice between power *of* the workers and power exercised *in the name of* the workers was made at the outset, even before the dangers became apparent. By this choice, the kitchen maid lost all hope of participating in the management of the state; indeed, Lenin was prompt to ridicule that utopia, which he characterized as a "fairy tale."[18]

Although the dictatorship of the proletariat very soon took on the form of a centralized state power from which workers' committees were excluded, the Bolsheviks nevertheless did not intend to restore a traditional state. The new state they created was not, in their mind, to assume the domination of one class over another. What is more, it could not, they thought, since the economic foundations of the traditional state (private ownership of the means of production) had disappeared. The Bolsheviks thought they embodied a totally unprecedented type of power. They owed the power they held neither to any measurable force, nor to a material base, nor to the social group from which they came, but to an intangible historical phenomenon: They were the consciousness of the proletariat, the product of the course of history. What justified their power was their certainty that the logic of history was on their side. Their power was legitimate because they embodied the proletariat, its historical interests and its will. The apparent contradictions among the diverse wishes of the workers (expressed in votes and in support for other political groups) hardly mattered. If there was any contradiction, it resulted from the fact that the proletariat was not always capable of determining where historical necessity was located. Lenin had already thought before 1917 that historical necessity and the proletariat's perception of that necessity were far from coinciding; he had concluded that, in order to remedy this situation, it was necessary to create a vanguard party, the guardian of a true vision of historical necessity and thereby responsible for leading the proletariat.

There is no need to emphasize that this absolute certainty of embodying historical necessity had a nearly religious character and that it was beyond any logical explanation. Nor is there any need to emphasize that the legitimacy that flowed from it was not fundamentally different from the legitimacy of Christian sovereigns "anointed by the Lord," who justified their power by the invocation of immanent necessity. These systems for the legitimation of authority, which call upon the conviction of those on whom the authority is imposed, imply the existence of a coherent ideological system, explicitly formulated and mobilizing society around clear common values. Ideologies of this type cannot be spread in a vague manner. They demand a weighty apparatus that directs, educates, and reassures society and keeps it constantly in contact with the certainties which are the basis of power. This explains the fact that ideology occupies a central place in the Soviet system, that it covers the whole spectrum of social and private activities, and that it penetrates all areas of individual and group existence. It also explains the fact that—whatever the real evolution of the U.S.S.R., whatever changes may have come about, and however great the distance may be between the fundamental principles of Soviet ideology, on the one hand, and reality and the convictions and reactions of the citizens on the other—the function of ideology has been to maintain an unchanged, immutable discourse, assuring society at every moment that reality and the original plan coincide. It explains, finally, the importance in Soviet society of the group that is the guardian of the ideology: the Party.

This initial choice (which was derived, it is worth recalling, from faith and not from a rational analysis of the facts) has involved specific constricting consequences for the Soviet system. It must be, and must remain, an ideological system; and a system with a monopoly on ideology, because admitting the existence of other ideologies would amount to accepting a challenge to the "truth" underlying the system. It must also be a system directed by a single political organization, because the existence of competing organizations would have as a corollary the competition among different kinds of truth. "Truth," when it is derived from faith, is indivisible and not subject to discussion. From Lenin's initial choice—power monopolized by the Party in the name of a historical necessity of which it was simultaneously the bearer, the arbiter, and the guarantor—flowed the entire Soviet system as it came to be organized: a single monolithic party, and an ideology in possession of a monopoly on the truth. From this choice also came the fact that the Soviet system might change its methods or choices, but the mono-organizational and mono-ideological system remained inviolable, for this inviolability was the source of its legitimacy and invulnerability.[19]

The Birth of Privileges

As the founder of the system, Lenin immediately recognized all its consequences. This is why he strengthened his party and assured its internal coherence by having the Tenth Congress adopt, in March 1921, the rule forbidding the establishment of internal factions. But growing authoritarianism was not the only side to Lenin's activity. As a minimum, he attempted to bring the "power of the workers," the only power certified by the ideology, closer to the workers themselves, to make the living conditions of those in power and those who produced the same, by means of material egalitarianism.[20] During the years Lenin was in control, we witness the development of an egalitarian ideology according to which the lowly, though deprived of power, nevertheless embody a social model. Thus, various measures taken at the beginning of the regime were designed to prevent those in power from becoming privileged figures, to remove any material basis from their power.

The model, for Lenin, was the Paris Commune, where those who exercised public functions were supposed to be paid less than the workers.[21] A decree of November 18, 1917, fixed a ceiling for the salary that could be received by a manager or an official of the new system. At this time, when a highly skilled worker earned approximately 400 rubles a month, the maximum authorized for a people's commissar or an official at the same level was set at 500 rubles, to which could be added 100 rubles for each nonworking member of the family. The right to housing was also strictly regulated. No one at that rank was entitled to more than one room per person. No doubt these rigorous provisions still left room for situations which, compared to the surrounding poverty and unemployment and to the crowding of the urban population in communal apartments, made those who gravitated to the spheres of power privileged beings. But Lenin was careful to reduce these privileges as much as possible, and his own austerity served as a model for those around him.[22] But even at this early stage the egalitarian impulse came up against two realities, one economic, the other political. The economic factor emerged at the end of the harsh period of "war communism," when the Soviet regime had been on the point of drowning in the poverty and discontent of a society which, in the spring of 1921, in town and country, was rising up against it. To save the system, to restore it to life, Lenin gave up war communism in 1921 and opted for the New Economic Policy (NEP). This choice was a pause in the march toward communism, giving time to restore the economy to life. For peasants to go back to work and for industry to start moving again, it was necessary to loosen constraints, to allow material incentives to operate, and to encourage initiative and ability. This meant, in the country, that peasants could grow richer provided they produced enough to feed the cities; and, in industry, that those who were absolutely necessary, the "specialists," would be attracted by the offer of wages appropriate to their skills. As currency, which had almost disappeared during the years of war communism, gradually resumed its role, these financial stimulants had real significance from the very beginning. They introduced into professional life a hierarchy that grew rapidly.

Was it possible to reward professional competence financially and at the same time keep political personnel and the growing bureaucracy apart from this hierarchical structure of earnings? As soon as equality was sacrificed to economic necessity, it was clear that political workers would benefit from the same advantages. Were they too not an absolute necessity for the system?

At this point, Lenin attempted to contain as much as he could the return to an inegalitarian system.[23] A decree of June 23, 1921, specified that the wages of political cadres were not to exceed 150 percent of the average wage of the enterprise where they worked. But these provisions were very soon superseded by a more rapid progression than had been foreseen in the pay received by political cadres, and also by the fact that the cadres often undertook extra work, thereby increasing their earnings. By March 21, 1925, a new decree drew the logical conclusion and widened the spread of political salaries, which were already known to oscillate generally between three and four times the average worker's pay.[24] But wages were not the essential question. From this period on, when the Soviet regime was hesitating between egalitarianism and an empirical approach to its problems, egalitarian proclamations and limitations imposed on the wages of those with political responsibilities had only minor significance, for money and pecuniary rewards were far from being the only means of livelihood. Penury has its laws in every set of circumstances. It creates circuits by which one acquires goods because one is in a position to acquire them, more than because of the money at one's disposal.

What counted in the years following the revolution in Russia was food and lodging. The food-rationing measures adopted in 1917 and extended in the following years had the function of distributing insufficient goods according to social and utilitarian criteria. In the workers' state, the worker was king and had the right to the largest rations. The various categories of survivors of the old regime—aristocrats, bourgeois, clergy, nonworkers—were on the lowest rung of the social ladder and were often not even taken into account in rationing provisions. But criteria of utility very soon complicated this pattern. The government first decided to favor the specialists, who were indispensable to the operation of the country. Because Russia was fighting against epidemic illnesses in 1919, a decree of April 10 granted special food rations to doctors and nurses. On April 30, 1920, blue- and white-collar workers in enterprises of particular economic importance, workers involved in dangerous activities, and non-manual workers with exceptional qualifications received in turn similar advantages. Was it possible to favor in the same way all public officials and those who gravitated around the government? Since this extension of privileges to the political sphere ran so counter to egalitarian ideology, the government chose, during the war communism period and even more in the following years, to combine official egalitarianism with the clandestine practice of special advantages. Members of the government and their families, members of the Party, the police, the army, the various bureaucracies resolved their material problems by creating a whole parallel economic system, which gave their members access to cafeterias, restaurants, and specialized stores closed to the outside world, indeed barely known to it. There was thus established a hierarchical order to society, following unwritten but perfectly functioning rules. For example, as early as 1918, there were special rations *(paek)* in the army that were so much larger than the norm that many nonmilitary applicants got themselves fraudulently enrolled on army registers in order to take advantage of them.

Because of penury, behind legal equality, a de facto inequality thus developed, and every social category that benefited from this inequality was careful to conceal it, because it was a complete break with the affirmation so strongly and constantly reiterated that the Soviet state was a workers' state. The only privileges that were admitted were those enjoyed by the specialists, precisely because they helped to justify the egalitarian thesis. The specialists were, in general, from the old privileged classes; their momentarily necessary advantages were a final sacrifice to a disappearing world, and the specialists themselves were destined to disappear.

To economic inequality, official or concealed, was added political inequality. As we have seen, Lenin restored repressive institutions in 1917. The years of civil war and struggle against the adversaries of the regime made the police an instrument of great strength whose functions (repressive and judicial) covered the entire society. However, these functions had a limit that Lenin had established at the outset. The Party was outside the scrutiny of the police.[25] By setting up a protective cordon around it, Lenin granted his Party a form of security that the rest of society was far from enjoying. He also granted it an impunity that allowed it to accumulate material advantages not always authorized by law. By thus shielding political circles from the common law and the common fate, Lenin helped widen the gap between this nascent political class and society; above all, he helped forge a homogeneous social body: Soviet bureaucracy.[26]

While inegalitarian practices were developing and privileged groups were being established, the ideology transmitted a social model in conformity with the aspirations of the revolution. What official speeches endlessly repeated, newspapers printed, and novelists were called on to express was the epic of the lowly, the fraternal universe of men sharing a single fate.[27] By its language and attitudes, the Soviet government denied the reality which was coming into being. It hung on to the myth of hard times in which the working class, triumphant on Russian soil, paid the price of its solitude on the international level. This was already a sketch for the later explanation that legitimated the differentiations beginning to take shape in the U.S.S.R.; since the revolution had triumphed in only one country, it had to adapt itself to this unexpected situation.

The years during which the Soviet state was created, the years marked by Lenin's personality, were in the end characterized by choices (willed or not) which oriented the Soviet system in a particular direction, foreign to the original utopia and to the objectives defined by the revolution. Power (political or technical) moved away from the rank and file; it became a matter for specialists. At the beginning of the century, when Lenin had attempted to define the means of revolution in *What Is to Be Done?*, he quickly concluded that the revolution had no room for amateurism and spontaneous initiatives, that it demanded professionals and rigorous organization. As master of the government in 1917, Lenin applied to the exercise of power the rules he had elaborated for the exercise of revolution. The professionalization and rigorous organization of power (foreign to revolutionary utopia) is a constant of Leninist thought.

The government which developed in the years between 1917 and 1923, when Lenin dominated the Soviet political scene, very soon became bureaucratic, authoritarian, routine. This evolution took place all the more easily because, from the very beginning, the government escaped from the control of society. From the ruins of the imperial state of 1917 emerged, almost immediately, a new state which, like all the states denounced by the revolutionaries, relied on instruments of constraint under its exclusive control.[28] The power and the field of operation of these institutions of constraint never ceased to grow.[29]

Dispossessed of power and of the means to control it, society from this point on had no means of expression outside the ruling party. The only possibility it had of bridging the gap which separated it from the government was to identify itself totally with the government and to assert that that government was an emanation of society. The ruling stratum, by establishing a hierarchy in the distribution of available material goods and by organizing privileges, had in a few years divided the social community into particular categories distinguished by their access to goods; they had thus given power a material base. To be sure, privileges were not granted in equal measure to all the categories that might benefit from them, and differences in status appeared among various categories. We can thus detect four varieties of status that created at least four social groups (each one unified around its particular advantages) that stood out from the rest of society by the early twenties.[30] The specialists, who could be openly favored because of their social origins, received high pay. Political leaders (Party, state, police), whose advantages could not be recognized, had strictly controlled wages calculated on the basis of workers' wages, but these salary limitations were compensated for by exceptional administrative advantages and by a system of distribution of rare goods (food, housing, transportation). The army very soon added to their material advantages (special stores, eating facilities, housing) a pay scale that was above average (and improved even more by the right to earn funds from supplementary work), a particularly advantageous pension system, educational privileges for the children of soldiers (priority of admission to higher education and exemption from fees), and so on. Finally, the creative intelligentsia (academicians, writers, artists, lawyers, doctors, researchers, and the like), to the degree that it agreed to cooperate with the government, was the object of the government's favors: special rations established in the early twenties, housing (the law of January 16, 1922 granted an extra room to researchers for their work; in 1924, that provision was extended to everyone whose intellectual activities "require the provision of appropriate quarters"), travel, and especially, from 1925, the presentation of prizes rewarding creative activities, prizes which, along with significant amounts of money, provided various advantages of prestige and status.

There was thus created in a few short years, on the margin of the workers' society, a society of the favored, who sometimes displayed their privileges and sometimes, as in the case of those with political responsibilities, concealed them behind the fiction of modest wages. Whether it was admitted or not, social differentiation had all the more weight because it was linked to a possible perpetuation of these differences through the opportunities for access to higher education.

In this area, too, the aims declared by the Bolshevik government were generous and egalitarian. On August 2, 1918, it proclaimed a general right to higher education and, in a first phase, set up a quota system to promote the admission of workers to workers' institutes (Rabfak, or preparatory courses leading to higher education for the workers).[31] At the same time, the universities were virtually closed to applicants from non-working-class backgrounds, who were subjected to a draconian system of selection and obliged to pay excessive fees (nearly ten times the ordinary fees, from which working-class applicants could moreover be totally exempted).

But these provisions favorable to the workers were soon limited, first of all because access to the universities was also a political privilege. The quota system gave to Party organizations (notably the Central Committee), to the Komsomol (the Communist youth organization) and to the unions the right to push their own candidates for higher education. It is clear that the political cadres were quick to use this privilege to assure the education of their children. As early as 1923–24, the government granted special privileges in this area to certain categories. Children of soldiers (generally of officers) and of the army's political cadres were placed on an equal footing with workers and poor peasants as far as rights were concerned. In succeeding years, the "creative" intelligentsia also benefited from ease of admission, the exemption from fees, and the provision of scholarships for their children, and in March 1926 they were even given a quota of places in the universities of the Russian Federal Republic. No doubt, workers were still encouraged to obtain higher education, but the Soviet state already felt the need to open the universities as a first priority to those who were the best prepared intellectually and politically. It is therefore hardly surprising that in 1930 only one third of the students in Russian universities came from working-class or peasant backgrounds.

The Soviet government in its early years established a difficult compromise between the ideals of the revolution and the problems it confronted. With the elimination of the czarist bureaucracy, the Bolsheviks still had to take care of the "management of things." Refusing to leave this management to society as a whole, monopolizing power (which they very quickly asserted was a matter for professionals), they had to find the cadres for the new state. And they could not find them in their own ranks. At the outbreak of the revolution, the Bolshevik Party included barely twenty thousand militants, and they were decimated by the battles of the civil war or absorbed by the emerging institutions. A popular government, the Bolshevik government recruited from the people those who would participate in the management and control of the country at all levels. The twenties were in this respect years of promotion *(vydvizhenie)*, when workers and peasants moved directly from field or factory to positions of authority. Through these promotions, the Party rewarded political fidelity, the adhesion to its doctrine and its rules by the "children of the people." By this desire to promote the "best" popular elements, the Party resolved, in its way, the dilemma of power. No doubt the popular revolution led in a few months to a political system confiscated from the forces "from below." But those who took care of its operation were, uncontestably, elements who had emerged from the people. When, after 1921, the government momentarily compromised with bourgeois specialists, it normally attached to the engineer or factory manager recruited in this way a "red director" who, by his very vigilant presence, indicated the fragility of the agreement with the specialists and the Party's distrust of them. The same thing occurred in the army, where the political commissar was set over the officer who had come from the czar's army. This government external to the people, but made up of those who had risen from its ranks, very soon faced problems of effectiveness because of the lack of training of these improvised leaders. The Soviet press of the time bears witness to the constant movement of cadres, which assured the promotion of a considerable number of workers and the simultaneous elimination of a no less impressive number of those who had just been promoted. In certain cases, the rate of turnover reached 50 percent for a few months.[32]

As the years passed, the Soviet regime nevertheless tried to establish an effective administration, and it conceded authority and privileges to those whose abilities or political loyalty were indispensable. But despite the inequalities that developed in the course of the twenties, despite the space carved out by "bourgeois specialists" in the economic system, despite the growing professionalization of the political personnel, these years were above all characterized by extraordinary social mobility, several aspects of which need to be emphasized.

In the first place, this mobility was more prevalent in the political domain, which was totally open to the rising popular strata, and more limited in the economic and intellectual domains, where a certain level of qualification was necessary. Moreover, despite the great insecurity of positions at the time, this mobility had lasting consequences for many of those it affected. The elites from the old regime who had been eliminated could scarcely, with a few exceptions, later reenter the spheres of power or intellectual activity. For those on the rise, despite the high rate of failure, promotion could definitively affect their place in society. Finally, and this is probably the essential point, these changes in status were not limited to those directly involved but in most cases affected the future status of their children. It was not individuals but whole families whose position on the social scale was thus changed. These changes were still only sketched out at the end of the twenties. But Stalin's great social revolution and his system of government by "permanent purge" completed the process of giving new contours to post-revolutionary Soviet society.

Stalinist Political Culture: Inequality and Insecurity

The industrial revolution of 1929 and collectivization suddenly gave social mobility unprecedented dimensions: geographic mobility, whereby peasants were moved to factories or construction sites and workers displaced as large projects required, and mobility of status, since peasants were excluded from development and considered enemies of progress, forced to participate against their will. Positions of responsibility were closed off to these permanent suspects. Conversely, the workers, leaders of industrial development, became as a result of the war the government declared against the peasantry in 1929, the only laboring class on which Soviet power could rely. Industrialization, collectivization, and the development of the bureaucracy required increasing supervision for all the political, repressive, and technical tasks. The possibilities of acceding to positions of responsibility had never been so great since 1917. But development has its inherent demands, chief among them being competence. From the early thirties on, competence became a central preoccupation of the Soviet government, and in order to stimulate it the government authorized a partial renunciation of the egalitarian ideal that had been maintained until then, at least officially. Stalin spoke clearly on this point as early as 1931, emphasizing that, when a country needs technicians, their usefulness must be taken into account in determining their wages, and he demanded that they be treated differently from common laborers. The consequence of this approach was a growing differentiation of wages which Stalin ratified.

There was differentiation of wages between categories and within each category. The position of three groups—political personnel, productive workers, and creative intelligensia—throws light on this evolution.

Little is generally known about the first group, for during Stalin's rule information about its material situation became rare, in contrast to what had been the norm in the twenties. But by juxtaposing various pieces of data, one can estimate that, around 1934, when the average worker's wage was 150 rubles a month, ordinary district or regional officials earned between 250 and 500 rubles a month, while the highest-paid members of this group earned approximately 800 rubles.

Although the earnings gap between average workers and political officials tended to widen, it was nevertheless not substantial and did not really contradict the practice of the preceding years. We can get a better sense of the Stalinist revolution by considering earnings policy in industry. Here the salary scale was constantly changing. While the average worker earned 150 rubles and the lowest-paid laborer earned 63, those at the top of the scale had wages above 1,000 rubles. Still more significant, bonuses granted to particular factories—to reward their efficiency, high levels of output, or the savings they were able to accomplish—were distributed within each factory according to hierarchical position. The highest paid received the largest bonuses, while the lowest wages were barely increased. During the thirties there thus emerged a rigid hierarchy of labor which was consolidated by constantly growing material differences.[33]

In certain areas of activity, the incomes of individuals considered particularly useful to society were still more striking. This was the case in the army; lower-ranked officers were already better paid than workers (approximately twice the average wage), and higher-ranked officers earned nearly 2,000 rubles a month. This was also true for intellectuals who joined the unions created in the early thirties (the Writers' Union, the first of these, was created in 1932) and whose official status as intellectuals guaranteed them an income that could exceed 2,000 rubles a month; but here too there were many inequalities.

A comparison of the incomes of various social categories in the mid-thirties leads to two immediate conclusions. The working class, theoretical holder of power in the U.S.S.R., was the great victim of the policy of income differentiation which was then rapidly developing. At the time, money and material incentives were no longer objects of contempt; quite the contrary, they rewarded competence and usefulness. And workers' wages suggested that their usefulness was evaluated at an infinitely lower price than that of soldiers or industrial managers. A second conclusion that can be drawn is that political cadres remained substantially more modest in their material demands than their equivalents in industry or than the intellectuals. But the truth lies elsewhere. The official documents on incomes policy reveal to those who consult them only one aspect, known monetary income. But the picture is complicated by what these documents leave out, the material or psychological advantages given to certain social categories. These advantages particularly affected the position of those who moved in the circles of power. Although Stalin was in fact inclined to sanction officially the inequalities linked to competence and knowledge in the economic sphere, he was not prepared to do the same for the distance that separated the working class from those who held political power in its place. In the case of the economy, he could invoke the necessities of development to justify his inegalitarian choices. But could he admit that the working class, disfavored by its lack of capacity and education, had been dispossessed of its natural power as well by a ruling group that derived the right to considerable material benefits from its function? To admit that political cadres had exorbitant economic rights could be to admit that nothing remained of the old utopia of justice and equality. This explains the government's remarkable discretion whenever the income of the "political strata" at all levels was at issue. This also explains why the hidden privileges of these strata multiplied and made their nominal wages completely meaningless.

In the thirties, problems of daily survival were crucial. The continuous fall in agricultural production from 1928 to 1934 and the destruction by the peasants, driven to despair by collectivization, of the Soviet stock of cattle had as a consequence a permanent shortage of food products, with particularly tragic episodes like the year of famine 1932–33. But even aside from those exceptional moments when it became absolute famine, the shortage of food was constant, not to mention the chronic shortage of shoes, clothes, apartments, and so on. In spite of strict state price controls, especially on food products, the inhabitants of the U.S.S.R. were daily confronted with price rises and severe shortages.

The government, incapable of providing for the most elementary needs of the whole society, chose on the one hand to carry on a general policy of rationing and, on the other, to reserve access to available goods for certain social categories. Everything in this system was selective. Rationing called upon criteria of utility or timeliness: In the early thirties, foreign specialists had the right to 48 kilos of bread a month, workers to only 24, and office workers and children to 12. For meat, the differences were even greater, the rations ranging from 14 kilos to 4.4 and 2.2.[34] These official rations varied not only in quantity but in reality. In some stores for common mortals, shortages made it impossible to honor customers' coupons. On the other hand, shops reserved for particular categories of Soviet citizens guaranteed their access to indispensable goods. The ordinary, badly paid citizen did not have access to any special shops, which proliferated to supply political cadres, the intelligentsia, the army, and the police. Nadezhda Mandelstam writes in this connection, "In this country, the privileged have always been rewarded not by envelopes containing their wages but by 'extras'—currency placed in sealed envelopes—by special rations, by access to *closed* stores."[35] These stores, established as we have seen during the first years of the regime, multiplied simultaneously with the growth of the bureaucracy. In the thirties they diversified. Sometimes they were stores whose existence was known only to those who could use them, stores hidden from all other eyes—these were known as closed distribution centers *(zakrytye razpredeliteli)*—sometimes there were "special counters" inside stores open to everyone where the privileged could place their orders. They were also served first and thus benefited from the dual advantage of never having to worry about supplies running out and being able to avoid annoying lines, the most typical and permanent characteristic of social life in the U.S.S.R. since 1917. Finally, in 1930, stores were established in which goods were paid for in foreign currency. These stores were supposed to be restricted to foreigners, but they were also open to those whose functions enabled them to travel or placed them in contact with foreigners. It was especially the upper levels of the political system who had access to this last kind of store.

In addition to the possible use of parallel distribution systems, there was at the time another decisive differentiating element, also mentioned by Nadezhda Mandelstam: the "sealed envelopes" whose contents improved the income of their recipients and enabled them to shop in the luxury stores outside the rationing system, stores with exorbitant prices like the Gastronomes, with their piles of goods unobtainable elsewhere. The use of these envelopes, called *pakety* in Russian, grew substantially under Stalin. It appeared in the early twenties as a means of improving, in special circumstances, the income of the leaders, which was still low. But it rapidly spread and became a regular practice, allowing the doubling or tripling of the incomes of principal leaders of the state and the Party without changing their official salaries and without including these extras in the tax system, which, in principle, was supposed to help reduce disparities in income.[36]

Thus the political elite that was established after the revolution enjoyed many privileges, through which it escaped from poverty and attained genuine comfort while hiding behind apparent austerity. But the growing gap between the living conditions of the average Soviet citizen and the conditions of those in power soon made necessary physical segregation in order to conceal the privileges. More and more in the course of the thirties, each category of privileged people was enclosed in its own living quarters, where it enjoyed precise rights connected with its particular status.

The memoirs and novels published inside and outside the U.S.S.R. since Stalin's death constitute the best historical material for judging these special positions and privileges, which were created on an ad hoc basis in the twenties but which by the thirties already followed an unwritten code. Yuri Trifonov, a noted Soviet writer, has described the lives and privileges of high-up party members in *The House by the River:* large well-furnished apartments in buildings with several elevators, guarded by deferential doorkeepers, where this society lived in extraordinary material comfort. The recognized writer, printed and honored in his country, is echoed by the banned testimony of Eugenia Ginzburg's *Journey into the Whirlwind.* The book's first chapters re-create the easy life of the dignitaries, in the Party's vacation houses, where children judged the respective positions of their parents by the kind of car they drove, and where New Year's Day 1935 was celebrated in evening dress with tables heaped high with food, while the rest of the countryside was dying of hunger and living in rags. These privileges also belonged to the police, described this way by the daughter of a high police official of the thirties:

> My father's new position made us one of the most privileged families in Moscow. His nomination was approved by the seventh department of the NKVD, which was in charge of all upper-level nominations in the Soviet Union. We then received a wooden dacha, and a five-room apartment in the building of the Foreign Affairs police station opposite a sub-

way station. We received a special ration book from the Kremlin which gave us the right to buy the best goods at the Kremlin Gastronome. This special book also allowed us to order dishes prepared in the Kremlin kitchens. The servants could bring complete meals (soup, chicken, meat, and ices) in special containers. In addition to his salary at the Foreign Affairs police station, my father, as an NKVD reserve officer, received a pension of 500 rubles a month. He had the right to a ten-week stay in Crimea [the Russian Riviera] and the Caucasus, all without spending a penny.[37]

Vast apartments, special stores, dachas, envelopes. These were the most common privileges of those who occupied important positions of command or control.

These "basic" privileges were supplemented by others which had an amplifying effect, accentuating still more the disparity between those who had these rights and the great mass of workers. This was the case for rents. Faithful to its egalitarian dream, the Soviet government in the twenties promulgated numerous regulations limiting rental costs. Working-class families crowded into one room of a communal apartment and sharing kitchen facilities with several other families had the consolation of paying a very low rent in proportion to their wages (35 to 44 kopeks per square meter for a monthly wage below 145 rubles—14,500 kopeks—according to 1928 figures).[38] But if we compare workers' rents with the maximum rents established for army and police officers or State and Party officials, we note that the privileged rents were equal to or lower than those of the workers, and they were for private apartments. From 1932 on, the Soviet government decided to offer free lifetime lodging to anyone who had rendered it exceptional service. The tax system developed in the course of the first five-year plan, 1928–32, added further to the injustice of the situation. Initially this system was designed to lower high incomes, and additional documents, like the law of April 3, 1932, limited the tax liability of the lower paid. But the practice of the thirties worked against the generous intentions expressed in the documents. The privileged categories also benefited from a complex system of partial or total exemptions, for the official part of their earnings, and hidden advantages escaped all taxation.[39] Thus, the army and the police had a particular system of taxation that finally left them almost all their salary, not to mention income from other sources.

From the thirties on, income and social status largely determined the possibilities of later promotion. Indeed, access to education, for which the children of the working classes had priority after 1917, gradually returned to being a social privilege. No doubt the right of everyone in the U.S.S.R. to an education was recognized, and the accelerated development in which Stalin involved the country in 1929 had as a corollary an increased effort to attract masses of adolescents toward higher technical education. During the first five-year plan, the number of students in the U.S.S.R. quintupled, and children of workers entered the universities in large numbers (there were 47 percent in Russian universities in 1932, compared to 30 percent in the late twenties.)[40] But in a very few years, university recruitment changed because the rules governing it changed. On June 23, 1936, new principles were adopted for admission. They specified that there was equality of access to the university for all, without consideration of social origin. The primary criterion became the school record and success on the university entrance examination. Children who had been able to follow a ten-year course of study and to work in favorable material conditions were from then on infinitely better prepared for the university than workers' children, who, after a brief course of study, received special preparation in courses designed for workers (Rabfak) and crammed in overpopulated rooms of noisy communal apartments.

If we consider that, beginning on October 2, 1940, the last three years of secondary education involved tuition expenses, and that the cost of a year's study in an institution of higher learning was equivalent to four to six weeks' pay for an average

worker, it is easy to understand how promotion through education soon became again a narrow path reserved for those who
had the material means.[41] In 1921 the head of the department
of professional education in the Commissariat of Education,
Preobrazhenski, had said, "At this moment, there is a veritable
class war at the gates of institutions of higher learning between
the worker-peasant majority of the country that wants to educate specialists from its ranks, for its own sake, and the ruling
classes and the strata connected to them. The proletarian state
openly sides with the people."[42] Barely ten years later, Stalin
denounced this attitude, which he called "petty-bourgeois
egalitarian," and supported a policy that closed higher education to the people on whom Preobrazhenski intended to base
the future elites of the country.

Stalin implicitly admitted, by various decisions, that the privileges of political leaders and professional elites included the
possibility of perpetuating their extraordinary status. His policies during this period seem at first sight very contradictory. On
the one hand, he involved his country in an economic and social
revolution of unprecedented magnitude that generated an
equally unprecedented social mobility. Because the U.S.S.R.
then needed innumerable technical and administrative managers, all active elements of society seemed to be able to benefit
from this mobility of structures, jobs, and needs. But at the same
time various measures ratified privileges and outlined the contours of a society that already included social differentiation and
was quickly becoming stratified. What was new under Stalin
was first of all that he accepted and ratified the existence of
differences in status. No doubt certain privileges remained concealed, especially those connected with political functions. But
in a general sense, Stalinist policies emphasized and gave official
status to the privileges of particular categories.

This official status came from the change that was then taking
place in the system of values promulgated by the Soviet state.
The post-revolutionary years had been dominated by egalitari-

anism, promotion of the lowly and the working class, and the depersonalization of history, reduced to the history of the popular masses in movement. In the course of the thirties, other values insidiously emerged, values linked to the demands of development. The competence and knowledge that Stalin constantly praised were not characteristic of the lower classes. They belonged to an elite, to those who had studied, who occupied a special place on the ladder of occupations, who did not blend into the mass. Reading what was published in the U.S.S.R. in the years before the Second World War is enough to provide an appreciation of the change that was taking place. Newspapers, literature, painting (all the arts were mobilized to express Stalin's plans through socialist realism) reflected the social and moral hierarchy of these years of the turning point. Out of the mass of the lowly emerged those whom society saluted as its most useful representatives: engineers, managers, experts, leaders. The crowd remained anonymous, but from this anonymous mass emerged individualized heroes. The manager of the factory had a name, a face, a history, abilities. This individualization of talents and exploits extended to the past, and the great figures of history who were restored to their places in books and schools justified by their past services the present privileges enjoyed by their successors.

After having exalted the army of the lowly for ten years, Soviet ideology hierarchized society according to utilitarian criteria. Privileges and high wages were now accepted as rewards for competence and social usefulness. In this way, the judgment of inequality changed. Just as, immediately after the revolution, it was appropriate to conceal privileges in favor of an austerity that placed all Soviet citizens at the level of the worker and made him their model, so after 1930 material success was no longer concealed and everyone dreamed of realizing the new social model, the privileged manager. Egalitarianism had thus given way to a morality of inequality and material success.

This new social model was strengthened by the introduction

of titles and rewards that created a new "socialist" hierarchy, but they were oddly reminiscent of the Empire's old "table of ranks." The first title created, Hero of Labor (July 27, 1927), provided substantial material benefits for its recipients: retirement pay, housing, exemption from taxes. But since the requirements for this award were stringent and those who obtained it were generally already privileged, Stalin added the following year the Red Banner of Labor, which was less prestigious, provided fewer concrete benefits, and was frequently awarded to entire factories. After 1930, the system was constantly diversified, ranging from Hero of the Soviet Union and Hero of Socialist Labor to the Order of Lenin and the Red Banner.[43] The army established its own particular order, the Red Star. The benefits tied to these various orders were diversified and hierarchized, but all of them in these difficult years brought their recipients prestige, a certain sum of money, and particular rights. These rights ranged from ease of access to the university to more modest benefits, like more or less free urban or even railroad transportation. Some of the titles—the most prestigious ones, Hero of the Soviet Union and Hero of Socialist Labor, which also provided the greatest benefits—were always reserved for a small number of people. Finally, the war led the government to distribute decorations widely, to multiply titles (especially military titles), ranks (on the model of military hierarchy), and uniforms and insignia.[44]

The Soviet system thus moved steadily away from the directives of Lenin, who had abolished this type of differentiation and condemned the use of traditional titles (like "minister" or "government"). But even before war broke out, Soviet society was strictly hierarchical, divided into categories with clearly defined prestige and rights, even though privileges were less and less public as one approached more closely to the top. What is remarkable in this period was the willingness to ratify officially, to legitimate, these differences. However, this radical change in Soviet political culture—for the renunciation of

egalitarian ideology and the "worker model" was a shift of decisive importance—did not imply that Stalin had returned society
to the path of tradition.

Despite apparent similarities between the past and the present, the formation of privileged strata during this period had
two characteristics without genuine equivalents in pre-revolutionary culture. First of all, Stalin extended to the working
masses the notions of elitism and privileges establishing a hierarchy in society. The Stakhauovite phenomenon allowed him
both to conceal his policy of social differentiation and to play on
worker emulation to change production norms.

Stalin's use of Stakhanovism is sufficiently interesting to be
looked at in detail, for it clarifies the complexity of his policies.
The fact that the productive exploits of the worker Aleksei
Stakhanov were completely fabricated in 1934—to provide an
accessible model for the working class (for Stakhanov, knowledge and competence were replaced by a profound Communist conviction and the will to go beyond his own productive
abilities) and to assure it that the paths of social promotion were
also open to it—has been known for a long time.[45] What is less
well known is the way in which Stalinist power seized on a
reaction of the rank and file against his inegalitarian policies in
order to use it for the benefit of those policies. Indeed, as early
as 1932, predecessors of Stakhanov appeared on the job. In
factories, the first shock-troop workers" were probably not
manipulated by the government but, on the contrary, embodied an effort by the most conscious elements of the working
class to compel recognition in the factory, to play a specific role,
at the moment when Stalin was proclaiming that authority and
usefulness were not working-class qualities. These first attempts
at increasing the status of the workers were not only ignored by
the government but reduced to silence. And a few years later,
when Stakhanov emerged from the darkness, he took great care
to emphasize the individual aspect of his exploit and the inspiration he had received from the Party and from Stalin. Socialist

emulation and the "worker model" then entered Soviet political culture. To be a shock-troop worker, a new category of the privileged, was a perspective that the Party opened to individuals taken out of the working masses, not a path that the working masses as a whole had chosen to follow. Moreover, the exploits and privileges of the small number of individuals who made up this category were paid for by the entire working class, on whom an increase in work norms was imposed each time a shock-troop worker showed the way.[46]

Stakhanovism thus completed the outline of the model of society that was imposed under Stalin. Stalinist society was not a community of equals, it was dominated by the "best," whose abilities justified, at every level, their authority and privileges. The higher one rose in the social scale, the greater were the privileges, and the easier they appeared to be to perpetuate.

But here we touch on second essential characteristic of Stalinism: the fragility of positions and privileges. Stalin was the creator of a proliferating bureaucracy, in which everyone who held a fraction of power was granted excessive authority and codified privileges, most of which were recognized; but he was also the systematic destroyer of that bureaucracy. In this system, the privileged were always in danger of being purged— that is, expelled from the universe of the privileged and annihilated. The purges which began in 1928 with the trial of the Dubass engineers ("bourgois specialists," they were accused of sabotage, and their elimination brought about a general purge of "specialists," of the economic machinery of planners, and so on) were to continue to the end of the thirties, and they systematically eliminated the managers of all the institutions on which Stalin based his power: Party, state, army, police, economic machinery, intelligentsia, and so on. If the first effect of these purges was to throw millions of people into the camps or simply to kill them, their political effect was to permit a constant renewal of managers at all levels and therefore to assure permanent upward mobility. The Party offers an excellent illustration of this mobility. Between 1933 and 1939, approximately five million Party members were purged; the higher one rose in the party, the bloodier the purges became. The rank-and-file militant could hope to get away with a simple expulsion; but for anyone who had any responsibilities at whatever level, a purge implied tragic consequences. Behind each leader who was eliminated, we can see an entire group disappearing, leaving open jobs that would immediately be filled. Tragic as it was for those who disappeared, the purges opened up extraordinary opportunities for rapid promotion for those who had succeeded in establishing solid positions. An instrument of social mobility which allowed Stalin periodically to renew totally the elite and to assure the rise of new elites loyal to him and in agreement with his conception of power, the purge thus appears to have been a central element of the Stalinist political system.

To the social mobility that was thus assured should be added three complementary characteristics of Stalinist practice. Lenin, who had established the repressive system, had made it a principle that the Party was to be protected. The Party used repression through the intermediary of the police, but the police could in no case attack the Party. Stalin abolished the immunity that the Party had enjoyed and thereby placed it, as a social body, on the same level as the other hierarchies of the U.S.S.R. He remained alone, above the repressive system. Moreover, in the course of the thirties, Stalin had granted an exceptionally privileged status to the institutions of law and order, army and police. The entire political culture of the thirties had in fact helped to glorify these two institutions. The Constitution of 1936, which marked the rebirth of the state and its attributes—territory and sovereignty—of patriotism and of the appeal to traditional national values, assigned to the army of the time a central role in the protection of the state. The restoration of uniforms, military discipline, and military traditions confirmed the army's place in society.[47] The same thing was true for the police. The development of the concentration camp system, which gave it the responsibility for convict labor, made it not only a repressive instrument but the principal Soviet enterprise. The publicity for police recruitment campaigns in the early thirties changed the negative image of this social body; it was officially presented at the time as a pillar of the Soviet system. Then, by making informing an obligation for the good citizen (the hero held up to Soviet youth at the time, Pavlik Morozov, was glorified for having denounced his own father to the police), the Stalinist system created privileged special relations between the individual and the police, which was the guarantee for everyone's security. It is significant that denunciations were not addressed to the Party but to the police, or to Stalin directly. This indicates the diminution in status of the Party, which was no longer the final recourse.

The privileges enjoyed by the army and the police were hardly concealed, and were presented as the normal counterpart to the social usefulness of the two institutions. But—and this is the third interesting aspect of the system—this status and these privileges did not protect their beneficiaries. No more than the Party were the army and the police sheltered from the purges. In the years 1936–38, the army lost a considerable portion of its officers, and, as in other institutions, repression was harsher the greater the responsibilities and privileges. In the officer corps as a whole, the rate of elimination seemed to hover around 25 percent, while at the higher levels it reached 80 percent (colonels), 90 percent (generals), and even 100 percent for field marshals.[48] The police, instrument of the repression, did not escape either, and two series of purges, in 1936 and 1938, eliminated its chiefs, Yagoda and then Ezhov, whose fall brought about that of a certain number of their colleagues.[49]

The precarious nature of every status and the lack of immunity for all social bodies at all levels suggest two conclusions about the system of power established by Stalin. First, Stalinist power, which lasted for a quarter century, did not create a viable political system. In fact, elitist political culture implies a consolidation of the elites. But Stalin constantly destroyed the elites as they were established, and we know that in the last years of his life he was preparing a new purge which would have reopened the infernal cycle of eliminations and upward mobility. This contradiction between a political culture stabilizing society around known values—competence, loyalty to the system—and a perpetual calling into question by periodic "cultural revolutions" was by definition intolerable to anyone who could, at any given moment, benefit from the system.

Second, Stalin's political practice was characterized by the total absence of rules. All Stalin's initiatives and changes of direction were, for this reason, unpredictable. One example provides evidence. In the late forties, when the future purge was in preparation, the police, as a first step, carried out massive arrests on the periphery of the Soviet state, in the regions where prisoners who had completed their terms were confined. These former prisoners, trying to understand the logic governing their arrests, finally discovered that it was simply alphabetical; because of the first letter of his name, an individual might escape from the purge or experience again the hell of a concentration camp.[50] These two characteristics, the absence of a real political system and the absence of any political logic, operated so that the system was held together by Stalin, but it obviously could not survive him intact. The very rapid political evolution after his death indicates that the Stalinist dictatorship, in its personal aspects, was condemned to disappear, like all other systems of personal dictatorship that had existed up to that point.

CHAPTER TWO
THE TIME OF HOPE

At Stalin's death on March 5, 1953, the course of events was dominated by two factors: the awareness on the part of his potential successors that the Stalinist system of power could not be continued as is, and the weariness of society.

The situation which the political elite confronted was totally unprecedented. Like its predecessors in 1924, it could call upon no rule of succession, no definition of actual power. With Stalin gone, who could say where power lay? But those who had surrounded Stalin in his last years were marked by the memory of Lenin's succession, by the experience of the total power Stalin had exercised, and by terror of the purges from which they had escaped. They were united by the fear of seeing a new Stalin emerge in their midst, who would accept power and destroy all of them. They were also united by fear of popular weariness. Might it not turn into revolt, as had often happened in Russian history, and might not this revolt sweep away the entire political system?

Out of this fear was born a consensus which united the political apparatus around two preoccupations: to set up a collective leadership replacing Stalin's personal tyranny, in order to block the path to another tyrant; but, at the same time, to resolve the problem of power within the political sphere, without the intervention of society, in order to prevent society from affecting or changing the system. In the interregnum from 1953 to 1957, Stalin's successors succeeded in maintaining their agreement to change the system and shelter themselves from its excesses; at the same time, they preserved its essential element, its absolute authority in the face of a society excluded from all these changes. Power remained a matter for those who possessed it, and the intervention of society was out of the question.

This consensus was facilitated by two factors. There was first the continued existence in 1953 of a police system at Stalin's service, escaping from any control by the other bureaucracies, and seen for that reason as a threat to the entire class of political figures which helped to unite them "in an alliance of fear." It was also facilitated by the absence of real divergences among the potential successors. When Lenin died in 1924, the Party was deeply divided over fundamental choices: Should the NEP be continued or not? How and how fast should they industrialize? What kind of society should they form? In 1953, the major choices had been made long before; collectivization, industrialization, a society without antagonistic classes were objectives that had all been more or less well attained. The age of great conflicts had thus come to an end, and the potential leaders could only adjust and manage the system. This explains why all the decisions of the years of transition pointed in the same direction: adjustment of the political system, and management of its relations with society.

The Emergence from Tyranny

To prevent the rise of a new tyrant, Stalin's successors tackled first the instrument of tyranny, the police, and the man who controlled it, Lavrenti Beria. On March 6, 1953, with complete agreement, they put into effect a first solution which removed Beria from the ruling group and entrusted the power of state and Party to Georgi Malenkov; then, a few days later, to prevent Malenkov from concentrating excessive power in his hands, they took authority over the Party away from him and turned it over to Nikita Khruschev. Thus, in a few days, a balanced power was set up which eliminated the most dangerous man of all to start with and also avoided the possibility that a single man could present himself as the successor. A few months later, Beria was arrested by his colleagues and killed.[1]

Achieving this result required lucidity on the part of Beria's colleagues, who had learned from the lessons of the past; their cohesion, to organize a plot concealed from police surveillance; and especially the support of the army, which alone could provide a counterweight to the military forces available to the police and their chief in 1953. For the first time in Soviet history, the army, humiliated and relegated to a secondary position after its victory in 1945, was called upon to participate in political life and to arbitrate the conflict over the succession.[2] And its help was all the easier to obtain because it was used to break police power. After having removed the police from the political scene and suppressed tendencies toward personal power, the leaders agreed to restore the authority of the Party and to return it to its central place in Soviet political life. No doubt Stalin had never explicitly challenged the Party's authority; but by subjecting it to police control, withholding the power of decision from it, doing away with all the regular public forms of its existence (congresses and plenums), and periodically downgrading and eliminating all its leaders, he had reduced it to the status of a mere mechanism. His successors were quick to restore the Party to its role, and the most resounding demonstration of the desire to do so was the Twentieth Congress held in 1956. This consensus, whose basic raison d'être was to undermine the possibility of a new tyranny, should not be underestimated, even if its inspiration was entirely negative. The Soviet leaders' fear in 1953 was at the origin of the most profound and long-lasting change that ever took place in the U.S.S.R. Since 1953, despite appearances, power in the U.S.S.R. has never again been personal or total power.

Along with this first change came another, no less important for the future: the search by Stalin's successors for political rules to regularize and institutionalize power. Beria's elimination in 1953, in obscure circumstances—officially, he was shot in December 1953 after a trial, but in all probability he was killed by his colleagues at the time of his arrest six months earlier—recalled by its violence the bloody rivalries of the Stalinist period. But the similarity was only apparent. Stalin arranged the assassinations of broken men who in no way threatened him, while his successors got rid of Beria because they were afraid of him. Moreover, this was the last bloody episode of Soviet struggles for power.

Two years later, the removal of Malenkov from his position as head of government gave evidence of the distance that had been traveled from the Stalinist tradition of violence. Malenkov was driven to resign in February 1955; he accused himself of incompetence and recognized the failure of an economic policy which his rival, Khrushchev, had incidentally sabotaged. But his self-criticism involved neither expulsion from the party nor dishonor. In 1957, when Khrushchev, then at the height of his power, in order to get rid of his opponents, whom he classified as "anti-Party" elements, attempted to bring extremely serious charges against them—factionalism, complicity with Stalin—the Party agreed to condemn them but not remove them totally, and especially not to return to the path of pitiless purges. The condemnations led to changes of status. V.M. Molotov became ambassador to Mongolia, Malenkov the manager of a factory in a distant region. Better than any other, Molotov's example explains the change that has occurred, and been maintained in this respect, since Stalin.[3] Condemned for "anti-Party" activities in 1957, systematically opposed to de-Stalinization and refusing to carry out self-criticism, Molotov died at ninety, forgotten, to be sure, but in comfortable retirement provided by the Soviet government, without having known dishonor, prison, or persecution. Since Stalin's death, Soviet leaders have thus had the right to be politically incapable, to make mistakes, and to oppose the Party's policies. No doubt the Party expels them from political life, but it no longer destroys them. Forced retirement and simple expulsion are practices that appeared in the U.S.S.R. between 1954 and 1957. They changed the system because they regularized it. They indicated that leaving power was not equivalent to death and thereby made competition for power less ferocious. This regularization of political life, which was one of the first gains of post-Stalinism, has also been a particularly long-lived one.

The Emergence from Fear

Protected from arbitrary power, Stalin's successors also attempted at the outset to reassure society. And they did so in the transition period by tackling two fundamental grounds of anxiety: the insecurity of life, and material difficulties. Insecurity was a problem shared by the political elite and by society in general. Everyone felt equally threatened by possible purges; all had suffered equally from past purges. To ward off future dangers, to eliminate a possible return of the purges, Stalin's successors, from the moment of his death, denounced his arbitrary rule and his plans by revealing that the "doctors' plot" was a police fabrication, that from henceforth the time of invented plots and purges had passed.[4] To this principled decision, important because it was a commitment about the future, should be added the measures taken by Beria to free prisoners. As head of the police and prison system, he countermanded the arrest orders issued in 1953, freed those who had just been arrested, and opened prison and camp gates—very prudently and partially, but he did open them.[5] In the struggle for power, in which he was as yet only half beaten, Beria attempted to acquire the image of a liberal, by using his police functions for this purpose. His colleagues feared this sudden liberalism just as much as his past cruelty.

On this point, too, the transition period was a clean break

with the existing system. Of course it was the government that decided to put an end to arbitrariness, to assure society that it could stop fearing arrests and hope for grants of clemency. Of course, too, no one called the system itself into question, and arbitrariness appeared to be the result of badly regulated decisions and of excesses. But by liberating prisoners, even in small numbers, and by recognizing excesses, the government involuntarily undermined what had been until then a veritable dogma: the idea that repression was just, that only "enemies of the people" were involved. This limited opening granted society a certain right to doubt.

Even more than for fear, the successors wanted to provide a remedy for the daily material frustrations of citizens. Malenkov concentrated his efforts on an economic program whose objective was, for the first time, to attempt to feed and clothe the inhabitants of the U.S.S.R. However timid and partial the decisions taken between 1953 and 1956, and even though they were designed only to reassure society, their effect should not be underestimated. No doubt Soviet society remembered the periods of calm between the waves of repression under Stalin. But if we read the memoirs of the time, we observe that society was becoming aware of the changes taking place, even if it could not and dared not measure their extent or the likelihood of their lasting.

Prelude to the Twentieth Congress

The country soon moved beyond these uncertainties, because the Twentieth Congress and Khrushchev's rise to power gave the still tentative efforts to adjust the system an unexpected, and in many respects devastating, turn. Unexpected because, until 1956, against those who argued for a new economic orientation favorable to the individual and for a certain relaxation of restrictions, Khrushchev seemed to be the representative of a rigorous tradition. He defended the authority of the Party and the priority of industrial development, and in the past he had ruled the Ukraine in a pitiless manner. He was, finally, the author of a plan for the reform of rural society, the project for "agrovilles," proposed in 1951, the only threat at the end of the Stalinist period of a new stage on the road of social revolution.[6] At the time, no one imagined that Khrushchev would attempt, for a period of several years, to turn the political system in a more egalitarian direction, to make it more open to popular participation, less centralized, and less authoritarian. Although the major economic and social choices had been made by Stalin, there remained a radical choice that could be made —to modify the political system by destroying its rigidity and opening it up to society. Confronted with this radical choice, Khrushchev did not fully carry out his intentions. His personal hesitations and the hostility of the Party soon revealed the limitations of his program. But, despite the failures, the fact remains that for several years the entire Soviet system—in the government sphere and in the relations between government and society—experienced an evolution that might have changed its nature.

If the constellation of political forces in the U.S.S.R. remained complex until the fall of Malenkov, beginning with his expulsion in 1955 and his replacement in the government by Nikolai Bulganin, the position and the importance of each successor became easier to evaluate. In the newly formed organization dominated by Bulganin and Khrushchev, Bulganin, the ersatz soldier, carried little weight, in the Party as in the army. Khrushchev on the contrary imposed himself as the highest-placed Party member, the one whose experience and clientele were most noteworthy. He had professional experience, thanks to his technical industrial training, and unequaled political experience. He had been at the head of the Communist organization of the Ukraine, the largest of the Soviet republics and the most significant economically; he had held the same position in Moscow, and on the eve of Stalin's death he had taken on the responsibility for managing the machinery of the Party in the Secretariat of the Central Committee. A competent administrator on national and local levels, a specialist in industrial problems but also expert in agricultural questions, tied to the army by his participation in the great battles of Stalingrad and Kursk, Khrushchev was, of all the survivors of the Stalinist period, the one who could lay claim to the greatest support.

This exceptional position explains Khrushchev's growing power and the means he used to solidify it and to carry out his programs. The Party was for him a privileged means of action. He had a certain degree of control over it, since, by calling on the Ukraine and Moscow organizations, he could dispose of one quarter of the votes at the Party congress. And the function of this congress was to elect the ruling bodies for the future. Khrushchev attempted, before the Twentieth Congress, to influence its future composition and its procedures. He wanted to introduce into the Party some elements that seemed essential to him: more flexibility, even internal democracy, and more innovation, which presupposed substantial renewal of political personnel. A series of measures taken before the Twentieth Congress indicates the constancy with which he pursued this program of change.

At the end of Stalin's life, the ruling organs operated under such irregular and capricious conditions that their entire capacity for action was undermined in advance. Stalin, who was an insomniac, called his colleagues together at any hour of day or night, especially at night, and cheerfully mingled working sessions and drinking bouts. No organ met regularly.[7] By the end of 1953, all the administrative bodies of state and Party had returned to regular and normal hours, which indicated that the machinery of power had begun again to function according to strict rules and not the whims of a dictator. The Presidium—the name given to the Politburo at the Nineteenth Congress in 1952 by a Stalin who thereby seemed intent on cutting ties with the old Bolshevik Party—began again to meet every week, and the Central Committee met six times between Stalin's death and the Twentieth Congress. The Supreme Soviet itself, the embodiment of state power, returned to periodic meetings—twice a year.[8]

Although this resumption of regularity in institutions, added to the regularization of changes in personnel, seems a matter of course a quarter century later, in the middle fifties it was the sign of a veritable political revolution in the U.S.S.R. Everyone who participated in these institutions, directly or indirectly, was reassured and gained from these conditions an authority that their earlier uncertainty of status had made impossible. Status and authority began to derive from belonging to an institution, no longer from the momentary favor of Stalin.

But the new weight of institutions presupposed, for those who aspired to real power, a greater degree of control over the people who worked in those institutions. As head of the Party apparatus, Khrushchev, like Stalin in the thirties, began to multiply shifts of personnel in order to strengthen his influence over the various Communist organizations. Between 1953 and 1956, the first secretaries of the Communist Parties were changed in seven of the fourteen federated republics and in forty-one regions of the Russian Republic (the R.S.F.S.R. had no republic-wide party; therefore, the secretaries of the obkoms, the regional organizations, had a position equivalent to that of secretary of a republic) out of sixty-nine. In all, forty-eight out of eighty-three first secretaryships changed hands at the time—that is, more than half the regional leaders of the Party, who normally had a *de jure* right to a seat at the Party Congress and who had substantial influence there, owed their promotion on the eve of the Twentieth Congress to Khrushchev.[9] In contrast to such movements of personnel under Stalin, the changes that took place after 1953 brought about no crisis and did not appear to be purges. For the first time in Soviet history, everything took place as though the appearance of new leaders automatically involved similar movements throughout the administration. This was a shift in procedures that has been too easily forgotten because of the more spectacular changes that followed the Twentieth Congress.

Finally, and this too was a change in political style, the Party began to open its debates and, timidly at first, to involve the public in them. The year 1955 was of capital importance in this respect. Economic policy was discussed at the Party plenum in May 1955.[10] The inefficiency of industry was subjected to criticism. The press opened its columns to a debate on the problems of efficiency and even indulged in comparisons with results achieved by capitalist enterprises. More specialized discussions developed at the same time among historians and military experts.[11] No doubt these forums were limited to groups of professionals and left the ordinary public unconcerned. But there was one common element to these debates: They led to a systematic critique of earlier positions, of the doctrinal rigidity which had prevailed until 1956, and they suggested that the revitalization of the U.S.S.R. would come about through radical changes. These debates—and this, too, is important—however controlled they may have been, were presented as a critique coming from specialists on the problems under discussion, and they were an implicit condemnation of excessive centralization. Thus, important changes in direction took place on the eve of the Twentieth Congress. The collective institutions of the Party had replaced the personal methods derived directly from Stalin's will, a new group of political personnel was moving up, and the right to criticize had been established.

The Time of Confessions

It was against this background of change that the Twentieth Congress carried out fundamental revisions. The "secret speech," read by Khrushchev in a dramatic atmosphere, and the confession of Stalinist crimes, have sometimes obscured those aspects of the whole congress that were so profoundly and irreversibly innovative.[12] They have also obscured the limits the Party imposed on the changes that were beginning to develop. What was particularly novel was the confession of crimes committed, which implied, whatever may have been intended, that the holders of power in the U.S.S.R.—that is, the Party in all its incarnations—could make mistakes. The theory of the Party's infallibility, which had justified all of Lenin's decisions and Stalin's excesses, could no longer be upheld after February 1956. What was also novel, and charged with consequences, was the confession that personal power unfailingly leads to error and crime. For the result of this confession was that only collective power was legitimate and without danger.

Whether or not Khrushchev intended to use the weapon of de-Stalinization against his colleagues, in order to consolidate his personal power, is of little importance from the perspective of history. By insisting on denouncing the effects of the personality cult, by drawing up a balance sheet of those effects (insufficient, to be sure, but terribly tragic), Khrushchev armed the party against future candidates for personal power, and in the first place against himself. Involuntarily, he set personal power in the front rank of the dangers threatening the Party, and in this sense he dealt a decisive blow to personal power in any form.

These were the gains of the Twentieth Congress. They were considerable, for they weakened the two pillars of the Soviet system: the infallibility of the Party and its consequent legitimacy. But these were the limits of the Twentieth Congress, limits that explain why the Soviet system survived such confessions, which ought to have brought it down. Khrushchev, despite an unquestionable desire to change the Soviet system, was first of all a creature of that system. He fully adhered to its central idea, that power belonged to the Party and that society must be excluded from it. What he wanted was to rationalize the government, to make it acceptable to society, and to establish the relationship between government and society on a new basis of confidence and nonviolence. But these adjustments did not imply any change in the essentials; the sphere of power was and must remain a closed world over which society had no control. This is why the "secret speech" and the confession of mistakes were reserved for the Party. It was up to the Party to carry out its self-criticism and to reform itself. This is why, in addition, no fundamental choice by the Party was called into question in 1956, least of all the choices of 1929 that had determined the social structures of the future.

According to the "secret speech," the Party, or rather Stalin, began to go wrong in 1934; but the collectivization imposed on peasant society by a decision "from above" fell on the positive side of the balance sheet. By dating the "cult of personality" from 1934, Khrushchev preserved intact the idea that it was up to the Communist Party alone to decide the fate of society and that revolutions could be carried out "from above," could be imposed on society. He thereby attempted to rescue another idea, the infallibility of the Party. In 1934, deprived of its old elites, subject to permanent purge, the Party was indistinguishable from Stalin. But in this area, Khrushchev and his colleagues were incapable of fully carrying out their intentions. No one in the U.S.S.R., and certainly no one in the rest of the socialist world, believed that a single man could bear total responsibility for a complete deviation of the system. It was clear that the entire Party had been wrong in the past, and this implied that it could be wrong in the future.

In 1956, Soviet society was turned toward the hopes of change opened up by the congress.[13] These hopes concealed for several years the fatal blow that had been dealt to Soviet ideology and the Soviet system. But when hopes had dwindled, the consequences of the congress became visible. Deprived of its aura of infallibility, of its legitimacy, the Party now seemed to be only the machinery of power, without other justification for lasting than its capacity for imposing its will, by persuasion or force. The myth of the "radiant future," already substantially weakened beforehand, lost all meaning in 1956. At that very moment, two socialist countries carried the analysis of the Twentieth Congress to its logical conclusion. Hungarian society revolted against the authority of the Party, which it attempted to reject. And the Chinese leaders, quite to the contrary, concluded that a party is wrong when it admits its right to be mistaken, and in the name of the infallibility of the Party they supported Stalin against his successors.

The Years of Change

But within the U.S.S.R., Khrushchev was in 1956 the man who embodied a possible evolution of the system. By that very fact he was attractive to a substantial segment of society; on the other hand, he terrified a large number of Stalin's companions who, having survived the years of the purges without mishap, wanted their acquired positions to be stabilized. These contrary reactions guided Khrushchev's actions to a certain extent and led him far beyond his initial projects. In the Party, he troubled his peers, who were aware of his position of strength in the organs of power and of his new popularity. They detected two dangers in the situation. First, Khrushchev might take advantage of his prestige as a "de-Stalinizer" to step into Stalin's shoes. After all, Stalin's example indicated that the path to personal power need hardly be accompanied by clear declarations of intention. Stalin had long taken refuge in his "loyalty to Lenin." When Khrushchev proposed a return to the "norms of Leninism," was he not pursuing the same ambitious ends? The second fear, equally legitimate, was that de-Stalinization, the necessity of which was admitted by all the leaders, would go beyond their intentions and overflow the framework of the Party. In the aftermath of the Congress, the delegates who had been present at the reading of the "secret speech" had the task of reading it to groups of Communists, and they were to manage, and supervise, its diffusion throughout the Party.[14] But there is no lack of testimony indicating that the "secret speech" was distributed outside the Party.[15] In this instance as well, Khrushchev's colleagues suspected either that he had acted imprudently or that he was using the "secret speech" to serve his personal ambition.

This is why a veritable conspiracy was organized against him in the Presidium, and it attempted to overthrow him in June 1957. In this period, pushed by the hardening opposition around him but also by his own vision of necessary change, Khrushchev followed two paths: he worked both to decentralize the system of power and to reduce the privileges of the leaders.

Centralization of decision and management had, from the outset, been an essential element of the Soviet system of power. Among other concerns, it satisfied the will of the Party, whether led by Lenin or by Stalin, to prevent any centrifugal movement in an immense country in which national passions, awakened by the revolution, had far from subsided in 1953. Khrushchev had three reasons for preferring a policy of decentralization.

There was first a desire for economic effectiveness. All Stalin's successors agreed at the time on the necessity of giving at least minimum satisfaction to social needs. Stalin had paid no attention, thanks to a repressive system that reduced society to silence. As soon as an appeal was made to social consensus, it became impossible to ignore the most elementary material needs of Soviet citizens. By decentralizing the management of the economy, Khrushchev hoped to improve its performance.[16]

Economic decentralization also allowed the introduction of peace and social consensus at another level, that of the nationalities. The Twentieth Congress had taken stock of the excesses committed against them. But it had not suggested a shift to a genuine federal status which would respect the various national wills. The implicit program of the Twentieth Congress was clear: to improve relations among nations in order to lead them to "Soviet unity" and not turn the clock back and recognize their aspirations to be different. In this case, too, the major choices of the past were adopted. But there was one domain where concessions could be made, in the area of economic administration, where national aspirations and the interests of the Soviet state could coincide.

Finally, decentralization of economic management would allow Khrushchev to break political strongholds that he could not otherwise touch. Everywhere in Moscow, in the ministries, in the State Committees, the privileged holders of power were disturbed by his activity and provided significant support to his enemies in the Presidium. Those who had survived Stalinism had often accepted de-Stalinization because it assured their security. Once this security was guaranteed, most of those who held a fragment of power were intent on stabilizing the system, halting change, and making their status and privileges permanent. This was the source of their anxiety over the initiatives of Khrushchev, who was attempting to consolidate his position through dynamic de-Stalinization.

The economic reform of 1957 (the Supreme Soviet approved it on May 10), imposed by Khrushchev after a difficult struggle with the Presidium, corresponded to these diverse intentions.[17] This reform created Regional Economic Councils *(sovnarkhozes)* to which were transferred the powers of most of the major central industrial ministries. Although the planning system and major options remained the province of the central government, the power to manage the economy genuinely moved to another level and to different personnel. Moreover, by this reform, Khrushchev greatly strengthened the power of the regional administrators of the Party—the regional secretaries. To this displacement of the levels of authority, which involved the rise of a new political generation—the first secretaries of the regions with economic skills, managers and technicians of the economy from a provincial background—was added a rapid change in political procedures, which culminated during the crisis of June 1957.

To impose his economic program on a hostile Presidium, Khrushchev multiplied his appeals to the Party's Central Committee and to the Supreme Soviet and defended his arguments in the newspapers.[18] That is, he went over the heads of his colleagues and addressed the broader organs of Party and State and—still timidly, but the tendency was already there—even public opinion. This represented a break with previous practice, in which political debate was concentrated at the highest level. The crisis of June 1957 persuaded Khrushchev to go even further in the direction of broadening the debate.

The facts can be quickly summarized. In June 1957, Khrushchev's enemies in the Presidium had succeeded in agreeing to eliminate him, and in the course of a carefully prepared meeting they informed him that they had decided to depose him. Until 1957, no Soviet leader had succeeded in opposing, on such a decision, the supreme organ of the Party. We need only recall that in 1924, following Lenin's death, when the Politburo had become aware of Lenin's "letter" urging them to keep Stalin from the position of general secretary, Stalin had offered his resignation to his colleagues. Khrushchev, far from resigning, demanded a meeting of the Central Committee, which, he said, had elected him, and he invoked rules that had never before operated. With the help of the army, the members of the Central Committee dispersed throughout Soviet territory were swiftly brought to Moscow, and they gave their support to Khrushchev (205 votes out of 309). The orators of the Central Committee grasped the opportunity to emphasize that it was their role to decide questions of nomination and dismissal, and that the time of hasty and irregular procedures had passed.[19]

While saving his position, Khrushchev had also carried out a political revolution. The Party had now clarified its rules of operation. Everyone knew where the power to decide who would hold the ruling positions lay. The Central Committee, elected by the representatives of the Party assembled in congress, expressed their will. The plenum of June 1957 occupies a very important place in the process leading toward a restoration of institutions and their prerogatives. In order to manipulate the Party, it was henceforth necessary to manipulate the Central Committee.

But the progress that had been achieved did not stop there. After his victory, Khrushchev sought to eliminate his opponents and to take control of the Presidium. To do this, he did not hesitate to resort to the methods he had condemned and, after having accused his colleagues of belonging to an "anti-Party group" (a factional activity which should at the least have brought about their exclusion from the Party), he tried to implicate them in Stalin's crimes and to destroy them in that way. The Party—that is, the Central Committee—which had saved Khrushchev, saved his colleagues in the same way from his pursuit by refusing to undertake a trial against them for "Stalinism." Eliminated from the ruling organs, the "anti-Party" members were not liquidated.

This new tolerance encouraged factional politics within the Presidium, where Khrushchev never succeeded, despite his efforts, in shaping a majority that would support all his enterprises. Seen in his years of glory as the true successor to Stalin (and his foreign activities encouraged that perception), Khrushchev had constantly to put forth considerable efforts to modify the political balance at the top and to shift the location of political decisions. In order to accomplish this, he changed the political personnel by means of renewal. In 1961, at the Twenty-second Congress, Khrushchev pushed through new statutes for the Party which required a periodic rotation of cadres.[20] From top to bottom of the Party, cadres were to be periodically renewed, following rules that were more restrictive for the lower levels than for leaders of the very highest ranks. At the same time, he attempted to broaden and democratize political debate. After having argued for the ultimate authority of the Central Committee over the Presidium, from 1960 on, Khrushchev went further by "broadening" the plenums of the Central

Committee and by involving in debates, if not in decisions, individuals or groups who did not belong to it.[21] Thus, in opposition to the ruling organs of the Party, Khrushchev progressively called upon particular capacities that diminished the role of those organs. What Khrushchev was attempting, in the end, against a Party that he could not totally manipulate, was to call upon the support of the rank and file that was constantly extended to new strata. In 1957, the "rank and file" for him was the Central Committee against the Presidium. From 1960 on, it was the "technicians" against a majority of the Central Committee which had grown resistant because Khrushchev's egalitarian reforms were affecting all privileges. Finally, in 1962, Khrushchev sought to impose himself beyond the Party, in a society based on "participation."[22]

The Struggle Against Privileges

Privileges were undermined in many ways. The first privilege claimed by the holders of power was security of employment. Beginning in 1954, Khrushchev displaced cadres wherever he could and thus created his own "clientele" in the Party. The reform of 1957 and the subsequent rules on the "rotation of cadres" accelerated these movements.[23] Confronting the clientele that Khrushchev had thus created was a growing faction of malcontents who had lost their positions. Stalin had resolved the problem of the mobility of cadres through the purges. Thrown into concentration camps, at best forgotten, the cadres who were eliminated could not constitute a threatening group. But in the late fifties, dismissal no longer involved tragic consequences, and this led to the formation of a coalition of the excluded. What is more, the principle of rotation implied that every cadre would eventually be removed, and they were therefore anxious in anticipation.

To the rise of discontent created by the Party reforms was added a profound hostility to Khrushchev's egalitarianism,

which attacked the tangible, material signs of social differentiation and the perpetuation of a dominant stratum through the
privileges connected with education.

One of the first privileges suppressed by Khrushchev was the
practice of "envelopes," particularly dear to the recipients because they were clandestine, allowed them to maintain an
image of disinterestedness, and were exempt from all taxation.[24] Khrushchev also attacked the hierarchy of ranks and
insignia established by Stalin for certain institutions. In 1954
and 1956 he abolished ranks (or classes) for factory managers
and members of the judicial system, which had been modeled
on the hierarchy in the military. He removed the stripes that
had decorated the uniforms of railroad officials.[25] These reforms
diminishing the prestige of the groups concerned also had, it
goes without saying, financial effects. Although he did not dis-
turb military titles and orders, Khrushchev decided on a reduction in the armed forces in 1960, which resulted in some early
retirements and their accompanying financial drawbacks.[26] In
a general way, he also attempted to limit some of the advantages then enjoyed by reserve or retired military officers.

But it was Khrushchev's educational reforms that might have
struck the strongest blows against the privileges of power.[27]
The effects of the Stalinist system of education could be assessed
in 1953. Beginning in the thirties, extended secondary education had stopped offering manual and technical training and
had systematically become a channel for admission to the universities and even a system of pre-university selection. The
disappearance of general polytechnical education coincided
with the appearance of "special" secondary schools, in principle
designed for children gifted in particular areas (such as sports,
art, or foreign languages). But they very soon became privileged means of access to the most prestigious universities. Entry
into these schools then became a widespread aim among the
privileged, and their social composition indicated that access to
them was determined by the social and material resources of

the family and not by the gifts of the children. Two totally separate forms of training thus channeled Soviet youth. For a minority, there was the royal road of a complete secondary education, "special" or general, leading to the university. The majority was oriented toward professional studies tied to the needs of industry. Even before 1953, the cost of studies and the selection procedure that exempted the best students of the extended secondary system (winners of gold and silver medals) from university entrance examinations had created a predominance of children of the most favored social categories in the universities. In 1953, a new factor complicated the problem. The number of students graduating from secondary schools suddenly increased to such an extent that competition to enter the university became fierce: at least six candidates for each place.

Aware of the segregating role played by education, Khrushchev, by a series of measures taken between 1956 and 1958, attempted to restore more equality to the system. At the outset, he attacked the network of "special" schools and preached a return to polytechnic secondary education adapted to the requirements of the world of work.[28] On June 6, 1956, he proclaimed free secondary and higher education and reserved a quota of places in the universities for candidates who came directly from the production lines. On August 3, he introduced into the system of scholarships for higher education the criterion of "resources," whereas these scholarships had previously been granted on the basis of the candidate's educational attainments. Finally, in December 1958, he had a law adopted which completely changed the admissions system and the method of study in the universities. All students had to spend time in productive labor, which thus became an integral part of the university curriculum; the number of places reserved for candidates coming directly from the working world was increased; and a complex system of "transfer points" and part-time or evening courses permitted movement from production to the

university at any time. The law of September 1959 asked factories to recommend workers as candidates for the universities.
Finally, exemptions from entrance exams tied to awards received in secondary school were practically abolished.[29]

These measures, in principle, placed all aspirants to higher
education on an equal footing, whatever their origin and whatever course of study they might have followed. But, as early as
1958, the reform was circumvented, and it provoked a coming
together of hitherto dispersed opponents. Those who had for
years supplied most of the clientele of the universities, the
teachers, and the heads of enterprises were united in their
hostility to this reform. They were all fighting for their privileges, in the name of the quality of instruction, the homogeneity
of the students, or else the effectiveness of productive enterprises. In a very few years, the effect of pressures from every
direction and general bad will was to make the failure of the
reform obvious. Long training periods in production had been
transformed into vacations, and candidates from the most favored backgrounds had used the channels opened for the workers for their own benefit. In 1964, when a general assessment
was made, it was apparent that the social composition of the
universities had hardly changed since the Stalinist period, and
that evening courses were used primarily by candidates from
non-working-class backgrounds who had not found places in
daytime university courses as a means of catching up and entering the regular system.[30] The measures democratizing education in the end served to broaden the clientele from the governing milieu by increasing, for their benefit, the number of
available places and the methods of access to the universities.

The battle around this reform was very significant. The notions of equality of opportunity, democratization of education,
and social mobility, dear to Khrushchev, could not be attacked
head on, to the extent that they lay at the heart of the Soviet
ideological system and to the extent that all Khrushchev's reforms tended toward a certain democratization. But the way in

which the traditional beneficiaries of education were able to turn to their advantage the measures designed to reduce their role in it indicates both the solidarity of the privileged and the solidity of their position. Although Khrushchev did not succeed in imposing his views in this decisive area, which governed social mobility or stagnation, he nevertheless provoked the hostility not only of those whose privileges he was attempting to reduce but also of those to whom he was attempting to transfer those privileges. It was because of disappointment and dashed hopes that the working class and, to a lesser degree, the peasantry, to whom Khrushchev tried to open the doors of the Party and access to schools, finally judged him to be, like his colleagues, long-winded and muddleheaded, incapable of fully carrying out a program.

Until 1962, Khrushchev attempted to adjust the Soviet system while remaining within its logic. Even though he broadened the forums of Party discussion and attempted to change the Party's social composition, he multiplied reforms in the name of the Party and of its privileged political function. In 1962, he was confronted with the Party's general hostility; it circumvented his reforms in every area, emptied them of their content, and recreated the fiefdoms that Khrushchev had tried to weaken and replace with more genuine popular participation.[31] This was true of the Party, which, at the top, refused to allow the operation of the rules of renewal of personnel imposed by its first secretary. It was true of the economy, where the transfer of central powers to the *sovnarkhozes* led to a doubling of bureaucracies, the ones that survived more or less legally in Moscow and those that proliferated in the economic regions and rapidly gave birth to new alliances and hence to new fiefdoms. It was also true of the educational system. Everywhere, Khrushchev came up against ruling strata determined to defend their positions and the benefits—official and concealed—that were attached to them. The common denominator of these discontents was the Party, and in November 1962,

aware that he was confronting merciless opposition, Khrushchev finally stepped outside Soviet logic, the logic of the Party
as absolute master of power. The reform of November 1962,
which organized the Party according to the system of production, cut it into two branches, agricultural and industrial, and
involved all Party cadres in the specialized activities of those
branches.[32] The Party, which until then had dominated the
economic system, which drew its strength and legitimacy from
its unity and uniqueness, which had thereby imposed on society
a mono-organizational and mono-ideological system of which it
was the justification, at that point lost its reason for dominating.

If there has been a moment, in the course of its six decades
of existence, when the Soviet political system was very close to
a radical transformation, that moment came during the two
years between the reform of 1962 and the fall of Khrushchev.
What saved the system at the time was its inertia, civil society's
lack of political experience, and probably Khrushchev's own
fear of crossing the Rubicon.

The inertia of institutions was a very important element in
the failure of the reform of 1962. No doubt it was applied at the
time, but it did not break habits at one blow. Very often, the
division of the Communist organization into two branches kept
in place the former chief official—regional or district secretary
—at the head of the sector which was more important locally.[33]
Thus, in regions where industry predominated, the former regional chief of the Party took over the industrial branch. Absorbed by his ever-increasing foreign travels, Khrushchev was
unable to direct the redistribution of officials in the framework
of the reform, and the administration of the Party had a certain
latitude to limit its effects. Because the mono-organizational
system had had a long existence, and because the Party was
determined to defend its unity, the reform seemed to come
down to a series of provisional measures.[34] And in the background could already be seen the plans designed to eliminate

the man who called into question the preeminence of the Party.

A second reason for Khrushchev's failure was the nonexistence of civil society. Only the Party, threatened in its existence, perceived the stakes of the reform. But society, and even its intellectual elites, saw only one more reform, in a sphere that was foreign to it since it had long been excluded from power. It was between 1962 and 1964 that the degree of weakness—indeed, of nonexistence—of civil society in the U.S.S.R. became most apparent. No one understood that the system was on the point of changing. No one was ready to contribute to that change, for political information, outside what was transmitted by the Party, did not exist. Similarly, there was no place, no structure for social gathering, that was not controlled by the Party. At the Twenty-second Congress, Khrushchev had called for popular participation. But it was the Party that discussed the forms and degrees that that participation could adopt.[35]

Finally, Khrushchev himself probably did not dare step over the border that separated him from change of the political system. In his iconoclastic undertakings, in his intuitions about the need for change, he remained dominated by his past, by the training he had received in the Party. He had glimpsed and forecast—within certain limits—a political system different from the one that had prevailed since 1917. "The state of the whole people," proposed as a model in 1961, opened the way to popular participation through multiple channels of expression and decision, like the local soviets and the unions which, since the early twenties, had been nothing but transmission belts for the Party.[36] The use that Khrushchev made of the competence of specialists was also at this time an argument for diluting the Party's authority.[37] But even after 1962, he never followed his proposals to the end. His inability to think outside the framework within which he had been trained helped to save the system, just as much as the desires of those who benefited from it.

In the last analysis, the questions that arise are: first, the degree of authority Khrushchev possessed in the years 1956–64 and, second, the nature of power during that period. It cannot be denied that Khrushchev's personal power was significant. This is easily confirmed by a consideration of the reforms he imposed. He was able to go very far on the way toward reducing the authority of the Party, and he did so without calling on institutional counterweights, like the army. Although the army permitted Khrushchev to reestablish his position in 1957, he never repaid it. In 1958, he eliminated the army's representative, Marshal Zhukov, from the Presidium, and in the early sixties, by reducing military strength, he struck a blow against many of this group's advantages.[38] In 1962, Khrushchev was as unpopular with military officers as he was in the Party apparatus. Because of his incoherences, moreover, he alienated support he might have found in certain social groups. This was true for the intellectuals, whose initiatives and freedom of creation he encouraged by imposing on the Party the publication of Aleksandr Solzhenitsyn's first book, *One Day in the Life of Ivan Denisovich*,[39] while almost simultaneously discouraging them by persecuting Boris Pasternak and insulting non-figurative painters.[40] An evaluation of the work accomplished by Khrushchev thus leads one to emphasize the openings he carried out in all areas—politics, culture, the economy, foreign policy—but also the incoherences in his decisions which often led his programs into dead ends. We note his unquestionable power, which allowed him, until 1964, to impose on a hostile Party measures that it did not want, but we also note his weakness, since the Party was capable of slowing or sabotaging his reforms and then of eliminating him. And eliminating him "peacefully," which is another indication of the limits of his power.[41]

What in fact was power in the U.S.S.R. in the early sixties? How can we understand the juxtaposition of Khrushchev's personal power and the Party's capacity to slow him down and eliminate him? This gives some indication of the road that had been traveled since the days of Stalin, who was able to impose his choices on his colleagues and to eliminate them physically.

Power in the years 1956–64 was no longer—as Khrushchev's fall and, before that, his frequent failures indicate—completely in the hands of one man. It was a combination of the power of a supreme leader and the authority of a collective apparatus, the Presidium, which joined together various hierarchies. Although this apparatus for a long time gave in to Khrushchev's initiatives, at the same time it got him to respect procedures. And when the apparatus revolted against Khrushchev, this occurred within the framework of the procedures developed and safeguarded during those years. Post-Stalinist Soviet power can be characterized above all by the multiplication of political agents—institutions confronting leaders—and by the way in which all participants restrained their capacity for action at moments of confrontation in favor of regular and peaceful procedures. On these two levels, and despite the continued manifestations of personal ambition, the Stalinist era seemed to be over.

But, although power relationships had changed considerably, the same thing was not true of the nature and consequences of power. In 1964, power was still distant from society, and especially from the workers. It remained concentrated in the Communist Party. And the egalitarianism proclaimed by Khrushchev had left intact a certain number of the privileges attached to power.

CHAPTER 3

POWER IN A CLOSED CIRCUIT

Who governs the U.S.S.R.? This question has haunted statesmen and sparked debate among political scientists ever since 1917. The most common answer concentrates on personalized power, on the supreme leader. In public opinion, Soviet power is usually identified with the four key figures who have punctuated the history of the U.S.S.R.—Lenin, Stalin, Khrushchev, and Brezhnev. And, behind the struggles and changes in direction, we have tended to rely on the idea that an authoritarian system necessarily has a leader, and that Russia always returns to its demons, substituting "red czars" for the dethroned white czars. The anecdotes that are so popular under the socialist regime have helped to reinforce this vision.

The Soviet Constitution of 1977 supplies a rather more sophisticated answer to the question. Power is embodied in the state, which is, according to the Constitution, the expression of the social will and one of the "ways in which the power of the people operates."[1] Behind this definition of power, apparently so limpid, lie concealed a concept and a reality that are infinitely more complex and difficult to grasp.

The Soviet conception of power, as specified in the Constitution, has three poles: the power of the people—that is, the power of the entire social body which has been transformed, educated, and homogenized by its long post-revolutionary history; political power, no doubt an expression of the social will but at the same time endowed with a separate existence and embodied in the state; and finally, and above all, the charismatic power of the Party, which the Party draws from Marxist-Leninist doctrine and from an innate awareness of the needs and wishes of society. No doubt the Constitution places the people at the point of convergence of these various kinds of power. It asserts that they are the true holder of power (chapter I, article 2) and that "the Party exists for the people and is at the service of the people" (chapter III, article 6). At the same time, the Constitution provides for the autonomy of the state in relation to the people, making it distinct from the people. Especially it asserts that the Party leads and guides society and thus places the Party above society.[2]

Soviet political life, in appearance at least, provides examples of this division of power among the people, the state, and the Party. The Soviet people elect a bicameral parliament—the Supreme Soviet—and the state exercises its authority through the intermediary of a government and innumerable administrative bodies. However, the reality is that the Soviet system is dominated by the Communist Party, which holds power and rules out the possibility of sharing it with any other institution. Neither the parliament nor the government is responsible for political choices. By virtue of an unwritten law—which is, however, the fundamental law of the U.S.S.R.—these choices are exclusively the domain of the Party. It is up to the parliament and the government to receive them, translate them into laws, and put them into effect. The Party is thus the real holder of power in the U.S.S.R., but it exercises this power through the intermediary of central institutions and regional bureaucracies.

The preeminent authority of the Party over parliamentary and governmental institutions has two complementary characteristics. First of all, at the top of the various institutions, there is no possible opposition or competition, for the men who lead them are all members of the central organs of the Party and maintain the link between the Party and these bureaucracies. Secondly, the Party's authority over institutions goes beyond the hierarchical and functional relation established by the system, and beyond the identity of personnel. The Party also possesses its own administration—secretariat and departments of the Central Committee—which encompasses all domains of state activity. To each ministry there corresponds a department in the Party with highly qualified specialists, who assure the Party's control and, if necessary, a means of participating in the actual operations of the policies the Party had decided on.

In the end, the best summary of the reality of power in the U.S.S.R. is this formulation by Merle Fainsod, which will serve as the guiding thread of our analysis: "The real Parliament of the U.S.S.R. is the Central Committee of the Party; the real government is the Politburo; and the real Prime Minister is the general secretary."[3]

The Central Committee of the Party

In the Soviet system, the Central Committee is a decisive link in the chain of power and the meeting place of the political elite. Whoever "rules the U.S.S.R." certainly belongs to the Central Committee.

This collective body, familiarly known as the TSK, has evolved considerably, in the course of the various periods of Soviet history, in the number of its members, its composition, and its procedures, and these changes have affected its role.

For Lenin, the Central Committee was simply the small group that led the Party. The Committee elected at the end of the Seventh Party Congress in 1918 included 23 members, only 15 of whom had voting rights.[4] In 1976, the Twenty-fifth Congress elected a Central Committee of 426 members, 287 of whom were voting members. To these large numbers was added the Central Control Commission of 85 members. At first sight, there is a strong impression of a very great expansion of the ruling elite of the Party: 23 people in 1918, 511 in 1976. But the Party membership had swelled so much in the course of Soviet history that it, too, bore few resemblances to Lenin's small organization: 300,000 members in 1918, 15 million in 1976.[5] A comparison of these figures indicates that the membership has less representation today—in numbers at least— than it had more than half a century ago. In 1918, there was one seat on the Central Committee for every 13,000 Party members; today, 35,000 members are required for each seat. While the Party has grown larger, then, its elite has tended to contract.

Numerical data are enlightening in an attempt to understand the evolution of the Central Committee and its place in the Party. Table 1 assembles these data for crucial periods of Soviet history.[6]

What can be concluded from this table? First of all, its numerical strength has changed the functions of the Central Committee. Under Lenin, this small body could meet frequently— twice a month—and fulfill the functions of a veritable cabinet. But after Lenin's death, when it was necessary to assemble more than a hundred people, meetings became less frequent and resembled the sessions of a small parliament. Although rules periodically set out the frequency of Central Committee meetings (in 1922 it was to meet every two months, in 1934 every four months, in 1952 every six months), the rules were for a long time purely formal. Stalin called few meetings of the Central Committee, sometimes forgetting its existence for years.[7] Khrushchev was responsible for restoring this institution to life. Despite its growing numbers, he called on its authority when there were conflicts between him and his colleagues on the Presidium.[8]

On the other hand, Table I may be deceptive, because it suggests stability and change that are both in contradiction with the facts. In the years 1934–39, between the Seventeenth and

Table 1:   Party Membership, Congress Delegates, and the Composition of the Central Committee

Congress	Party membership	Number of delegates		Central Committee	
		Voting	Non-voting	Members	Candidates
VII *(March 1918)*	between 300,000 and 400,000	46	58	15	8
X *(March 1921)* Prohibition of factions N.E.P.	732,521	694	296	25	15
XII *(April 1923)* Beginning of conflicts for the succession	386,000	408	417	40	17
XV *(December 1927)* Turn toward collectivization	887,233 +348,957 candidates	898	771	71	50
XVII *(January–February 1934)*	1,874,488 +935,298 candidates	1,225	736	71	68
XVIII *(March 1939)* After the purges	1,588,852 +881,814 candidates	1,569	466	71	68
XIX *(October 1952)* Stalin's last congress	6,013,259 +868,886 candidates	1,192	167	125	110
XX *(February 1956)* De-Stalinization	6,795,896 +419,609 candidates	1,349	81	133	122
XXII *(October 1961)* Program of transition to communism	8,872,516 +843,489 candidates	4,394	405	175	155
XXIII *(March–April 1966)* After Khrushchev	11,673,676 +797,403 candidates	4,619	323	195	165
XXV *(February–March 1976)*	15,058,017 +636,170 candidates	4,998		287	139

Eighteenth Congresses, the number of Central Committee members and candidates did not change. However, the faces of these committee people changed from top to bottom, for these two congresses framed the period of the purges that decimated the Party. Over 70 percent (98 out of 139) of the elected members of the 1934 Central Committee and more than half the members of the Congress (1,108 out of 1,961) were physically liquidated.[9] Thus, the 139 members of the Central Committee in 1939 had almost no one in common with those of 1934.

The situation that has prevailed since Stalin's death is exactly contrary to the apparent Stalinist stability, and the political changes that have taken place in the U.S.S.R. have shown themselves first of all in the composition of the Central Committee. It has been characterized both by a continued increase in numbers—even though this was less substantial than the increase in Party troops—and by the stability of its membership. The Committee elected at the end of the 1976 Congress was made up essentially of members who had belonged to the body for a long time. Of the 287 titular members, 10 percent had been repeatedly reelected since 1956; half of those elected in 1961 were survivors from the preceding congress; from congress to congress, the rate of survival rose to 79.4 percent at the Twenty-third, held after Khrushchev's fall, 76.5 percent at the Twenty-fourth in 1971, and 83.4 percent at the Twenty-fifth in 1976. The enlargement of the Central Committee has had the primary function of permitting the rise of new cadres, since the old ones have held firmly to their positions. And we should emphasize that, however spectacular it may appear from the raw figures, the enlargement of the Central Committee has introduced less and less new blood, precisely because the proportion of old members, reelected at one congress after another, has continued to increase. The most massive entry of new members took place not after Stalin's death but in 1952, when he was still at the head of the Party. The 92 new arrivals in the Central Committee in 1952 represented a change of three quarters of the membership. Since then, although the Twenty-second Congress elected new members to the Central Committee representing 62 percent of the total, the proportion of new entrants declined in the course of the following congresses to 24.6 percent (1966), 36.5 percent (1971), and 29.6 percent (1976). Thus, in contrast to the Party, which has almost doubled its membership since 1961, the top of the Party has withdrawn timidly around an elite which has been reelected from one congress to the next and accepts new members only with difficulty.

A second remark concerns the moments when the Central Committee opened up, which were often out of phase with great historical moments. It was not the Twentieth Congress and de-Stalinization that modified the Central Committee, nor was it the Twenty-third Congress following Khrushchev's fall. In the periods when the leadership of the Party changed (Stalin, Khrushchev), its ruling organ was extremely stable. And, although Stalin almost totally renewed the membership of the Central Committee through the purges and the postwar opening, and although Khrushchev, using peaceful means, also attempted to change its composition in 1961 when his power was at its height, it is noteworthy that the Brezhnev period has been opposed to these tendencies. In sixteen years of power, the group which succeeded Khrushchev in 1964, far from disrupting the Central Committee, assured its continuing stability, while opening it up slightly in order to allow new arrivals to strengthen the institution.

This policy of stabilization appears even more clearly if we look at the list—rather short, it is true—of the members of the Central Committee whom the Congresses of 1971 and 1976 did not reelect.[10] Of the 81 who disappeared in these two congresses, more than a third had simply died (the average age of Central Committee members made this predictable); 15 others had retired, most of them because of their advanced age, but a few because this euphemism has come to be used to disguise political disgrace (this was the case for V.P. Mzhavanadze, first secretary of the Georgian Communist Party, dismissed for embezzlement, and for P.Y. Shelest, whose fall was a resounding episode in the nationality struggles). For the others, there are no explanations. But, if we take account of the dead and the retired, we note that political longevity tends toward the figure of 90 percent. This fact is all the more remarkable because aging, and the consequent natural disappearances, is a recent phenomenon in the composition of the Central Committee, which would not have affected it in the same way in the past. The effects of aging have in fact made themselves felt more and more clearly. Between the Twenty-fifth Congress and the summer of 1978—that is, in a year and a half—the Committee elected in 1976 buried 17 more members.[11]

As for the new entrants, they too have been representative, more than may appear at first sight, of this desire for stability. Forty-five of the 87 new titular members of 1976—that is, more than half—were already candidates (candidates are nonvoting members of the Central Committee).

The growth in numbers and the pattern of renewal in the Central Committee indicates the stability and, beyond that, the peace that has ruled in political circles since 1964. To the crises, purges, and expulsions of earlier years have succeeded relationships of a new type. The fact that the principal cause of changes of personnel in the institution has been their physical condition is an indication of an equilibrium that had never existed before. The social composition of the Central Committee confirms the impression.[12]

Why is one elected to the envied—and privileged—position of member of the Central Committee? In Lenin's time, the answer was clear: for the personal qualities represented by each individual, as a revolutionary before 1917 and as a political man thereafter. With Stalin, the criteria changed but remained just as personal; what counted was loyalty to the general secretary. At the present time, it is clear that personal virtues have nothing to do with being elected, except for a few marginal cases.

The composition of the Central Committee represents a careful balance of institutions, responsibilities, and nationalities, a balance that no longer varies.

The institutions which are best represented on the Central Committee are obviously the Party apparatus (40 percent of the total) and the apparatus of the state (31 percent in 1976, 30 percent in 1971, 28 percent in 1966). Thus, these two hierarchies, with 70 percent of the membership, have always dominated the supreme organ of the Party.[13] Then, follow three groups whose respective proportions have varied over time but whose importance has been affirmed in the course of the Brezhnev period: army, diplomatic corps, and police. Among these groups, representation of the army has experienced the greatest variations, as a function, one may well imagine, of the international situation and, at certain moments, of its participation in internal political problems. The military held 4 percent of the seats on the Central Committee in 1934, 14 percent on the eve of war in 1939, 11.5 percent in 1952 when Stalin was devoting himself to reducing the place that victory had given them in the Party, 7 percent in 1956, but 10 percent again in 1961. Thereafter, their representation has decreased with regularity: 9 percent (1966), 8 percent (1971), 7 percent (1976).[14] This decline of military representation hardly corresponds to the legend which has made the army the arbiter of the political situation in the U.S.S.R. Nor do the police occupy the place they are often assumed to hold in the highest institutions of the Party when real data are ignored: 3 percent of the seats in the years 1934–39, which is not very many, but the Central Committee was only a phantom at the time; 4 percent in 1952, when Stalin was preparing a new purge; the proportion of the KGB fell to 1 percent in 1956, 0.5 percent under Khrushchev, and has now risen again to 1.5 percent.[15] But we must further note the fact that this rise is due to the proportion of police among the candidates, while their representation among the titular members is one sixth as large (0.5 percent of voting members, 3 percent of

candidates). The military, on the other hand, have equal representation in the two categories. Although the Party is perfectly
willing to grant places to the police, it does not intend to restore
it to the role of major agent in political life which it held under
Stalin. The diplomats, for their part, are in a rising position
which coincides with the development of Soviet foreign policy.
From 3 percent in 1956, their representation has increased to
5 percent; but, significantly, the proportion of titular members
among them is much larger than, sometimes double, that of
candidates. The diplomats are thus visible and respectable
members of the highest organs of power.[16] These differences of
representation express differences in social and psychological
status in contrast with the practice of the Stalinist period. They
also express, and we will return to this point when we consider
the composition of the Politburo, the respective weight and
autonomy of each institution in the process of decision making.
Finally, the unions occupy a minor place in the Central Committee, where they hold only 1.5 percent of the seats, most
without voting rights, which is a measure of their power in the
Soviet system.

If we leave the domain of institutions to consider social status,
we observe—despite constant calls to open the Party to the
laboring classes—the very small proportion of workers and
peasants, who hold 4.5 percent of the seats on the Central
Committee, but only 3.5 percent of those with voting rights.[17]
Writers—those who are legally recognized as such—and scientists have representation roughly equivalent to that of the workers.[18] If we refer to the social composition of the Party in the
seventies, which was 41.6 percent workers and 13.9 percent
peasants, we are forced to note that the summit of the Party is
far from reflecting the social composition of the rank and file of
the Party, or that of the U.S.S.R. Nor does the Central Committee reflect the social composition of the Supreme Soviet, the
highest organ of the state, which contained at the same period
18 percent workers, 17 percent peasants, but only 16 percent

officials of the Party apparatus and 14 percent officials of the government apparatus.[19] In other words, the Central Committee reflects the structures of authority, while the Supreme Soviet tends to a representation of Soviet society which comes closer to reality.

The representation of diverse institutions and social groups of the U.S.S.R. is not enough to give a complete picture of the Central Committee. Hierarchies of another type, national and regional, also very clearly affect its composition and permit, through the Central Committee, an evaluation of the respective importance of various nationalities and regional entities in the system. The representation of nationalities at this upper level of the Party is not always easy to define, inasmuch as the information available is not the same from one congress to the next. In 1976, the Central Committee contained a majority of Russian delegates (approximately 60 percent). The national republics were represented in very unequal proportions, in numbers and in the hierarchical positions of their delegates (titular members, candidates, or members of the Control Commission), as well as in their functions. By considering these various criteria and looking at the place assigned to the principal political leaders of each republic (first and second secretaries of the Communist Party, president of the Council of Ministers, president of the Presidium of the Supreme Soviet) in the various institutions of the Party, it is possible to evaluate their respective importance.[20] The Russian Federal Republic was unmistakably in the first place, in both numbers and rank of its delegates. It was followed by the Ukraine and Kazakhstan; then by Uzbekistan and Byelorussia; then by Georgia; finally, by all the rest of the republics represented in smaller numbers. The Ukraine and Kazakhstan had the following in common: the first secretaries of their Parties on the Politburo, voting seats on the Central Committee for their three other major political dignitaries; second secretary of the Party, prime minister, and president of the Presidium of the Supreme Soviet. Hierarchical differentiations of status begins with the three following republics. All national republics (except for Russia, since it has no Communist Party of its own) have the right to a full seat on the Central Committee for their first secretaries, and those from Uzbekistan, Byelorussia, and Georgia are also deputy members of the Politburo. The principal leaders of Uzbekistan and Byelorussia all have voting seats on the Central Committee. But Georgia has only one candidate's seat for its second secretary, and its chief of state has to be content with a seat on the Central Control Commission. The other republics of the Union, beyond the seats for their first secretaries, have nonvoting seats for their prime ministers; their other dignitaries sometimes sit as candidates on the Central Committee, but more often on the Central Control Commission.

In general terms, this describes the delegates to the Central Committee. A look at this institution prompts one immediate observation. It is a body that brings together not individuals but functions. What qualifies an individual for entry to the Central Committee is the position occupied elsewhere, which provides automatic access to the highest institution in the Party. It is an evident fact that the dead are almost certainly replaced by their successors in the other positions they occupied, and the same holds true for those expelled.[21] In this perspective, promotions and exclusions can be explained by the "professional" history of Central Committee members and not by sudden disfavor of their electors—that is, the members of the congress. The balance on the Central Committee now represents a certain balance of forces in the U.S.S.R., among the bureaucracies, the regions, and the republics. Considered in this light, the Central Committee is a genuinely collegial organ.

But at the same time, it is not by a long shot an assembly of equals, each one with the same political weight. Between Aleksei Kosygin, head of the Soviet government and member of the Politburo, and M. S. Ivannikova, who worked in a Moscow cotton factory, there was little in common.[22] More than their personalities, it is the functions they carry out and the bureaucracies they represent that gives them weight within the Central Committee. The head of the Soviet government is an ex officio member of the Central Committee and the Politburo. The worker Ivannikova is certain never to join the Politburo. Moreover, it is significant that the same orators are frequently heard at plenary sessions of the Central Committee—namely, the representatives of the major republics, who hold the record for the number of speeches and the extent of subjects treated.

Of course, the Central Committee is elected at each congress by a secret ballot, on which, in principle, the delegates may maintain or cross out the names proposed to them. But they cannot change these names, which are those of candidates holding positions which automatically qualify them for seats on the Central Committee. Thus, well before becoming a member of the Central Committee, a Party or state official named to a particular post knows that that appointment will lead to a seat on the highest organ of the Party. So the Central Committee has tended to become the meeting place for the elite of Soviet politics and to reflect the respective weight of the various institutions which dominate the life of the U.S.S.R.[23]

This evolution of the Central Committee, which has made a ruling institution into a purely representative body, is reflected in its procedures. Central Committee meetings, to which Khrushchev had at first given a certain prominence and greater frequency, since then have tended to be less frequent and shorter and are not reported in detail.

During Khrushchev's first two years of power, from December 1956 to December 1958, the Central Committee met eleven times, and the average session lasted three days. During the following six years, 1959–64, the Central Committee held fourteen plenary sessions, an average of slightly more than two meetings a year. The time devoted to these sessions each year was ten days, or approximately four days per session.

In the Brezhnev era, the Central Committee at first seemed

to be engaged in significant activity, but this has tended to diminish as time has passed, and the shortness of the sessions indicates the formal character of the meetings (see Table 2).

This table prompts several observations on the evolution of the Central Committee's activities. Whatever the number of meetings held by the Central Committee each year, the total time devoted to them no longer ever exceeds four days and the number of sessions seems for a long time to have hovered around an annual average of two or three. Another significant fact is that the length of working sessions of the Central Committee seems less and less affected by important events, either in the political life of the U.S.S.R. or in foreign affairs. In this period, the Central Committee was most active in 1964, 1965, 1966, and 1968. In each of these years, the link between the activity put forth and important events is very clear. In 1964–65, the Party got rid of Khrushchev and liquidated his reforms. In 1966, it held the Twenty-third Congress, the first dominated by the new group. Finally, in 1968, the Czech affair mobilized the Party. On the other hand, the following congresses, 1971–76, seem to have had little effect on the activity of the Party. Nor did major international events: the two Arab-Israeli wars in 1967 and 1973, the Soviet penetration of Africa in 1975, or the invasion of Afghanistan in 1980. The great moments of détente (SALT in 1972, summit conference of 1973, Helsinki conference in 1975) do not appear on this table either. No doubt it is now impossible to have a clear idea of the debates of the Central Committee because stenographic reports have not been published since 1966.[24] And press coverage does no more than mention the subjects of the major reports. Thus we know that two orators spoke at length in June 1980: Leonid Brezhnev, to announce the date and agenda of the Twenty-sixth Congress to be held in February 1981, and Minister of Foreign Affairs Andrei Gromyko, who discussed the international situation.[25] If there was a debate—and the Afghan affair probably provoked one—it is doubtful that it could have taken up much time in the course of a one-day meeting. The evolution of the Central Com-

Table 2:   Periodicity of Central Committee Plenums[26]

Years	Plenary Sessions	Number of Days
1964 (Oct. to Dec.)	2	2
1965	3	5
1966	6	8
1967	2	3
1968	4	6
1969	2	2
1970	3	4
1971	3	4
1972	2	2
1973	2	4
1974	2	2
1975	3	3
1976	3	4
1977	3	4
1978	2	3
1979	2	4
1980 (first three quarters)	1	1

mittee's activities—the annual meeting in the autumn is almost certainly devoted to the presentation of the plan and the following year's budget—seems to have transformed the institution into a sounding board for the most important members of the Politburo.[27] Could such an assembly still save a leader in difficulty, as it did in 1957, or depose him, as in 1964? In other words, can it arbitrate conflicts at the top?

It is all the more important to determine the relations between the Central Committee and the Politburo, because their complementary or potentially antagonistic character largely determines the way in which the system functions in what remains the most imprecise area, the choice of its principal leaders.

The Real Centers of Decision: Politburo and Secretariat

The Politburo, unlike the Central Committee, has changed relatively little in the course of Soviet history. From the mo-

ment he came to power, Lenin used it as a real center of political decision.[28] It was at the time the most manageable body
because of its small size: eight members in 1919, only five of
whom had the right to vote. Amid the general increase in membership of institutions, it is striking to note how close the Politburo has remained to its origins, closed to every attempt at
enlargement and thereby capable of holding on to real power,
which has gradually escaped from the Party Congress and the
Central Committee. In 1980, at the conclusion of the June plenum, the Politburo consisted of twenty-three members, fourteen with voting rights and nine candidates.[29] The very small
increase in numbers occurred chiefly at moments of crisis,
when leaders attempted to swamp colleagues who were difficult to manipulate with a massive influx of new members. In
1952, Stalin increased it to thirty-six members, twenty-five of
whom had voting rights; Khrushchev made it twenty-five,
fifteen with the vote. Since the early seventies, the size of the
Politburo has stabilized, even though one may detect a certain
instability in its composition.

Like the Central Committee, the Politburo more or less systematically provides seats for holders of the highest positions in
the hierarchies of the state and the Party.[30] The head of government of the U.S.S.R., his first vice-president, and the head of
state are automatically included, as are a few secretaries of the
Central Committee and a few first secretaries of Communist
Parties of the republics. Here, too, a republic's political weight
defines its place in the Politburo. As a general rule, the Ukraine
and Kazakhstan, and also Byelorussia, whose predominant positions in the Central Committee have already been indicated,
have the right to full seats; other republics (like Georgia and
Uzbekistan) must be satisfied with nonvoting seats.[31] Certain
bodies, like the army and the police, have had varying fortunes
in the Politburo.[32] Since the early seventies, however, they
have been assured of continuous representation. We should also
note the personalized character of membership in the Polit-

buro, which is in only apparent contradiction to the institutional and geographical balance which can be detected in its makeup. The higher one rises in the hierarchy, the more power tends to be personalized, and the members of the Politburo, outside their function, possess authority and personal prestige that are only increased by various public aspects of political life.

A body with restricted membership, made up of personalities holding one of the highest titles in the state and the Party, thereby possessing significant weight, the Politburo is a veritable government which imposes its decisions on the other political institutions. By law, however, the Politburo is only the permanent executive organ of the Central Committee, whose authority it assumes when the Committee is not in session. This theoretical dependence on the Central Committee finds expression in the way the Politburo is named. It is elected in open vote by the voting members of the Central Committee, at the end of a congress in which the latter body has just been chosen by secret ballot. Expulsions or nominations of new members are also carried out by the Central Committee, which can thus change the composition of the Politburo in the course of its plenary sessions.[33]

As an emanation of the Central Committee, the Politburo resembles it in many respects, but certain traits are specific to it and point to its originality. First of all, the Russians have an even larger majority than in the Central Committee, particularly among voting members (ten seats out of fourteen), and this preeminence has grown stronger in recent years.[34] A second characteristic is the relatively significant renewal of this body since 1964. The Politburo of 1980 contained only four "veterans": Kosygin, elected for the first time in 1948, Suslov (1955), Brezhnev (1957), and Kirilenko (1962); as well as two deputies: Rashidov and Demichev. Three quarters of its members had thus been named to seats on this body under Brezhnev, and five of them after the Twenty-fifth Congress. Of the members who have left the Politburo since 1976, half the departures were due to death (Grechko, Kulakov), while the other half were the result of disgrace (Podgorny, Mazurov). Despite this far from negligible rate of renewal, the Politburo is noteworthy for the high average age of its members: nearly seventy for titular members and sixty-six years and eight months for candidates. Still more noteworthy is the Party's systematic tendency to promote old men. An examination of the average age of voting members confirms this fact. In 1966, at the end of the Twenty-third Congress, the average age on the Politburo was fifty-seven; in 1971, the Twenty-fourth Congress sent men to the Politburo who rejuvenated it, since the average age declined from sixty-two years and six months to sixty years and six months. Quite to the contrary, the elections at the Twenty-fifth Congress in 1976, despite the change in personnel, ratified an increase in age to nearly sixty-six; and despite the changes in the years 1976–80, the average age of the body has increased by one year for each year that has passed. If this tendency continues, we can imagine the Politburo on the eve of the Twenty-seventh Congress. This tendency also leads to imbalances in relation to the Party's political base, to which we will return.

The sociological characteristics of Politburo members are naturally connected to their age. These men, members of the first generation educated by the revolution, mirror their whole generation. Sons of workers and peasants for the most part—the Russia of 1920 drew its elite from these two social classes—they were generally trained in technical schools; for them, political activity in the Party apparatus was a road to social promotion. This is in fact one of the general characteristics of political personnel under Brezhnev, for whom the criterion of selection is more and more frequently the fact of having had a career as an apparatchik.

Like the Central Committee, and to an even greater extent, the Politburo is not a society of equals. Several factors differentiate its members from one another, the first of which is the hierarchy of their functions and the simultaneous possession of

several positions in the Party. Dual membership in the Politburo and the Secretariat and extended areas of responsibility
help to define the place of individuals (see Table 3). It is impossible to understand the role played by the Politburo, its functioning, and its shifting balances without at the same time considering the Secretariat of the Central Committee.

In theory, the Secretariat is not a decision-making body but
rather an administrative arm of the Central Committee, whose
primary function is to "manage routine matters, notably problems of cadre selection, and to see to it that Party decisions are
executed." As is often the case in the Soviet system, where
explicitly formulated principles and reality diverge, the Secretariat, which is scarcely mentioned in Party statutes, is almost
as important as the Politburo.[35] Elected, like the Politburo, by
an open ballot of the Central Committee at the end of each
congress, the Secretariat is also an extremely restricted body:
eleven members at the end of the Twenty-fifth Congress in
1976; only ten in 1980, six of whom had seats on the Politburo
(four with voting rights, two without). Even more than the
Politburo, the Secretariat has been subject to frequent renewal.
Of those who belonged to it before 1964, the only survivors are
the unshakable Suslov and Brezhnev, who was elected to the
Secretariat at Khrushchev's fall.[36] Since the Twenty-fifth Congress, the Secretariat has lost three members, only one of them
(Kulakov) for natural reasons. In the same period, three new
members joined its ranks, one of whom (Riabov), elected to the
Secretariat at the October 1976 plenum, was eliminated at the
July 1979 plenum. Like the Politboro, too, the Secretariat,
which sometimes has had younger-than-average individuals in
its ranks, seems to have been afflicted by a tendency toward
rapid aging. In 1980, its members' average age was sixty-seven
years and eight months; it too had been changed in the direction of increasing age by the disappearance of younger members (Riabov was fifty-one when he was eliminated, and Kulakov died at sixty).

Table 3   Politburo and Secretariat: Members' Positions in 1980

Name	Date of Birth	Number of Years in Office		Present Position	Date of Election or Nomination	Area of Responsibility	
		Full Member	Candi-date			Domestic	International
Politburo Members							
Andropov	6/15/14	7	6	President of State Security Committee (KGB)	May 1967	Security	Intelligence
Brezhnev	12/19/06	23	2	General Secretary of the Communist Party of the Soviet Union	October 1964 (First Secretary) 1966 (General Secretary)	Supervises all policies	Supervises all policies; international relations
Chernenko	9/24/11	2	1	President of the Presidium of the Supreme Soviet Secretary of the Central Committee	June 1977 March 1976	Work of the cadres of the Politburo	
Grishin	9/18/14	9	10	First Secretary of the Gorkom of Moscow	June 1967	Supervises Moscow Party	
Gromyko	7/18/09	7		Minister of Foreign Affairs	February 1957		International policy
Kirilenko	9/8/06	18	4	Secretary of the Central Committee	April 1966	Party organization; industrial organization	
Kosygin	2/21/04	24	5	Prime Minister	October 1964	Economic administration; finance	Economic problems of the socialist camp
Kunaev	1/?/12	9	5	First Secretary of Kazakh Party	December 1964	Supervises Kazakh Party	Foreign trade; international relations
Pelshe	2/?/99	14		President of the Party Control Committee	April 1966	Party discipline	
Romanov	2/7/23	4	3	First Secretary of the Leningrad Obkom	September 1970	Supervises Leningrad Obkom	

Name	Date of birth	No.	Position	Date joined	Responsibility	Foreign military operations
Tikhonov	5/14/05	2 (promoted 11/27/79) 4	First Vice-Prime Minister	September 1976	Economic administration; industry	
Ustinov	10/30/08	11	Minister of Defense	April 1976	Defense; space	Foreign military operations

Politburo Candidates

Name	Date of birth	No.	Position	Date joined	Responsibility	Foreign relations
Aliev	5/10/23	4	First Secretary of Azerbaidzhan Party	July 1969	Supervises Azerbaidzhan Party	
Demichev	1/3/18	16	Minister of Culture	November 1974	Culture	
Gorbachev	2/3/31	(promoted 11/27/79)	Secretary of the Central Committee	November 1978	Agriculture	
Kuznetsov	2/13/01	3	First Vice-President of the Presidium of the Supreme Soviet	October 1977	Assistant to Brezhnev as head of state	
Masherov	2/13/18	14	First Secretary of Byelorussian Communist Party	March 1965	Supervises Byelorussian Party	
Ponomarev	1/17/05	8	Secretary of the Central Committee	October 1961		Relations with foreign Communist Parties not in power
Rashidov	11/6/17	19	First Secretary of Uzbek Party	March 1959	Supervises Uzbek Party	
Shevarnadze	1/25/28	2	First Secretary of Georgian Party	September 1972	Supervises Georgian Party	
Solomentsev	11/5/13	9	Prime Minister of the R.S.F.S.R.	July 1971	Economic administration and finances of the R.S.F.S.R.	

Secretariat Members Not in Politburo

Name	Date of birth	Position	Date joined	Responsibility	Foreign relations
Dolgikh	12/5/24	Secretary of the Central Committee	December 1972	Heavy industry	
Kapitonov	2/23/15	—	December 1965	Party cadres	
Rusakov	12/31/09	—	May 1977		Relations with the socialist camp
Zimianin	11/21/14	—	March 1976	Culture	

Despite their difference in status—membership in an organ of permanent power versus an administrative organ—members of the Politboro and the Secretariat are indeed a group apart. The responsibility each man has over precise sectors of activity —which, taken together, cover all domains of Soviet life—and the authority each exercises through his own apparatus (the general secretary of the Party has a personal cabinet, some members of which have seats on the Central Committee),[37] on through the intermediary of the specialized departments of the Central Committee, give each leader control over several networks.[38] Finally, the Soviet system, as it has developed in the course of the last two decades, emphasizes the role of individuals, even if this role is presented as an integral part of collective power. The election of these higher leaders at the end of congresses is an opportunity to measure their popularity. When the press reports the event, it indicates a hierarchical ranking of each figure's prestige by noting the order in which each election was announced and the length of cheers and applause which greeted it.[39] Since 1964, there has always been a single winner in this popularity contest: Leonid Brezhnev.

Is the hierarchy of political organisms in the U.S.S.R., their overlapping and their complexity, in the last analysis only an ingenious screen for a personal dictatorship? The authority Brezhnev commands and his real place in political life deserve examination. For on the answer to this question depends to a large extent the analysis that can be made of the Soviet system as a whole.

Personal Power or Personalization of Power

In 1956, when it undertook a condemnation of Stalinist excesses, the Twentieth Congress of the Party attributed them to the cult of personality.[40] And it thereby admitted that the essence of Stalinism was an excess of personal power. With personal power removed, communism should recover its virtues and its legitimacy. Eight years later, in 1964, when his colleagues eliminated Khrushchev from power, they accused him with admirable unanimity of having restored personal power. And once again the Party's judgment was clear: Personal power carries within itself the seeds of all excesses and all deviations; it is contrary to the Party's vocation and to the interests of society. With Khrushchev removed, his colleagues swore never again to leave room for personal power, and to rule the Party and the country collectively. But a few years of political stability seem to have led, by the early seventies, to a well-known phenomenon: the emergence of a single personality once again dominating the system. From the group that took over in 1964, one man has stood out, Brezhnev, and he has polarized attention and given his name to the entire period. The honors he receives in his own country, the attention granted him by international society, everything seems to indicate that, despite the repeated condemnation of personal power in the U.S.S.R., it exists again as it existed in the past.

In theory, there is no place for personal power in the U.S.S.R., both because the Party condemns it and because nothing in the political system—the Constitution or the Party statutes—provides for the concentration of power in the hands of one man.[41] However, since Khrushchev's fall, Brezhnev has imposed himself as supreme leader. He has done so because, gradually, everyone who might have been a rival has disappeared from the political scene, because he has concentrated the principal powers in his hands, and because the cult that has developed around him has given him a political stature and a legitimacy enjoyed by none of his colleagues.

In 1964, Khrushchev was replaced by a group within which power was carefully balanced. No one in the group dominated the others. Brezhnev was at the top of the Party, but Podgorny had at least equal authority, for he was responsible for questions of organization and personnel in the Party, while Kosygin was in charge of the state apparatus. To this small group must be added Aleksandr Shelepin, president of the Party Control Commission.[42] The balance of positions was strengthened by a mixed distribution of responsibilities. No individual was in charge of a single area of activity. Thus, all members of this troika had international activities, in which Kosygin played the primary role.[43] In 1965, when the U.S.S.R. attempted to bring the Indians and Pakistanis together at the Tashkent conference, this spectacular mediation was conducted by Kosygin. Two years later, he was again the one who traveled to France and England and then met President Johnson at Glassboro. Thus, Kosygin dominated the first Soviet-American summit conference of the post-Khrushchev period, and the government seemed to be the place where international relations were worked out.

Brezhnev was in charge of another sector of foreign policy on the border between domestic and international affairs. As head of the Party, he dealt primarily with Communist countries and secondarily with the Third World. In 1969, out of the ninety-two days he devoted to international relations, only nine involved countries outside the Communist world, and they were almost all Third World countries.[44] Until the end of the sixties, Kosygin very clearly dominated the foreign policy of the U.S.S.R., and he was the leader most visible to the external world. In domestic affairs, the distribution of tasks was just as equitable. In the summer of 1965, when the Party celebrated the twentieth anniversary of the victory over Germany by naming "heroic cities" and granting them medals, Brezhnev's presence in Leningrad was balanced by Kosygin's in Volgograd (the new name for Stalingrad) and Suslov's in Odessa.[45] Collective government was then at its height. But, imperceptibly, the situation changed. As had happened in the past, Brezhnev first acquired a stronger position than his colleagues within the ruling organs of the Party, by peacefully displacing those who formed a counterweight to his authority. Thus, Podgorny moved from the Secretariat to the presidency of the Supreme

Soviet, which was in 1965 more an honorific position than one with genuine power.[46] From then on, Brezhnev was the real master of the Party, since he was responsible for choosing the cadres, and he received the title in 1966 when the Twenty-third Congress restored the position of general secretary, held from 1922 on by Stalin.[47]

What were the meanings and implications of this change of nomenclature, this return to an inegalitarian, hierarchical title, charged with such tragic memories? As early as the Twenty-third Congress itself, we can glimpse the immediate consequences. Brezhnev was accorded exceptional status by his peers. He will "lead the Central Committee," declared K. F. Katushev, a rising star of the party who had recently been promoted to first secretary of the important Gorky region. "He will lead the Politburo," explained another delegate to the congress,[48] and the first secretary of the Kirghiz completed the portrait by hailing Brezhnev as the "political head of the Party."[49] From that point on, the cult of Brezhnev grew steadily, first of all in the way he was referred to. For his seventieth birthday, his colleagues hailed his as the guide *(goid')* of the Party, a title to which only Lenin and Stalin had had the right in the past.[50] To emphasize his connection to Lenin, and probably even a certain form of equality, his colleague Kirilenko defined the Soviet political community in these terms: "The Central Committee, Leonid Ilyich [Brezhnev] personally, and all his companions in arms *(soratniki)* of the Politburo." Here, too, the parallel with Lenin was striking.[51] The acknowledgment of his *personal* position in the Party, the familiar designation by first name and patronymic with the omission of his last name, the term "companions in arms," which had been used for Lenin's associates—all seemed to come directly from the hagiographical books about Lenin and sometimes even went beyond the Stalinist vocabulary. To complete the picture, we can also cite "The leader in the style of Lenin,"[52] the man whose "life and work have been devoted to developing and embodying

Lenin's cause,"[53] who has "creatively developed Marxist-Leninist theory"[54]—these and an endless number of ever more glorious terms of praise have constantly accompanied the invocation of Leonid Brezhnev's name. In addition to this praise are the honors which he receives more frequently than is usual even in the rather expansive Soviet tradition. The U.S.S.R. is accustomed to the celebration of personal and political jubilees. Every ten years, it celebrates its leaders' birthdays with great display and much distribution of decorations, which can be seen on the leaders' chests at major ceremonies. Widely celebrated and decorated on his sixtieth and seventieth birthdays, which was normal, Brezhnev was honored again for his seventy-second birthday on December 19, 1978, which is out of the ordinary.[55] At the ceremony held at the Kremlin on that day, Brezhnev received the Order of Lenin for the seventh time and the gold medal of Hero of the U.S.S.R. for the third time. If we add to these three medals, which marked his sixtieth, seventieth, and seventy-second birthdays, the medal of Hero of Socialist Labor granted him in 1961, and the Karl Marx Gold Medal, we note that he is the most decorated man in the U.S.S.R.—for the present, it goes without saying, but also for the past, since he has gone beyond Stalin, who was hardly stingy in decorating himself. (Stalin received the Order of Lenin only three times, Hero of the U.S.S.R. only once, in 1945, and Hero of Socialist Labor once, in 1939.) There is only one example of someone receiving the medal of Hero of the U.S.S.R. more often, and that was Marshal Zhukov, who was decorated four times for his victories in the Second World War.

Brezhnev's written work—memoirs and political writings—has contributed to his cult. This work, greeted "with immense interest by the Soviet people and all of progressive humanity," "read, re-read, and enthusiastically studied," "a school of life for each new Soviet generation,"[56] earned its author the Lenin prize for literature on April 22, 1979 (which is abnormal, because the prize was not supposed to be given until 1980), and fabulous press runs (the trilogy of Brezhnev's memoirs had already been printed 180 times with a total printing of 18 million copies, and 65 million copies have been printed of his complete works).[57] Finally, although the Twentieth Congress had prohibited statues of living leaders, the rules were loosened in 1973 when the Party agreed that the exceptional cases of those who were "twice named Hero of the U.S.S.R." could be honored in that way. The first beneficiary of this exception was of course Brezhnev, whose bust was unveiled in his native city, Dneprodzerzhinsk, in May 1976. By holding this ceremony on the thirty-first anniversary of victory in the Second World War, the Party cleverly mixed the cult of Brezhnev with the celebration of an event that still had mobilizing force, concealing to some extent the exorbitant character of the honor that was granted, once again, to Brezhnev alone. The space given him in the press is just as revealing about this cult. At party congresses, the press notes the constant growth in the ovations he has received (twenty-five seconds of applause in 1966, twenty-eight in 1971, forty-two in 1976), which are much longer than those received by his most popular colleagues (Kosygin, who was always in second place, reached eleven seconds in 1976; as for the others, three or four seconds are enough for their admirers). The newspapers take no note of the fact that this "vehement and prolonged" applause is to a large extent directed by Brezhnev himself, since he is the one who reads the list of delegates, and he can therefore choose to leave space for the Congress to demonstrate its enthusiasm by the rhythm he adopts. For his seventieth birthday, *Pravda* devoted six pages to him out of an issue that had been extended to eight pages for the occasion.[58] As for his speeches, they are often published in full, whatever their length or content. Thus, for the 1971 elections to the Supreme Soviet, *Pravda* presented candidate Brezhnev's speeches in thirteen columns, beginning on page one. This privileged treatment contrasts with the five columns generally granted on page two or three of *Pravda* to the principal members of the Politburo, with the exception of Kosygin, who was close behind Brezhnev (nine columns on page one), and Suslov and Kirilenko (six columns, but on page two).[59] The preeminent place given to Brezhnev was all the more remarkable because there was no justification for it in 1979. During the 1974 elections, Brezhnev had in fact delivered long speeches which required that *Pravda* give him three pages. The brevity of his electoral presentations in 1979 meant that, in reality, it only filled half the space assigned to it and had to be surrounded with photographs. On the other hand, Kosygin's long speech was cut, so that in its published form it would be shorter than that of the general secretary. One can see how much this formalism and respect for precedence reveal about the political hierarchy.[60]

The object of an official cult, Brezhnev is responsible for a violation—and a substantial one—of the norms of Soviet political life, by his introduction of a certain nepotism into it. The founders of the Soviet regime were careful not to favor their relatives and not to create dynasties. Khrushchev was the first to break with this reserve, and he was criticized at the time of his fall for the role he had given to his son-in-law Adzhubei.[61] Although the general secretary's family remained in the background until the mid-seventies, since then two of its members have benefited from accelerated promotions better explained by their connections to Brezhnev than by their career profiles. Yuri Brezhnev, the general secretary's son, a foreign trade specialist, was elected to the Twenty-fifth Congress in 1976, an honor justified neither by his position in the Party nor by his administrative position; a few months later he was named deputy minister for foreign trade of the U.S.S.R, in charge of transport, and in March 1979 the first deputy minister for foreign trade.[62] These successive promotions of a young man (he was born in 1933) in a political system fiercely attached to the practice of giving ministerial positions to old men were clearly the result neither of chance nor of merit. Moreover, like his father,

Yuri Brezhnev collects decorations. Another family promotion, equally discreet, has been that of Yuri M. Churbanov, Brezhnev's son-in-law.[63] At fifty-four he was promoted to first deputy minister for domestic affairs of the U.S.S.R., replacing General Paputin,[64] whose death mysteriously coincided with the invasion of Afghanistan in December 1979.[65] This rapid progress of the male representatives of the Brezhnev family toward high positions in the Soviet administration contrasts with the general tendency of the children of leaders to turn to para-political or intellectual careers. What is noteworthy here is that nepotism is a rare phenomenon in Soviet political circles, and that it has appeared late in the Brezhnev period.

Brezhnev thus seems to have accumulated all the signs of the personal power his Party so severely condemned in 1956. But if the cult of personality and nepotism have been given free rein, is this not because they express Brezhnev's position of exceptional power? Here, too, the change that has occurred in relation to 1964, and even in relation to the Stalinist period, seems to designate Brezhnev as the most powerful man in all of Soviet history. The powers that he has gradually concentrated in his hands have no precedent.

By becoming general secretary in 1966, in principle, he acquired control over the entire Party. In fact, he has preponderant authority in the Politburo—since 1976 he has ordinarily been called its "head," a completely irregular title, because the general secretary has no right to direct the Politburo.[66] But this title and the fact that he is always placed at the head of the list of the Politburo, even when the members are arranged in alphabetical order,[67] emphasize the general secretary's personal authority over this organ. His authority over the Secretariat is more normal; he is officially in control of its meetings and its agenda, and he is also in control of all nominations inside and outside the Party, through the *nomenklatura.*[68] The entire Soviet bureaucracy thus depends on the authority of the general secretaryship; in the past, this instrument had allowed Stalin to manipulate the Party completely and to reduce it to complete passivity.

No doubt the separation of powers between government and Party, decided on for the first time in 1953 to weaken Malenkov and a second time in 1964, has been maintained. But this separation of powers has to a large extent lost its meaning, because Brezhnev has seized control of foreign policy and has become the real head of the Soviet state in the eyes of the external world; also because, in 1977, he received the title of head of state.

Since 1956, foreign policy has been a means used by Soviet leaders to affirm their authority. Khrushchev persuaded his colleagues to make him *also* head of government in 1958, by appealing to the consideration that a Party head was in a bad position to negotiate with non-Communist heads of state.[69] At the beginning of the post-Khrushchev period, a division of the international realm seemed to be a reasonable response to the problem. The head of government dealt with non-Communist heads of state, while the head of the Party was in charge of relations with Communist states and the Third World, which the U.S.S.R. classified in a special category.

But in this area, as well, the situation changed in the early seventies, when Brezhnev gradually replaced Kosygin on the scene. By 1971, relations with the non-Communist world took up nearly one third of his time. He turned some dealings with the Third World over to Podgorny, the head of state, and took charge of relations with the most important representatives of the Western world, those involved in détente: the United States, France, Germany. In 1974, nearly two thirds of his foreign activity was devoted to the Western world, the rest to assuring the cohesion of the Communist world and ties with a few Third World countries considered close to the U.S.S.R. With Podgorny's fall in late 1966, Leonid Brezhnev became the master of the totality of Soviet foreign policy.

At this point he took on a new responsibility: direction of the state. The presidency of the Presidium of the Supreme Soviet had long been a purely formal function, and the occupant of the position was kept apart from all responsibility. But Podgorny had attempted to use the position to hold on to some elements of power. By electing Brezhnev to the position in 1977, his colleagues resolved the problem, already posed by Khrushchev, of the international status of the man who embodied Soviet foreign policy. But at the same time they avoided placing the government apparatus, which certainly represented a real instrument of power, into the hands of the head of the Party. They thus avoided reinstituting a focus of political power that had been condemned and evoked unpleasant memories. They also avoided a dismissal of Kosygin, whose popularity was demonstrated at every Party congress and was based on a constantly emphasized economic competence. The conditions in which Brezhnev was raised to the head of the Soviet state are, moreover, not completely clear. He was elected president on June 16, 1977, during the meeting of the Supreme Soviet, on the nomination of Suslov, who invoked the superior interests of the state.[70] Discussing this election again two years later, Suslov explained that the decision to nominate Brezhnev for this position had been made at the plenum of the Central Committee in May 1977.[71] But if we read the report of this plenum in *Pravda,* we note that, although it reports Podgorny's expulsion, it is silent on the problem of his succession.[72] These contradictions indicate either that political decisions made in the U.S.S.R. are often announced with some delay to the Party as a whole, or that the level at which they are made is not always the Central Committee.

More than his position as head of the state, which is a matter of prestige, Brezhnev's military powers deserve consideration, because they raise the question of relations between civilian authority and the army. From 1974 on, we can detect a veritable "military turn" in Brezhnev's preoccupations and his career. In his New Year's Day speech, where he expressed his desire to pursue a policy of coexistence, Brezhnev insisted at the same time, on three occasions, on the imperatives of defense and the necessity of strengthening Soviet military potential.[73] From that moment on, Brezhnev, whose military career had been essentially in the political services of the army, rose through all the ranks of the military hierarchy at great speed and reached supreme leadership in two years. In April 1975, for the thirtieth anniversary of victory in the Second World War, Marshal Grechko, Minister of Defense, named him general of the Army, skipping over the intermediate rank of colonel general.[74] In May 1976 he was named Marshal of the U.S.S.R., and his compatriots discovered in passing, in a radio report, that he was also president of the State Defense Council,[75] which made him the supreme head of Soviet armed forces and placed him at the summit of the entire military-industrial complex.[76] From that point on, everything contributed to the strengthening of Brezhnev's military stature. His war activities were glorified, both in his own work *(Malaia zemlia)* and in commentaries on his past.[77] To the civilian honors he had already collected, Brezhnev now added the highest military decorations. A golden saber, an extremely rare decoration called the "arms of honor," was given to him on his seventieth birthday in December 1976; then on February 20, 1978, the Presidium of the Supreme Soviet, of which he was and remains the president, granted him the supreme military decoration, the Order of Victory,[78] reserved in principle for those who have held "positions of command at the highest level" and whose activities at the front "radically changed the military situation."[79] The least that can be said is that Brezhnev's military past scarcely meets these criteria. But it was in fact as supreme head of the army, covered with honors and titles, that he conducted a tour of inspection of the troops of Siberia and the Far East, in the company of the Minister of Defense. His inspections of the most advanced units in the U.S.S.R. (rockets in Novosibirsk, the Vladivostok naval base), the insistence of the press in pointing out that the trip was concerned primarily with the defense and security of the U.S.S.R., everything indicates the importance of Brezhnev's military role.[80]

Thus, after a period of relative effacement, in the course of the seventies Brezhnev had suddenly begun to accumulate powers, honors, and praises, to the point of becoming at the end of the decade "the dominant political, state, and military personality of our age,"[81] the man who had established a link with Lenin, overarching all of Soviet history.[82]

Can this emergence of Brezhnev at the summit of the Soviet political pyramid, a position which designates him to world opinion as the real master of the U.S.S.R., be considered the reality of Soviet political life, or is it a deformed image of that reality? It is remarkable that this concentration of power, for which there indeed are precedents in the U.S.S.R., has come about without affecting the stability of the political system. When Stalin seized absolute power, he imposed his decisions on his colleagues by dishonoring them and then by liquidating them. He held uncontested domination over a Party that was terrorized by the permanent purges to which it was subjected. When Khrushchev in turn tried to impose himself on his peers, he was obliged, insofar as possible, to change the composition of the Party's ruling group; and his peers, hardly inclined to be dominated and then eliminated, got rid of him within a few years.

Brezhnev's rise to supreme power bears no resemblance to these precedents. No doubt, the renewal of personnel in the ruling organs was an aspect of his rise, but—and we will return to this—the process had specific characteristics in sharp contrast to the political crises of the past. Moreover, the most prestigious figures of the Soviet political system, Kosygin and Suslov, far from being affected by these changes, seemed to have contributed to them to a great extent. Finally, the duration of Brezhnev's power—by 1980 he had already been in power twice as long as Khrushchev, nearly three times as long as

Lenin, and his political longevity was approaching that of Stalin
—suggests a certain consensus. This leads to two questions: (1)
Are all the elements of Brezhnev's power that have been described—cult of personality, concentration of powers—in constant and actual development? and (2). What kind of balance is
there in the relations between this all-powerful leader and the
Party apparatus which surrounds him and which elected him?

There is one particular area in which there can be no doubt
about the real effects of the cult of Brezhnev: the concrete
benefits that go along with it. Brezhnev is unquestionably in an
extraordinary position, and because of this special status he can
practice nepotism without incurring criticism. But it is important to indicate the limits of this privilege. Careers in the
U.S.S.R. can be unmade as quickly as they are made, and because they are based on political decisions no one can guarantee
their stability; Adzhubei, whose fortune had been assured by
Khrushchev, experienced a rapid fall. As for the rest, Brezhnev
derives from his diverse functions and decorations material benefits that cannot be evaluated. One example may indicate this
difficulty of giving exact figures for the income of Soviet leaders:
author's royalties. Brezhnev owes the fabulous print runs of his
literary work to his political position. It is impossible to evaluate,
even approximately, the income he derives from this source,
but his *Trilogy,* of which more than 10 million copies have
officially been printed, must have brought in a minimum of
500,000 rubles. (We should note here that the average annual
salary in the U.S.S.R. in 1980 was less than 2,000 rubles.) There
has been complete silence on this question and on the use to
which such sums may be put. But it is obvious that power in the
U.S.S.R., if it is not connected to capital at the origin, can have
considerable financial effects, effects from which Brezhnev's
whole entourage has benefited. No doubt the original austerity
of the Soviet leaders and the frequent calls by Brezhnev himself
for economy make it impossible for him to make any glaringly
obvious changes in his way of life. His only apparent luxury is

the use of the fleet of automobiles given to him by foreign heads of state. But whatever remains of egalitarian aspirations in the U.S.S.R. has been effectively demolished by the fortunes that have been built up by those in power.

Beyond these obvious material inequalities, it is a questionable procedure to analyze the scope and the meaning of the cult of Brezhnev without introducing nuances into the analysis. For nuances exist, and when they are taken into consideration they change the outline of the man and his political weight. While Stalin's colleagues hailed him as a man out of the ordinary, "the greatest man of all time,"[83] a man with incomparable personal virtues, the praise offered to Brezhnev emphasizes especially human qualities which are those of the average man and his ability to work in a collective body. It is precisely his most fervent admirers who emphasize these unexpected traits in the portraits they paint of their guide. What is exceptional in him, said Eduard Shevarnadze at the Twenty-fifth Congress, is his modesty: "He does not play at being a superman, and never tries to take another's place." His great virtue is "to have established good human contacts in the Party," "to have created a good working atmosphere and developed consultations and cooperation."[84] What is more, periodically—and especially when Brezhnev's cult or his prerogatives are progressing—the Party over which he has authority reaffirms the importance of the collegial principle: "The general secretary of the Party is not a chief, he cannot give orders. He is only the first among equals in a collective leadership elected by the Communists."[85]

All the texts that have established the cult of Brezhnev can thus be read in two senses. On the one hand, there is the abundance of the material, the considerable number of times he is quoted, applauded, or praised for his qualities, and the space the press gives to his every action. But on the other side there is the content of these praises, which make Brezhnev a man of great merit, to be sure, but a man who is representative of the political group around him: the son of workers, promoted by the Party to the highest duties and determined because of that to defend the interests of the Party.[86] Nothing in these praises or this terminology suggests the portrait of a charismatic leader. The charismatic leader, as Max Weber has described him, feels himself, asserts himself to be charged with a mission about which he is accountable only to himself. This is why his legitimacy depends on no one, and the attitude of the masses toward him counts for little.[87] Brezhnev's legitimacy, as it can be determined from his cult, is radically different. He claims no mission, he is only the representative of the Communists, and his authority depends on the confidence they have in him. This ordinary hero is in the image of his peers: elderly men who continuously affirm, in domestic and foreign policy, their concern for stability and security. Just as his cult is slightly ambiguous, so the powers concentrated in Brezhnev's hands are not, as they clearly appear to be at first sight, the instruments of total power. The position of general secretary of the Party—incidentally, barely defined by the statutes—carries with it considerable elements of power. But, even in this position, Brezhnev seems to possess limited power because of the continuous presence since 1964, in the Politburo and the Secretariat, of colleagues like Kosygin whose governmental responsibilities give them, too, great authority. Since 1964, Soviet leaders seem to have split into two groups: those affected by no change, who represent permanence, and those whose authority is limited by the brevity of their careers. The permanent figures are precisely those who share Brezhnev's past, who have roughly the same history and the same political profile. This similarity in experience and political longevity gives each one of them considerable authority in his particular domain.

It is significant that Brezhnev has on many occasions, for reasons of health but sometimes without that pretext, been replaced by someone belonging to this group of veterans. The Central Committee plenum held in April 1979 illustrates the division of labor that sometimes occurs in the ruling organs. It is the rule in these plenums that important questions of organization are treated by the Party's general secretary. The April plenum was to present the Politburo's proposals for the work of the new Supreme Soviet. Although the voice of the Politburo was in these circumstances represented by the general secretary of the Party, it appears clearly from the report in *Pravda* that Brezhnev merely provided a brief introduction to the debate and that Suslov spoke in the name of the Politburo.[88] This replacement of Brezhnev by another leader was repeated a few days later, on April 18, 1979, at the inaugural meeting of the tenth session of the Supreme Soviet. Here again, Suslov proposed the reelection of Brezhnev as head of state for approval by the legislators, but also, clearly trespassing on Brezhnev's prerogatives, the election of Vasily Kuznetzov as vice-president and the election of the entire Presidium.[89] These proposals are normally reserved for the general secretary, and the procedure had always been respected in previous legislatures.[90] The variation indicated not that Brezhnev had suddenly fallen out of favor but that the Politburo was acting together. The election of a vice-president to assist Brezhnev was immediately translated into action. The day before the opening session of the Supreme Soviet, Kuznetsov chaired the joint session of the Council of Elders of the two assemblies and the meeting of the outgoing Presidium.[91]

Brezhnev has been replaced by his peers on many other occasions, something which would have been unthinkable under Stalin, and which, under Khrushchev, would have clearly indicated a political setback. In the late seventies, this division of labor among the most prestigious figures of the Politburo clearly corresponded to the constant affirmation of collegiality which underlay all the compliments addressed to Brezhnev.

We thus get a sense of the real nature of Brezhnev's powers. He has been given power by his peers, he has not seized it from them. He was chosen by his peers after deliberation, on the basis of objective criteria and a common will to define the limits of personal power. The objective criteria are connected to his career. Of all the potential successors to Khrushchev, only Brezhnev had such extensive political experience in both professional and geographic terms. He was, above all, a man of the Party apparatus, within which his entire career had taken place. He had worked in every area—cadres, agriculture, industry, the army. Moreover, he had to his credit three types of experience covering all geographic levels of power in the U.S.S.R: responsibility for a region (Dnepropetrovsk), for republics (Ukraine, Kazakhstan, Moldavia), and in the center. Thus no categorical or regional-national aspect of the U.S.S.R., no problem of coordination or differentiation, was unknown to him. A glance at the biographies of Soviet leaders is enough to indicate that Brezhnev was in this respect an exceptional case among his peers. To this criterion of necessity, the "best choice," was added in 1964 an agreement on a certain number of requirements which Brezhnev has always respected. There would be no concurrent holding of Party and government powers; there would be restoration of the stability of positions; there would be restoration of the authority of all his peers—that is, the Presidium (the ex- and future Politburo); and there would be acceptance of a certain division of labor between state and Party.

These criteria and requirements provide the outlines of a stable political system governed by rules. Within the framework of these requirements, Brezhnev has unquestionably established increased authority and means of exercising power. His colleagues have left him free to increase his advantages in two areas. In the matter of prestige, the multiplication of titles and decorations bothered no one, and as a counterpart, to lessen their visibility, Brezhnev has decorated his colleagues as well, which gives them, too, many material and social privileges.[92] His colleagues have also left him a certain freedom of action in the area that demands the greatest amount of personal activity—that is, foreign policy, from which he gradually eliminated Kosygin and Podgorny. As for his military functions, as we shall see, they are probably based on a broad consensus in the Politburo on the function of political power. But through all these manifestations of authority, Brezhnev, from all the evidence, has respected the system established in 1964, which, because of the requirement of stability, has considerably limited his means of action.

It seems possible, at first sight, to reduce the Soviet political system to a personal dictatorship concealed behind the alibi provided by the Party and its ruling institutions, or else to a permanent struggle between Brezhnev's ambitions and programs and the wishes of his colleagues. But if we look more closely, we recognize that the system in its very structure has changed profoundly. Lenin was a veritable charismatic leader of the U.S.S.R., exempt from any drive for personal power—in fact, he attempted to depersonalize power. But, as Zbigniew Brzezinski has correctly pointed out, personal power exists in a one-party system when the man who embodies it is simultaneously head of the Party, its theoretician, and the head of the state organized by the Party. Without any question, Lenin combined all those roles, and this is why, after October 1917, he was able to leave the Party in his colleagues' hands and to govern the state. His moral authority over the Party remained preeminent. Stalin fit into the same mold of tripartite authority by eliminating or weakening anyone who might have formed a counterweight. But the successors of Khrushchev, after his failed attempts to restore the same unity of leadership, took great pains to separate these functions. It hardly matters that Brezhnev is both head of state and head of the Party if the government—that is, the management of public affairs, the economy, and the carrying out of plans—is separated from his power and if another individual embodies the government hierarchy. It hardly matters that his colleagues praise his merits as a theoretician and writer if the duty of expressing Communist orthodoxy is the general responsibility of the Party and

specifically of its spokesman, Suslov. The extreme personalization of Brezhnev's power, to which his colleagues have consented and contributed, does not coincide with real personal
power. And the stability of the ruling group, the continued
occupation by his colleagues of the essential positions limiting
his power, to which Brezhnev has consented, provides a true
picture of the system—that is, the persistence of collective
power. (See Appendixes I and II for the composition of the
Politburo and the Secretariat of the Central Committee since
1952.) An analysis of the background of power—the political
succession—and its manner of operation should permit a determination of how far this transformed power has consolidated
itself.

CHAPTER 4

THE POLITICAL RESERVOIR

The leaders of the U.S.S.R., because of their very great powers and their longevity, tend to monopolize attention and thereby help to give a distorted impression of the country's political organization. In fact, Communist systems, and the U.S.S.R. above all, more than liberal systems have done, have developed behind the central authority, at every level, a huge bureaucracy whose organization and coordination are essential for the functioning of the systems themselves.

There are several reasons for this state of affairs. The immensity of Soviet territory and the differences among populations no doubt have something to do with it, but it is much more a result of the nature of the system itself. The Communist organization of society places all collective and individual activities under the authority of a single, highly centralized party. There are no parties in the political realm, no market in the economic realm, no organizations in the social and cultural realms that can play an autonomous role. The immensity of the tasks that devolve on the Party and the state in so large a territory implies a very high degree of centralization. Finally, and this is not a minor argument, the political tradition the Bolsheviks adopted helped to orient them toward a bureaucratic system of power. Lenin's favorite model of organization was the army, as all his writings indicate. In the early twentieth century, economic development, the Bolsheviks' primary ambition, had been carried out in the framework of military societies: Prussia and Japan. And from its earliest years, the Soviet system was rapidly militarized, in its organizational principles and in the structure it imposed on society.

The power of the leaders is manifested through the bureaucracy, which is responsible for the supervision of society and the application of decisions made at the summit. It is also—and this is essential—the political reservoir from which will arise the new leadership of the U.S.S.R.

The Communist People

The Party, spinal column of the Soviet system, is both an organ of decision and an administrative organ. Sometimes it participates in, and sometimes it is totally identified with, the management of the U.S.S.R. at all levels and in every sphere of activity. This is why it is important first of all to define briefly its organization and ruling principles.

A first characteristic of the organization of the Soviet Communist Party is that it coincides exactly with the territorial and political organization of the country.[1] The U.S.S.R. is divided into fourteen national republics, regions *(oblast)*, cities, and urban or rural districts *(raions)*. The first entity, the national republic, corresponds to the desire of the founders of the U.S.S.R. to recognize—temporarily, at least—national differences and the aspiration of national groups to see these differences translated into statutory differences. For the same reason, there are two other types of political-territorial entity in the U.S.S.R.: the autonomous republic and the territory *(krai)*. Their size and political organization are the same as those of the regions, but they provide for the recognition of certain special rights of the national groups which make up the majority in each political division. Four republics stand out in this group:

Russia (R.S.F.S.R.), Ukraine, Kazakhstan, and Byelorussia. Because of their size, they are subdivided into regions, autonomous republics, or territories.[2] Most of the other republics do
not have such subdivisions, for they are of the same size as a
region in Russia. Because Party organization coincides with this
territorial division, each level has its corresponding Party organization, with a full complement of institutions—a committee,
a bureau, and a secretariat.

The Party's local institutions are modeled on the central organizations, with similar functions; only the names, the size, and
the scope of responsibilities vary. What is important is that,
from the center of the Soviet Union—Moscow—to the smallest
village, the same executive institutions are found—a Party bureau and a secretariat—and that from top to bottom a network
of rigid relations has been established, the rules for which were
established by Lenin in the concept of democratic centralism.[3]
According to the terms of this concept, Party organization
moves in two directions. The rank and file, through the rule of
elections at every level, sends its representatives to the top and
always has the right to receive reports of activity from those
representatives. In the opposite direction, the top of the Party
controls all the activities of the rank and file and has the power
of decision. This organization, characterized by both centralization and the capacity to penetrate to the most remote areas, is
particularly important at the level of the region, the relay point
between the center and lesser organizations. By its size, its
human makeup, and its economic functions, the region is really
a small-scale state. It is not an accident that one of the best
American specialists on the Soviet Union, Jerry Hough, has
presented the region as an equivalent of the French department and compared the first secretary of the regional Communist organization—the obkom—to a French prefect.[4]

In the U.S.S.R., even though nothing in the Constitution
stipulates it, the Communist Party is conceived of as the political reservoir from which the system draws all its cadres. This

reservoir is, by definition, the place where the "best," most aware citizens of the U.S.S.R. come together, and the essential criterion of recruitment—in theory, at least—is a high degree of political consciousness and adhesion to the system. By considering the current composition of the Party and the possibilities of promotion it offers its members, we can measure the evolution of the Soviet system and grasp its present tendencies.

Conceived by Lenin as a party of professional revolutionaries, what does the Party now represent in relation to society? To what extent is it a faithful reflection of society? What do political consciousness and loyalty to the system mean today? The composition of the Party is revealing on these points.

The Communist Party has become—this is worth emphasizing—a mass party; it has more than 16 million members, 10 percent of the active population.[5] These figures suggest that joining the Communist Party assures a certain degree of political participation. However, a consideration of the evolution of Party recruitment from one congress to another indicates a slowing down and some sociological changes. The rapid growth of Party membership characteristic of the years 1952–65 is now a thing of the past. From 1961 to 1966, the Party grew each year by 760,000 members; from 1966 to 1971 this rate was reduced to 600,000; and by 1966 the average had fallen to 450,000.[6] There are natural reasons to explain this decline. After a period of rapid growth, the Soviet population, like the populations of all industrialized countries, has experienced a definite demographic decline. Above all, the U.S.S.R. has paid in the seventies for the Second World War. The decimated generation can be seen in the proportion of those between twenty and thirty, who represented 18.5 percent of the total population in 1959 but only 12.18 percent in 1970.[7] And this is precisely the age group from which the Party recruits the majority of its new members. Finally, in the mid-sixties, the Party became more rigorous in its admission procedures and forced its members, once they had been admitted, to undergo more thorough political training than in the past. If we add that the procedure of exchanging cards in the early seventies gave rise to a thorough examination of members' qualities and activities and that, at the conclusion of these verifications, 347,000 Communists were expelled from the Party, it is easy to understand why the Party has been progressing more slowly.[8]

But the change in the social composition of the Party is more interesting. All the congresses of the post-Stalinist period have repeated that it is necessary to bring the Party closer to society by opening it to the workers. By comparing the figures indicating the social structure of the Party to that of the U.S.S.R., we can observe both the progress accomplished in "workerization" and the limitations of that progress. (See Tables 4 and 5.)

The juxtaposition of these tables immediately shows that the Party gives excessive representation to the broad and imprecise category of white-collar workers;[9] the working class remains underrepresented, despite a slight increase; and the only group whose representation in the Party seems to coincide approximately with its place in Soviet society is the peasantry.

But, here as in other cases, the figures express a slightly truncated reality. This is true first of all for the peasants, to whom the Party has not been nearly as favorable as the figures would suggest. If there is now a certain balance between the size of the peasantry and its representation in the Party, this is the result of a statistical transfer of a significant fraction of the peasantry into the group of workers. Indeed, one of the constants of Soviet agricultural policy in the seventies was the proliferation of sovkhozes—state farms—at the expense of kolkhozes—peasant cooperatives.[10] This structural modification of the countryside which has now placed more than half the peasant population under the authority of a single employer, the state, has brought about the statistical transfer of peasants to the category of workers. The countryside still employs many people, but under different names. Thus, a first conclusion becomes unavoidable: The countryside remains very underrepresented in the Party.

A second distortion of the figures derives from the fact that

Table 4:   Social Composition of the U.S.S.R. (percent)[11]

Year	Workers	Peasants	White-Collar Workers
1959	48	31	20
1976	61.2	16.4	22.4

Table 5:   Social Composition of the Soviet Communist Party (percent)[12]

Year	Workers	Peasants	White-Collar Workers
1961	33.9	17.6	48.5
1971	40.1	15.1	44.8
1976	41.6	13.9	44.4

the classification of Party members in a professional category does not always take into account their real activities. Moreover, the Party often preserves in its statistics an individual's activity at the moment of joining and "forgets" the subsequent evolution of that career. The first reservation is particularly important in considering peasant recruitment. If we consider the matter in detail, we observe that, of the Communists who in theory have come from the peasantry, half are in fact technicians (such as tractor operators) and only half of them are peasants working the land, while the first category represents one fifth, and the second four fifths, of rural workers.

As for this second point, it is impossible to measure its real implications for the social definition of Party members' origins. But many signs suggest that the men who are most firmly established in the apparatus, like Brezhnev, are still classed in the category of workers because of a brief period in production. This is why it is risky to attempt to compare society and Party with any precision.

On the other hand, we are on more solid ground when we

refer to criteria other than professional ones, such as sex, age, militancy, and education, which provide a clearer sense of how and why one becomes a Communist in the U.S.S.R. Sexual equality, a fundamental principle of Soviet law, does not appear in Party membership, and in this case no statistical transfer is possible. In 1976, the Party included 3,793,859 women, less than 25 percent of the total Communist population.[13] No doubt there had been progress in relation to the past, since in 1966 the proportion of women in the Party was 20.6 percent.[14] But if we compare the relative influence of men and women in Soviet society, we observe that in 1959 a woman was only one fifth as likely as a man to join the Party, and in 1974, one fourth as likely. Sexual equality, seen in this perspective, clearly has more to do with theory than reality.

The average age of Party members is difficult to judge, because the data published in the U.S.S.R. are imprecise. But on the other hand, we can compare the distribution of age groups in the Party and the population. The juxtaposition of the available data leads to two important observations of fact. First, the Party is chiefly represented among those between thirty and sixty and leaves little space for those younger than thirty, particularly those between eighteen and twenty-five. It is a mature Party. Second, within each age group of ten years, the average age in the Party is slightly older than in the population. In 1971, the Party decided to raise slightly the age at which members were admitted, and that measure has led to a general aging.

This belated recruitment is also related to another change: the increased importance of the Komsomol in a militant's itinerary. This organization of Communist youth, which accepted the "best" adolescents into its ranks, has at all times been considered as a means of access to the Party. But until 1972, the path was far from being of the first importance, and the proportion of komsomols admitted into the Party varied from 40 to 50 percent. We can observe a clear change in 1972, because since that date 70 percent of new members have come from the

Komsomol. It is appropriate to note that, here again, women confront a barrier, and their time in the Komsomol is not enough to open the gates of the Party more widely to them.[15]

But what is perhaps most characteristic of the Party today are its educational requirements. The progress of education in the U.S.S.R. has been constant, and the Party has more and more presented itself as the vanguard of an educated society. In 1956, when 2.9 percent of the Soviet population held higher degrees, the proportion was 11 percent in the Party, approximately four times that of society as a whole.[16] By 1977, the difference had diminished slightly, because the proportion had become 8 percent for society as a whole and 25 percent for the Party, approximately three times as many;[17] the reduction of this difference has to do with the general progress of education in the U.S.S.R. and with the relative progress of workers in the Party. But this ought not to conceal the fact that possessing higher education has become a very important element in admission, especially insofar as diploma holders have begun to constitute a significant Party group.

A final inequality in the composition of the Party, one that is not social, is related to the national differences characteristic of the U.S.S.R. The Party has never recruited equally among all national groups, and until the early sixties there was a disparity as large as five to one in the representation of various nations: The Russians, Georgians, and Jews were best represented, and the Kirghizes, for example, the worst represented.[18] For the favored nations, these differences can be explained both by historical reasons (socialism had been introduced early into Georgia; the Jews founded the first Social-Democratic organization in Russia, the Bund) and by the central position of the Russians in the whole political system. On the other hand, it is easy to see why peoples attached to their religion, long ignorant of Marxism or still largely rural and badly educated, came belatedly to the Party. But in the course of the last two decades, a long common education,[19] the progressive equalization of ways of life, and the desire to make admission to the Party more equal have unquestionably improved representation of the nations. In 1976, the disparity between the most represented (Georgians) and the least represented (Moldavians) was only three to one.

This unquestionable progress of all nations in the Communist Party of the Soviet Union cannot however result in equitable representation or avoid imbalances whose political meaning is obvious. We can foresee that the most badly represented people, those on the Islamic periphery, will remain that way for a long time to come, despite the efforts that have been made to improve their position. The Party is attempting simultaneously to increase all national representations and to limit the growth of its membership. But the populations of the Moslem republics have much faster demographic growth than that of the U.S.S.R., especially faster than that of the people with the highest levels of education;[20] these peoples will grow more quickly than they will join the Party, which will thus remain imbalanced. To this imbalance, which victimizes the peoples of the periphery, add the recruitment policy adopted—intellectual criteria of selection and the geographic criterion—which favors the large capitals and the economic metropolises located in the European part of the U.S.S.R.. This allows the Slavs to be overall the best represented. From 1961 to 1976, they fell from 75.8 to 72.8 percent of the Soviet population, but they still represented 80.2 percent of the Party militants, down from 81.2 percent.

We can thus see what the Communist population is like and what leads an individual to join it. Ideally, the Party is the Party of the whole people, and it should reflect their makeup and their progress. In reality, it is a party that carefully controls its development and in which cooptation is an inviolable principle which allows it to direct its choices. Being a worker is theoretically a decisive element leading to Party entry. But the position that has recently been granted to recruits from the Komsomol indicates that workers, too, are subject to a selection process.

Only the best educated politically, the most active, those who have passed through a preliminary barrier, can join the ranks of applicants to join the Party. Moreover, workers and peasants are graded according to their technical skills. The Party chooses specialists, people who have already risen to a certain level in their trade, over rank-and-file workers. And if white-collar workers (a category which, together with specialists, makes up the tertiary sector) are very likely to enter the Party, the kolkhozniks are very unlikely to do so. It is also better to be a man than a woman, to be over thirty, preferably around forty or a little older, and, most importantly, to have gone through higher education. In 1976, one third of those with higher-education diplomas were in the Party. Finally, it is better to be a Slav or to live in Moscow.[21]

The contradictions between the repeated objectives and the facts are striking. The Communist Party, by enlarging its ranks, far from becoming a mass party, has closed itself to the masses and tends to accept those who, in each professional category, have already begun their rise. The "wretched of the earth" are by definition excluded from this Party, which opens the path to upward mobility. In order to join it, you must already have some chance of rising on the ladder of success.

The Aktiv: Nursery of Cadres

But all these traits, which depict a mass Party open in reality only to those situated at the top, become even more pronounced when the object of attention moves from the rank and file of the Party to its more active levels. The Party comprises three categories of actors: the ordinary militant (as we have seen, it is not so easy to become one), the activist, and the permanent cadre.

The activist is one of the essential, and too easily forgotten, cogs in the Soviet system. Activists carry out particular, part-time, unpaid activities for the Party which has chosen them for these responsibilities. They do this either within permanent institutions, rank-and-file Party organizations in factories (committee, secretariat of a cell), or in the very apparatus of the Party or the state. This apparently voluntary work is not voluntary, for it is up to the Party whether a militant enters this category, in which many positions are part of the *nomenklatura.* The internal organization of the Party, with its complex hierarchy of elected positions, makes it easy to understand the Party's need for cadres and the place held in it by activists. Table 6 juxtaposes the hierarchy of Party organizations and the hierarchy of those who are responsible for its operation.

Two observations can be derived from this table. According to the figures of the Twenty-fifth Congress in 1976, the Party included 4,311,144 elected officers.[22] This meant that more than one fourth of the membership had some responsibilities in the Party. A second striking fact is that the mass of those elected were in the rank and file, and the higher one went in the hierarchy, the smaller the number of responsible officials. The pyramid of cadres, which is very wide at its base, since 24 percent of them are found in low-level organizations, narrows immediately afterward. We can see the difference in responsibilities and prestige between a group organizer *(partgrouporg),* in charge of putting together an organization in a workplace where the small number of militants would make the establishment of a regular rank-and-file organization impossible, and the first secretary of a region with authority to control and coordinate the activities of a considerable number of Communist organizations of the first three categories. On the level of general responsibilities, the *partgrouporg* or secretary of the rank-and-file organization operates in the field of a factory, a workshop, or a work group, but the secretary of an obkom acts within the framework of a region, which is both a political and an economic unit.

In these conditions, it is easy to understand that activism is confined to the lower levels where the Communist can recon-

Table 6:   The Party Organizations[23]

Number	Organizations	Number of Elected Personnel	Party Membership
	Level I		
528,894	Party groups		
400,388	Factory organizations	2,002,200	12%
	Level II		
390,387	Rank-and-file organizations	1,892,700	12%
	Level III		
2,857	Rural district committees		
571	Urban district committees		
813	City committees		
10	National district committees	385,532	2.46%
	Level IV		
150	Regional committees (two are cities)		
6	Territorial committees		
14	Central committees of the republics	30,201	0.19%
	Level V		
1	Central Control Commission of the Communist Party	85	0.005%
1	Central Committee of the Communist Party	426	0.0027%

cile personal and political activities: 90 percent of the activists work at the first two levels, 9 percent reach the third, and 1 percent go beyond that.

The decisive step for an activist is precisely to reach the third level, where many positions are reserved, ex officio, for permanent members of the apparatus. Here again we rediscover the elitist tendencies which have been continuously developing in the Party and the imbalance between the impulse to integrate workers and the real opportunities for promotion the Party offers them. In the rank-and-file organizations, the human, intellectual, and social characteristics of the activist correspond pretty well to those of the ordinary militant. Workers, women, people under thirty, and people without university diplomas are rather numerous. But as soon as the next level is reached, the activist changes form; now usually a man, closer to forty than thirty, he has passed through the higher education system and is rarely a worker. Here, the holders of *nomenklatura* positions in factories or Party functionaries occupy considerable space.

The obstacles to the activists' advancement should not obscure their place in the system. As driving forces of the Party among the rank and file, they help to identify the people around them whom the Party will coopt. They are also responsible for the preliminary ideological training of new militants, and they conduct propaganda sessions for non-Party members. Finally, they are the ones who mobilize a whole factory to meet its assigned production goals, and at this stage they exercise control over both workers and managers. Through this intermediary of the millions of activists in rank-and-file organizations, the Party controls from within all organizations, institutions, and bureaucracies scattered throughout the Soviet Union that are not already identified with it. Through this device, no one escapes the eye of the Party. The activists are one of the central elements by which "Big Brother" controls the society that Orwell so perfectly described in *1984.*

The Aktiv thus fulfills several functions.[24] It allows the Party to function with a relatively small group of permanent members, compared to the number of all its cadres. It assures a certain participation by militants in the management of economic and political life, at the lower levels. It is an instrument of control over society and over officials. Finally, it is a nursery for the political system. Does the Aktiv play its role fully? It is, from all the evidence, a complement to the Party apparatus and an instrument of control. But its right of control is limited by the competence of activists in any particular area. Can a worker enter into conflict with a factory manager who has been named to his position because of his competence? Another limitation goes along with the inequality of competence: The Party preaches simultaneously the need to control the managers of the economy and to strengthen their authority. Caught between contradictory imperatives, the elected leaders of rank-and-file organizations are often in a difficult position.

Another area in which activism does not fully carry out its function is as a nursery for the system's cadres. No doubt some of the lower-level elected officials manage to cross all barriers and move from unpaid activities to the status of permanent member of the apparatus, or even to one of the positions of the *nomenklatura.* But, to be able to do this, in general, one has to fulfill certain precise conditions, particularly of intellectual training. In fact, the career of a militant is laid out from the moment of entering the Party: toward continued upward movement or toward the extensive domain of unpaid activism, from which the chances of rising are relatively slender. The Aktiv thus presents itself with a dual face, seductive and repellant, for the ambitious militant. It is a means of acceding to positions of greater or lesser responsibility, of breaking out of militant anonymity; but unless certain conditions are fulfilled, the world of activism, for most of those who enter it, is already a closed world.

The Men of the Apparatus

Finally, above the Aktiv is located the sought-after category of permanent members of the apparatus, paid on a full-time basis, men—rarely women—for whom opportunities for advancement really exist in the Party, but also in all the administrative or intellectual structures of the U.S.S.R. The qualification of "permanent member," a bad translation of the Russian term "apparatchik," should not be understood in the light of what it involves in Communist parties not in power. In that case, the apparatchik lives in a closed system, in a countersociety in which he reproduces—in rehearsal—the operations of a power he has not attained. The apparatchik of a Party in power finds himself in a diametrically opposed situation. Society is organized around him and modeled on him, and all the functions of power are assumed by the apparatchiks and withheld from the surrounding society.

The role of the Party's permanent officials is easy to determine, but their numbers are harder to discover because the Party is very discreet on the question. At the Twenty-fifth Congress, published statistics indicated that 8.6 percent of Party members were employed in the apparatus of the Party, the state, the economy, and various other bureaucracies.[25] These 8.6 percent represent 1,349,700 members, but their distribution among the diverse institutions that employ them is not clear. Estimates of the number of apparatchiks are, for this reason, extremely variable, going from more than 400,000,[26] to 200,000,[27] and even to just over 100,000.[28] Although it is almost impossible to make a precise judgment on this question, the fact remains that we can with some probability estimate the number of militants paid from the Party budget (both full-time and part-time) at between 400,000 and 500,000.

The activity of real apparatchiks takes place not at the level of the factory but at the level of a territorial entity. Whatever the size of that entity—from district to republic—the extent of the tasks they are responsible for is the principal aspect of their activity. They are really the "leaders" at the territorial level because they are responsible for social mobilization, they supervise the operation of all institutions, the successes and failures of the economy are their affair, and, above all, through the system of the *nomenklatura,* they control the selection of those who have genuine responsibilities in the most diverse areas. At every level, one secretary is specifically in charge of problems of organization—that is, selection of cadres and control over the organs at a lower level.

The "Prefects" of the Party[29]

All these powers come together and solidify at the most significant territorial level, the region. At that level, among the apparatchiks, there is a narrow group, situated just below the central leaders, who play a decisive role and almost certainly represent the future source of political leadership. They are the first secretaries of regions, republics, and territories. Because of the range of their responsibilities, their position at the top of a pyramid of organizations, and the career profile and special qualities required to reach that position, the members of this group emerge from the interchangeable mass of the apparatchiks and command our attention.

The role of these secretaries depends, in the first place, on the importance of the organization that has elected them, the regional organization of the Party which, as we have seen, reproduces the structure and acts as a representative of the organization at the top. Like the Communist Party of the U.S.S.R., the organizations of the republics hold congresses every four years, and the regional organizations hold conferences every two years. The principal function of these meetings is to make an assessment of regional activities of Communists and others and especially to elect the executive organs of the Party: the Central Committee for republics, the Regional Committee (or Obkom) for regions. Both bodies are regular assemblies on the model of the Central Committee of the Communist Party of the U.S.S.R. A few examples of the committees elected in 1976 indicate this: between 200 and 265 members in the central committees of the larger parties, like Kazakhstan (248, of whom 179 were titular members and 69 candidates) or the Ukraine

(265, with 191 titular members and 74 candidates). Elsewhere, the membership was slightly smaller: in Georgia (192, of whom 60 were candidates), or in Moldavia (149, 43 of whom were candidates).[30] The size of the large regional committees is of the same order. Thus, in 1979, the Regional Committee of Leningrad included 130 members and 44 candidates, to which should be added the 26 members of the Control Commission. Although Leningrad and Moscow are exceptional cases, even more modest regional committees almost always have more than 100 members. Following the model of the Central Committee of the Soviet Party, these assemblies bring together representatives of the regional elite: the apparatus of the Party, the state, factories, the army, the police, unions, and cultural institutions.

The committees of republics or regions have no major activities, beyond holding plenary sessions that publicly demonstrate Party mobilization. In the end, real power, as is true everywhere in the U.S.S.R., belongs to the permanent organs: the bureau and especially the secretaries. The committee bureaus in republics and regions have an average size of 15 or 16 members (14 in Kazakhstan, 15 in the Ukraine, 13 in Tadzhikstan, 17 in the Leningrad region, 13 on the Moscow City Committee).[31] As for the periodicity of meetings at this level, the bureau holds at least two sessions each month, but permanent operations are under the control of the secretariats. Within the secretariat, two officials have specific titles, the first and second secretaries; the others are called simply secretaries, even though their functions are not always interchangeable. The first secretary is the real authority at this level, comparable to a French prefect, to use a Western reference, and also to the *governa* of the old regime in Russia.

Because there are so few of them, 170—148 regional secretaries, 2 secretaries of cities statutorily aligned with the regions, 6 of territories, and 14 of republics—the first secretaries are the only figures, except for the central leaders, who lend themselves to analysis. Their biographies are published, their activities inventoried. They make up a sufficiently coherent body to be examined as a whole.

It is obvious that they are the successors to power, as is clearly shown by the composition of the ruling organs of the U.S.S.R. The first secretaries represent the largest group in the Central Committee elected in 1976 (36 percent of its members).[32] The Politburo reserves significant space for first secretaries in office in the larger regions and republics (seven out of twenty-three in 1978). The biographies of Politburo members indicate that two thirds of them—beginning with Leonid Brezhnev—have been first secretaries for at least five years, and the same thing is true for three quarters of the members of the Secretariat. A glance at the past composition of the ruling organs of the U.S.S.R. reveals the constant importance of that position. The men who held a central place in the political system beside Stalin—Molotov, Khrushchev, Kaganovich, Mikoyan, Kirov, Zhdanov—had all been first secretaries at one point or another. These men, whose status gives them ex officio positions on the supreme organs of Soviet power, do not in any way resemble the "noncommissioned officers" of the Party or the rank-and-file activists. Eighty percent of them have completed higher education, which has become characteristic of men of this rank and is, moreover, adapted to their ultimate functions. For a long time, many first secretaries had received higher education in agriculture. Now, although there are still a number of graduates from schools of agronomy or rural engineering, industrial training has become predominant. It is true that even the regions that used to specialize in agriculture have increasingly turned toward industrial activity, and the first secretary encounters industrial problems everywhere in his efforts to control the economy. With this training based primarily on the two major sectors of the economy, there remains little room for other areas, and there are only a few holders of education degrees. Before reaching these high positions, most first secretaries in office have had some professional experience, often of short duration. But if we consider the facts closely, we note that, although some of them really come from production—agriculture or industry—the majority have earned their stripes in other areas: government, soviets, Komsomol, even in teaching.[33]

This primacy of apparatchiks over professionals is a relatively recent phenomenon. During the Stalinist era, the very rapid rotation of cadres and the habit that had developed from the beginning of the Soviet regime of "parachuting" cadres from the center into the regions and of displacing competent Communists according to need took the place of rules of recruitment. After 1952, on the contrary, we can get a clearer sense of the principles that governed nominations to these decisive positions. The desire to rationalize the Soviet economy led Khrushchev to make competence and the needs of the economy the chief criteria for selecting these high-level leaders.[34] From that point on, the Party has looked in its ranks, often at the lowest levels, for militants with a long professional past behind them and has propelled them without transition into high positions. Better still, it has introduced this criterion of choice into its recruitment policies, coopted the specialists it considered necessary for its general policies, and immediately given them significant responsibilities. But this evolution of Party policy has not taken place without difficulties. The promotion to these rare and sought-after positions of men from outside the apparatus has provoked the rancor of all those who hoped, after a slow rise through the ranks, to reach the highest positions of power through that process. Moreover, the penetration of the Party by specialists has created two distinct categories of higher leaders, thereby producing considerable tensions within the group, but also between the members of the group and their entourage. While the professional apparatchiks tend to identify with the apparatus, the newcomers identify more with the specialized elites from which they have come.[35]

Another change was added in 1962, generating even more hostility among the apparatchiks: the change brought about by reform of the Party. By dividing the Party at all levels into two organizations patterned on economic organization—industry and agriculture—Khrushchev no doubt hoped to make the apparatus more functional in economic terms. But above all, he counted on breaking the resistance of all the Party professionals by doubling their numbers and naming an elite of specialists to the positions thereby created. The first secretaries, as well as the officials who were victims of the division at lower levels, reacted in the same way, found themselves in competition with the economic managers and deprived of half their former responsibilities. This division, which reduced the work and the authority of all the apparatchiks, was particularly deeply felt by the secretaries of the obkoms, whose total authority over a region was thus abolished.[36] This is probably the source of the change that took place after Khrushchev's fall, on two levels, a change which established a new profile for these Communist proconsuls.

In the first place, under Brezhnev, the recruitment of cadres —first secretaries, but also other Party cadres at regional and lower levels—has tended to take place within the apparatus. With increasing frequency, cadres have been chosen on the basis of their career in the apparatus, whatever their professional past.[37] However, the constant increase in the Party's intellectual requirements and the professional character of the training received by young Communists have meant that these recruitment criteria have assured the promotion of competent Communists. The first secretaries (and they resemble the other permanent recruits), because of this new policy, have identified with the Party apparatus from which they have risen more than with specialized elites. At the same time, the training they have received and their professional experience have often given them a competence that allows them to feel on an equal footing with the specialized elites in carrying out their work, and sometimes even to dominate those elites.[38]

The second change, and by its consequences the more important one, derived from the desire to provide stable careers for
the Communist elites. After Stalinist arbitrariness, the Party
cadres aspired to stability in their positions. But far from assuring them of that stability, Khrushchev's policies condemned the
cadres to permanent insecurity. From his Stalinist training and
the organizational functions he had held in the Party, Khrushchev had developed an authoritarian and personal conception
of his relations with the apparatus. From the moment he
reached power, he felt he had the right of patronage, of intervening in appointments, which he constantly exercised, thus
practicing contradictory policies. On the one hand, he affirmed
his desire to decentralize responsibility and the management of
affairs. On the other, he constantly manipulated the political
cadres, thereby showing that in matters of choosing men centralized decision retained pride of place. The situation of the
first secretaries allows us to measure the extent of that contradiction.

At the Twentieth Congress, less than three years after Stalin's
death, thirty-nine first secretaries of the Russian Republic—that
is, more than half—were changed. Five years later, at the
Twenty-second Congress, only two first secretaries remained of
those in place at Stalin's death, the secretaries of the distant
autonomous republics of Tuva and Daghestan. All other positions had changed occupants, and often several times—thirty-
three positions had had two occupants, sixteen had had three,
and two had had four.

No doubt, not all these changes were unpopular. Certain
cadres too closely tied to Stalinism disappeared without provok-
ing great emotion around them. Many of those promoted were
not from outside the apparatus but were companions of Khrushchev who had worked at his side when he led the Ukrainian
Party from 1938 to 1949 or the Moscow organization in 1949
and 1950. It was inevitable and normal that Khrushchev promote the cadres who were close to him, since they constituted
a group on whom he might rely. By becoming an advocate of

decentralization, he could moreover give this group significant powers that would satisfy them. And this explains how in 1957, when Khrushchev was threatened with expulsion from the Presidium by his peers, he could call upon a new Central Committee where the apparatchiks who owed their promotion to him gave him unreserved support.

It was at this point that Khrushchev's policies shifted radically and his innovative initiatives alienated the support of regional cadres who had been loyal to him at the beginning. Scarcely had they been appointed when they discovered that their position was precarious. The rules of rotation promulgated in 1961 automatically limited their tenure of office.[39] Moreover, beginning in 1958, because his power was growing and he was active in various areas, particularly in foreign policy, Khrushchev gradually turned over the problems of Party organization—that is, appointments—to his colleagues. A. B. Aristov until 1960, and then Frol Kozlov until 1963, took hold of the question, proceeded to "parachute" cadres into the provinces, and appointed men who had no particular obligations to Khrushchev but who felt threatened by a policy that undermined their positions, a policy for which they held Khrushchev fully responsible. A master of the apparatus and its members in 1957, Khrushchev had provoked its hostility by the early sixties. His fall followed logically from this revolt of the apparatus, which he did not perceive. His unsuccessful appeal to the Central Committee in 1964 indicates as much.

The first secretaries had three causes of bitterness in 1964: the limitation of authority brought about by the reform of 1962, the total confusion created by the permanent "reformitis" of the Khrushchev period, and, above all, the insecurity of their positions. These complaints were made explicitly enough for the leadership of the Party to echo them.[40] It affirmed that regional officials should be assured of security of tenure and began by restoring the unity of the organizations.[41]

In 1964, the group that took power had to make a difficult

choice. They had to reassure the cadres, particularly those at the level of regions and republics whose weight in the Central Committee was decisive. But they could not reassure everyone at once. Khrushchev, by dividing the Party in two, had in fact doubled the number of officials at every level. Who would be placed at the head of the reunified organizations? What should be done with the losers in this new reform, which would in any case provoke rancor? Finally, by "recuperating" the largest possible number of cadres from the Khrushchev period, would they have to refrain from promoting newcomers and establishing an administrative corps tied to the new leadership?

In response to these difficult questions, the group in power, and first of all Brezhnev, head of the Party, came up with a graduated series of steps which, taken together, amounted to an extremely coherent policy for cadres. After 1964, the Party undertook to combine a policy of stability with one of openness, reassuring the cadres about their future and allowing for the rise of new groups. After having reunified the Party organizations, the central authority carried out a systematic change of regional leadership. But it did this in stages, with most cadres moving on to other positions, and especially by carrying out these changes in the name of the openness necessary to promote "young" members. These changes were not carried out in confusion but were announced to the Party as a measure for reorganization and housecleaning in preparation for the stabilization of careers. This program, presented by Brezhnev at the Twenty-second Congress, was executed between 1966 and 1971, the year when the period of stabilization began.[42] When we examine the situation of the regional first secretaries in Russia, we observe that, in 1980, this body was made up of four groups, corresponding to the periods of their recruitment. A first group of seventeen secretaries were those who had survived from the Khrushchev period, appointed (with two exceptions) between 1960 and 1964.[43] The second and smaller group, five members, was made up of first secretaries appointed between Khrushchev's fall and the Twenty-third Congress. (In fact, the changes had been greater than this figure indicates, since eleven positions had changed hands in a few months, but only five secretaries in this wave had remained in place.) The third and largest group, twenty-two people, was composed of secretaries promoted in 1966–71, between the Twenty-third and the Twenty-fourth Congress. (In this case, too, the change had been of greater magnitude: thirty-two for those five years, more than two thirds of whom remained in place.) Thereafter, a certain stability was established: Nineteen positions changed hands between 1971 and 1976, and eighteen of the new secretaries were still in office. Finally, between the Twenty-fifth Congress and the spring of 1980, thirteen newcomers completed the picture. It is clear to how great an extent the body of first secretaries had been renewed, since out of seventy-five positions considered, only seventeen were occupied by men appointed by Khrushchev. More than three quarters of the first secretaries owed their advancement to the current leadership.

At the same time, this shows the extent to which the Party leaders had attained the two objectives they had set for themselves. Definite opening up of the system went along with genuine job security for those appointed to these positions. Since 1971, aside from the fact that the rate of rotation of cadres has considerably diminished, the reasons for these rotations have also changed. If we examine the history of the secretaries who have left their positions, we note that natural causes (retirement, death) explain about twenty shifts. More than half of those who left were sent to Moscow, where they assumed positions in the central organs of the Party (one third) or in government (two thirds). Few of them, in this period, have disappeared without trace. No doubt, not all of them have benefited subsequently from equal promotions. Although certain careers have been spectacular,[44] propelling first secretaries into the Politburo or the Secretariat, and being appointed to a major ministry or the embassy of a major Western country represents a definite promotion, a middle-level ministry or an embassy in a small Third World country is a dead end. But in most cases, the sending of an upper-level cadre to Moscow represents definite advantages, notably in the standard of living implied by the transfer and the educational possibilities it provides for the secretary's children.

Not only have the rules for recruitment of first secretaries been regularized, but the methods used by the Brezhnev group have shown a significant change from earlier practices by leaving room for the expression of aspirations. The Party now leaves a greater latitude of action to the organizations concerned in the choice of their leaders. No doubt the central organs govern promotions, in the last analysis, but they have substituted "supervision" and a certain power of influence for pure and simple centralized decision making. The consequence has been that first secretaries are now recruited locally.[45] In the Khrushchev period, only a little more than half the first secretaries had had a career in the apparatus of their region. The present group rarely resorts to external promotions (one out of ten, approximately) and allows local organs to advance their own cadres. Only the proportion of first secretaries sent to Moscow has remained more or less stable (one out of twelve) through both periods. Careers now unfold in a relatively homogeneous framework well known to obkom secretaries. This geographical continuity contrasts strongly with the constant "parachuting" of the past, where a single cadre could develop a specialty as secretary of a national obkom and move from Tashkent in the fifties to the Communist Party of Lithuania in the following decade (this was the case, for example, for B. V. Popov, who was finally elected first secretary of the Arkhangelsk Obkom in 1967 and has settled there). The growth of local responsibility for the appointment of first secretaries corresponds to a real demand on the part of Party organizations obvious from the response of the Twenty-fourth Congress to Brezhnev's emphasis on this new tendency in the selection of cadres. Thanks to this policy, regional cadres can predict their future. They know that a position as first secretary that becomes available opens up possibilities of promotion primarily for officials of a slightly lesser rank in the same region. The order of succession for this position is now from second secretary of the same obkom to president of the executive council of the local soviet. Aside from these two jobs, which almost certainly lead to the position of first secretary, three others make candidacy possible, but with much less chance of success: a simple secretaryship in the same obkom, and the first or second secretaryship of another obkom.

In the end, in the Brezhnev period, the body of first secretaries and the regional leadership of the Party in general have obtained the stability they wished for and the possibility of predicting the evolution of individual careers. From these certainties, the regional cadres have derived increased authority, solidarity with the whole apparatus of which they are a part, and extended control over all the promotions dependent on their own *nomenklatura*. The central authority could not in fact have two distinct policies, one recognizing the competence of the regional levels of the Party to name their own cadres, and another involving heavy-handed intervention by the central authority whenever the *nomenklatura* entered the picture.

Now reassured and rooted in their particular locations, these secretaries, more than in the past, can form clienteles, since they have working for them the stability of their positions and a certain degree of autonomy in appointments. The development of local and regional clientelism is without doubt one of the characteristics of Brezhnev's Party.

If we finally try to define the first secretaries of today, we can see clearly both what connects and what differentiates them from their predecessors. They are a political body composed exclusively of men.[46] No position as first or second secretary of a region, a republic, an autonomous republic, an autonomous region, or a territory is or ever has been held by a woman. This continuity in the refusal to allow women to attain high positions in the Party deserves to be emphasized. Another permanent fact has to do with the balance of nationalities in the distribution of positions of first secretary. The Russians occupy a preeminent place. They are present in every Russian region, where they sometimes give way to Ukrainians (seven in 1980); in the national territories, as a general rule, the first secretary comes from the local nationality, while the second is systematically a Russian. But in two cases—the autonomous region of Karachayevo-Cherkess and the autonomous republic of Checheno-Ingush—this order is reversed; first secretaries are Russians and second secretaries are nationals. These cases are all the more significant because the Russian first secretaries of these national territories were named recently, at a time when the opposite rule had prevailed almost everywhere.[47]

But, although the composition of this body has remained the same in certain respects, it has changed in one important aspect: the average age of the first secretaries. The stability they enjoy and their more or less systematic recruitment from the next rung down in the regional apparatus have together increased their age. In 1965, 20 percent of them were over fifty-five. Now, more than 60 percent are over that age, there are none under forty, and the average age is fifty-eight. The Communist past of this group is in general quite homogeneous. Most of its members joined the Party during and after the Second World War, after the purges and the losses of the war had opened wide the gates of the Party and provided opportunities for advancement for the newcomers. There remain only two who entered the Party before 1939. At the other extreme, the number of those recruited in the post-Stalinist period has not grown very rapidly and has not gone beyond 15 percent.

But this analysis of the policy designed to reassure and stabilize the body of regional first secretaries loses all value outside the Russian Republic, when the choices made by Soviet leaders have to do with the nationalities. Here the situation is entirely different, characterized by permanent instability, in a climate of veritable purges. The upper-level Party leaders of the nationalities are divided into two groups: the first secretaries of Parties of republics (which do not exist in Russia) and the secretaries of regions, where they exist, or of autonomous republics and autonomous regions. The number of officials is only slightly higher than for Russia: 94 people, 14 of whom are first secretaries of Parties of republics, 72 of regions,[48] 4 of autonomous republics, 3 of autonomous regions, and 1 for the committee of the city of Kiev, which has a special status.[49]

If we consider the political longevity of the first secretaries of republics, we note that out of a group of fourteen, only three were in office before Khrushchev's fall, all incidentally elected after 1953,[50] six first secretaries were elected between 1964 and 1971, and five after the Twenty-fourth Congress. But this rate of rotation, which is already quite high, is nothing in comparison with the rate of renewal of regional first secretaries of the republics. Of the twenty-five regions of the Ukraine, only one has kept a first secretary elected before 1964, the other twenty-four having changed first secretaries, sometimes on several occasions. The first secretary of the gorkom (urban committee) of Kiev, elected in 1964 in the immediate wake of Khrushchev's fall, was displaced in 1979. In Kazakhstan, where the first secretary of the republic, D. A. Kunaev, took office in the weeks following Khrushchev's fall, only one region out of nineteen has kept the first secretary elected in 1959. One can get a sense of the instability of political positions in Kazakhstan by noting that in March and April 1978, in the course of ten weeks, five regional first secretaries were dismissed.[51] In Uzbekistan, although the autonomous Kara-Kalpak republic has kept its first secretary, the eleven administrative regions have changed leaders since 1968, six of whom have been removed since 1976. In the six regions of Byelorussia the first secretaries have been removed, twice in two regions. Just as complete a change has been carried out in Turkmenia, Tadzhikistan, Kirghiz, Georgia, and Azerbaidzhan. This means that, of the 94 high Communist officials in the republics, 88 have been changed under Brezhnev.

This is very far from the stability that reigns in Russia. But the most serious thing for these republics is that this rotation of cadres has not been carried out in a period of general change as in Russia, and it was not accomplished under the auspices of opening and renewal. The years 1976–80 have been marked by continual changes. The first secretaries who were dismissed were frequently accused of bad management in the best cases,[52] but much more often of flagrant abuses of power,[53] and corruption.[54] The displacement of these regional first secretaries was, moreover, only one aspect of the constant rotation of the cadres of the republics which, taking place in a climate of scandal, seemed to involve a rather systematic purge of the national cadres. In two large republics in particular, the Ukraine and Kazakhstan, expulsions and displacements from one position to another have occurred with extraordinary frequency in the last decade and have affected all higher offices—secretaries of obkoms, national central committees, and ministries. The consequence of these frequent shifts was that the replacement of cadres could not be carried out in the relatively logical and local manner that can be detected in Russia. In Kazakhstan, in the spring of 1978, there was a veritable ballet of first secretaries moving from one region to another, and in no instance did a second secretary whose immediate superior was removed replace him; he went to fill a vacant position in another region.[55]

In December 1979, in Kazakhstan again, there was another movement out of the ordinary: A. G. Korkin, the second secretary of the republic, a position of great importance, was transferred to the position of first secretary of a region, a definite fall.[56] This also indicates that the positions of regional first secretaries in the republics do not have as prestigious a status as their counterparts in Russia. These differences in status can be shown first by a consideration of the makeup of the Central Committee of the U.S.S.R. The compact group of first secretaries in that body is not equally distributed throughout the Soviet republics. The first secretaries of the R.S.F.S.R. are almost all (71 out of 75) elected to the highest offices. In 1976, 57 of them were voting members of the Central Committee, 13 were candidates, and 1 was elected to the Central Control Commission. The position of the first secretaries in the republics was clearly less favorable, since, out of a group of 94 first secretaries, only 44 had been elected. Moreover, they were less well placed than their Russian counterparts. Although all the first secretaries of republics (14) were automatically elected as voting members of the Central Committee, the secretaries of regions and autonomous regional entities of equivalent rank had only 17 elected members (14 elected at the Twenty-fifth Congress, to which were added 3 candidates promoted to voting membership at the plenums of October 1976 and October 1977).[57] The others included 12 candidates on the Central Committee (only 9 of whom remained after the promotions of 1976 and 1977), and 4 members of the Central Control Commission. In the hierarchy of the Party, the weight of the first secretaries of Russian obkoms is unquestionably preeminent, and membership in this body almost certainly guarantees a seat on the Central Committee.

Thus we can see that what characterizes the group of first secretaries of Russian obkoms is their direct and automatic access to the highest positions in the Party. The local authority they derive from this is increased; they are the unquestioned representatives of the central authority, to which they can moreover appeal on all matters. In this regard, their only equivalents are the first secretaries of the parties of the republics, who are assured full membership on the Central Committee. They are comparable to a lesser degree to the first secretaries of the regions of the two other Slavic republics, the Ukraine and Byelorussia, men who are hierarchically superior to their colleagues in other republics, since a majority of them are voting members of the Central Committee. However, access by the latter to the center of power is, despite all this, only through the mediation of the leaders of the Party of the republics, which places them in a slightly less favorable position than their colleagues in Russia.

The special advantages the regional secretaries have in gaining access to the highest positions are obvious if one looks not at the Central Committee but the more exclusive organs; the Politburo and the Secretariat. No doubt the Politburo automatically admits some first secretaries of republics, because it must unfailingly represent the composition of the Party. But the Secretariat accepts only those who have been regional first secretaries in Russia. The fact that the Ukraine is an exception to this rule in indicated by the careers of Brezhnev and his former colleague Chernenko. Many of the current (Brezhnev, Kirilenko, Chernenko) or recent (Katushev, Riabov) members of the Secretariat gained their experience in the field by directing regional organizations.

The Nomenklatura[58]

One of the principal functions fulfilled by the leaders whose duty it is to supervise regional affairs in general is the selection of cadres, for the Communist apparatus and for all other domains of economic and social activity. The *nomenklatura* at their level gives them considerable power in this respect, which they exercise with all the more authority because the stability they now enjoy, their knowledge of regional circumstances, and the central power's desire to function rationally all give them means and criteria for choices that their predecessors did not always have.

The *nomenklatura*—because it is surrounded in mystery by the Soviet authorities, who never publish the names of those who are on it—is often presented as a central, essential element of the Soviet system, outside of which there is no authority and no freedom of action. It is important at this point to see what it is intended to be, but also what it is in reality.

Since its birth, the Soviet system has considered that the selection and assignment of cadres *(poddor i rasstanovka kadrov)* had to be under the control of the Party.[59] This concern had led to different practices in different periods. In the Stalinist years, the *nomenklatura* was largely centralized and the positions left to regional authorities were limited. On the contrary, since 1956, great progress in decentralization has been made and there has been increased communication among the *nomenklaturas* at the various levels of the Party. The *nomenklatura* is by definition the Party's right to examine appointments to any position which is considered important. The *nomenklatura* covers political, administrative, and intellectual positions, among others. In fact, there are various kinds of *nomenklatura*. The most important, where real power to confirm or deny a nomination is located, is that of the Party. Every level of the Party, from the Central Committee down to district committees (but not below), has a list of positions within its sphere of control. The more important the post, the higher the organ in whose *nomenklatura* it is located. In addition to the Party *nomenklatura* there are particular ones. Each administration has its own, but, in these cases, every position in a *nomenklatura* outside the Party must be approved by the Party organ at the corresponding level. In any case, important positions are in the Party's *nomenklatura*.[60]

Although there is a particular *nomenklatura* for every level of the Party, this does not imply that a committee is aware only of its own *nomenklatura*. Besides its right to examine those outside the Party, each committee has a second list, "for its information," called *uchetnaia nomenklatura,* for which its approval is not necessary but through which it must be kept informed of all personnel shifts.[61] This complementary list extends the area of control of each level of the Party over people and their careers. Moreover, it allows those in authority over each *nomenklatura* to obtain deeper knowledge of the individuals who are not automatically under their control and, if necessary, to choose officials among them for their own *nomenklatura*. They thereby establish, in addition to the cadres proposed to them, a "professional reserve."

If the general rules that govern the *nomenklatura* are known, its content is not, for this is where the mystery begins. The Soviet authorities never publish the Central Committee's *nomenklatura*, and it is only by approximations, considering scattered information and testimony, that Western experts have arrived at a figure of around 40,000 positions.[62] Jerry Hough, in his work *The Soviet Prefects*, has brought together the limited data available on particular *nomenklaturas*.[63] In Moscow in 1958, the city committee and the district committees of the region alone were responsible for 17,000 positions, including 9,000 in the Party, 3,000 in economic administration, and 1,200 in the soviets. In 1966, the Riga city committee had 660 positions in its *nomenklatura*, distributed as follows: Party organization and soviets, 253; industry, 107; administration and finance, 85; ideological work, 83; education, 71; construction and municipal services, 61. These few examples suffice to indicate the particular areas of the Party's concern and vigilance, and they suggest something about the hierarchy of jobs in the U.S.S.R. Political leadership and administrative management represent more than half the *nomenklatura* positions; the economy comes next; education, associated of course with ideological work, also occupies a significant place; while construction and municipal services, on which the well-being of citizens largely depends, are relegated to the background.

We can see what determines whether a position appears in the *nomenklatura*: the importance attached to it by the Party. The list of nonpolitical positions in the *nomenklatura* has certainly varied over time as a function of the Party's priorities. The level to which each position is attached also depends on its significance, and this level at which the choice is made is reflected in the status of the appointee. Dependence on the Central Committee's *nomenklatura* confers on the holder of such a position authority and prestige not enjoyed by those dependent on lower-level *nomenklaturas*. [64] This explains the extensive overlapping of *nomenklaturas* at every particular territorial level and within each organism. Party cadres at the regional level do not all depend on the Central Committee; for many of them, their fate is in the hands of their Party committee. We can see the mingling of various levels of the *nomenklatura* within a single factory. The director of a large factory may depend on the Central Committee *nomenklatura*, his closest colleagues on that of the obkom, and the heads of divisions on that of the district.

What is important to understand is that this system covers appointive positions (an economic job, for example) as well as those subject to election in basic Party organizations, soviets, unions, or any other social organization. But in these two situations, the authority of those in charge of the *nomenklatura* is not the same. Appointments to "professional" positions call on criteria of competence and effectiveness which are sometimes differently interpreted by the Party and the economic—or intellectual—organization where the position is located. In a case like this, the Party is required to ratify or contradict a choice which is the result of a dialogue between it and the administration concerned. The situation is much simpler for "elective" positions: The candidate's name is "recommended" by the Party, which has absolute power in these instances. The Party statutes are explicit on this point. The Party's responsibility is in the first place not to allow elections to take place in "an unorganized way," and one of the most frequent criticisms addressed to Party leaders dismissed from their positions is their faulty organization of the selection process for candidates in elections or for appointed cadres.

In this respect, the regional first secretaries have considerable responsibilities, because the names not included in the Central Committee's *nomenklatura* are on their lists. Attempts at decentralization and the desire to find appropriate candidates have led the Party to give extended authority to regional officials in this system. Because their careers have unfolded in the region, the first secretaries generally know the candidates for *nomenklatura* positions quite well. Their intellectual and professional qualifications allow them to carry on useful discussions with heads of administrations on the question of nominations. And their political stability gives them the weight to impose their preferences both locally and at the center.

If the *nomenklatura* positions are difficult to identify, we are on the other hand better informed as to what gives an individual the possibility of occupying such a position. The best-placed candidates, in ascending order, are: members of the Party and the Komsomol, a commitment which guarantees in itself a "responsible" political attitude and something the Party organizations are aware of, since these are individuals the Party has coopted; and being an activist places one in an even more favorable position, but less than having been placed by the Party in the category of promotable cadres *(rezerv na vydvizhenie)*. [65] The Party itself has explained what this reserve is by giving instructions to draw future leaders from it more frequently. The deputy director of the "organization" department of the Central Committee, an expert in the matter, has said that it ought not to be limited only to the second in command of the positions to be filled. It is necessary to look for good leaders among the activists as a body: 4,300,000 elected officials in the Party, among whom first consideration should be given to the 400,000 cadres distributed among the Communist organizations—from the district level up to the republic—to those elected to the soviets, and finally to Komsomol members.[66]

Thus it emerges clearly from these instructions that to have any real chance of acceding to a *nomenklatura* position, one must be within the system. For a long time, belonging to the Party was the essential criterion for entering the system. But the post-Khrushchev years have been characterized by the combined criteria of political loyalty and education, which is a distinguishing trait marking Party members off from the rest of the population. Those who reach *nomenklatura* positions are better educated than the average members of the active population and also than ordinary Party members. Within the *nomenklatura,* education is also a differentiating element, since Party functionaries have attained, with increasing obviousness, a level of education superior to that of *nomenklatura* cadres at the same level. It is significant that, in 1976—and this tendency will probably be confirmed in the future—47.8 percent of the secretaries of low-level Party organizations had received higher education, compared to 99.2 percent of the district and city secretaries, and 99.4 percent of the regional and territorial secretaries.[67] Education has thus become an absolute criterion for social advancement, in both professional and political areas. Progress within the Party depends on a higher education degree: 70 percent of Party secretaries at all levels had one in 1976.

Being in a *nomenklatura* thus means that one is located in a particular category, defined by several characteristics: It is preferable to be a man, to have a higher level of education than the average, and to be relatively old because of a long period of study and the now rather late age of joining the Party. To be associated with the *nomenklatura* is to belong to the elite, recognized as such and endowed with established privileges—material privileges, of course, but above all access to education, which implies that this group has the opportunity to perpetuate itself.

If Soviet power is explicit in recognizing the existence and usefulness of the *nomenklatura,* it is much less so on the question of the privileged position of Party members in the *nomenklatura* and the privileges associated with it.

The Communists have no special rights in the U.S.S.R. Every position in the state, the economy, cultural organizations, or any other institution can be and is held, without distinction, by a Communist or a non-Communist. The only criterion is personal and professional qualification. Communists and those outside the Party are rewarded the same way for their merits at work or for exceptional actions in the domains of literature and the arts. Communists have no privileges in the form of wages or social status.

This was announced by a commentator on Soviet radio on August 20, 1978, but one of his colleagues made minor corrections in this ideal picture of an egalitarian society: "But Communists have certain special duties. It is a Party member's duty to take an active part in political life, in the administration of the state, and in economic and cultural development." In sum, if Communists have no particular claim to priority in holding positions of responsibility, they must "convince the others that the Party's policies are just. And to do this they must take an active part in putting them into operation. The only privilege of a Party member is to work harder and better than anyone else, to be an example by being at the heart of public life."[68] These slightly contradictory definitions situate the problem clearly. The duty of Communists remains that of guiding Soviet life in all areas of activity, and to do this they must take on responsibilities.

The *nomenklatura*, which gives access to the political reservoir and adds a professional dimension to it, which outlines the contours of a political, economic, and cultural ruling class, is sometimes called into question, for purely technical reasons, but also to "moralize" the Soviet system.[69] The great technical defect in the functioning of the *nomenklatura* is that it is an extension of the Party in composition and training, and it is thereby more conservative than dynamic. Despite the place it has given to education, the Party has not yet taken into consideration the changes of the elite in general. While a large technical intelligentsia has been developing in society, the Party has emphasized political training. This intelligentsia has found no place in the Party and no place in the *nomenklatura* either. Andrei Sakharov, in his various proposals designed to revive the Soviet system, has recommended doing away with the *nomenklatura,* demanding that specialists be appointed uniquely on the basis of professional criteria and that the election of all officials be the rule. It goes without saying that these proposals have met with the hostility of the Party, which vigorously defends its right to be a privileged path for social advancement and to control access to positions of authority according to its own criteria.

The consequences of this policy appear clearly in the political composition of the various areas of activity and in the respective positions given within each area to Communists and non-Communists. Communists occupy nearly 70 percent of the positions in Soviet institutions as a whole (Party, state, economy), 18 percent in science, 13.9 percent in industrial production, 12 percent in agricultural production, 9 percent in commerce, 7.7 percent in public services (such as community services). Thus it is the bureaucracy, from which everything can be controlled, that is their privileged domain, and we may note, if we combine the Communists present in all the bureaucracies and the non-Communists appointed to *nomenklatura* positions for reasons of competence, that the Party has completely taken over the centers of decision and administration, leaving the tasks of executing policies to those outside the Party.[70]

Is Communist power the power of an elite? And what content does the term "elite" have with reference to the U.S.S.R.? Does it cover just the small group of a few hundred people in the Kremlin who embody the leadership of the Party in its permanent organs and the Central Committee that elected them? Can it be extended to a particular category of cadres or to the entire Party? What is there in common between a small group turned in on itself, with considerable powers, and a Party of 16 million members involved in society, even if their role is to be the most dynamic part of that society? In the answers that can be given to these questions, what characterizes the Party of the Brezhnev era?

There is no doubt that we can apply to the entire Party the notion of an elite, even if it covers many different meanings and thereby leads to confusion. If we argue that an elite is "a group defined by its functions, which has a particular status within society,"[71] then clearly the Party is an elite in Soviet society. It is an elite involved in society because it penetrates all areas of social activity, in different degrees according to the importance it gives to each one, but an elite which has a specific function in society: to be the embodiment of, and a substitute for, civil society. Even though the Communist population has grown and represents a broader range of society, it is not identical with the Party. And this concern to preserve the elite character of the Party probably explains why—once the phase of increasing membership passed—the leadership adopted a strategy strictly limiting access to the Party.

An opening and then a closing of the Party: These are two characteristics of the current leadership. Through permanent purges, Stalin constantly changed Party membership. But these variations were of little importance, to the extent that the Stalinist party was only one bureaucracy among others, whose theoretically privileged status was called into question in practice. Khrushchev simultaneously opened the gates to the Party and attempted to attach it more closely to a society in which citizen participation in public life was growing. In this time, the elite went substantially beyond the confines of the Party. For the current leadership, the enlargement of the Party corresponds with the desire to make it coincide with the elites a modern society needs. But at the same time, the restrictions imposed on this opening indicate the desire to preserve a precise line of demarcation between Party and society, leaving intact the privileged, extraordinary status of the Communist Party. This is the first time since Lenin's death that the Party's vocation not to be indistinguishable from society has been so clearly indicated. In this sense, the Brezhnev group can legitimately invoke the continuity that joins it to Lenin.

Beyond that, we must emphasize several traits that characterize this elite and indicate its distance from society. The Communist population does not form a homogeneous group but is itself differentiated in function, status, and chances of promotion. Its homogeneity exists only with reference to the world outside it; within the Party, a number of elements create differences, some of which can be overcome—such as education and previous career—but others of which—particularly national origin and sex—determine, often definitively, the possibilities for advancement in the hierarchy of the system. In its own sphere, the closed world of communism has its juxtaposed worlds, and if, as a whole, the Communist population occupies the first place in society, all Communists are far from equal and far from capable of becoming equal.

Secondly, this system of promoting elites operates in a closed circuit. Here, too, the Brezhnev period has been decisive in restoring mechanisms that Khrushchev had partially called into question. The summit of the political hierarchy is in the end organized on the basis of the regional apparatuses. There, the powerful army of regional secretaries can influence final choices, because they determine the selection of delegates to the Party congress, which elects the Central Committee, which in turn elects the supreme organs of power and to which these organs are in theory answerable. Given that the electoral system amounts to authoritarian choices, according to which the first secretaries depend on the Central Committee, which is in turn the product of a list drawn up at the summit, in the end a balance is established between these supreme organs and their rank and file, the regional organizations. All power circulates from one level to another, passing through the electoral fictions of the assemblies. The evolution of the system depends in the last analysis on the relationships established among the three levels: regional apparatuses, Central Committee, and the narrow organs at the summit, which may be reduced to a single supreme leader. From this system, Khrushchev had drawn the conclusion that he could play each element against the others to increase his personal share of power. But the various players of the game reacted by expelling Khrushchev. His successors managed to understand the solidarity that existed within this circular system of power and to stabilize the positions of each group and its respective influence. It is probably this acute understanding of the hierarchy of the Communist population, this sense of a power based on various balancing acts, that explains the political longevity of the current leadership. Here, too, the generation of leaders under Brezhnev has rediscovered the path traced by Lenin. But noting the Leninism of Brezhnev and his colleagues, noting that they have succeeded in stabilizing and normalizing the powers of the elite, does not at all resolve the problems posed by the nature and dimensions of this power. In other words, is the power exercised by the elite at the summit total, unchanged, equally spread through all spheres of existence, and uncontested?

CHAPTER 5
THE VICTORY
OF THE MANAGERS

The Party has jealously held on to the power it confiscated from society in the aftermath of the revolution; there is no doubt about that. But what is this power? And what does the Party do with it? No authoritarian political system can remain fixed for long, because it must adapt itself to changes in the men it embodies and to a social environment in transformation. The death of Lenin and that of Stalin unavoidably called the legitimacy of the rulers into question. No one after Lenin could invoke the charismatic legitimacy of the founder of the system, nor, after Stalin, could anyone invoke legitimacy founded on violence and the grand design of a radical transformation of society. Despite his efforts, Khrushchev's critical work undermined another source of legitimacy: the infallible Party. Khrushchev's successors had to confront the formidable task of legitimating the authority of their Party with a weakened ideology, while trying to revive the ideological and political systems by subjecting them to the tests of rationality and competence, in order to take into consideration the intellectual progress and material needs of society.

Their enterprise can in the end be summed up in this problem: How can the system be modernized without at the same time weakening the sources of its legitimacy? Like Khrushchev in 1956, they have tended to rationalize the system, to bring out new norms. But, unlike the situation that existed in 1956, the 1964 group came together around several explicit points of agreement: the necessity of preserving a collective power, of keeping all problems and possible crises under the control of the highest organs of the Party, and, finally, of giving the system rules which would allow it to function smoothly. The 1964 consensus was evidently much more positive than the one established at Stalin's death. Khrushchev's successors got rid of him to preserve and institutionalize a political system whose essential characteristics they defined. This was an essentially political consensus. It was a question of the system, of power and its relations to society. All the hesitations of the post-Stalinist years over the possible intervention of society in political change gave way to a certainty: Power must be preserved from any intervention by society. What Khrushchev's successors have rejected above all is the confusion he had introduced into the political system: confusion among the various levels of power, confusion between the Party and what was outside the Party.

Unlike Khrushchev, his successors had extended experience: the experience of his mistakes—ideological disturbances, divisions in the ruling class, discontent in the Party—and the experience of the strength derived by them from agreement in the ruling group. They knew that collective decision making would allow them to establish a normalized political life assuring their security. Khrushchev's fall was in fact a *political* event, the first one in Soviet history in which threats and open or disguised violence played no part. The successors' first concern was to consolidate this gain and to institutionalize political life. This institutionalization covered three areas. For the highest level of power, it was necessary to define the relations among individuals and to settle once and for all the problem of personal power. A second area was the balance among the various bureaucracies and their relations with the summit of power. Finally, there remained the difficult problem of the devolution of power. A political system is not functioning normally, has not reached its maturity, unless it does not stumble periodically over problems of succession, the transfer of power from one group to another and eventually from one political generation to the next. On all these points, until 1964, the Soviet system operated without rules, at the whim of the solutions devised by those on the road to power whenever they confronted an obstacle. The consequence of this political empiricism was that the Soviet system for a long time compensated for the absence of rules by violence, endangering the lives of the political elite but also the life of the entire system.

The "Mini" Succession Crises

When they eliminated Khrushchev in October 1964, his colleagues intended to put an end not only to his innovations but also to any attempt to establish personal power. The key phrase of the period following the expulsion was "a return to collective leadership," the principle which seems to have served as a guiding thread for this group.[1] At the same time, Khrushchev's successors encountered two irreducible phenomena of political life. In the first place, there were personal ambitions, all the more difficult to suppress because collective power, despite pious assertions, had never, since 1917, been anything but a transitional formula in the U.S.S.R. The reality of Soviet power had constantly been characterized by the rise of a leader, concealed behind collective leadership and protected by the silence of the documents. The second political phenomenon, going beyond the Soviet framework, was the personalization of power which characterized the international political scene and contemporary international relations. How could the U.S.S.R., which had played an active role in international relations since 1956, escape this tendency? What collective power could be heard by the heads of state who increasingly personalized their policies and their contacts? It was clear as early as

1964 that the future of the new group in the Kremlin depended largely on the manner in which it would accommodate the personal ambitions of most of its members, and also on its capacity to combine a certain degree of personalization of power with the preservation of collective power.

The collective leadership of 1964 was hardly spectacular. There were no colorful figures like the great rivals of 1953, Khrushchev, Malenkov, and Beria, whose powerful presences —physical and psychological—and whose incompatibility were striking. There was nothing like that in 1964, but rather an apparent colorlessness. It is not surprising that the experts who contemplated the calm success of this badly known group with astonishment predicted with admirable unanimity that they were a transitional one. However, this unspectacular Politburo harbored some personalities who were more striking than others, either because of their powers or because of the organizations they could manipulate.

In theory, the collective leadership contained two balanced powers, which were to remain separate and around which the Politburo as a whole, then known as the Presidium, was organized: Party power and governmental power. If the government had a single leader in Kosygin, whose economic skills as an industrial administrator had been recognized since 1941, Party power was in many hands. No doubt the Secretariat, the center of the system, was dominated by Leonid Brezhnev, whom Khrushchev had sometimes presented as his successor. But his functions as coordinator did not cover everything. Ideological authority was separated, for the first time in a long time, from organizational authority. The man who embodied it, Mikhail Suslov, had joined the Party under Lenin in 1921 and entered the Politburo under Stalin in 1947.[2] At the summit of the Party, he represented a continuity that few men—except for Mikoyan, whose influence was not great, and N. M. Shvernik, who was already seventy-six[3]—could claim. He had survived the Stalinist purges and the subsequent elimination of Stalinists and had been for more than thirty years his Party's chief expert on ideological problems. The stability of his status and the permanence of his functions assured him a particular position in 1964. He possessed and has constantly continued to possess one of the symbols of power: ideological rigor. At Brezhnev's side, another organizer was in competition with him in his own domain: Nikolai Podgorny, who had long been responsible in the Secretariat for problems of Party structure and organization.[4] The two men had in common their present functions in the Party apparatus and long experience in the most important non-Russian republic, the Ukraine. Each of them had a stronghold there, Brezhnev in the industrial region of Dnepropetrovsk, Podgorny in the equally important region of Kharkov. One had subsequently led Moldavia, the other the Ukraine. Brezhnev's experience was above all that of a Party man, interested, through his functions, in heavy industry and defense production; Podgorny's experience was as a professional of light industry, snapped up by the Party apparatus because of his competence.

Finally, behind these four men who seemed to possess the principal powers of the Party and the state, another figure appeared in 1964: Aleksander Shelepin. No doubt, when the collective leadership was established he was not a part of it, because he was not a member of the Presidium, which attracted all the attention. But, at forty-six, he had behind him a rapid and full career which, in many respects, differentiated him from Presidium members.[5] First of all, he was better educated than most of them who had had quick technical training; Shelepin had had a genuine higher education in literature and history, and, what is more, at the prestigious University of Moscow. His career, also unlike those of most of his colleagues, was a true career of a man of the apparatus, without economic or regional experience, carried out entirely in Moscow. The Komsomol had been his first site of activity. As first secretary of the organization of Communist youth in 1954, when the Soviet government launched its virgin lands campaign, he mobilized "volunteers" to carry out the grand design. The energy he displayed led to his being named, at forty, to head the Central Committee department in charge of organizational problems in the republics and then in the same year to be named president of the State Security Committee, or KGB. Even though gerontocracy did not yet characterize the Soviet system, his career is astonishing in its rapidity and uninterrupted success. From the KGB he moved to the secretariat of the Central Committee, most probably with a special area of concern linked to problems of security, and the following year he was vice-president of the Council of Ministers.

When Khrushchev was eliminated, this forty-six-year-old man accumulated different powers. He had three official positions: secretary of the Central Committee, president of the Control Committee of the Party and the State created in 1962, and vice-president of the Council of Ministers. These functions assured him considerable power. As head of the KGB, he had used that instrument to strengthen his position with the supreme leaders. In 1961, when Khrushchev wanted to revive de-Stalinization, Shelepin was one of his most ardent supporters. At the Twenty-second Congress, he spoke against the Stalinists, who were then "anti-Party" elements, and used documents in the possession of the KGB against them.[6] By using the police to launch a purge, he was only resuming the tradition of the Stalinist police, but he cleverly emphasized what distinguished him from them. In 1956, he helped to distribute the "secret speech" to the Komsomol, and in 1961 he put police power at the service of the Party against Stalinism and its excesses. On leaving the KGB he did not break all his ties with it, but left as a replacement Semichasny, who had been his colleague on the Komsomol and who now owed him two promotions: the leadership of the Komsomol and that of the KGB. The past collaboration of the two men, his contribution to Semichasny's rise, and his supervisory duties over the KGB on the

Central Committee all enabled Shelepin, even though he was no longer head of the KGB, to keep close contacts with it, contacts he used in October 1964 to assure the help of the police to the group that expelled Khrushchev. His functions as president of the Control Committee were also of exceptional importance. Thanks to the committee, he exercised some control over the entire administration. It is worth recalling that these were the functions exercised by Stalin in 1922 at the head of the Rabkrin (inspection service of workers and peasants).

Thanks to these multiple functions, Shelepin was the only person in 1964—at the moment when the Party decided that state and Party powers should be permanently kept separate—to appear in both hierarchies. His colleagues had no alternative but to recognize that power and the service he had done them by neutralizing the KGB. At the November 1964 plenum, they appointed him a full member of the Central Committee without his ever having gone through the candidate stage.[7] Further, when it was necessary to explain Khrushchev's fall to the Egyptians, who were panic-stricken by the event, Shelepin was sent to reassure them on November 23, 1964, because he had been close to Khrushchev and might embody a certain continuity in the eyes of these allies.[8]

In the balance of forces that existed in October 1964, nothing indicated that Brezhnev would become the most visible if not the most powerful personality on the Presidium. With Shelepin's entrance, one can estimate that half the members of the Presidium (it contained ten members in October 1964 and increased to eleven in November with the arrival, in addition to Shelepin, of P. Y. Shelest, first secretary of the Ukrainian Communist Party, to compensate for the loss of Kozlov, who had been very ill since 1963)[9] made up the real ruling group, because of the great responsibilities of its members and the apparatuses or functions they represented. Within this narrow group, a series of changes in the positions of individuals created, in a few short years, an entirely different balance of power.

These changes took place in the course of repeated crises, the two characteristic traits of which were that they occurred in the Presidium without involving larger bodies, and that they unfolded in a *political* way—that is, peacefully and, in general, preserving the honor of those involved. In Soviet political life this constituted another step in the institutionalization of the system.

The first crisis unfolded at the end of 1965, and its consequence was the simultaneous weakening of two figures who were in appearance all-powerful, Podgorny and Shelepin.

The weakening of Podgorny was brought about in two ways: The subordinates who had been associated with his past activities and enabled him to control the selection of some Party cadres[10] were displaced and subjected to criticism; then criticism was directed at the management of the Kharkov Party, Podgorny's former stronghold and still one of the bases of his power.[11] This questioning of the Kharkov organization was carried out all the more easily because the Party took steps to reconstruct it, because it was necessary to rectify the errors made under Khrushchev, and because this reordering could not be confused with a reprisal. But this was only a prelude to the direct elimination of Podgorny, accomplished at the Central Committee plenum in December 1965. At that time, Anastas Mikoyan offered his resignation on the grounds of his age—seventy—and his health; his departure left the presidency of the Presidium of the Supreme Soviet vacant, and Podgorny was immediately elected to the position. Moving from the secretariat of the Central Committee, which organizes the political life of the U.S.S.R., to a position without real power represents a considerable political defeat. But it is notable as a break with the political tradition of the U.S.S.R., where falls are generally spectacular, that the collective leadership took great care to make Podgorny's fall honorable. (Mikoyan later emphasized this desire to give a "legal" cast to competition for power. In confidential remarks to close associates, he said that his resigna-

tion was the consequence of a secret resolution adopted by the
Central Committee in the months following Khrushchev's fall
that forced the retirement of all leaders who reached seventy.[12]
If this resolution really existed, it is clear that it served only
once, to allow the Party simultaneously to get rid of Mikoyan
and Podgorny.)

At the same moment, Shelepin, another strong man of the
Presidium, was weakened by a purely administrative measure.
The December plenum abolished the Party and State Control
Commission,[13] from which he ruled as a supervisor of the administration, thereby taking away his position and the vice-
presidency of the Council of Ministers that went along with it.
No doubt Shelepin remained a member of the Secretariat, but
now on the same basis as the others, without exorbitant
prerogatives. But his fall had only begun. In July 1967, he left
the Secretariat for the presidency of the Central Council of
Unions, a position as devoid of power as the presidency of the
Supreme Soviet offered to Podgorny. A month earlier, his former colleague Semichasny had been eliminated from the KGB.
Shelepin was thus deprived of all his links to the bureaucracies
that held real power.[14]

The weakening of these two men coincided with other
changes in the composition and organization of the ruling organs. The Twenty-third Congress, which met early in 1966,
restored to the Presidium the more prestigious title of Politburo, and it also reestablished the general secretaryship of the
Party—abolished at Stalin's death—and appointed Brezhnev to
the position. Gradually, the Party seemed to restructure itself
around him, as can be seen in the duties he was given and the
appointment to the ruling organs of some of the men connected
with his career in the Ukraine and Moldavia. The most important of these changes was the appointment to the Secretariat of
Kirilenko, a voting member of Khrushchev's Presidium,[15] who
inherited the functions of organization and appointment recently held by Podgorny. Kirilenko is in many respects a double

of Brezhnev.[16] Like the General Secretary of the Party, he was born in 1906, and, like him, he joined the Party in 1931. He was an engineer in the aeronautics industry and thus had behind him a dual career, as a professional and an apparatchik. And a substantial part of his career unfolded in the area of Brezhnev's power, Zaporozhye and Dnepropetrovsk. Like Brezhnev, he was a specialist in questions of heavy industry and defense. At the same time, once the former occupants had been forced out, the decisive positions of the Ministry of the Interior and the KGB went to men like Shchelokov (Minister of Interior of the Union in September 1966), whose careers had been closely linked to Brezhnev's.[17]

In less than two years, this movement changed the composition of the Politburo and the Secretariat, but it did so in a very insidious manner. Between Khrushchev's Politburo, which had eighteen members (twelve voting members and six deputies), and the Politburo elected at the Twenty-third Congress, which contained nineteen (eleven and eight), twelve members remained the same. Looked at closely, the changes were not dramatic. Of the four voting members who left, two were eliminated by natural causes (Kusinen died shortly before Khrushchev's fall, and Kozlov shortly afterward), and two septuagenarians (Shvernik and Mikoyan) retired. Only one of the deputies, L. N. Efremov, was eliminated. The new Politburo was apparently satisfied merely to replace those who had left with new men (A. P. Kirilenko; Shelepin; P. Y. Shelest, first secretary of the Ukraine; K. T. Mazurov, first vice-president of the Council of Ministers who had an ex officio seat on the Politburo and was promoted to voting member; and, finally, Arvid Pelshe, an old Bolshevik of sixty-seven who had joined the Party in 1915 and represented, after the departure of Mikoyan and Shvernik, continuity with the Party of Lenin).

The changes were clearer among the deputies. Three of the four newcomers had characteristics worthy of note. Two first secretaries of republics, P. A. Masherov (Byelorussia) and D. A.

Kunaev (Kazakhstan), increased the "regional" weight of the Politburo. Moreover, Kunaev and another newcomer, Ustinov, had had careers associated with heavy industry, close to Brezhnev's interests.[18]

The changes in the Politburo were thus significant but discreet. Central Committee secretaries increased from four to six, and their representatives were generally younger, since, under Khrushchev, two of the four secretaries on the Presidium (Khrushchev and Kuvsinen) were seventy or older. The number of first secretaries of republics increased from four to five. But, at the same time, the principal changes affected the group of deputies. The disappearances because of death or old age and the general decrease in age among the secretaries gave this renewal a peaceful appearance. It was also carried out with the Party's complete agreement, because of two factors: the general policy on cadres followed by the collective leadership (which can be measured by the Twenty-third Congress) and the concern to present everything with the label of "collective leadership."

After the plenum reestablishing order in November 1964, the first political task the ruling group set for itself was in fact to do justice to the cadres displaced by Khrushchev and to appease them. The problem arose in the most urgent way at the level of obkom secretaries—taking into account their weight in the Central Committee. As we have seen, solutions were quickly found that calmed everyone's anger.

The collective leadership distinguished two men of this group and assured their promotion to the center. F. D. Kulakov, first secretary of the territory of Stavropol, became head of the Agriculture Department of the Central Committee; and I. V. Kapitonov (former first secretary of the Obkom of Ivanovo) was placed at the head of the Central Committee department in charge of Party organs for the Russian Republic. Both were soon named to the secretariat of the Central Committee. The bitterness created by Khrushchev was thus quickly erased, and the new group—which had, in declarations to the Party apparatus, linked its fate to the idea of stabilization—assured the support of the largest group on the Central Committee by guaranteeing them stability of employment.[19]

To this measured and calming policy was added an extraordinarily collegial attitude at the summit. Not only were the changes made in the Politburo and the Secretariat carried out without apparent drama (at the Twenty-third Congress, Podgorny, who had been demoted, was applauded "long and noisily," just as much as Suslov and Kosygin),[20] but—and this is the novelty of the period—the losers remained associated with power and preserved the means to struggle. Moreover, neither Shelepin nor Podgorny gave in; neither one fell into a political void. Quite the contrary, from the secondary positions to which they had been relegated, they attempted to play a political role and by their activity to give real content to functions which until then had been rather empty. In foreign policy, the Politburo presented itself collectively on the international scene. There is much evidence of this in negotiations with Middle Eastern countries, particularly with Egypt. While Nasser was alive, Kosygin, Gromyko, and Podgorny went to Cairo one after the other, each one explaining that he was only a representative of the Politburo, which was solely responsible for foreign policy. The Arab delegations to the U.S.S.R. were generally received by a majority of the Politburo. In 1968, during the Czechoslovakian crisis, all the indications are that decisions were made on the basis of collective responsibility. This insistence on collective power was precisely what allowed Podgorny, representative of the collective head of state which was, by law at the time, the Presidium of the Supreme Soviet, to embody the power of the Soviet state. From 1967 to 1976, Podgorny played an increasingly important role in the external affairs of the U.S.S.R.; he was the one who signed the treaty with Egypt in 1971, the first bilateral friendship agreement between a non-Communist country and the U.S.S.R. Similarly, once Shelepin had been relegated to the unions, he tried to make them an instrument of power; in 1967, he seemed to represent a force which the collective leadership took seriously.[21]

The second "succession" crisis of the post-Khrushchev period arose at the end of the decade. As undramatic as the first, its consequence was to show more clearly where the center of power was located. The crisis went back to 1967, when Khrushchev's successors had to confront the international difficulties they had inherited from their predecessors. In the assessment of Khrushchev's record they had made in 1964, one area of success stood out among many weaknesses: the policy of increased involvement in the Middle East. Although the Soviet position in Egypt and Syria did not counterbalance the conflict with China or the tensions in Eastern Europe, it nevertheless indicated that everything in Khrushchev's international activity had not been in vain. This is why the rapid collapse of the Arab states in June 1967, totally unforeseen in the U.S.S.R., had a powerful impact. We know that the Politburo was divided at the time and that Brezhnev, because he was general secretary, had to confront serious criticisms, a calling into question of the whole policy that had been followed in the region since 1964.[22] He also had to fight over the definition of future policy: to continue Soviet involvement or abandon it. And he was forced to accept future army control over a policy for which the principal argument was arms deliveries. Hardly had the Arab storm passed when the Prague spring arrived. The choice it imposed, to intervene militarily or not, once again divided the supporters of firm methods from those who wanted to pursue a moderate policy.

We must, however, avoid the simplistic vision of a "hard" or interventionist clan and a "conciliatory" clan that these two episodes suggest. Although it is in fact clear that in both the cases of Egypt and Czechoslovakia there was opposition between those who wanted to defend Soviet positions and those who wanted to present a conciliatory image of the U.S.S.R., the interventionists were far from identical in the two cases. Those who argued in 1967 that the U.S.S.R. should maintain its presence in the Arab countries—that is, rearm and control them—were precisely those who were troubled by the idea of intervening in Czechoslovakia in 1968. For they thought that such an intervention would frighten the Arab states. It is not an accident that the only head of state of the Third World, and probably of the non-Communist world, who was informed of Soviet intentions in Czechoslovakia a few hours before the invasion was Nasser.[23] Nor is it an accident that, in 1968 as in 1967, despite the internal debate, the Politburo loudly proclaimed its solidarity. After the Arab defeat, when Podgorny went to Cairo to reopen dialogue with an Egypt that accused the U.S.S.R. of having abandoned it, Brezhnev escorted him to the airport: an unusual demonstration in such a situation.[24] In 1968, all the documents said, "The Politburo has decided," and there were no personal declarations on Czechoslovakia.

Although it concealed its division on these two problems, the Politburo was less discreet on internal problems. The plenum of December 1969, which discussed economic problems, attests to the existence of a veritable group of malcontents—Shelepin, Mazurov, Suslov, Shelest—united by a common hostility to the general secretary. Their criticisms were directed at economic priorities, but we can probably see in them Shelepin's desire to recover lost ground by joining with Suslov, who was troubled by the ideological crisis, and with Shelest, leader of the Ukraine, who was hostile to the priority given to Siberia at the expense of his republic and to a shift in foreign policy toward détente that weakened the peripheral republics.[25] An indication of the crisis troubling the Politburo was the postponement of the Twenty-fourth Congress to a later date not according to statute. The Twentieth Congress had established that regular periodicity of congresses was indispensable to assure the normal functioning of the Party. This violation of the principles of 1956 indicates the difficulties the leadership was experiencing.[26]

Institutionalized Collegiality

But at this very moment a solution to the crisis was emerging. It involved an affirmation of the role of the general secretary and a series of changes in the composition of the ruling group.

Like Khrushchev, Brezhnev was able to strengthen his position in 1970 thanks to foreign policy. Until then, the foreign policy of the U.S.S.R had been turned toward the Third World and the Communist countries and had served as a field of action for the representatives of the state (Podgorny) or the government (Kosygin). The reorientation of foreign policy toward the Western world and toward détente introduced Brezhnev into the foreign policy circuit and enabled him to play a personal role in it. Because Brezhnev was concerned with foreign policy at the time of détente, it has generally been concluded that he was the author of the policy.

If we look more closely at the course of events, we observe that he was above all its spokesman. But it is very risky to deduce from this that he initiated it or that it expresses his preferences. At the origin of the opening to the West, we find the policies of General de Gaulle at a time when foreign policy in the U.S.S.R. was largely a government matter and was carried out by Kosygin. In 1969 again, when there was an incident with China to settle, it was Kosygin who communicated with Mao over the seldom-used hot line.[27] But in 1970, when détente was affirmed, Brezhnev strengthened his position at the expense of Kosygin. Criticized for the Politburo's economic choices in 1969, he became a critic in his turn, at the Twenty-fourth Congress in 1971, of the economic policy that had been followed under Kosygin's direction.[28] It was Brezhnev who presented to the Congress a plan designed to resolve simultaneously the economic problems "of individuals, groups, and the whole society."[29]

Foreign policy accentuated this advantage of Brezhnev's. In

the preparatory phase of the SALT talks, and then in the Indo-Pakistani war of 1971, it was Brezhnev who was the principal negotiator with President Nixon and who adopted alternately intransigent and conciliatory attitudes. In January 1972, it was with Brezhnev that Nixon carried on a correspondence, barely courteous on both sides, about Vietnam.[30] It was Brezhnev again who negotiated with Nixon in Moscow in May 1972. At that point, there was no longer any doubt that the foreign policy of the U.S.S.R. was embodied by Brezhnev. The desire to personalize it appeared as much on the Soviet as on the American side. If Nixon proposed as an example for their bilateral relations the memory of the relations between Roosevelt and Stalin, Brezhnev let it be known, with respect to the exchange of gifts between governments, that he would hope that his passion for luxury automobiles would be kept in mind.[31] But, although these personal relations were established, Nixon never had the impression that he was confronting a single negotiator, and the way in which Brezhnev, Kosygin, and Podgorny relayed and supplemented one another led him to conclude that this was a group, dominated, because of his age and his more expansive and conciliatory character, by the general secretary of the Party.[32] Although Nixon glimpsed differences in attitude, in this golden age of détente, he never considered that Brezhnev was its personal guarantor.

Brezhnev owes his place on the political stage in the end to his respect for the collective leadership, in which, while developing more influence and commanding increasing support on the Central Committee, he has introduced no brutal changes. The mini-crisis of 1970 was settled without the appearance of any losers, even though Brezhnev was the victor.

In the following years, particularly after 1973, the Politburo and the Secretariat were progressively renewed. But in this case, too, the changes were carried out gradually, without any climate of crisis, generally as the results of particular episodes. Most of the seven men excluded from the Politburo in the

seventies were excluded for good reasons. Mzhavanadze, because he was accused of serious misappropriation of funds, lost
the leadership of the Georgian Party and thus his seat on the
Politburo. Shelest and Voronov, open adversaries of a conciliatory foreign policy, which Brezhnev defended in the name of
the Politburo[33] and which, all the evidence indicates, had the
support of a majority of that body, quietly lost their seats in
April 1973. The departure of D. S. Polianski in 1977 and the
later departure of Mazurov took place against a background of
agricultural difficulties. The long resistance of Shelepin and
Podgorny gives a sense of these attenuated crises. Politically on
the defensive from 1965 on, Shelepin disappeared from the
political scene only in 1975, after an inglorious trip to England.
The disdain with which he was treated by the English unions,
more sensitive to his police past than to his position as union
leader, finally provided the Politburo with a pretext to decide
that he badly represented the Soviet unions. Podgorny, too, was
finally forced out. But it was a man of seventy-five that his
colleagues sent into retirement.[34]

A consideration of the composition of the two organs of the
summit, Politburo and Secretariat, and their variations, leads to
several conclusions. Despite changes in personnel which seem
to be frequent, the Brezhnev period is characterized by stability. In the years 1923–30, the Politburo left by Lenin was totally
renewed, with the exception of a single member, Stalin. From
1953 to 1962, the Politburo inherited from Stalin lost all its
members except for two, Khrushchev and Mikoyan.[35] On the
other hand, six voting members of the Presidium in 1980 had
been members at the time of Khrushchev's fall, and four of
them have held the decisive positions since 1964: Brezhnev,
Kosygin, Suslov, and Kirilenko. The permanence of the real
holders of power, representatives of the Party, the government,
and the ideology, is particularly noteworthy. Although the Secretariat has experienced many comings and goings, what is
evident there too, beyond sudden rises and falls, is the stability

of the most important group, the secretaries who are also members of the Politburo. Three out of the four—Brezhnev, Suslov, and Kirilenko—have continuously maintained this status, which provides them with exceptional means of control over the Party apparatus. This stability of a group which has long been associated with the central apparatus, but also with "fiefdoms" in the regions or republics, limits the significance of the movements that have periodically affected the composition of these two organs.[36]

A second conclusion concerns the nature of the crises that have brought about these changes. At no point in the Brezhnev era has there been an open political crisis, marked by confrontations like those under Stalin, or like the dramatic episodes of Khrushchev's struggle against the "anti-Party" group in 1957 or 1961. The muffled crises of the Brezhnev era have been characterized either by the very slow erosion of the positions of Shelepin and Podgorny—that is, by a belated resolution of the succession problem of 1964 which finally assured the triumph of a group from which those two members were excluded—or by a series of scattered expulsions that allowed the opening of the summit of the apparatus to two categories of men: representatives of regional fiefdoms whose careers had been very closely connected to that of the general secretary (Chernenko, Kunaev, Shcherbitski) and the representatives of other apparatuses to whom we shall return. But in 1965, as well as 1970, 1973–75, and 1978—moments of the principal changes—there was no open debate and no sign that the leadership of the Party was involved in serious struggles. In each case, the leadership seemed to be expelling a body that had been badly or only partially integrated.

A third conclusion touches on the "normalized" character of these movements of people, which give evidence as well of new political practices. No doubt, some leaders were eliminated in the context of a criticism of their policies. But that criticism remained moderate. Polianski left the Secretariat in 1977 because the results of the agricultural policy for which he was responsible were bad.[37] But Polianski was not directly accused, and his position had been weakening since 1973. The only two men excluded who were subject to strong attacks were Mzhavanadze, whose corruption was a matter of public knowledge,[38] and Shelest, whose loudly nationalistic positions were in opposition to the integrationist theories of the Party after the Twenty-fourth Congress.[39] The other exclusions often seem to have been the result of weakening positions. This was the case for Shelepin, who was forced at the elections for the Supreme Soviet in 1974 to give up a prestigious urban electoral district for a rural district. His final expulsion in 1975, carried out during a plenum which was announced only after the fact, thus seemed to be a sanction for the failure of the trip to England.[40]

To repeat, the most remarkable fact of this period is not only the muffled character of the crises but especially the normalization of the status of the excluded. Under Stalin, a political fall implied death or, in the best cases, a loss of freedom and dishonor. Khrushchev had tried to maintain the dishonorable character of political defeat (the "anti-Party" group were "factionalists," and most of them were accused of "complicity with Stalin"). But in the seventies, Mazurov withdrew on the grounds of deficient health,[41] and Podgorny asked to retire. And the ultimate fate of the excluded has not always been "political death." Aside from the fact that they have preserved the material advantages they enjoyed when they held office, they have sometimes been appointed to other positions (Polianski was named ambassador to Japan), and sometimes they have become honorable retirees. Thus, Podgorny was present at the Kremlin ceremonies in November 1979 for the sixty-second anniversary of the revolution.[42] The presence of a high-ranking leader who had recently been dismissed at ceremonies which brought together the Soviet political leadership indicated the existence of new political mores. We can also include among these innovations the fact that Soviet leaders are now absent for long periods for unexplained reasons without that giving rise to widespread speculation about their political fate. In autumn 1976, Kosygin was absent from all political functions—of the Party and the government—for eighty-seven days and then reappeared, without any explanation. These periods of absence, like Podgorny's reappearance, indicate above all the ruling group's confidence in its capacity to preserve power.

Calm, stability, and consensus are in the end the dominant characteristics of political relations among the leaders in the Brezhnev period. The era of pitiless struggles among individuals seems to have passed, to be replaced by self-perpetuating solidarity.

Army and Party: Conflict or Cooperation?

The evolution of the kinds of relations among leaders went along with a deeper change: The supreme organs of the Party became more representative.

The Central Committee had for long assured the representation of specific groups: the Party bureaucracy, institutions, regions. The stability characteristic of this body meant that each group tended to preserve its place there. Until the early seventies, this representative function was irrelevant to the composition of the Politburo, to the extent that the weight of individuals was decisive. But if we examine the changes that have taken place, we can observe that there too it is bureaucracies rather than individuals that were appointed, and the Politburo has expressed the interests of those bureaucracies. This turn of the Politburo toward becoming more representative dates from 1973. At that time, membership was granted to the leaders of the three institutions closely related to foreign policy: the Minister of Foreign Affairs, Andrei A. Gromyko; the Minister of Defense, Marshal A. A. Grechko; and the President of the KGB, whose functions also include internal security and espionage, I. V. Andropov. Although the men at the summit have changed since 1973, the bureaucracies they represent have preserved a stable position. And this raises to begin with the problem of the weight of those bureaucracies, particularly the army and the police, in the ruling organs and in the decision-making process. Behind the leaders of these bodies, in fact, there exist apparatuses—the police, for example—that have long carried on autonomous activities and whose capacity to become again bodies acting on their own initiative or weighing decisively on the Party is one of the problems of Soviet power. The possibility of military power or growing pressure by the army or civilian power also resurfaces periodically in the U.S.S.R. And the seventies, when the U.S.S.R. reached the status of a global power through an even more active foreign policy, left room for the development of the activities of the army and the KGB. Was the arrival of their leaders at the summit of the ruling apparatus in 1973 a sign of that progression? What capacity does the political apparatus have to contain collective ambitions, much weightier than personal ambitions? This is all the more a question because collective ambitions have been strengthened by the general evolution of Soviet politics.

The place of the army in Soviet political life must be evaluated on the basis of several elements. There is the more or less substantial representation of the military in the various apparatuses, of course. But we must also consider who these military men are, the tone of the relations between civilian and military power, and finally the domestic and international objectives of the U.S.S.R. The weight of the military in State and Party apparatus is at first sight impressive. In the Supreme Soviet of the U.S.S.R., military representation has been fairly constant since the beginning of the Brezhnev era: 56 deputies in 1962 and 1966, 58 in 1970, 56 in 1974, and 55 in 1979.[43] In relation to the total number of deputies, which has oscillated from one legislature to another between 1,442 and 1,517, the proportion of the military has practically not changed, going from 3.9 percent in 1962 to 3.6 percent in 1979. Those elected by the people, since the Supreme Soviet is elected by universal suffrage, are practically all invested with this dignity because of the positions they occupy. The body of deputies from the military corresponds to three groups which are all systematically represented: the holders of the highest positions in the Ministry of Defense and the commanders of the large military regions, of the forces stationed in Eastern Europe, and of the navy; the "marshals" who survived the Second World War; and military men representing the national minorities of the U.S.S.R.[44]

In the Party, where real power is located, the representation of the army is more spectacularly provided for, as was demonstrated by the thirty men elected to the Central Committee in 1976. With one representative on the Politburo—the Minister of Defense—or three more if one counts military titles (Brezhnev, Ustinov, Andropov), the army seems to be a privileged body in the sphere of political power.

These quantitative indications become clearer when we move from the figures to the recent history of relations between the Party and the army, a history which, in the Brezhnev years, does not follow a straight line but twists and turns.

After Khrushchev's fall, the army, which he had disappointed and angered, immediately took on new importance. Not that it had played a role in his elimination, which was essentially a political act, but its neutrality had served Khrushchev's enemies. As in other areas, the successors denounced his choices and thereby satisfied the army on the essential question of economic priorities.

In December 1964, Kosygin declared to the meeting of the Supreme Soviet, "The Communist Party and the government have decided to strengthen the economic and defense potential of the country by strengthening heavy industry."[45] In this proposition, presented solemnly under the dual authority of the Party and the government, what Kosygin rejected implicitly was the decision—heretical in the eyes of the army and all other "eaters of steel"—made by Khrushchev on October 10, 1964, to abandon the eternal priority of sector A. The following year, Kosygin was still more explicit in his rejection of Khrushchev's positions, about which he said, "To economize on military expenses is to go counter to the interests of the U.S.S.R."[46] The army could consider itself satisfied on this point. The economic policy limiting military investments was abandoned, and military interest and national interest became synonymous.

But the latent conflict between the army and civilian power which arose in the early sixties, far from subsiding, became more acute. Armed with the assurances it had received, armed also with the idea that periods of transition are favorable to such steps, the army tried to impose itself as an autonomous force. From November 1964 to 1967 an almost open struggle—the struggles of individuals were thoroughly effaced by this conflict between apparatuses—continued between the two powers, with Party and government united in a common desire to limit the rise of military ambitions. This opposition can be observed in two areas: foreign policy and political control of the army. Moreover, the two areas overlapped, because in both cases the army was attempting to assert its autonomy and its right to participate in decision making.

The opposition in foreign policy broke out during the first weeks after the collective leadership came to power. The leadership affirmed at the outset its attachment to the policy of peaceful coexistence, which, said Brezhnev, is a central element in Lenin's legacy, and emphasized that, to achieve a reduction in international tension, "the Soviet Union is ready to develop Soviet-American relations."[47] The United States was presented as a "country of many Americans drawn toward peace and weary of the cold war."

At the same moment, the supreme leader of the army, Marshal R. Y. Malinovski, Minister of Defense, was taking quite different positions. In Red Square, during the military parade of November 7 and again at the later reception, he asserted that the United States was the center of world imperialism and that it threatened the U.S.S.R. and peace. These declarations were in such disagreement with Brezhnev's speech that when *Pravda* published them it censored Malinovski's anti-American remarks.[48]

The second area of conflict between army and Party, autonomy of the army or submission to political authority, also appeared right after Khrushchev's fall. In the days following the event, Marshal Malinovski succeeded in having Marshal Zakharov appointed chief of staff—he had been removed from the position in 1963 by Khrushchev for having opposed his military policies, particularly his desire to control the army. A fortuitous combination of favorable circumstances made the position available at the very moment when the new leadership was establishing itself.[49] This appointment very soon revealed its meaning, because Zakharov, as he had done under Khrushchev, became an advocate of the responsibility of the military command in all areas, emphasizing how the intervention of the Party was inappropriate to the requirements of the army and how much it had damaged the interests of the U.S.S.R. in the past.[50] "The army for the soldiers," this was the demand clearly expressed by the military professionals. The Party responded to this demand by trying to strengthen the influence of the Political Administration of the Army by naming its head, General Epishev, to the rank of titular member of the Central Committee at the November 1964 plenum. Through this promotion, the head of the political control services of the army suddenly attained equality of status with the Minister of Defense. Two wills came into collision. A self-confident army in an internationally difficult period—the American air raids on North Vietnam began in February 1965—drew arguments from the international context and the solidarity that the U.S.S.R. had proclaimed with Vietnam[51] to defend the weight of the army in the nation, its responsibilities, its importance in political decisions. From this flowed the unique role of the military command[52] and the importance of investments in this sector.[53] Con-

fronting the army, the Party, which expressed itself in this critical period through its military intermediary, the Political Administration of the Army, was not nearly as clear in its positions.
A comparative reading of the newspaper that expressed the
views of the professional army, *Krasnaia zvezda* ("Red Star"),
and the organ of the political authority of the army, *Kommunist
vooruzhonykh sil* ("The Communist of the Armed Forces"),
indicates the unequal force of these desires. No doubt *Kommunist vooruzhonykh sil* referred to Lenin to argue that "the
principal source of organization of the Soviet army is the leadership of the Communist Party"[54] and that the "single command"
demanded by the military could be accepted only "in the perspective of the Party."[55] For that organ, the defense potential
of a country did not lie only in the armaments at its disposal but
in morale—that is, the nation's ideological training.[56] Up to that
point, the political cadres of the army supported positions contrary to those of the professionals, but thereafter hesitations
began. In fact, the higher-ranking political cadres shared the
positions of the professionals on the size of the armed forces.
The army had reacted violently to Khrushchev's proposals to
reduce military forces, and it had been supported by its political
cadres. In 1963, General Epishev had made his own contribution to the debate by asserting that the wars of this age call for
mass armies and a reinforcement of all military sectors and all
categories of armaments.[57]

After Khrushchev's fall, the military professionals could not
fail to observe that, although they were in absolute disagreement with the political head of the army when he advocated
the preeminence of the Party's authority, they found an ally in
him when it came to defining military needs. And the first
months after Khrushchev were dominated by debates over economic priorities and the economic needs of the army. The discussion of preparation of the five-year plan posed a crucial problem: Should the rise in Soviet living standards be accelerated?
This was Kosygin's suggestion,[58] and Podgorny explained its

consequences. He emphasized that, although for a long time "the Soviet people had accepted material restrictions in the interest of giving priority to the development of heavy industry and defense capability," social wealth and social needs had not placed in the forefront "the daily interests of the workers."[59] This concern to favor consumption was far from unanimous in the Party, and it considerably troubled the army. This is why the army was attentive to the traditionalist position advocated by Suslov.

Without denying that the Party had to take social needs into account, Suslov asserted, against Kosygin and Podgorny, that the age of sacrifices was not over, because "objective reality"— that is, the external world—made it necessary to pursue a policy of giving priority to strengthening defense capability.[60] We can see in this instance how complex the political picture of the U.S.S.R. was in this transitional phase. The Party was divided between supporters of the traditional priority of heavy industry and supporters of a veritable consumerist politics. To defend its needs, the army had to rely on the former. But these were precisely the ones who were most passionately attached to the theory of Party dominance over the army, which the army challenged. It is not an accident that General Epishev, like Suslov, was both a supporter of controlling the army, which was his function, and a defender of its economic needs, which he considered a first priority. To defend its right to autonomy, the army would certainly have gained more if it had banked on Kosygin and those who, with him, wanted to create a link between society and government by a rapid improvement in the standard of living; for this purpose, in every area, they adopted an empirical approach for which the centralizing Party might have to pay. Of the two tendencies, the army chose in the end the one that guaranteed satisfaction of its economic needs and its capacity of development, hoping by this support to gain the power which would enable it to loosen the grip of political control. Although this conflict over the relations between army and political power, which unfolded at the beginning of the post-Khrushchev period, was less spectacular than the individual quarrels that occupied center stage, it was infinitely more important for the future of the system. What was at issue were the major economic choices. And the quarrel oriented the future political balance between the Party and the army.

In 1966, the army seemed to be the winner in this struggle for influence. The Party leadership reversed itself on announced reduction in military expenditures and reestablished the 1965 budget at the level that had been originally estimated.[61] The Twenty-third Congress, despite a conciliatory tone and a constant insistence on the theme of peaceful coexistence, marked a clear hardening in comparison to the positions adopted in international matters after 1956. This hardening was the affirmation of the priority of Soviet defense needs[62] and a clear delimitation, in spatial and political terms, of peaceful coexistence. Khrushchev had allowed doubt to linger about the area where coexistence applied. Did it concern only the relations of the U.S.S.R. with the developed world or also Soviet relations with developing countries? The formulations of the Twentieth Congress and the policies subsequently followed in the Third World suggested that the class struggle could everywhere be relegated to some distant and unpredictable future.[63] The Chinese had not been mistaken when they accused the U.S.S.R. of having abandoned the path of revolution. The Twenty-third Congress was much clearer in this respect: Peaceful coexistence, said Brezhnev, should apply to Soviet-American relations (it goes without saying that the other industrialized countries fit into this scheme). Elsewhere, competition and the progress of international socialism would be delayed at no moment, because the progress of the revolution in the Third World and the fate of the socialist camp were inseparable.[64]

Thus in 1966, at the moment when it was beginning to consolidate itself, the Brezhnev group clearly indicated its views about the world—coexistence, no doubt, but within very precise limits—and its priorities: strengthening Soviet power. To affirm their objectives, the Soviet authorities spoke with a single voice: the voice of general secretary Brezhnev, the voice of head of government Kosygin, the voice of the army. No doubt one can note some differences of emphasis between the army and civilian power. If Brezhnev and Kosygin both celebrated peaceful coexistence in their speeches to the congress, the military men who spoke, Marshal Malinovski and General Epishev, both forgot to mention coexistence and devoted themselves exclusively to threats, the power the U.S.S.R. needed, and its resources.[65] But these differences should not conceal the essential point. From its very first solemn manifestation—Party congresses are designed to "publish" the line being followed—the group of Khrushchev's successors defined a political vision which it would follow without deviation in the future, a vision of a world in which coexistence and progress are closely connected, where the domain of coexistence has limits, while the domain of progress has none.

Could the army be fully satisfied with the choices of the Twenty-third Congress? In appearance, yes. The world described by the Party demanded a large and powerful army. Politics would continue to depend on military power for a long time. Just as it was recognized in Soviet priorities, so the army found a significant place in institutions. It was represented at the Congress by 352 delegates, 7.1 percent of the total. And the Congress had elected 32 of those delegates to represent it on the Central Committee. In the supreme organs, Politburo and Secretariat, it saw the rise of a man close to its interests: D. F. Ustinov. He had, in fact, been People's Commissar for Armaments in 1941 and had specialized since then in questions of heavy industry. His appointment to the Secretariat and his presence among the candidates of the Politburo, if they did not provide the direct presence of the army, nevertheless created a situation more favorable than the one that had existed since the expulsion of Zhukov in 1958.

Perhaps, if we look at it more closely, we can observe that the progress of the army in the Party apparatus was only relative. The army's delegation to the Congress had increased by only 2 members from 1961 to 1966, while the total number of delegates from one congress to the other had increased by 225. And although the 32 delegates elected to the Central Committee represented a numerical progress, the enlargement of the Central Committee at the end of the Congress finally slightly reduced the army's representation in relation to the whole. But the most remarkable point is probably that the only progress the army accomplished was that made not by military professionals but by the Political Administration. The latter had had, in fact, a single delegate on the Central Committee in 1961, General Golikov, titular member of the Central Committee and passionate defender of the theory of the Party's preeminent authority in the army.[66] In 1966, this body was represented among the titular members of the Central Committee by its head, General Epishev, and by two candidates, the head of military administration for the Moscow district and the head of strategic missile forces.[67] No doubt, the "political" men of the army represented only a minor fraction of its delegation on the Central Committee (3 out of 32), but their progress indicated a tendency, the desire of the Party not to leave the army outside its control. At the end of the Congress, this tendency was barely visible, and the army understood it in its own way. Malinovski had said it to the Congress: The officer corps, up to the highest level, was 93 percent members of the Party or the Komsomol.[68]

The army thus realized within itself a synthesis between political power and military power, and this justified its autonomy. Armed with this conviction and the budgetary concessions it had obtained, the army was struggling to have the Party recognize in every respect its right to be a specific social body, different from all others in society.[69] And it gained this recognition in a domain in which the Party, since the elimination of Khrushchev, had been very careful not to weaken itself, the delicate domain of rehabilitations. In the "secret speech" and in the course of the years following the Twentieth Congress, the rehabilitation of the military had been exceptionally important. The great leaders liquidated by Stalin in 1937 (including Tukhachevski, Iakir, Gamarmik, and Blücher) had been restored to their place in Soviet history. Similarly, the role played by the military command in the Second World War had been reevaluated. But, in the late sixties, the army wanted to go beyond what the Party had accepted—that is, a disavowal of Stalin. It obtained a partial rehabilitation of Zhukov, victim of the "political purges" of the post-Stalinist era,[70] and especially—and this is extraordinary—the rehabilitation of a major executed under Lenin for having "conspired against the Soviet regime." Now, if there is a boundary the Party intends not to cross in confessing past mistakes, it is the boundary of the Leninist period. Lenin's Party was infallible—that is, the guarantee of the infallibility of the Party in general. In these circumstances, there cannot have been any unjustly condemned victims under Lenin. The rehabilitation of Major Dymenko indicates the army's combativeness but, even more, a clear desire to point out the Party's failings and thereby the exorbitant character of its pretensions to control everything.

The balance sheet of Party-army relations before 1967 is difficult to draw up. It seems nevertheless to lean in favor of autonomy of military power. The Party multiplied declarations affirming the primacy of ideology and of its authority. But it was led, by its international choices and by its traditions, to economic decisions that strengthened the army, reassured it, and led it to be demanding on other levels.

This uncertain balance between the two powers was strongly called into question by the death of Malinovski in the spring of 1967. Who would succeed him as Minister of Defense, another military man or a civilian? The question was far from easy to resolve, especially considering the political tradition of the U.S.S.R. The Party had long succeeded in dominating the army, by placing it under the authority of nonmilitary ministers or fake military men like Bulganin, an apparatchik whom the Party had made into a marshal. The army had been under the authority of a man from its ranks for only twelve years, between 1955—when Bulganin became prime minister and was replaced by Zhukov, who was in turn replaced by Malinovski in 1957—and 1967. The question was thus raised again. Would Malinovski be succeeded by a military man? For the army, the answer was not in doubt; it intended to preserve the positions it had gained in the post-Stalinist period. For the Party, the answer was no less clear, but it went in the opposite direction. "The leading role of the Party in the construction of the army and in the armed forces must grow,"[71] for "the experience of the last two wars proves that leadership can not be entrusted to the military alone."[72]

For ten days, an acute conflict opposed the Party to the army. This conflict, which was not apparent because it involved bureaucracies rather than people, nevertheless represented the second serious crisis of the post-Khrushchev period. Beyond the appointment of the new Minister of Defense, the discussion, traces of which can be found in military publications, dealt with the decisive problem for the system of the army's right to live outside the Party, or at least to consider that its own Communists were enough to embody the Party's authority. The Party had a candidate for the succession, Ustinov, whose industrial background justified his appointment and who was a veritable apparatchik. But again in 1967, the political leadership was unable to impose its decision. At the conclusion of the debate, the army had won; its minister was a professional soldier, Marshal A. A. Grechko, whose experience went back to the civil war and who was one of the military cadres whose advancement had been substantially helped by the Stalinist purges. A genuine military man, Grechko was also an old Communist, since he had joined the Party in 1928, at twenty-five, and had been a member of the Central Committee since 1952.[73]

The victory of the military was reinforced in the following period by the Arab-Israeli war of June 1967 and the Czechoslovakian crisis. In June 1967, considering the fate of the Soviet military supplies that had been delivered to the Arabs, the army was in a strong position to say in its turn that military matters are too serious to be left to nonspecialists. Faced with the defeat in the Middle East, the political authorities could only agree with the army on the necessity of strengthening Soviet military capability. The theses published for the fiftieth anniversary of the revolution, the celebratory speeches,[74] everything indicates that the military's positions had carried the day. Brezhnev said at the time that the policy of peaceful coexistence must be based on an "invincible defense capability."[75] The theme of Party control over the army was blurred in the military press; when the subject was treated, military leaders generally expressed vigorously their certainty that it was "necessary to strengthen the unity of command" but that this was "the privilege of the military leaders and of them alone."[76] What can be found above all in the press is the army's insistence on the military needs of the U.S.S.R. The military reform of 1967, which brought about a certain militarization of society, also helped to increase the specific powers of the army.

The Czechoslovakian crisis completed the process of pushing the army onto the political stage, which does not at all imply that it had argued in favor of a military solution. During the feverish months that preceded the invasion, Kosygin, as well as Marshal Grechko, appeared in Czechoslovakia. An analysis of the Soviet newspapers representing the various bureaucracies (*Pravda* for the Party, *Izvestia* for the government, *Trud* for the unions, *Krasnaia zvezda* for the army) points up the hesitations and doubts of each group rather than definite attitudes.[77] The only military argument suggesting an intervention was made by the political head of the army, Epishev, on April 23, 1968.[78] One may imagine that the military professionals were not very inclined to support an intervention carried out in the

name of ideological interests and involving the army's "ideological" tasks. But the Soviet army participated in the changes
imposed on Czechoslovakia. On April 13, 1969, four days before
Alexander Dubcek was replaced by Husak, Marshal Grechko
went to Prague with the Vice-Minister of Foreign Affairs of the
U.S.S.R., and from there he went to Germany. This activity of
a military leader outside his domain, these political meetings
(with Ludvik Svoboda, Husak, and Ulbricht) suggest that the
army was then tempted, as it had been in the Middle East, to
go beyond its role and to intervene by the side of the Party, on
the latter's terrain. The Soviet leaders had learned long ago that
one does not call on the army without having to pay a price. The
political authorities have never accepted this price, and every
period of growth in military autonomy has been followed by a
bitter struggle between the Party and the army which the Party
has always won.

Until the end of the decade, the army continued to assert
itself, profiting from the transitional phase of the succession,
during which the leaders were still uncertain of their power;
profiting as well from the international problems which the
new group had to confront. But in the early seventies, the
situation began to reverse itself. Soviet power had reached a
certain degree of equilibrium among individuals. International
problems—the armed conflict with China on the Ussuri River
in March 1969, the world Conference of Communist Parties in
June, and especially the policy of an opening to the West—
demanded a unity of views, or else each event in international
life would further the political progress of the army. The Party's
will to impose more political discipline on the army came out
less in the traditional declarations on the primacy of politics
than in the spectacular decision made in April 1969 to do away
with the classic May Day military parade and to hold only one
annual demonstration of military power, for the anniversary of
the revolution.[79] This was perhaps a signal to the United States
with which the U.S.S.R. began strategic arms limitation talks

(SALT) in November 1969. And Brezhnev, in his May Day speech, avoided any allusion to "American imperialism."

From this point on, relations between the Party and the army entered an entirely different phase, in which the Party attempted to be reassuring about the implications of the policy of détente while at the same time tightening its authority over the army. In one respect, the army could consider itself satisfied: The Central Committee elected Marshal Grechko to the Politburo. For the second time in the history of the U.S.S.R., and the first had been very brief, a military professional, supreme leader of the armed forces, had a seat on the Politburo. He took his place beside two other newcomers, the head of Soviet foreign policy, Gromyko, and the chief of police, Andropov. These simultaneous promotions suggested that, this time, the army was present in the Politburo as a group, and not to reward services rendered by one man to a group (which had been the case for Zhukov). It was the importance of foreign policy and détente (which had to be "balanced" by a strong army and extreme internal vigilance) which had brought to the supreme organ of power not three men but three heads of apparatuses. Détente implied, from the military point of view, that the U.S.S.R. approach it from a position of strength. Grechko's promotion was, in this respect, both a stick—discreet but real—brandished in the direction of the Western negotiators, who were thus informed that détente did not mean actual or potential weakness of the U.S.S.R., and a guarantee to the army that it would not pay the price of that détente and that it would be discussed with the army. The presence of the army in the Politburo had, moreover, a considerable advantage for the political authorities. In their relations with the United States, when the United States doubted Soviet will to apply seriously a policy of arms limitations and pointed to Soviet military expenditures,[80] they could accuse the army. And, in fact, the army, with the voice of its representative in the Politburo, constantly insisted on the necessity to link détente and power.[81]

The Party had thus succeeded, by including the army in its decision-making organ, in presenting to the outside world the convenient image of a leadership divided between the politicians "who want peace" and the military who are by definition "warmongers." The representation of the military at the summit thus serves many purposes. But this time the Party did not loosen its grip; it maneuvered the army and indicated its intention of gradually imposing its supremacy.

At the Twenty-fifth Congress (where the number of military representatives in the Central Committee suffered a sharp reduction), military problems were not treated by the army leaders but by the general secretary of the Party. The silence of the Minister of Defense was unprecedented, all the more so because Grechko was present at the congress and was very active during this period.[82]

This silence can be explained in the light of the events that followed, events that marked a veritable seizure of power by the Party over the army. Marshal Grechko died on April 26, 1976.[83] But, contrary to what had happened at the death of his predecessor, his successor as Minister of Defense was no longer subject to debate. Three days later, the new minister was appointed. There had been a return, after twenty-one years, to the classic formula of an apparatchik at the head of the army. The new minister, D. F. Ustinov, whose candidature had failed in 1967 because of military opposition, was in a position of strength in 1976. The Twenty-fifth Congress had just appointed him to titular membership in the Politburo, and his long experience with the problems of the arms industry was particularly important for the military men themselves, at a moment when armament problems were again on the agenda. It hardly mattered that Ustinov was not a military man; he was appointed, by a degree of April 29, 1976, general of the army, and three months later, he became a marshal of the U.S.S.R.[84]

The granting of high military titles to the dignitaries of the Party did not stop there. By a decree of May 7, 1976, the Supreme Soviet appointed Leonid Brezhnev Marshal of the U.S.S.R.[85] The Tass communiqué said that this appointment was in recognition of the role of the general secretary "in the presidency of the Defense Council of the U.S.S.R.," an organ unknown until then. The decree and the revelations it included are very important for an understanding of the evolution of the relationship between civilian power and the army in 1976. In suddenly revealing to the Soviets the existence of the Defense Council and the role played in it by Brezhnev, the authorities informed them, at the moment when the Ministry of Defense slipped out of military hands, that in any case the supreme head of the armed forces was the general secretary of the Party. Could one express more clearly the army's subordination to the Party? At this point, we can understand how the conflict between Party and army that had lasted for years had been resolved. The army, as a group, was broadly represented in the Party. Its supreme leader was the general secretary. The Politburo contained three high-ranking officers: Marshals Brezhnev and Ustinov and General Andropov. The army was present in the Secretariat itself for the first time, since the marshals of the Politburo were also members of the Secretariat. At the same time, the number of military titular members of the Central Committee also increased from twenty to twenty-two, since we must add to the group the general secretary of the Party and Andropov (with Ustinov replacing Grechko). Once again the figures are deceptive, for they conceal a weakening, not a strengthening, of the army. The high military command included a large number of "politicians," who occupied all the positions in the supreme organs of the Party. Of the nine living marshals of the U.S.S.R., two were men of the apparatus, and of the eleven generals of the army, three were also apparatchiks (Andropov, president of the KGB; Shchelokov, Minister of the Interior; and Epishev).

The army of the late seventies thus found itself in a contradictory position. Foreign policy gave it a considerable role, and domestic policy, as we shall see, tended to blend the values of the army with the social values of the Party. The highest dignitaries of the Party, by putting on uniforms, further glorified it and affirmed the symbiosis of Communist interests and military interests. But at the same time, the Party had confiscated military prestige for its benefit and often spoke as though it represented the army. Minor incidents clarify this confusion of the two hierarchies. In 1976, when Brezhnev received his marshal's stars, only the Politburo attended the ceremony, in which the army was after all an interested party.[86] In 1978, when he received the Order of Victory, the only speakers were himself and Suslov.[87] Did the absence—or the silence—of the military express their displeasure, or was the Party pushing them aside? Whatever the answer, one unknown persists: Who really benefited from this evolution? For all that, were there winners and losers in this reordering of the bureaucracies?

It is difficult to answer these questions without examining briefly the weight of the defense industries in the political system. They are the primary concern of six federal ministers: defense industry (Zverev), aeronautics industry (Dementiev), naval construction (Iegorov), electronic industries (Shokin), radio industry (Pleshakov), and construction of strategic, ballistic, and space program materials (Afanasiev). Aside from those ministries that work directly for the army, four others have closely connected activities: chemical industry, automobile industry, automation and control systems, and tractors and agricultural machinery.

These various ministries have certain characteristics in common, among which is the very great stability of their leaders, who all have long experience in their fields. Thus, the Minister of the Aeronautics Industry of the U.S.S.R., Dementiev, has been in his position for more than twenty years. In general, the ministers connected to defense were appointed under Khrushchev and have not been affected by political changes at the top. Almost all of them have voting seats on the Central Committee.

But, unlike the situation that prevailed under Khrushchev (when Pervukhin and Saburov represented the defense industries on the Politburo), the ministers in this sector are excluded from the Politburo. Finally, they have adapted to economic reforms, notably to financial accounting *(khozraschet)*, perhaps the better to defend their prerogatives before the central authorities.

We can thus see the development of the broad outlines of a "military-industrial complex." The defense industries, like the army they serve, are a privileged sector in comparison to industry as a whole. Their leadership has solid job security and considerable means of action, but also the will to acquire a certain degree of independence, by invoking their experience, competence, and adaptive ability. Their place on the Central Committee, like that of the military, assures them of representation in the institutions of power. But, like the army to which they are connected, the defense industries are present at the highest level through the intermediary of an apparatchik, Ustinov. In a general fashion, three men are in charge of liaison between the enormous sector of defense industries and the political authorities, none of whom is a leader of industry. They are, aside from Ustinov, L. V. Smirnov (titular member of the Central Committee and president of the Military-Industrial Commission, whose function is to coordinate the activities of the Ministry of Defense, the Ministries of the Defense Industries, and the institutes of the Academy of Sciences carrying on research in this field) and I. D. Serbin, who has assumed the leadership of the department of defense industries in the Central Committee of the Party. This organization of defense industries shows the cohesion between the army and the industrial sector that serves it, at all levels of the apparatus of power (Politburo, Presidium of the Council of Ministers of the U.S.S.R., apparatus of the Central Committee). Even led by civilians, the army and its interests hold a considerable place at all levels of the political hierarchy. We can see in the end how, after a long period of trial and error, the present relations between the political authorities and the army were established, at a moment when foreign policy had opened substantial room for the military.

The army is really a closed social body, endowed with many unquestioned privileges and certain of being able to preserve them and to reproduce itself as a group. The material and psychological world of the army is distinct from the world of Soviet society as a whole, and the army is determined to perpetuate that specificity. The political authorities have granted it a growing role in carrying out foreign programs,[88] and no longer present it, as they used to, as a simple defense force for the socialist fatherland. There is of course a limit to this role of the army's: The Party decides on its activity. However, this limitation, which has been constantly emphasized by Soviet policies in the years 1976–80, should not conceal everything that unites the army and the Party rather than opposing them.

There is first of all the political culture of the contemporary Soviet Union, to which we shall return. It is characterized by broad agreement between the Party and the army on the objectives of the Party's activity, the legitimacy of its power, and the importance of the mission the Party has given to the army.

The process of decision making in defense matters is another area of agreement. Although the Party has, in fact, the prerogative of defining general policy, it appears from particular examples, especially in the Middle East, that it often delegates its power of decision to the army whenever the army is involved. Moreover, because it is represented at all levels of power, even though its representatives may be civilians, the army has the means to make itself heard. Probably more than any other group, it also has the possibility of expressing positions that are sometimes different from Party theses. It is enough to read *Krasnaia zvezda,* to see how, as the years have passed, the military leaders have strongly asserted their conception of a unity of command which would eliminate political authority, to see the distance between the positions defended by that newspaper and its Communist counterpart, *Kommunist vooru-zhonykh sil*—all this is enough to indicate the military's freedom of tone and the degree of tolerance they enjoy. But it is appropriate here not to confuse the defense of the interests of categories and debates on major political choices. The Brezhnev Party has accepted the fact that the army, as a group, may assert its particular interests. On the other hand, when a Brezhnev preaching détente and conciliation is opposed by the demands of the military for increased vigilance and more armaments, we must ask if, behind this apparent disagreement, there is not a knowing division of labor, which allows the U.S.S.R. to pursue its armament program while asserting that its *political* choice is to stop it.

Cooperation between the Party and the army is obvious in many areas. The fact that most military leaders belong to the Party, the penetration of the army by the political bureaucracy —everything imposes, beyond whatever resistance may exist, the collaboration of the military with the Party. No doubt they rarely participate in the regional life of the Party and in government organisms, but administration has offered them many fields of cooperation: conscription, transportation, paramilitary training, education.

Although the army, like the defense industry, is headed by apparatchiks, they are nevertheless vigilant in defending military needs, in the area of arms production, in the improvement of careers, and in the preservation of the various privileges the army enjoys. Moreover, the central authorities charge it only with the defense of the nation from external attack, and sometimes with domestic economic tasks. In fact, the army has helped in certain major projects[89] where civilian manpower was inadequate, like the construction of the Baikal–Amur railroad, help in the harvest,[90] and the organization of transportation. But the thankless tasks of the maintenance of internal order, intervention against demonstrations of social discontent (strikes), and the repression of opposition are all the exclusive province of the KGB. The army is a social model, a body whose privileges make it attractive, and its prestige is not tarnished by any repressive function. Dominated by the Party, it also owes a lot to the Party, in its post-Stalinist metamorphosis.

The KGB: Dependence and Prestige

The entry of the president of the KGB into the Politburo in 1973 and the spectacular activities of that organ in the repression of dissidents have led to the conclusion that, in the U.S.S.R. of Brezhnev, as in that of Stalin, the KGB is a central element of the system. However, political reality does not at all confirm such an analysis. Although the army represented a perennial problem for the central authorities and it has taken years to assure the preeminence of the Party over the army, the case was entirely different with the police.

As soon as Stalin died, the political authorities decided to reduce the police again to the role Lenin had assigned to them: a powerful instrument of control over society, but an instrument controlled by the Party. This was the first point around which a consensus was established in the post-Stalin years, and this consensus was long-lasting. To resume control over the police apparatus, whose power was based on the fact that it had its own armed forces, the political authorities proceeded in two stages.

In 1954, the KGB, which had come out of a reform of the police, was placed under the authority of General Serov, originally a soldier who had moved to the police around 1930. Nevertheless, by this choice, the Party, which had been helped by the army to get rid of Beria, was still using the army gradually to take control over the police. It also defined the limits of police power. Independent of the soviets, the police were dominated on the one hand by the procurature (the supreme procurator of the U.S.S.R. and his subordinate representatives),[91] on the other hand directly by the Party. Since the separation of powers does not exist, the supreme procurator is elected by the Supreme Soviet but his position depends on the *nomenklatura* of the Central Committee. He in turn appoints the procurators of republics and regions and controls appointments made in smaller territorial units by people he has appointed. The *nomenklatura* operates everywhere—that is, the Party controls everything. As long as the Party was disorganized by Stalin and its mechanisms were irregular, the police took advantage of the situation to assure its independence. But in the U.S.S.R. after Stalin, the Party's control over the mechanisms of appointment and election once again became effective because the Party was stable. The Party's control was strengthened at the center by the dependent relationship between the KGB and the Central Committee department in charge of administrative organs, which supervised the police. In the field, the subdivisions of the KGB were under the authority of the corresponding Party organ.

In 1958 began the second phase, the one which was to place the police under the direct control of the Party. While General Serov was put at the head of the information service (GRU), he was replaced successively by two apparatchiks who had come from the leadership of the Komsomol: Shelepin from 1958 to 1961 and Semichasny from 1961 to 1967. Finally, in 1967, Y. V. Andropov, a secretary of the Central Committee, became president of the KGB.

The appointment of Andropov was a striking event. For the first time in the history of this organ, a man of very high rank had been called on to lead it. Until then, it had been leadership of the KGB that had given one the right to a seat on the Central Committee. In 1967, the opposite occurred, and to emphasize further this unprecedented situation, Andropov was appointed a candidate of the Politburo, of which he became a titular member in 1973. The change occurred, then, not in 1973, but in 1967, and its meaning is clear. By placing a high-level official at the head of the KGB, the Party was giving its representative considerable authority over the police he was called on to lead. The Party's authority over the police could not be challenged, because Andropov did not owe his rank in the Party to the police. On the contrary, thanks to him, the police were present in the Politburo, a situation it had not recovered since the death of Beria. But Andropov's deputy, Simon Tsvigun, who was a professional policeman, the first one since Beria who had been promoted so high from the inside, had to be content with a candidate's seat on the Central Committee. The police as a body thus had rather weak political representation. There is another reason which explains Andropov's appointment and his elevated personal status—he was appointed General of the Army, and his two principal deputies, Tsvigun and G. K. Tsvinen, vice-president of the KGB and candidate on the Central Committee, received the same title in 1978[92]—and this was the Party's desire to restore prestige to an institution whose excesses had been publicly displayed by de-Stalinization. After the period of attacks against the police and the reimposition of control came the time of reconstruction. This policy was urgent in 1967, when Soviet intellectuals were attached to the notion of "legality," and to the rights given to them by the Constitution, and attacked the KGB directly. For the Party, the moment had come to stop the erosion of police authority and to give this discredited body the support of Communist authority. Directed by military men, even though they did not really belong to the army, ruled by the Party, the KGB discovered a new respectability. It was significant that in 1967 the fiftieth anniversary of the creation of this body was celebrated with solemnity.[93] Andropov loudly proclaimed that it was an honorable body and attempted to recruit not dubious characters, as in the past, but an intellectual elite. The recruitment campaigns of the KGB indicated this change in orientation.

The police are also a military force, and this further explains the Party's desire to control them. The KGB's own forces (in charge of security and guarding the borders) include approximately 130,000 men. They are equipped like infantry units and are under the authority of an army general (the KGB's fourth), Morozov. In order to have an idea of the forces of law and order, we should add to them the troops under the authority of the MVD[94] (Ministry of the Interior), which include 800,000 men whose function is to guarantee security in the rear, protection of strategic points and communications networks, and surveillance of foreigners. Finally, the MVD also has a militia of 250,000. The KGB and the MVD, whose troops are armed like regular infantry units, have their own supply of tanks, armored vehicles, and helicopters. Although these perfectly equipped and disciplined troops serve the authorities as a powerful means of maintaining order, one can understand that the authorities no longer accept that such a military force and such a network of surveillance over society escape from their control.

The status of the police in Soviet society is thus far from comparable to the status of the army. Calmed by the homage they have received and by the muzzle that has long been placed on denunciations of their excesses, and endowed with material privileges, the police have forgotten their post-Stalin bitterness and recovered a place in the system. But this place is rigorously defined. The police preserve considerable exorbitant powers over society, and the call for "socialist legality" is not enough to limit them. But they are without resources in the face of the central authorities. They are a tool for maintaining order but certainly not active participants in the political system. Indispensable to the authorities, strengthened in prestige in the eyes of society, the police occupy an important place in the Soviet political system but at the same time a limited place, because Soviet power, quite willing to use them, has no intention of recreating a state under their domination. One of the most obvious successes of Stalin's successors is to have continuously maintained their understanding on this point. They have integrated the police, as they have integrated the army, into

Party institutions. But, now, it is the Party and the Party alone that is the dominant bureaucracy.

From Stability to Petrification

In 1964, Khrushchev's successors placed their power under the sign of the stability and job security of the political personnel. The promises made in 1964 have been kept, and the consequences of that stability in the early eighties are among the principal characteristics of the Soviet system. It is a gerontocratic system whose leaders are among the oldest in the world. In this respect, the system of the U.S.S.R. is paradoxical. The right to retire at a relatively early age (fifty-five for women, sixty for men) is an achievement to which Soviet society is firmly attached. It has vigorously defended this right, even though demographic decline in the U.S.S.R. in the seventies has led to a shortage of manpower, and premature retirement has slowed down Soviet economic development.[95] But as soon as it is a matter of political or administrative functions, the age of retirement no longer exists. The dispositions adopted in 1965 to force Mikoyan's retirement have fallen into disuse since then. This problem is so striking that the press sometimes evokes it, by noting the ages of leaders in passing,[96] or else by emphasizing the need to promote "young cadres." However, this observable gerontocracy[97] is more differentiated than at first appears. It involves two distinct problems, the advanced age of the ruling elite but also the generational differences that exist within the ranks of power.

The fact that a gerontocracy rules the U.S.S.R. is a direct consequence of political stability. A politburo whose central core has not changed since 1964, among whom no titular member has budged since 1966, and a Central Committee that changed by less than 20 percent in 1971 and less than 10 percent in 1976 are institutions in which the average age can only increase regularly. But, more than just the highest institutions of the Party, it is the "ruling group of the U.S.S.R." that is revealing about the consequences of political stability. This ruling group, analyzed by S. Bialer[98] (from whom Table 7 is borrowed), includes sixty people, distributed among the Politburo and the Secretariat of the Party, the Presidium of the Council of Ministers, and a part of the Presidium of the Supreme Soviet. In these three groups are assembled the holders of political and administrative power, and they all belong to the generation of those over sixty-five.

A comparison of these figures leads to several remarks on the age structure of the narrowest group, the group which has the highest responsibilities in the U.S.S.R.

First, in 1980, the proportion of the ruling group over sixty was over 75 percent and the number of those over seventy tended toward 30 percent. The sexagenarians no doubt represented nearly half the ruling class, but if we examine each institution, we note that their place was not identical everywhere. In the Politburo, the septuagenarians are more numerous than the sexagenarians among the titular members and three times as numerous as those under sixty, who are almost all in their fifties. In the Secretariat, even though changes have been frequent, the septuagenarians are as numerous as their sexagenarian colleagues and twice as numerous as those under sixty. Finally, in the Presidium of the Council of Ministers, where men in their sixties predominate, those over seventy are five times as numerous as those under sixty. In only two groups does the proportion of those under sixty reach one third, among the candidates on the Politburo and the members of the Presidium of the Supreme Soviet.

From this we can derive a second important observation. Among the rulers of the U.S.S.R., one's age is all the older the higher one rises in the hierarchy to the regions of greatest stability. The very relative youth of the candidates on the Politburo and the Presidium of the Supreme Soviet goes along with a lesser degree of importance. On the other hand, the age

Table 7:   Ruling Group of the U.S.S.R.

Institutions	Number of Positions	Average Age	Distribution by Age Group (in %)	
			Over 70	Under 60
Politburo				
Titular members	13	68.1	46.1	15.4
Candidates	8	64.7	25	37.5
Secretariat of the				
Central Committee	10	66	40	20
Presidium of the Council				
of Ministers	14	67	35.7	7
Presidium of the Supreme Soviet				
upper segment				
entire group	15	64.2	26.6	33.3
Averages		65.2	27.4	25.5

record is held by the titular members of the Politburo, followed by the members of the Presidium of the Council of Ministers. This aging, all the greater the higher the responsibilities, can be seen within each institution. Although the average age of titular members of the Politburo was seventy in 1980, the ages of central core of the group—Brezhnev, Kosygin, Kirilenko, and Suslov—which is the collective artisan of the history of the Brezhnev period, totaled 302, for an average age of seventy-five and a half.

The Soviet gerontocracy is exceptional in two respects. First, real responsibilities are assumed by the oldest elements of the ruling class. Aged leaders survive in many political systems, but their power is reduced as the years pass. Moreover, they are often surrounded by younger colleagues who assume all or some of the responsibilities. This was long the case in the U.S.S.R. At the Nineteenth Congress in 1952, Stalin had reached seventy-three, but the ruling class around him had an average age of fifty-four (fifty-three for the Politburo, fifty-two for the Secretariat, fifty-five for the Presidium of the Council of Ministers). In 1964, when the Khrushchev period came to an end, the situation was roughly the same. Khrushchev was seventy, but his political entourage was on the average fifty-six. Aging could be observed most clearly in the Presidium (the ex- and future Politburo); its titular members had an average age of sixty-one. This body had, in fact, put up the greatest resistance to the renewal of cadres that Khrushchev wanted to impose. But the almost unchanged average age of the ruling group (it had grown two years older between 1952 and 1964) indicates the degree of renewal Khrushchev had imposed on it. In comparison, one can measure the degree of stability of the Brezhnev period. The entire ruling group has grown older. In 1980, Brezhnev was seventy-four, Stalin's age at death and a few years older than Khrushchev when he was eliminated, and the entire ruling group around him had reached an average age of sixty-seven. It is this harmony between the aging of the chief and the aging of the whole ruling group that really characterizes the evolution of Soviet power, and it poses crucial problems of succession to which we shall return.

The different degrees of aging observable in the ruling group, according to the level of responsibility one considers, differentiate in the same way the political elite, understood broadly, according to institutional and regional distinctions.

Take the institutional distinctions first. When one moves downward from the narrow ruling group to a broader central elite (ministers and presidents of state committees of the U.S.S.R., administrative officials of the Central Committee, high-ranking military commanders: approximately 120 people), one obtains an almost equivalent average age: sixty-four and a half for the group as a whole, compared to almost sixty-six for the highest leaders. But here, too, there are differences within each group, according to the degree of importance. The body of the ministers of the U.S.S.R. clarifies this "strategy of old age."

In 1980, this group underwent slight modifications because of the death of three ministers in office.[99] The average age of this body was sixty-five, with considerable differences in age (from eighty-one to forty-six), but two characteristics of its age structure need to be emphasized. First, there was a relative homogenization through aging (twelve ministers were under sixty, thirty-three between sixty and seventy, and fourteen over seventy). Further, and here we find a constant, the heads of the principal ministries were substantially older than the average: At Defense, Ustinov was born in 1908; at Foreign Affairs, Gromyko was born in 1909; at Foreign Trade, Patolichev was born in 1908; at Interior, Shchelokov in 1910; and at Finance, Garbuzov in 1911. However, there was a certain degree of renewal at this level, if only to replace the ministers who had died in office. But an examination of the way this renewal functioned indicates that the concern to appoint younger men was far from dominant among the rulers. In 1976, when it was necessary to replace the septuagenarian Minister of Defense, Grechko, they chose Ustinov, who was sixty-nine. The Minister of Naval Construction, Butoma, who died the same year at sixty-nine, was replaced by Egorov, who was exactly the same age. This policy predominated everywhere. Thus, Shvernik, who was asked to retire in 1966 when he was seventy-eight, was replaced as president of the Party Control Commission by Arvid Pelshe, who was still in the position at eighty-one. Similarly, in 1965, Mikoyan at seventy was considered too old for a president of the Presidium of the Supreme Soviet. But in 1977, Brezhnev, who had reached seventy-one and was already quite ill, was elected to that position. This refusal to make the political personnel younger has sometimes taken absurd forms. Thus, in 1976, to relieve Kosygin, who was then seventy-two and openly spoke of his weariness, a second position of first vice-president of the Council of Ministers was created (one such position already existed, occupied until 1980 by Mazurov). But the new position was given to N. A. Tikhonov, who was seventy-one.

Just as the average age of the leaders gets lower as one goes down the ladder of power, the ladder of positions and institutions, so it gets lower as one moves away from the center of power toward the authorities of republics or regions. The holders of major positions in these cases (first secretaries of republics, regions, and republican regions; second secretaries of republics; presidents of councils of ministers of republics: approximately 160 people in all) are on the average under fifty-seven. Similarly, the commanders of military districts are on the average fifty-seven, while the average age of the high command at the center is sixty-five. This difference among both political and military cadres emphasizes once again that real power in the U.S.S.R. is at the center, and that peripheral and regional powers are powers of transmission and management.

The age of the political leaders confirms, if this is necessary, the breadth of the centralizing phenomenon in the U.S.S.R. There are really two elites, one at the center, the other in the republics and regions. The central elite, which holds all the important positions in the party and the various bureaucracies in Moscow, is a mirror image of the small ruling group. It constitutes the framework of the Soviet system, and it has come from a single generation with a single career pattern. It has enjoyed a stability almost as great as that of the group at the top. It has demonstrated extraordinary determination in holding on to the positions it occupies, which only biological laws have been able to overcome.

Unlike this central elite, the elite of the regions and republics is of an age that corresponds to its responsibilities. According to Soviet criteria, this elite is extremely young, but it is, in fact, as old on the average as the central elite was when Khrushchev left power.

This age structure which is peculiar to the U.S.S.R.—a very old ruling group, a central elite almost as old, an elite in the regions and republics substantially younger—raises three questions. How did these differences between center and regions come into being? To what extent do age differences imply differences in mental ability? To what extent will these differences influence succession problems?

The generational difference between ruling group and central elite on the one hand and regional elites on the other is without any doubt a result of the conditions and reasons that determined Khrushchev's fall. His colleagues, who reached an understanding to get rid of him, based their alliance on a desire for stability. No doubt, that desire extended to the lowest rung of the apparatus, but it was a decision at the top, and in the Party, that set it in motion. In the Party apparatus, especially at the intermediate levels and in the administration, before guaranteeing job security, the new group had to liquidate the reforms that had affected the status of the cadres: the *sovnarkhozes* and the division of the Party. This explains why the stability that was immediately established at the top was accompanied, at first, by a considerable movement of cadres in the regions and republics. Moreover, the cadres of the republics (secretaries of national Communist Parties, presidents of councils of ministers, even ministers) were constantly much less stable than the regional cadres, for in their case the problem of the elites was complicated by the national tensions and was resolved by frequent purges. The first consequence of this gap between center and periphery was that, while approximately 25 percent of the central personnel were changed, there was a much larger renewal of the regional and peripheral personnel. Unlike Khrushchev, who intended to apply the principles of renewal of the ruling apparatus to all levels and all institutions, his successors changed the rules of renewal. The degree of protection decreased from the top to the bottom of the hierarchy; it also decreased institutionally, in the following order: Party apparatus, government, military command, nonpolitical elites integrated into the ruling organs. We can see this differentiation clearly by comparing the way the movement affected the summit of the Party with the way it affected the upper layers of the government from 1966 to 1980. A third of the members of the Politburo and the Secretariat were changed, but in the government, the rate of change was close to half its members. Among the members of the government who had retained their positions after 1964, nineteen ministers died in office.[100]

These differences in the renewal and the age of political leaders are expressed in differences of experience and career. As Jerry Hough has correctly pointed out, the Soviet political elites belong to four groups, born in the space of thirty years—between 1900 and 1930—and yet very unlike one another.[101] The first, born before 1910, is the group to which the principal leaders of the Politburo belong, in any case the core of the irremovable—Brezhnev, Kosygin, Kirilenko, Suslov—and a few newcomers—Gromyko, Ustinov—the holders of important positions. This group is a genuine product of the revolution. If the revolutionary leaders of 1917 were intellectuals, often of bourgeois origin, the generation that next rose to power derived advantages from the elimination of earlier elites. They were the sons of workers (45 percent) and peasants (41 percent) whom the Party recruited in its egalitarian phase. They are the ones whom the Party trained rapidly in the Rabfak and steered toward belated technical studies and diplomas that rewarded more their qualities as Communists than the training they had received. The title of engineer that they displayed covers especially their rise in the apparatus and their quickly acquired specialization.

The generation born in the years immediately preceding the revolution is already quite different. When it reached adolescence, the Soviet regime had stabilized and had turned toward criteria of competence and quality, progressively giving up its will to promote the oppressed of the past. The bureaucracy that had been installed wanted to favor its own in the universities, where the price of tuition and the difficulty of entrance examinations established a system of selection based on money and

social background. There is nothing surprising in the fact that
the working class and the peasantry are no longer the only
reservoirs of cadres and that more than a third of the elites (35
percent) of this age group have extended the privileged status
of their equals. This political generation, unlike the preceding
one, has often been through secondary school, and the older
members, whose studies were not interrupted by the war, went
to the university. They entered the Party at the end of regular
studies which, by the quality of the curriculum, designated
them for positions of responsibility. In this group are men like
Andropov, Grishin, Kulakov, and Mazurov.

Next comes a group that the war decimated or whose training
it stopped. Those who were born between 1920 and 1925
hardly had the time to complete their secondary education. If
they survived the war, it was too late to resume studies. They
encountered the competition of those whom the war had not
removed from school, and their military experience did not
help them to submit to the discipline of study.

Quite to the contrary, the last group, born about 1930, despite the political upheavals of those years and then the war,
benefited from all the possibilities for normal education. We
find in this political generation the children of the elites who
rose with the help of the purges or who escaped the purges. It
was the first Soviet generation to be normally educated, having
received a complete secondary education and carried on higher
studies, where the criteria were qualitative rather than social.

The first of these four generations rose quickly to power in
the mid-thirties, when the purges were decimating the preceding elites and drawing toward the top all who could demonstrate their Communist past and their competence. Having
arrived at the top forty years ago, this generation often escaped
from the war because the U.S.S.R. had to continue to function.
This was the generation that assumed political and administrative control over the country between 1941 and 1945 and that,
in the absence of massive purges since then, has succeeded for

nearly four decades in holding on to its positions of power. The force of this group lies, above all, in Stalin's annihilation of the preceding political generations. Having arrived at the highest positions at an early age, it has been able to keep itself there, first because there was no competition, then because it had control over the rise of the following generations. It later called to its side to assist it the best-educated group of the immediately following generation, which entered the Party at the end of the war and with whom, despite a slight difference in education and experience, it has in common a relatively advanced age and the tragic memory of the Stalinist years and the war. The septuagenarians and sexagenarians who are still in power in the early 1980s, while they blithely advance to the age of seventy or eighty, form a group with relatively strong solidarity, determined to preserve power. It is significant that when this group has opened itself to younger elements (for example, Katuchev entered the Secretariat at forty-one in 1968 and Riabov was promoted to secretary at forty-eight in 1976), it has quickly rejected them.

In the same way, the Politburo has often excluded from its ranks the youngest of its members, those under sixty (Shelepin, Polianski). When there has been renewal at the summit, the group that dominates the U.S.S.R. and that belongs to its first political generation has arranged for this renewal to operate against the younger men and to preserve the generational unity at the top.

The generation of men who have just reached fifty, the postwar generation, is not absent from the system, but it finds itself confined to regional positions.

Power is now distributed among three groups (while there are four generations), each one of which occupies a determined and stabilized place on the ladder of responsibilities. The old guard that dominates Party and state apparatus was once the very young political generation propelled upward by the Stalinist purges, and in its maturity it refused to be eliminated by

Khrushchev. Having survived these two difficult phases, it jealously guards the system's immobility which guarantees its own
position. As a support group, it has given all the decisive positions at central and regional levels to men who are a few years
younger, and it has guaranteed them job security. But this system has as a counterpart the blockage of the system at all levels.
The holders of these positions are now separated from total
power only by the irremovable old guard. It is not surprising
that their voices are sometimes raised to suggest that the solution of many problems would come through an unblocking of
the system. This was done by G. V. Romanov, for example,
Leningrad Party leader and a representative of that generation.[102] These men who are all close to the summit are moreover under pressure from a third group, their deputies, the
younger generation of men of fifty, who would like in their turn
to move from the secondary posts in which their elders have
confined them to greater responsibilities.

Security of employment, for which the apparatus fought in
the early sixties, is now a brake on many ambitions. On this
point there is, of course, no agreement among all those who
have been waiting impatiently at their posts for years. Those
who are first in line wish for a rapid unblocking of the system
that would allow them to replace the old generation at the top,
but they dare not preach the necessity of renewal too forcefully,
for they are aware of the ambitions of those behind them, and
they wish later to enforce against them the stability that has
blocked their own advancement.

The distribution of generations and positions has blocked the
political evolution of the U.S.S.R. and distorted the process of
succession. The succession is inevitable, considering the average age of the leaders. However, the older they grow, the less
the men approaching eighty who rule the U.S.S.R. show any
intention of confronting this problem. At the Twenty-fifth Congress in 1976, when the Politburo took on the appearance of a
hospital—Brezhnev, Grechko, and Kosygin were all in very
weak health—the Congress members reelected almost the

whole of the Central Committee, and the promotions to the top were of men of seventy-five (Kuznetsov) or sixty-five (Chernenko). Clearly, the leadership did not wish to open up any problem of succession. Nearly five years later, on the eve of the Twenty-sixth Congress which was to be held in February 1981,[103] the Central Committee announced in advance[104] that the two major reports would be presented by Brezhnev and Kosygin. By thus placing in advance at the center of the congress, in a role that requires energy, the heads of Party and government, the Central Committee indicated that the hour of the succession had not arrived.

This unexpected procedure suggests continuity, not change. The succession, which has become inevitable because of the age of the leaders, is not a succession of individuals; it will be marked by a total shift of generations. This shift will be all the more important because, if there has been a generational continuity of leaders since 1953 involving a continuity of experience and training, there is now in the race for power a generation totally different from its predecessors, removed from them by age and experience. This rupture is the logical consequence of the absence of the intermediate generation, the generation the war decimated or tore away from its education and which is not in a position, because of its small numbers and its hasty and insufficient education, to join the competition. This gap in generations accentuates the differences between the two generations in place and the one that aspires to rise to major responsibilities. On one hand, there are men still conscious of a tragic past, shaped by Stalinism, for whom the external world is disturbing and who try simultaneously to defend themselves against it and to compromise with it. On the other, there is a generation for whom Stalin and the war are uncertain memories, a generation that was exposed very early to the external world, whose seductions and weaknesses it knows, and that began its political career in a universe where dialogue is based on the military power of the U.S.S.R. Still very distant from power, this generation no doubt has less wish for stability than its predecessors, for its promotion depends on destabilization. We can see how alliances have been forged among all the septuagenarians and sexagenarians who have reached the rungs of central power and for whom stability means they will hold on as long as they are able, wherever they may be, and will automatically replace those who disappear. An implicit solidarity unites them against those who embody youth and impatience. At the point of intersection of the two age groups, and the two levels of responsibility, we find once again the group of the first secretaries. By their age, most of them are already in the camp of the older men who will take over. But the regional positions they occupy and their difficulties of advancement place them still far from power and badly placed to reach it, so true is it that in the U.S.S.R. centralization dominates everything. Loyal for the moment to a leadership that put them in office and has guaranteed them virtual permanence, they may at any moment swing over to the camp of those made impatient by the system's immobility.

This accumulated impatience probably explains why the old guard of the Party, far from preparing mechanisms for succession, has avoided raising the problems and suppressed alternate solutions, by blocking each generation at a particular level of the pyramid of power. But this system, which was in the sixties the origin of the loyalties aroused by the current leadership, which has assured the cohesion of the political elites of the U.S.S.R., has as a counterpart the effect of prolonging indefinitely a major weakness of the system: the uncertainties of succession. The maturity of a political system is measured largely by its capacity to assure the transfer of power according to fixed and functioning rules. In this respect, the Soviet system is far from having ripened.

We can now measure the changes in the functioning of the system brought about by the Brezhnev group and what it failed to carry out.

It has contributed, above all, job security for the political elites. In this, it differentiated itself from Khrushchev. Stalin's successor attempted—and succeeded—to reassure all his fellow citizens and colleagues and to give them the security of survival. Khrushchev's successors have been concerned above all with the political world in which they operate, which they have shaped by taking account of the urgencies that de-Stalinization brought to the surface.

The power they established is the power of a coalition of interests, and this coalition has steadily persevered since 1964. The political struggle that existed, which is inherent in every political system, unfolded between this coalition and the individual elements it rejected. The stability and firmness of the coalition have allowed the political struggle to be given a peaceful and institutional character. The coalition, claiming legitimacy in the name of the Party, could be more assured and more magnanimous toward individuals. The personalization of power should not conceal what is essential. Brezhnev's power is derived from a consensus. One of his functions is to express the existence of the coalition from which he emanates and to be the bearer of its interests and its views. In the end—and this is its primary characteristic—the Brezhnev period has succeeded in forcing individual conflicts into the mold of institutions, thereby making them not at all threatening to the whole system.

Another gain of this period, to be added to the institutionalization of conflicts, is the institutionalization of the entire system. The Soviet bureaucracies now have deep social roots, routines, expertise, and, thereby, unquestionable influence. These bureaucracies have all found places at the summit of the system in the organs of real power—Central Committee, Politburo, permanent apparatus of the Central Committee and the Secretariat—where their representatives are present not, as in the past, because of their prestige, or because they fought bloody battles for a place, but because they embody the interests of the groups who have assured their advancement. This evolution of the system toward the representation of groups and not men has been encouraged by the political stability of the last decade. The elites are now more assured, and they try to rely on stable structures and to speak in their name. Every group has its particular interests, but the system is ingenious in balancing them and bringing them together under the authority of the Party, which assures common representation of all interests. To reinforce his power, Stalin played on all the bureaucracies in turn. In this game, Khrushchev stumbled over most of them. The major work of his successors is to have recognized the importance and the interests of every group and to have given them all a status. The representation of each bureaucracy in the organs of real power allows them to defend their interests. But at the same time, the Party has placed them under its control. The ruling coalition at the top is now the expression of the Party's authority and the representation of the bureaucracies. No doubt this adjustment of the system does not exclude the possibility that one day a bureaucracy—the army, for example —may again demand an autonomous role. But it would thereby risk losing the place it holds in all the institutions, even though that place is held by men of the political apparatus who are representing it.

This evolution toward the institutionalization of conflicts and interests has been made possible by the stability or immobility of the system. The counterpart of success is that the system has become frozen. Even more than the immobilism of men and generations, it is the immobilism of debate that characterizes it. The consensus that keeps the coalition in power, that also keeps everyone at his rank, has as a condition that there be no debate about problems dividing the various bureaucracies, in which a compromise would be difficult to find. This explains why the group in power has devoted itself—within the U.S.S.R., because foreign policy is another problem—to management without confrontations or discussions and has relegated to an indefinite future all the serious problems from which could arise conflicts that would shake this unanimity based on permanent compromise. The technique of power of the Brezhnev group can be summed up in two propositions: (1) balance and stabilize all powers and (2) avoid any debate or decision that might change the distribution of power.

The progress of the system has thus been paid for by immobilism, the refusal to confront pressing problems—above all, the problem of the transfer of power—because it would affect the balance that has been achieved between men, bureaucracies, and generations. In their search for a viable political system for those who are within it, the leaders have chosen—is it an effect of age? of the tragedies they have lived through?—to ignore the future, to reject any dynamism in the system. Will a generation without the knowledge of fear accept forever the choice imposed by the memory of past fears? And will the immobilism that ignores society and has resolved none of the problems that have arisen always be accepted by society?

At the plenum of the Central Committee in October 1980, Aleksei Kosygin was allowed to exercise his right to retire because of the state of his health. He was replaced, predictably enough, by his deputy, N. A. Tikhonov, who was one year younger than he.

CHAPTER 6

THE MANUFACTURE

OF SOULS

More than sixty years of socialism in the Soviet Union have produced results that are very distant from the original utopia. The political system—whether the personal dictatorship of the past or the dictatorship of a collective leadership—is character- ized by the omnipotence of the state, power operating in a closed circuit, and a society which has been unable to organize itself according to its own wishes but depends entirely on the central powers. In certain respects, this situation recalls the state of Russia at the beginning of the century that provoked the explosions of 1905 and 1917. Is it experienced in this way by society? Does society find it intolerable?

Although observation of the Soviet system shows these appar- ent similarities between past and present, it also leads to the recognition that the social reaction has been radically different from the one that was expressed in 1917 by rejection of the system. When the Communist Party proudly proclaims that "the Party and the people are united," it expresses a feeling that is still rather widely shared by a society which theoretically holds power but which is obviously kept apart from it. Despite the distance between political theory and reality, despite the existence of a power beyond the reach of society held by an extended category of leaders *(nachal'niki)* whose social status and privileges differentiate them radically from the mass of ordinary citizens, until now society has adhered to the system. Since Stalinism has been liquidated, and violence and repression are now applied only selectively, social consensus, the extent and reasons for which must be explained, is the basis of the relations between power and society. This consensus functions around a political culture that is defined by power and that has penetrated the entire life of individuals.

Every political system is organized around a political culture[1] whose values, symbols, and solidarities allow the system to maintain contact with society and to acquire legitimacy, and which allows society to identify with power. But while, in pluralist systems, political culture is relatively open and heterogeneous, in authoritarian systems it is characterized by homogeneity and the refusal to compete with other ideas and values.

In this regard, the Soviet system has given a particular place to its particular political culture, Marxism-Leninism, and it is not content to affirm its superiority implicitly. This political culture is the privileged instrument for social integration and for the formation of consensus. It is coherent and closed to any external ideological contributions, even though it has changed substantially over the years and accommodated itself to circumstances and to social evolution. But the way in which this political culture is brought to bear on society, far from changing with the Soviet system of values, has only reinforced its essential characteristics. This is why, in order to understand society's adhesion to the system, we have to consider the content of the political culture, the means of socialization, and the measurable effects of that socialization.

The "New Man" and His Universe

Marxism-Leninism is in principle the beginning and the end of the system of values with which Soviet society is identified.

It proclaims the emancipation of man, a "radiant future,"[2] that of communism, where necessity is no more[3] and where, by working together to construct this future of freedom, man gives a sense to his life, on earth and in the course of history, as he once assured his salvation beyond the temporal realm in the Christian vision. Marxism, like Christianity or any other religion, thus opens onto an eschatological vision of human fate and claims to answer the problem of the last things.

However, as soon as one moves from this utopian vision of Marx to the real arena of a socialist state, the emancipation of man is carefully defined and limited. The ideology developed by the Bolsheviks since 1917 has done nothing but make more precise what is meant by human freedom and development, and the Communist Party Program developed in 1961[4] gives it precise contours. The new man of the radiant future is one who is in harmony with the community. Happiness and emancipation are not individual gains but the fruit of a common effort, of common ideas, of an adhesion to the project and the values of everyone. The center and guarantor of the project is the Communist Party, and individual development is attained by adhesion to the values of the Party. The unity of the Party and the people *(splachennost)* is both the path and the goal of the emancipating project of Marxism-Leninism. Everything is ordered within this conception. Individual rights and freedoms,[5] which are never absolute but relative, depend on social progress, on the advance toward the radiant future. In this general vision of human fate, Soviet political culture has gradually incorporated values adopted from the common heritage of societies or from the Russian heritage. First of all is work, a central value of Christian society, a redemptive value. The 1961 program made it a veritably moral, not material, need of Communist man, and the Constitution of 1977 gives it considerable space.[6] It is not an accident that one of the most repressed forms of deviance, to use an epithet that is widespread in the U.S.S.R., is parasitism.[7] The opposition between worker and parasite (parasites are those who claim to define their participation in social life according to their own norms) gives a measure of the ideological evolution of the Soviet system.

The glorification of "socially useful" work goes along with the glorification of the family. At the dawn of the Soviet regime, the family had lost its rights, but since the early thirties, it has been considered an indispensable link in society, the privileged space for the development of early infancy. The rehabilitation of the family has gone along with an adhesion to traditional moral values, with the rejection of permissiveness and any form of marginality. The stereotype of the "good" Soviet citizen conveyed by the media is the worker who labors for the good of his family and the common good, indistinguishable from one another, who is disciplined, and who adheres totally to the system, whose values he transmits to his family.

The third term of traditional systems, patriotism, has also made its reappearance in Soviet political culture in the past several decades. Soviet citizens may love and adhere to their fatherland, but this is not by virtue of an archaic attachment, but because of what it represents on the road of historical progress. The socialist fatherland is the property of everyone, while the traditional country belonged to the ruling class. Didn't Marx proclaim that the workers had been stripped of their country?[8] Soviet political culture is thus an amalgam of "Marxism-Leninism" and the traditional values around which societies have been constructed. It tries to maintain the vitality of the Marxist tradition in the demonstrations and the symbols of its ideological components. The U.S.S.R. has thus made November 7, the anniversary of the revolution, the national holiday, which reconciles the idea of revolution with that of fatherland. And after having made a tabula rasa of all pre-revolutionary history, the Soviet system has now, on the contrary, assured continuity with it, presenting the revolution as the outcome of a long and glorious history and placing the pre-revolutionary leaders and the heroes of the revolution side by side in the pantheon of men who have contributed to the evolution of Russia.

In principle, the "new man" adheres totally to the political culture that is offered. He works less because he must than because he wants to. He is honest and moral. He wishes to be useful and participates in every way in the common work of constructing socialism and defending the fatherland. Individual happiness melts into collective happiness, and the community, represented by the Party, represents each individual and his interests.

Despite its traditional elements, the political culture is thus oriented toward the present, designed to answer all of the Soviet citizen's questions, to shape each person according to a uniform mold. This vision combining past and present is directed toward everyone, from the leaders with their privileges to the peasants who represent the rear guard of society and have no access to the sphere of power, from the Russians who rediscover in the unitary vision of the Party the *sobornost* of the traditional Russian Orthodox community to the Turkomans who find in it no counterpart to the values of the nomad society to which their ancestors belonged. Soviet power has given itself the task of forming a "new man" in harmony with this political culture, of creating a uniformity of minds. Have the writers who were called on to contribute to this effort of shaping, transforming mentalities not been called "engineers of souls"?[9] No authoritarian political system in this century has invested more than the Soviet system in this "manufacture of souls," whose mechanisms we must now examine.

Permanent Socialization

It takes considerable time and effort to change mental attitudes. Lenin had quickly discovered that the destruction of the old order, the abolition of private ownership of the means of production, and the abolition of exploitation did not bring about a revolution in thinking.[10] From the beginning, the Bolsheviks set themselves the task of making explicit a political culture that reflected their project, but they also understood that this political culture would change mental attitudes only if two conditions were met: that it be alone in permeating people's minds, and that it permeate them permanently—that is, that the socialization of the Soviet citizen be total and cover the totality of existence.

The official political culture does not have an absolute monopoly of ideas and values, insofar as the Soviet system concedes freedom of conscience to individuals in their private capacity.[11] It also concedes to national groups the freedom to preserve national "forms," but these must express, in terms appropriate to the traditional culture of each group, a common system of values: Soviet political culture. There is a great distance between religious freedom and cultural freedoms. In one case, it is a question of the whole system of values; in the other, freedom is reduced to the means of expressing the system. Nevertheless, these concessions function so that the monopoly enjoyed by Soviet political culture is not absolute. On the other hand, the political culture enjoys a unique right of diffusion. Religious freedom is an individual, strictly limited right, excluding any possibility of diffusing and propagating religious values and loyalties. In the face of these restricted rights, with no possibility of collective expression, the privileged position of Soviet political culture is strengthened by the unlimited means of socialization at its disposal. The Soviet citizen is subjected to intense and continuous socialization, all the more effective because there is no, or almost no, counterweight. For every stage of individual life there is a corresponding means of socialization.

This active exposure to the political culture begins in earliest childhood. No doubt small children who remain at home are in part protected from it, but only in part, because families are accountable to the state for the education given their children. The family must prepare them for socialization and not instill into them ideas and values that might contradict the dominant political culture. In particular, parents, who are free to practice a religion, must not expose their children to religious ideas.[12] In recent years, the increasing number of cases of Baptist children taken away from their parents in order to shield them from their parents' religious influence indicates that, for the authorities, the role of the family in early childhood is to relay the institutions of socialization.[13] Family education, to which Soviet pedagogical experts attach considerable importance,[14] must in no case be separated from the political culture. We can see how this return to family values is distinguished from the place given to the family in Russian tradition. Without any doubt, in every society, the family is a cell of the global society which is an extension of its system of values and authority. But in Russian tradition, the institution of the family, despite the changes it experienced in the course of the nineteenth century, remains very strong, marked by the religious tradition much more than by state influence.

Once early childhood is past, school life begins at the age of seven; it has a dual function. It must transmit knowledge of course, but also, and perhaps first of all, the school shapes the Soviet citizen. The school, far from being neutral, is explicitly the first place where the collective attitude of mind is formed, where common values are instilled. The influence of school is very great for several reasons. Compulsory schooling and its extension permits it a long-lasting impact on the world of children.[15] Systematic cooperation between school and family, which is part of the Soviet school system, gives the school a means of exercising continuous surveillance over family life and its contribution to the spread of common values. The world of the school is paralleled by that of the youth organizations, which the child must join to avoid immediate "marginalization" and which are controlled by the Komsomol and therefore actively spread Communist ideas. From seven to nine, children are members of the organization of "Little Octobrists" (Oktiabriata); then, until fourteen, they are pioneers.[16] The moral code of these organizations, the responsibilities that weigh on the children as a function of their age, everything helps to insert them, from this early stage, into a clearly Communist universe. Their adhesion to the values offered by these organizations no doubt depends on the fact that children are malleable, but also on a powerful stimulant: the future. From the ranks of the pioneers, in fact, come the elect, the komsomols, who are now the "Party's reserves."[17] If joining the Komsomol does not condition one's school and university career, we must note that intellectual merit and political activism often coincide. The function of the school is thus to a great extent—directly and indirectly, with the help of the youth organizations—to "arm childhood ideologically."[18]

Beyond school, political socialization becomes more elaborate, using many networks, all under Party control.

The organizer of this socialization is the department of propaganda of the Central Committee of the Communist Party of the Soviet Union, on which depend, at every territorial level of the Party, the departments of agitation and propaganda, led by a member of the secretariat of each organization. These departments organize political training at their level and supervise the activity of political socialization of educational institutions and the local press. The spread of political culture is not, and by far, a product of improvisation.[19] If there is an area where liaison between the central authorities and the regional institutions has developed, it is certainly this one. Political penetration of society takes on various forms: direct political education in Party establishments, agitation among the workers, and the spread of atheism.

The Party schools are designed for Party cadres, but also for the rest of society. The Party has a whole network of schools[20] distributed throughout Soviet territory. They are, in ascending order of importance, 141 permanent courses for Party and government cadres, 9 Party and government schools, 14 republican and inter-regional Communist universities, and the institutions of higher education dependent on the Central Committee.[21] Until 1978, the Central Committee was in charge of three advanced schools: the Academy of Social Sciences, the Upper School of the Party, and its equivalent by correspondence. This network was open to a small number of the elect, since the graduates of all schools amounted to about 250,000 for the years 1971–75. As always, the pyramid narrowed at the top. Among this number, there were 510 graduates of the Academy of Social Sciences, 1,646 for the Upper School of the Party, and 18,862 for higher education by correspondence.[22] But the establishments at the top, which recycled the system's higher cadres, had been criticized so much that, in 1978, "the Central Committee of the Communist Party of the Soviet Union asked the rectors of the Party's upper schools . . . to raise the ideological, doctrinal, scientific, and methodological level of lectures, seminars, and student work, to be dynamic in introducing new teaching methods, to make more use of audiovisual techniques."[23] These criticisms also provoked the reorganization of the education offered under the direct authority of the Central Committee. The three schools were combined in a single institution: the Academy of Social Sciences of the Central Committee,[24] inaugurated with great solemnity on September 1, 1978.[25] In his inaugural speech, Suslov emphasized the significance of this change. The Academy had to prepare the highest Communist cadres to confront not only political responsibilities but economic and international responsibilities as well. But the Party, as we have already pointed out, after having widely opened its ranks to professionals, was again engaged in a policy of favoring the promotion of apparatchiks. In these circumstances, it was obliged to develop the political training of those professionals who had already reached high-level positions and to "professionalize" the apparatchiks. Moreover, according to Suslov, it was to serve not only to improve Soviet cadres but to admit cadres from other Communist countries. It thus had a dual integrating purpose: It was to provide cadres shaped according to the same mold, trained in the same disciplines and informed with the same certainties, both to the U.S.S.R. and to the entire socialist community.

Communist teaching addressed to the apparatus is far from representative of the Party's methods of socialization for the mass of Communists and for all those who gravitate around the Party without being members. The Party offers them advanced and diversified political education organized on three levels. At the elementary level, for five or six years, adults meeting in groups of fifteen or twenty receive, through lectures and discussions *(beseda),* basic notions of politics and economics and are familiarized with the biography, thought, and legacy of Lenin. At the intermediate level, courses last for six to eight years and are devoted to theoretical study of Marxism, political economy, the Communist program, and the activity of the Communist Party of the Soviet Union. At this level, students must supplement theory with political activism. Finally, at the higher level, students are directed either to Marxist-Leninist universities or to schools for activists. In every case, at this stage they receive advanced theoretical training and are prepared for responsible positions of political or economic management in local or regional organs. The length of studies depends on the degree of general education. For those who have completed higher education, it lasts for two years; for the others, four years. Anyone may supplement this training with theoretical seminars which extend the period of study for another year or two. This system, created on the eve of the Twenty-third Congress, was also revised and modernized in 1978.[26] Because the general educational level of the Soviet population has improved, perhaps also because interests have shifted, the Party has attempted to accentuate the concrete aspects of education, those linked to practice, at all levels. In every case, it is a matter of explaining the world of "advanced socialism" and the tasks the Communist Party has set itself, domestically and internationally. In other words, through this educational network, as it has in the past, the Party is attempting to interest and involve students in the concrete policies it is pursuing and in the results of those policies. The increasing attention given to foreign policy in these courses is a recognition of the growing orientation of Soviet power toward foreign activity as a compensation for domestic immobility. But it also corresponds to the necessity recognized by the Soviet leaders of erecting a barrier against the mirage of the external world, which now forms a part of the Soviet citizen's fund of knowledge. This Communist training has reached a large and growing segment of society, as the assessment established at the Twenty-fifth Congress indicates. In 1966, 13 million Soviet citizens participated in these various courses, but by 1976–77 their number had reached nearly 21 million.[27] Several factors in this progress of participation in Communist training should be emphasized. There is, first, its hold on those outside the Party. More than 8 million participants are not Party members.[28] Moreover, the higher levels now attract half the students, whereas the elementary level accounts for only one tenth (it represented more than a third in 1966).[29] This means that the educational system has increasingly been established in the best-educated circles (a shift upward that mirrors the general evolution of the Party) and that it has reached a growing number of educated non-Communists.

If we add to the 20 million students enrolled in Party schools the 7 million studying under the aegis of the Komsomol and the 35 million who receive economic training, we become aware of the magnitude of this phenomenon of permanent socialization. Its cohesion is assured by the Party under the management of 2,200,000 qualified propagandists.[30]

Political Training in the Field

But the Party's work of socialization does not stop with this advanced training for the benefit of the better educated. The work is rooted in the depths of society, in the masses, for whom an immense labor of popular education is carried on by three methods—agitation, political instruction, and lectures[31]—which supplement each other and enclose the masses in a complex system of information and propaganda, the aim of which is to respond to all their questions, their curiosities, and even their discontents, in order to leave no place for any other source for the diffusion of ideas. Consider the following.

Agitation is closely connected to the world of work. Agitators, who come from a work group, "agitate" their companions on the job. They must in the first place give impetus to work by explaining its aims and by uncovering, if necessary, the professional and also personal problems which might trouble a work community. The agitator is thus simultaneously a kind of teacher who watches over everyone's activity, morale, and morality and almost a social worker who creates a link between the worker and the Party, sometimes smoothing over minor problems, and allowing the Party to know the workers, their reactions, and even their frustrations. All this is because the agitator, despite political commitment, is a member of the community, distrusted but living in such proximity to everyone that nothing can really be kept hidden. Agitation has many forms: talks with individuals or the whole group, direction of the "red corner" where wall posters and other information are provided, and so on. Agitators belong to the working community, and they are at the same time members of a community of similar people, the collective of agitators *(agitkollectiv)*, within which their plan of action is developed.[32]

Above the agitator, who is in principle a specialist in the worker's everyday problems, is the political instructor *(politinformator)*,[33] who delivers to the workplace very specialized information on various themes: politics, economics, international relations, ideological and cultural problems. Better educated than the agitators, they are generally not members of the work community, even though their activity takes place in that setting. Finally, at the top, is the professional lecturer *(doklad-*

chik), a graduate of one of the Communist academies, perhaps even an important Party cadre, who deals very seriously with a wide variety of topics, specialized or not.

This activity of popular education requires considerable personnel. According to the records presented to the Twenty-fifth Congress in 1976, the U.S.S.R. had 3,100,000 agitators, 1,800,000 political informers, and 300,000 lecturers.[34] Counting propagandists in the Party's educational establishments, agitators, and so on, 8 million people in all are permanently charged with supervising and instructing Soviet society. In this network of convergent training systems and activities, all of which spread the same ideas and the same values, the life of the ordinary citizen, as one may imagine, leaves little room for personal reflection and the search for other sources of information. As we shall see, "over-politicization" has negative effects; it often leads to the desire to escape from all politicization.

The Party's effort is supplemented by a theoretically voluntary organization which is in fact under Party control: Znanie (knowledge), the purpose of which is to propagate scientific knowledge and, especially, atheism. In the first decades of the Soviet system, the Party multiplied direct efforts to uproot and ridicule religious convictions.[35] Emelian Yaroslavski, a specialist of militant atheism, created the League of Militant Atheists in 1925, produced a number of publications propagating atheism, founded museums of atheism (generally churches transformed for the purpose, like Kazan Cathedral in Leningrad), and organized imitation ceremonies subjecting religion to ridicule. This immense mobilization of men and means—atheism had its brigades—was abandoned during the war because it was thought inopportune, and since then it has been totally changed. In the postwar years, and especially with de-Stalinization, the authorities concluded that militant atheism was anachronistic, because it was too primitive to suit the broadly educated society of the sixties and seventies, and also because the authorities considered religion as a simple survival of a distant and faded past to which only old men and badly educated peasants clung.[36] To practice militant atheism was to continue to grant importance to religion. This is why active, propagandistic atheism gave way to the diffusion of the scientific approach to the universe. But religion remains at the center of the preoccupations of Znanie, which publishes series of brochures (twelve series covering all the major areas of human thought), books, newspapers, and particularly a monthly which frequently sums up religious affairs in the U.S.S.R., *Nauka i religia* ("Science and Religion"). In 1978, the total press run of this association's publications was 100 million copies. This powerful association had more than 3 million members in 1975 and was given hours on both radio and television (327,000 lectures broadcast in 1978). Every year it organizes thousands of lectures throughout the U.S.S.R., mobilizing millions of listeners. (According to the *Great Soviet Encyclopedia*, 26 million lectures were delivered in 1978, and they were heard by 1,262,000,000 people, which suggests that every Soviet adult heard several lectures in the course of the year.)[37]

The Soviet masses are compelled to undergo this permanent education, which reaches first of all those who lead an active life, since the workplace is its privileged location. They are, moreover, subject to periodic mobilization for celebrations and an intense visual propaganda. The authorities take great care periodically to bring society together for collective celebrations, both because civil celebrations have the function of responding to the human desire occasionally to break the monotony of ordinary life and because religious holidays or the religious celebration of the great events in human life—birth, marriage, death—used to represent serious competition for the Party.[38] Two kinds of celebrations are thus designed to combat the attraction of religion: collective celebrations—May Day, the anniversary of the revolution, Victory, Women's Day, Lenin's birthday, the New Year—and personal celebrations—solemn civil weddings (in which the wedding palaces and flowers laid on Lenin's tomb or the tomb of the unknown soldier are attempts to link the event to Soviet history) the ceremony "of the name" (which has replaced baptism), and Communist funerals. Everything is calculated so that at fixed dates or at certain moments the life of the citizen flows solemnly into the rituals organized by the Party. These festivities, which break up human life and its activities into "Communist" periods, also have the advantage of involving in the process of socialization the inactive, the retired and housewives, who in large measure escape from the educational activity centered on the workplace. Finally, in the U.S.S.R. there is an intense visual propaganda which involves the display on avenues and crossroads, in parks and factories, of banners carrying slogans, portraits of the leaders, thematic posters, and honor rolls on which are hung photographs of outstanding workers. No one can take a step without coming up against this repetition of themes in honor of the Party or in glorification of those whom the effort of "socialist emulation" has driven to great exploits. What is constantly repeated in all this are the certainties the Soviet citizen must possess, the ambitions the Party assigns to him or her, and the models it offers.

The media—press, radio, television—help to magnify this educational effort. Newspaper circulation is considerable (seven copies for every ten inhabitants), 80 percent of the households have a television (almost 100 percent in areas with adequate reception), and almost everyone has a radio.[39] No doubt, purely cultural or entertainment programs occupy more air time than news and agitation.[40] This evolution of programs is connected to the evolution of expressed needs and also to the desire of the authorities to control their citizens' leisure. A radio and especially a television schedule that was excessively politicized might divert the audience to other activities, notably reading, less subject to control. On the contrary, programs that correspond to the desires expressed by society attach it to the media and permit the exercise of some control over the use of leisure time.

Adding all this together, it seems that there is no room for other influences in shaping Soviet attitudes of mind. However, in parallel to the Party, the army has undertaken a program of manpower training whose importance has been constantly growing.

Socialization through the Army or Militarization of the Society?

The development of the army's socialization activities is a recent phenomenon in the U.S.S.R. But the ambition to mold minds is an old one in the army. In the early twenties, Mikhail Frunze expressed his conviction that it was the army's vocation to educate men not only in the handling of weapons but in social and moral behavior. The idea of a social model in the keeping of the army comes out clearly in his writings.[41] But despite the militarization of society and of labor characteristic of the U.S.S.R. in the thirties, neither Stalin nor, later, Khrushchev allowed the army to play the educational role to which it aspired. The monopoly of the training of minds has always belonged to the Party. In this area, too, the Brezhnev years have been marked by a gradual shift, long difficult to detect, but that has now created a new situation, in which Party and army play an at least equal educational role among certain strata of the population.

Specialized Training for the Military

Like the Party, the army (and this is conceded to it) has its own network of instruction designed to train its cadres. The system of military education that has developed and improved in the decades following the Second World War is now composed of four levels:[42] military schools, at a level comparable to that of the secondary technical schools, where the course lasts for two years; higher military schools, with a four- or five-year program and diplomas equivalent to those in ordinary higher education; sixteen military academies, with three-year programs involving the preparation of one of the two categories of thesis in the U.S.S.R.: the candidate's thesis (at perhaps a slightly lower level than an American Ph.D.) and the doctorate (equivalent to the French *doctorat d'État*); and, at the same level as the academies, seven institutes, highly specialized in various disciplines (such as foreign languages, finance, or management).

The weight of this military training in the Soviet educational system can be determined from the figures. In 1972, of the 811 higher education establishments (VUZ) in the U.S.S.R., 125 were military, including the twenty-three academies and institutes with a rank equivalent to that of the most prestigious establishments. This means that one out of seven higher education institutions depended on the army; at the highest level— military academies and major universities—the proportion of military education reached 30 percent.

This general organization of military education has undergone several shifts in recent years that have improved all the more the place of the military elite in society. First of all, the privileged level of military education has shifted. For a long time, the educational activity of the army was concentrated primarily on the intermediate schools. But the general rise in the educational level in the U.S.S.R. has meant that now the higher military schools are the ones with a privileged role. Since they accept fewer students than ordinary schools of higher education, the student-teacher ratio is more favorable and the quality of teaching shows the effects of that fact.

The training program of the officer corps has recognized this shift in educational level and the increased quality of the education that has been received.[43] Now, 45 percent of officers in general and 75 percent of missile specialists have the training and title of an engineer. All brigade commanders and all officers above that rank have university degrees, which is also the case for 80 percent of the officers who have not yet reached that rank.

The army has not left to the traditional university a monopoly on the training of engineers and high-level scientists. It actively trains them, and it also sends military men to regular universities, so that the degree of scientific competence of the military has been constantly increasing. The consequences of this effort are obvious. More and more military men, on professional grounds, have joined the Academy of Sciences and various scientific institutes. And the penetration of the traditional academic world by the army has been further increased in recent years by the creation of "military departments" in the universities.[44]

The Training and Supervision of Civilians

Training its elites, joining the university world, the army has also gone beyond its bounds and taken charge of the training of civilians in three ways: through secondary schools, through military training, properly speaking, and by the organization of a civil defense system. The military law of 1967[45] seemed to reduce the place of the army by lowering obligatory military service from three to two years.[46] But this shortening of military service, aside from the fact that it was partly contradicted by a decree issued in 1977 that extended the time of service for graduates of higher-education institutions,[47] actually shifted a part of military training into secondary schools. This law provides that all secondary schools give military training to the boys in the two last years (the ninth and tenth). This training is placed under the authority of a military man—generally a retired officer—assigned to the school and paid by it. This officer is in theory subordinate to the director of the school, but conflicts often arise because the school system has difficulty in absorbing this supplementary constraint.

Despite these conflicts of authority, and despite the fact that the system falls far short of reaching able young men who might be in the final classes, because the "long" course of study has not yet been generalized, this extension of military training to the school has had several important consequences.

First of all, it provides the elements of an answer, if not a true answer, to the labor problem. Long military service would remove too large a mass of men from production, and this is now intolerable, in consideration of the Soviet shortage of manpower. In this way, the army avoids weighing too heavily on economic life. But at the same time, through the school system, it is able to set up a reserve force. Moreover, since the long course of study has developed in the cities, this reserve force is recruited in an urban setting where the population is better educated, and this corresponds very well with the needs of a modern skilled army. The military constantly insists on the necessity of enlisting educated recruits.[48] Finally—and this point is not negligible either—through this cooperation, the army has introduced its own system of values into the school. It corresponds essentially to that of the Party—discipline, a sense of hierarchy, patriotism—but it is also different inasmuch as it places national values and attachment to the army at the top.

In reality, all this is not new for the students in the last two years of school, for their childhood in the organization of pioneers was marked by encounters with the army. The pioneers (25 million children participate in the movement) devote time to various patriotic-military activities: meetings with war veterans, visits to sites of Second World War battles, and conversations with soldiers on active duty. The pioneers also organize large-scale paramilitary exercises, designed to give children a preliminary contact with the preparation they will later receive. Thus in 1969, 15 million children between the ages of ten and fourteen participated in Operation Zarnitsa, half game and half genuine patriotic and military exercise.

But the pioneers' military notions and the preparation received in school are not the essential. Real military preparation, which is an obligation for all boys over sixteen,[49] subjects them for two years to a common training, supplemented by specialized instruction. Ordinary military preparation includes a minimum of 200 hours of training. University students for their part are required to undergo longer preparation, involving 450 hours of classes in five years, supplemented by two months in a military camp. If we are to believe Soviet military publications, two thousand "specialties" are offered to these students.[50]

This preparation is entrusted to a voluntary association, the DOSAAF (Voluntary Society for Support of the Army, Air Force, and Navy), which works under the supervision of the Komsomol. The association's president is an air force marshal, A. I. Pokryshkin, born in 1913 and elected as candidate on the Central Committee in 1976. His presence at the head of the organization shows that retired military men play an important role in it. The tasks of preparation imposed by the military law of 1967 and taken on by the DOSAAF have greatly increased the resources and membership of the association.[51] In the five years following adoption of the law, the organization's budget tripled[52] and its membership increased by at least 25 percent.[53] No doubt the association is not very concerned with giving precise indications about its activities. But in 1973, one of its lecturers declared that the DOSAAF numbered 65 million members in its ranks—that is, one quarter of the people in the U.S.S.R. and half its active population. If this figure appears excessive, we may nevertheless accept as a base figure 40 million adherents, according to another estimate by the organization. We should especially remember that 70 percent of the members of the DOSAAF are komsomols. In the end, even though many young men slip through or shorten military training, the DOSAAF plays a very important role. It provides special training for many future recruits and general training for the majority of young men. It even trains those who, for various reasons, are exempt from military training and who, through its mediation, are nevertheless brought into contact with the army. The DOSAAF is thus a veritable appendage, often misperceived, of the military sector, particularly in budgetary respects. The association's own budget and the budgetary grants it receives are not included in the military segment of the Soviet budget, and yet it is the army that benefits from them. And finally, the DOSAAF is an institution for social mobilization implanted by its responsibilities and its large numbers in every social milieu and every geographical area, which guarantees its effectiveness.

A final link in this system that introduces the army into society is the organization of civil defense. The memories of the Second World War and the popular disarray of the early days of the invasion which made the Soviet system falter remain in the minds of those who lived through that period. By starting from these memories and permanently raising the question of society's capacity to organize itself to survive in case of a new war, the authorities have justified a considerable effort of education and popular mobilization. Since 1961, the question of civil defense, its means and its importance, has been constantly present in the media and in the leaders' speeches.[54]

The organization of civil defense has constantly developed and improved since then. In 1972, it was endowed with a specially coordinated structure based on two principles: strengthening of the role played by the Ministry of Defense and systematic cooperation at every level between the army and the civilian bureaucracies.

In practice, civil defense is primarily a sector of the military organization. At the top, it is placed under the authority of a special department of the Ministry of Defense whose head has the rank of deputy minister and who has sat as a titular member of the Central Committee since 1976.[55] This department has direct authority over those in charge of civil defense problems in each Soviet republic. The head of each military district also has a department of civil defense within his area of responsibility. We can see the centralization of this system, supervised as it is by the army at every level of Soviet territory. Civil defense is made up above all of special units[56] under military authority, organized on the model of regular troops. To set up these units, which play an active role, the civil defense administration can call on any man between sixteen and sixty and any woman between sixteen and fifty-five. These units are used in emergency situations to supplement the efforts of the regular bureaucracies. Thus, they helped in the fight against the forest fires that ravaged the Moscow region in the summer of 1972. In addition to special units, civil defense also organizes "groups" in workplaces, schools, and so on. These groups are under the direct authority of a civilian head and are required to engage in periodic training and defense exercises, so that no sector of civilian life is left out of this preparation for a possible war.[57] If we consider the extent of the system and the considerable role the army plays in it, we can propose two conclusions. First, civil defense, in spite of the adjective, is a sixth army that should be added to the other five (land forces, air forces, air defense, navy, strategic missiles) to have a reasonable idea of Soviet military capability. As for military preparation, civil defense is an invisible extension of the area of responsibility and the material possibilities of the army. Material support is provided by the civil sector (ministries, factories, and the like), but authority over the system as a whole is held by the army. Second, civil defense is a veritable system of peacetime mass military education. Considering the overlap between the army and the bureaucracies and the very dense network of organizations that depend on it, few citizens of any age, in this instance as well, can escape from a certain military influence.

In the end, from young pioneers to adults involved in production, every Soviet citizen—male or female, since civil defense makes no sexual distinctions—is permanently confronted with defense problems, asked to become actively interested in them, put in contact with the army, and led to experience its influence. There is hardly a place or an area of activity where one can totally escape the presence or preoccupation of the military. Even those who study and are interested only in music come up against the army in the Moscow conservatory, in the form of a department of military music.

Years ago, civilian power imposed its preeminence on military power. But during the same period in which civilian power was loudly asserting that decision making in every area was exclusively its concern, the army was taking a growing place in society, participating more and more in the shaping of attitudes of mind and penetrating ever more extensive areas of civil life. Soviet society and Soviet life have unquestionably grown more militarized. But does this imply an opposition between the Party's work of socialization and that of the army? These two organs do not spread conflicting ideas because, for a long time now, patriotism and the greatness of the U.S.S.R. and its interests have been central values in the political system. The Soviet Constitution of 1977 indicates as much when it includes in the section on the duties of the citizen, immediately after work and respect for socialist property, the duty of "defending the socialist fatherland" and strengthening the power and authority of the state.[58] The army thus confirms the action of the Party in forging the collective mentality of Soviet society. Subjected to such a coherent and continuous enterprise of supervision and mental training, is the Soviet citizen now a "new man" who offers evidence of the effectiveness of this effort of socialization?

The "New Man" Seen Clearly

Soviet power is not alone in asserting that it has created a "new man" and thereby carried out an unprecedented cultural revolution. Among those who study the system from the outside, there are many who are fascinated by this revolution in mental attitudes and who consider that the U.S.S.R. offers a spectacular and unprecedented example of organized cultural change. This judgment is shared, in cruelly ironic terms, by certain dissident like Zinoviev, who believe that the Soviet system has managed to deform and destroy the humanity of man and to replace him with a robot it can maneuver as it pleases. "New man" or "ruined man"; which is true? And how is the "new man" supposed to be and behave in the first place?

This human product of the revolution, education, and advanced socialism has precise characteristics freely propagated by the media. He is a man whose desires and actions are those of the entire community; who thinks of the Party's objectives before his own ambitions and objectives; who not only has internalized the system of Soviet values but forcefully testifies to his ideological conviction and his adhesion to the system; who sees no difference in nature between manual labor and other activities; who is ready to accomplish all tasks in which he will be useful without concern for their financial rewards; whose behavior, finally, in personal and professional life is always stamped with comradeship for others and enthusiasm for his country.

Can one meet this human model in the U.S.S.R.? And how? No doubt, collective behavior lends some credence to this edifying image of the "new man." Doesn't the massive presence of workers at agitation sessions or at the lectures of the Znanie association indicate agreement between popular concerns and the objectives of this mass socialization? Doesn't the fact that 140 million Soviet citizens participated in the debates on the Constitution of 1977[59] prove the high degree of society's social consciousness, as do the increased membership in Party and Komsomol or the massive enrollments in voluntary organizations like Znanie or the DOSAAF? Soviet newspapers devote substantial space to examples of voluntary action by the young in economic life. Putting the virgin lands into production under Khrushchev, today's construction of the second Trans-Siberian railroad, or the realization of great projects in the under-populated northern regions of the U.S.S.R. require "spontaneous" help that the Komsomol takes charge of bringing together. Each group of komsomols provides its team of volunteers to compete in this activity, and posted or published honor rolls indicate clearly that popular enthusiasm greets the projects of the government.

But can we consider collective behavior totally representative of attitudes of mind? In every society—including those in which constraint is not the determining element in behavior—collective attitudes are largely shaped by education and environment, and a substantial gap can exist between individual convictions and their collective expression. In the Soviet Union, where social pressure on individuals and groups remains great, the difference between the external attitudes, behavior, and convictions displayed in groups on the one hand and personal certainties on the other is without any doubt substantial. Given that fact, to attempt to define the "new man" even superficially, it is important to point to two questions. To what extent does collective behavior express real adhesion to proclaimed values? To what extent are the systems of values that individuals sometimes recognize in harmony with the culture transmitted by the Party and its auxiliaries?

In the U.S.S.R., how can one go beyond attitudes to grasp their meanings? Inquiries carried out in the field remain subject to the decision of the authorities and are therefore irregular and partial. Since 1945, two waves of emigration have released from that country Soviet citizens who represent a privileged means of apprehending the moral universe of the society. The first wave was made up of deportees and prisoners who did not want to return to the U.S.S.R. after the war. They provided considerable documentary material to Western specialists, and the studies on the U.S.S.R. in the years 1945–60 are first of all the product of their answers. The second wave, the emigration of Jews and dissidents authorized or forced to leave their country (more than 150,000 left in the seventies), also provided, because it was made up of Soviet citizens of sufficiently diverse ages and levels of education, a certain number of answers to help understand mental attitudes. But these inquiries must take account of several elements. Distance often deforms, as does ethnic origin.

Recent émigrés practically all belong to the "European" part of the U.S.S.R., and very largely to the Slavic part. The greatest number of them also belong to the best-educated circles. Thus, the limits of this kind of opinion research are clear.

A final and very precious source, even though it is difficult to handle, comes from Soviet publications themselves. Newspapers, through the criticisms they transmit, and Soviet literature present an image of the Soviet mental universe that is far from being a simple reaction of the political culture the system relies upon.

Soviet power, even though it holds a monopoly of communication and opinion formation, has always been aware that public opinion as it comes out in behavior could not be identified with real opinion, that it had to achieve knowledge of the real society. The only period when reality was totally obliterated by appearances was the Stalinist period, for two reasons. For Stalin, coercion replaced knowledge of society, and it forced society to conform to an ideal model. Social consensus then depended completely on terror, which produced an apparently homogeneous society and a homogeneous public opinion which identifies itself with the social project. "Socialist realism" was nothing but the esthetic expression of that suppression of reality in favor of a fiction that invaded everything. Solzhenitsyn's *Cancer Ward* is both the concentration-camp universe and the generalized lie, the fiction that overflows reality and swallows it up. At the time, nevertheless, there was a simulacrum of investigation of public opinion. The newspapers published readers' letters; in Party meetings "the questions and reactions of the ordinary militant" were always encouraged and praised; there was also encouragement of great collective demonstrations: rallies, meetings to discuss the Constitution of 1936 or the abortion legislation of the same year. The authorities carefully controlled and directed all these expressions of popular opinion. Sometimes, however, manifestations of public opinion escaped from its control. This is what happened at the time of collectivization, when the peasantry's reactions of despair revealed to the authorities the magnitude of popular hostility to its policies and led it at first to retreat and then to rely on still more violence.

Stalin's successors, because they had abandoned violence, knew that they had to pay attention to society and understand it. This explains the sudden wave of public opinion surveys in the early sixties, when the authorities asserted that the dictatorship of the proletariat had given way to the state of all the people. However, this curiosity, this impulse toward social investigation, does not indicate a radical change in the nature of the regime but only in its methods. The Khrushchev government had no intention of considering society in order to conform to its wishes. What it was looking for was to establish a new mode of relations with society that would be contractual and peaceful. But the goal remained the same. The authorities intended to use opinion surveys to bring out a social model. These surveys also had an educational aim: They were to help shape collective consciousness. They were also a means of controlling individual behavior by measuring it against a public opinion which became a reference point for everyone.[60]

The first and perhaps most important opinion survey carried out in the U.S.S.R. was launched in 1961 by the organ of the Komsomol. Its theme was youth, and they asked the young twelve questions concerned with their opinion of their generation.[61] After that, surveys proliferated, particularly centered on the young but also on specific questions (attitude toward work, toward the country, and so on). Once the early enthusiasm of the investigators had passed, the socializing function of the opinion survey was clearly accepted by everyone. One of the best Soviet specialists recognized as early as 1967 that knowledge of public opinion is a necessity for decision makers, because they can thereby integrate popular reaction into their choices.[62] According to him, knowledge of public opinion should allow the system to function smoothly, with the support of society. This function appeared so useful that in 1967 a center for the study of public opinion was established in the Academy of Sciences. It was abolished two years later, but its necessity as a regulator of the system had been widely accepted.[63]

In the late sixties, the effects of Khrushchevism were felt in every area, and particularly in the knowledge available about the average Soviet citizen. The closing of the Public Opinion Institute did not result in an abandonment of research but in a new orientation. Broad general surveys gave way to more precise, more scientific empirical research which, in certain areas —knowledge of the peasantry, for example, or of certain ethnic groups—was very thorough.

Literature also helped to explain society. Socialist realism often gave way to the social reality of the U.S.S.R. The rural writers in particular seemed to give themselves the task of describing as precisely as possible an everyday reality that was absolutely distinct from the triumphant statements of the leaders. They gave room to individuals and their personal aspirations, while the Soviet community and its great projects faded into the background. In this literature of everyday life, the future often gave way to nostalgia about the past and to those things that indicated the continuity between past and present. The "new man," for many writers, disappeared, to be replaced by the "old man," or just "man." Even letters to newspapers, sometimes despite the controls, reflected this change.

What can be drawn from these surveys, published literary works, and letters to newspapers to explain patterns of behavior and their deep reasons?

A first area of investigation, one in which the authorities were very interested because it allowed them to measure the effects of their policies, was the real level of participation in socialization activities. Many surveys tried to understand what drove Soviet citizens to participate in agitation groups, lectures, and rallies, and what they gained from doing so. To the question, "Why are you involved in political education?" it sometimes, though rarely, happened that the group questioned answered that it was from conviction.[64] Much more frequently, the answers referred to a feeling of obligation: "administrative pressures" or "Party discipline." It was normal for at least half the individuals surveyed to answer that they were receiving political education against their will.[65] A first characteristic that came out in the surveys published in the U.S.S.R., and this is what makes them significant, was the generally expressed indifference to the activities of political socialization. They formed a part of one's social obligations, but there was no agreement between individual aspirations and the attitudes that were adopted.

A second trait which came out in the answers was that this passive, indifferent reception of political culture characterized first of all those who ought to have inspired the rest of society by their example: its best-educated elements. But political indifference also affected the working class. In a survey carried out in the early seventies in a Lenigrad factory, 75 percent of the workers questioned about what motivated their attendance at political training sessions answered that they attended meetings because they were forced to, and 5 percent among the remainder expressed the wish to be courteous to the propagandists. Thus, only one worker out of five agreed that he or she felt an interest in these political sessions and attended them purely voluntarily.[66]

The Soviet authorities could not, moreover, take refuge in the comforting idea that Soviet society was divided into a fraction of active and conscious citizens, the Communists and komsomols, and a mass of passive citizens, for the surveys indicated that the political elite as well demonstrated indifference to these collective manifestations of solidarity and ideological conformism. We find this attitude expressed explicitly by a third of the Party members questioned in the course of one survey.[67] The situation was still worse when, in place of questions addressed directly to those concerned, the investigators presented the answers of the propagandists who were asked to define their public. A survey carried out a few years ago in the

Kursk and Mogilev regions on the participation in education organized by the Party revealed that the komsomols were the most indifferent and that, at all levels, at least half the participants showed little interest in the training they were receiving.

Has this generally involuntary participation in political education produced any results? What do Soviet citizens retain from teaching that is imposed rather than accepted? Propagandists questioned on this point have often shown great skepticism. In a survey conducted in the Moscow region, more than half the propagandists asserted that their students had retained practically nothing of what they had heard; among those who did not share this pessimistic view, only 9 percent thought that the political education received had an influence on the conviction of those they had trained.[68] The low level of political and theoretical knowledge of the beneficiaries of systematic political education—not to mention the effects of agitation sessions on the job—was very widely attested to by the propagandists, who readily pointed out that their listeners were permanently incapable of saying what was meant by proletariat, dictatorship of the proletariat, or détente, not to mention more complex notions like nationalization (which three quarters of those questioned were incapable of explaining).

What is more, the interest of the participants in these sessions, when it existed, was rarely directed toward fundamental matters helping to forge a socialist consciousness. A survey carried out in Taganrog[69] on subjects likely to excite the curiosity of listeners showed that they were chiefly interested (94 to 96 percent positive answers) in international problems—that is, in the outside world—in local affairs, and in domestic policies, primarily economic policies. On the other hand, answers showing an interest in problems of Marxism, the history of the Communist Party of the U.S.S.R., or economic theory in general were below 35 percent. And we must also recognize that it is difficult to say openly in the U.S.S.R., even to a researcher, that one is not interested in Marxism.

From their various investigations, the authorities concluded that the ideological training of their citizens was badly conducted; that its quality was deplorable; that the spirit of routine and the negligence of those in charge of ideology, at various levels, revealed themselves clearly in a simple fact: only 7.2 percent of the citizens thought that agitation and propaganda provided them with new knowledge.[70] Moreover, those who participated attentively in the various political training courses were precisely those who were already the best trained.[71]

The masses' lack of enthusiasm for the institutions of socialization and their obvious indifference to the subjects treated impressed Soviet authorities sufficiently to lead them to undertake a veritable mobilization of the ideological services. At the Central Committee plenum on November 27, 1978, Leonid Brezhnev announced that the Politburo had decided to create a special commission to consider a reorganization of all the institutions charged with the ideological training of society.[72] The Party press has subsequently echoed this anxiety of the authorities in the face of social apathy, understood as a failure of the work that had been undertaken.

Does this apathy, which is real and unmistakable, mean for all that that the authorities' efforts have been futile and that social consciousness has remained unchanged despite the pressures that have been exercised? Does the system of values to which individuals adhere really differ from the model of the "new man"?

The best-known group, because it is most closely followed by the leaders, is the young. Their answers are important because their numerical weight in Soviet society is considerable (nearly half the Soviet population is under thirty); in addition, the young are really a product of the Soviet system and have been brought up by parents who themselves have known only that system. The surveys carried out in the last few years have shown that the young wish above all for material comfort (well-paid work), social status (diplomas), access to the outside world (travel), and warm human relations (friendship, children, love). In answers providing a hierarchy of the wishes of young people, we do not find the desire to help in the development of the country, or be socially useful, or conform to a model established by the community.

A detailed survey carried out in the Novosibirsk region confirms and particularizes this general orientation of the aspirations of young people.[73] A group of adolescent secondary-school graduates was asked to classify seventy professions by order of their personal preferences. At the top, the majority placed scientific researchers (physicists first), engineers, geologists, mathematicians, airline pilots, biologists, and the like. In the middle of the pyramid were doctors, officers, and teachers; and at the bottom, employees of various services, followed in last place by laborers and workers.

No doubt young people in every modern society have similar ambitions, and the attraction exercised by the prestigious professions of the scientific world is in part due to the progress of science. But in the U.S.S.R., this hierarchy contains some distinctive traits. First, the greatest attraction is felt for prestigious professions rather than for money. This magnetism of prestige can be understood to the extent that Soviet society is a society where dividing lines are predicated on status rather than wealth. Money does not permit the perpetuation of privileges, but the status of a profession does. Moreover, money, as we have already said, has only relative value. The situation of the individual has less to do with financial resources than with the privileges enjoyed. In addition to material things, physicists enjoy a certain degree of freedom. They meet foreigners. They have access to foreign publications. They may be able to travel. By that very fact, their status is exceptional. A second characteristic of this choice, also found in all modern societies but in contradiction with the ideology of Soviet society, is contempt for manual labor. This attitude cannot be totally explained by the lure of material goods, for the wages of skilled workers are higher than those of ordinary office employees, higher even than those of more prestigious professions (such as elementary education or medicine). Soviet authorities have moreover reduced salary gaps and improved the position of workers on the salary scale. But what they have not been able to change is the social status of the worker and the possibility of moving from that category to another. Surveys devoted to the Soviet family have shown that marriage consolidates social differences. A manual worker has every likelihood of marrying in his milieu, of having a way of life determined by his work,[74] and of seeing his children carry on his work and his way of life. The rejection of manual labor is largely dependent on the fact that it is perceived as a definitive social choice.[75]

A final remark concerns the absence of political functions from the ambitions of young people. Although they are subject to constant political pressure, and the notions of commitment, usefulness, and responsibility converge to form the social model that is proposed to them, their choices seem to brush aside everything that has to do with politics. Here too, the explanation has to do with status and the possibility of perpetuating social advantages. In 1917, the Soviet regime abolished titles and the symbols of deference that the old regime had used abundantly. However, since 1917, titles and distinctions—meritocratic in origin and not hereditary, to be sure—have sprung up again. And it is precisely the careers that attract young people that have generally produced these titles. Intellectual positions—researcher, biologist—presuppose the acquisition of the university title of doctor or professor and lead in special cases to the particularly envied (and profitable, because of the tangible and hidden privileges it involves) title of academician. It is in the extraordinary professions that one has the greatest chance of becoming a Hero of Socialist Labor, and the complicated hierarchy of titles granted to artists is clear testimony to the Soviet tendency to distinguish and classify. The professions that young Soviet citizens choose first are precisely those in which distinctions go along with success, and those in which status is not only most prestigious and richest in privileges but also the most stratified.[76]

A second reason that makes these careers more attractive than the political world is that they imply stability of status. Soviet political history has been too agitated and tragic not to teach those attracted by power about its dangers and uncertainties. The political fall of a leader was for a long time accompanied by the simultaneous fall of a whole network of clients and associates. The absence of clear rules for the political process has maintained the uncertainties and instability of political-bureaucratic positions. Conversely, professions linked to a high degree of competence are perceived as stable. This perhaps explains why the children of Soviet leaders generally move away from the sphere of power and turn toward intellectual careers.

This attachment to values located in the background of the official political culture, or condemned by it as "petty-bourgeois" manifestations—individual happiness, the acquisition of material goods, security—is not restricted to the young. The interests and behavior of all of Soviet society give evidence that, on the fringes of the political culture transmitted by the authorities, there exists an implicit culture that the authorities cannot be unaware of. Its signs are obvious. A good example is provided by a reading of the newspapers placed at the disposal of Soviet citizens by clubs and libraries, which are vehicles for the Soviet system of values. The authorities have always attached considerable importance to the means of communication offered by institutions to their citizens, for collective readings open the way for the influence of agitators and propagandists. In 1980, on the occasion of the annual subscription campaign for newspapers and periodicals,[77] it was possible to note a change in the press runs of—and hence the demand for—various publications. This shift is expressed above all in the decline of political organs. The publications of the Central

Committee of the Party *(Kommunist, Partiinaia zhizn', Agita-tor)*, of the Komsomol *(Molodoi kommunist, Smena)*, and the unions *(Sovetskie profosozhuzy)* registered declines sometimes as high as 10 percent of the original run.[78] On the other hand, literary reviews *(Zvezda vostoka,* organ of the writers of Uzbe-kistan, *Novyi mir, Inostrannaia literatura)* progressed spec-tacularly. Still more remarkable was the veritable leap forward of three magazines: *Za rulem* ("At the Wheel"), *Roman-gazeta* ("Novel Magazine"), and *Molodaia gvardia* ("The Young Guard"). The popular success of these three publications, which already had very large press runs, is revealing of the passion for automobiles that has seized the Soviet people, of novelistic day-dreams, and, in the case of *Molodaia gvardia,* of the progress of the Russian nationalist or even chauvinist ideas that it trans-mits. If we analyze the interests of Soviet citizens in detail, we note that they prefer anything that is distant from ideological education. Thus, of the two history journals, *Voprosy istorii* ("Problems of History") and *Voprosy istorii KPSS* ("Problems of the History of the Communist Party"), it is clearly the second that has been abandoned. If the general-history journal has lost one reader out of thirty-three, the one devoted to Party history has lost one out of nine. The Znanie society has also registered losses, and readers have clearly lost interest in the publication of the soviets, *Sovety norodnykh deputatov,* which lost 93,000 copies out of 752,000. But readers increased for film *(Sovetskii ekran)* and sports *(Sovetskaia fitzkultura)* and remained stable for most art and humor publications.

This orientation of readers[79] has been confirmed by surveys concerning the attitudes of readers toward the content of news-papers. Questioned on this point, the readers of *Izvestia, Pravda,* and *Trud* answered with near unanimity that the editorials interested them little (only 30 percent of the readers of *Izvestia* indicated interest in the editorial), and that their interest was drawn essentially to international problems (74 percent for the readers of *Pravda,*[80] 69 percent for those of

Izvestia), moral problems (75 percent *Izvestia*, 57 percent
Pravda), unusual events, and humorous articles (64 percent
Izvestia, 57 percent *Pravda*). The surveys indicate that the
reader of *Pravda* glances first at the official bulletins that may
deeply affect the life of the Soviet citizen; then, reassured by
the absence of serious decisions, turns toward news of the external world, culture, and morality. Readers have adopted a skeptical attitude toward the news published by all newspapers, and
an attitude of indifference to political positions. Television,
watched by nearly all Soviet citizens for one or two hours a
day,[81] and radio, present in every household, although they
give much time to political preoccupations, also encourage Soviet citizens to avoid them, since nearly 40 percent of the
schedule is devoted to entertainment programs.[82]

Who is the Soviet citizen of today? And does the "new man"
whom the authorities have taken such pains to form exist?

If we consider Soviet society through surveys, testimony from
various sources, and the image it gives of itself, we are constantly confronted with two extreme truths. On one side, there
is the immense apparatus of education and social mobilization
placed at the service of ideas that are simple and, in some cases,
traditional. How could a society escape from this apparatus? On
the other, there is the society, in which much behavior—and
this is more and more the case—reflects attachment to a system
of values that does not belong to Soviet political culture, that is
located beyond ideological boundaries. Who are the real Soviet
people? Those who attend agitation meetings by the millions,
who are militants in the Party and the voluntary associations,
who confirm the slogan, "The Party and the people are
united"? Or is the U.S.S.R. a universe of open or silent dissidents, who submit to a power with which they never identify?

The truth of the Soviet citizen coincides with neither of these
extreme hypotheses. It is clear that the effects of a very long and
powerful effort of socialization cannot be nonexistent. On cer-

tain points—patriotism, fear or distrust of the external world, the assurance of security in everyday life (even at a low level) —society has internalized the official culture. Who in the U.S.S.R. would dream of preaching a return to private ownership of the means of production? The ascendancy and the omnipotence of the state are accepted all the more readily because what exists is connected to the pre-revolutionary tradition, when the state enjoyed unquestioned authority and was the greatest entrepreneur. The absolute authority of the Party and the absence of mediating institutions between society and Party, capable of confronting power—all that also belongs to the past as well as the present. The "new man" and the "old man" can come together here and recognize the elements of the legitimacy of power glorified by the present political culture.

But at the same time, behavior and convictions have evolved, and this evolution indicates the limits of popular consensus. Imperial legitimacy did not rest on a confusion between power and society but on the sacred character of power and authority. Soviet legitimacy flows on the contrary from a confusion between the authorities and their citizens, power and society. It is because society is identified with power that power exists and has legitimacy. And this is precisely where socialization has missed its goal. A better-educated society—which, moreover, no longer depends entirely on Soviet authorities for its information—has learned what separates the two. Aside from progress in education, two factors have in effect begun to affect the evolution of mental attitudes.

The first is access to foreign news. Foreign radio stations can be heard over a large part of Soviet territory. Finnish television reaches the Baltic states. Soviet citizens can now subject the news the authorities broadcast to criticism. And all the testimony converges to show that the ordinary Soviet citizen, who accepts with indifference the political training to which everyone is subjected domestically, avidly seeks the political information that comes from outside. The ideological monopoly that has blocked the mental horizon of *Homo sovieticus* for nearly six decades is in the process of erosion, if not of disappearance. And one of the foundations of Soviet political culture was its coherence and its impermeability to anything brought from outside.

A second element changing Soviet mental attitudes is precisely the rise of individual values. And here the Soviet system itself has contributed to the change. As long as the Soviet people lived with deplorable housing conditions and in fear of their neighbors, two characteristics of the Stalinist universe, family life and personal relations were very weak and could not serve as a refuge for the individual from the authorities. The improvement of housing conditions—an apartment no longer shared with strangers—and the disappearance of systematic informing —Pavlik Morozov is a character of the past—have restored strength to the family. The individual has rediscovered a protective cocoon against the external world. The family milieu also protects against socialization. It is very significant in this regard that Soviet people, when they are questioned on this point, say that agitation and political information should be reserved for the workplace and kept from the home. More and more, the home, even if it is a one-room apartment, has become again the place for individual life and no longer a place for collective political activities. Two cultures have thus begun to come into open juxtaposition: collective political culture, which is a matter for the authorities, and the culture of individuals, which registers their deep feelings, their solidarities, and some of their behavior. These two cultures mean that once again a split exists between power, *vlasti,* and people, *lzhudi,* between them, the ones who decide at the top, and us.

There is no doubt that this dichotomy exists in every political system. But the legitimacy of the Soviet system and the political culture that affirms that legitimacy rest on a fiction: the disappearance of the dichotomy. As soon as society begins to become aware that this was a fiction, then Soviet power becomes the same as all the others and must find a new legitimacy. This progressive coming to consciousness does not mean, however, that the U.S.S.R. is populated with opponents of the regime; it does imply that one day the consensus may be called into question, the leaders must justify their power, and the fideist explanation—that of the inexorable laws of history—is obsolete. The emperor has no clothes.

From this there follow two questions that are decisive for the future. Do the authorities possess political structures permitting them to channel and satisfy the social consciousness that is slowly awakening and is not the pure product of the "manufacture of souls"? And, for its part, does society possess methods and institutions to transform this confused awareness into action, to reach the status of a civil society worthy of the name, and thus to have an influence on the sphere of power?

CHAPTER 7

SUBJECT OR CITIZEN?

The contradictions the observer of the U.S.S.R. detects between ideological statements and reality, between power and society, are contradictions the Soviet system wants to ignore. Even more, it has demonstrated an extraordinary capacity simultaneously to affirm the coexistence and the compatibility of these two extremes. The Constitution of 1977 says:

> Having completed the tasks of the dictatorship of the proletariat, the Soviet state has become the state of the whole people. The leading role of the Communist Party, vanguard of the whole people, has increased.
>
> It [advanced socialist society] is an authentically democratic society, whose political system assures effective management of all social affairs and continuously more active participation by the workers in the life of the state.[1]

The dialectic of Party power and popular power is thus resolved in theory by the unity of the Party and the workers and in practice by the participation of citizens in public life. Soviet society, say its leaders, is characterized precisely by this very high degree of participation, which is gradually leading to social self-management or to Communist self-management *(obshchestvennoe samo-upravlenie* or *kommunisticheskoe samo-upravlenie).*

There is general agreement in the U.S.S.R. that social self-management is the goal toward which society and the Soviet system are tending. But the definition of self-management and the methods and limits of popular participation have gone through many variations in the Soviet debates of the post-Stalin period.[2]

Beyond the theoretical debates, there remains a reality. Workers' participation exists in the Soviet system. It has existed from the origins of the system. The soviets and the taking charge of all problems by society were the first steps of the revolution. The Bolshevik Party arrived only later.[3] Since 1917, it has institutionalized its relations with its citizens, within the framework of participation. In order for there to be identification between the citizen and the authorities at the level on which the citizen lives—that is, at the local level—dialogue and cooperation have to be established. These organized relations are also required because of the exclusive authority of state power over all aspects of individual life. The state is sole employer, sole educator, sole source of news, sole supplier of goods. Thereby, it is indissolubly united to society. It must recognize society's needs, discontents, and aspirations and organize with society a system of signals and contacts at the local level where precise expression can be given to needs and frustrations.

This popular participation in the life of the state, these relations between state and citizens, are expressed in two ways: universal suffrage, which in principle gives society the choice of its representatives; and local institutions, where the citizen takes part in management and thus plays an active role in public affairs.

By examining these two modes of participation in the Brezhnev period, we will attempt to answer the fundamental questions raised by this participation. Through the channels of participation that the system encourages, are the Soviet people in a position to accede to the sphere of decision making and thus to have an effect on political decisions? Or is this participation merely a supplementary means of socialization that the political system uses for its benefit? Has participation, whatever its real means and purposes, gradually changed, or may it possibly change the Soviet political system? Is it an element in the formation of the collective consciousness, and in what sense? Does it permit the authorities to control political subjects, or does it transform subjects into real citizens? Finally, to what extent is participation recognized by the elite as a road leading to the formation of a civil society?

Elections = Socialization

Elections in the U.S.S.R., as in most contemporary states, are considered the normal and natural manifestation of political participation. What differentiates the Soviet Union from many other states is the extension of the electoral system, the very high degree—in quantitative terms—of electoral participation, and the unanimity the elections reveal.

Let us first consider the general character of elections. Since the Constitution of 1936, the right to vote has been guaranteed to every Soviet citizen over eighteen.[4] This is a very extensive right, since universal suffrage designates the representatives of the people at every level of state power, from the Supreme Soviet (the bicameral legislature) down to the last village soviet. Voting is frequent in the U.S.S.R., considering the large number of assemblies that have to be elected. Voters are asked to vote for three kinds of assemblies, in the following pattern:[5] election for the Supreme Soviet of the U.S.S.R., for the supreme soviets of the federated republics and the autonomous republics, and for the local soviets. The Supreme Soviet and the thirty-five soviets of the republics (fifteen federated republics and twenty autonomous republics) are elected every five years. The local soviets are elected every two and a half years. The authorities take great care so that there is never any confusion among the three groups of elections, and the electoral campaigns are al-

ways distinct from one another. This system leads to the juxtaposition of "great electoral years," in which the voters vote
twice in twelve months, and years marked only by elections to
the local soviets. Thus, from March 1979 to March 1980, the
U.S.S.R. lived through a complete electoral year (March 1979,
elections to the Supreme Soviet; March 1980, elections for the
soviets of the republics and the local soviets).[6] In September
1982, the voters again go to the polls to reelect all the local
soviets, after a single electoral campaign, and from March 1984
to March 1985 they will once more be confronted with a great
electoral year.

The frequency of elections and the multiplicity of electoral
campaigns should not lead us to conclude that the U.S.S.R. lives
in a permanent climate of electioneering. Although each campaign lasts for two and a half months and is the occasion for
large-scale social mobilization, its political impact is minimal,
and that impact grows even less as one descends the ladder of
importance of the institutions elected. The central newspapers
devote considerable space to the candidacy of major political
personalities (that is, the members of the Politburo and the
Secretariat), and their speeches are abundantly printed, according to a pattern of precedence strictly linked to their place in
the hierarchy of the system.[7] But the regional and local newspapers are infinitely less prolix. In all circumstances, elections are
much less a matter of concern for the Soviet press than Party
congresses. The differing degree of attention reveals the difference in importance. Articles devoted to elections are also revealing about the electoral process. Aside from the electoral
speeches of the leaders, what the press makes public is first of
all the social image of the candidates. Why was the "super
milking woman" from a distant Russian village chosen to sit on
the Supreme Soviet? Behind that question, the place of a super
milking woman in Soviet society, her efforts, and her professional exploits are brought to the attention of the entire U.S.S.R.
Electoral news has in part the aim of showing the representa-

tive character of the electoral system and to glorify the rank-and-file candidate at the same time as the member of the Politburo. In this system, "the unity of the Party and the people" is expressed. At the same time, this electoral publicity concentrating on the extremes—Brezhnev and Kosygin on one side, the super milking woman on the other—tends to demonstrate that the voters' choice goes to the "best" at every level of community life.[8] The system's elitism finds substantial room for display in these campaigns. On the other hand, the electoral campaign is never an occasion for debate. Political and economic choices have already been made by the Party, and the texts and speeches published offer no matter for discussion.[9] Nor is the choice of candidates up to the voters, and this explains the unanimity that ratifies the results. The authoritarian and centralized character of the choice of candidates is, moreover, a point that Soviet authorities do not conceal. Quite the contrary, they consider that the capacity for future action by the soviets depends on this method of selection. However, since there are in the U.S.S.R. approximately two million representatives "elected by the people," it is clear that the process of selection varies according to level.

Two rules govern the selection of candidates: There must be only one candidate designated for each available seat, and the choice of a candidate for election is theoretically the province of every social organization endowed with legal existence[10] (the Communist Party is in principle in the same position as the unions, a workers' collective, a military unit). Generally speaking, this choice is made at a work collective meeting, organized in the factory, at an hour when all workers can attend so that the consensus of the collective may become evident. This consensus makes the candidate the single representative of the "bloc of Party members and non-Party elements."

Certain positions automatically designate their occupants as deputies. This body of "notables" represents nearly 80 percent of the Supreme Soviet and the soviets of the republics, but only a 25 percent of the regional soviets and perhaps even less for the lower level soviets. But the local soviets, one of whose essential functions is to work for the realization of the plan, would be quite ineffective if they excluded those who have local economic responsibilities (heads of kolkhozes or factories) to make room for workers. A study of local soviets shows that the president of a kolkhoz is by that very position almost certain to be a deputy, and the same rule prevails for anyone with responsibilities in the economy or culture. In this process of candidate selection, the Party is obviously not an organization equal to others, even though its intervention is often discreet. It is exercised by means of previous contact with social organizations,[11] but also through a certain self-censorship within each collectivity that is asked to select a candidate. These collectivities know that it is impossible to push a candidate unacceptable to the Party or to oppose a Party candidate. This self-censorship is not total; in certain cases—rare, to be sure—the work group has protested against the candidate who was proposed to it,[12] and—though this is not very common either—voters have even not ratified the choice of the social organizations.[13] In 1979, for the elections to the Supreme Soviet, there were 185,422 ballots cast against candidates for the Soviet of the Union and 150,754 against candidates for the Soviet of Nationalities. Seventy-two blank ballots were counted for the two assemblies. All the candidates were nevertheless elected.[14] To avoid expressions of this kind at the time of elections, the Party has attempted to give candidate selection a rather broad base in order to make sure that the choice made is acceptable to the voting community.[15]

Who can and deserves to be elected? What qualities designate an individual as being the best? What makes a good deputy, being an extraordinary worker, an activist, or demonstrating special qualities (ability to understand a situation and to manage problems)? These points are often debated in the U.S.S.R., precisely during electoral periods, but the answer provided is never clear. The fact remains that, through this process of preliminary selection, candidates are elected by crushing majorities. The almost total unanimity of the vote is a phenomenon common to both the Stalinist era and the Brezhnev period. Under Stalin, no one would have dared to cross off a name in sight of the officials or to go into a booth to do it, for that was a visible sign of disagreement with the Party's choice. This explains the absence of negative votes before 1953. On the other hand, the Khrushchev period, in this respect, was a veritable break with the past. The idea of the possibility of choice had advanced in men's minds; it had been publicly expressed in preelectoral debates and echoed by Party publications. In 1962, 750,000 voters—that is, more than one in 200—crossed off the name of the candidate proposed to them. In 1966, fewer than 600,000 did so.

The unanimity the voters demonstrate in their choices is reinforced by the very high degree of electoral participation, which is generally higher than 99 percent of registered voters. For the elections to the Supreme Soviet in 1979, participation reached 99.99 percent.[16] This spectacular result is remarkable in two respects. First of all, the rate of electoral participation has improved in the post-Stalin period, while generally the most terroristic regimes are credited with the capacity to obtain the highest rates of participation. Second, this rate of participation was not the result of police coercion but of social pressure, which is still a form of participation. As far as the level of voting in elections is concerned, one can only be struck by the constant "progress" the system has registered. In the elections of December 1937, participation was only 96.79 percent.[17] But since that moment the rate of participation has progressed continuously: 99.74 percent in 1946; 99.98 percent in 1950. The post-Stalin period was marked by a very slight decline in electoral participation, but not comparable to the rate of 1937 (99.95 percent in 1962, 99.94 percent in 1966). Since then, participation has regularly risen to reach the record noted of 99.99 per-

cent in 1979. At the last election in the U.S.S.R., there were
officially 23,952 abstentions out of a total number of voters of
174,944,173.[18]

How are this record participation and the unanimity it expresses obtained, if not by force? Must we accept, in the absence of violence, the image propagated by the Soviet press of
great popular jubilation and voters hurrying before dawn to
participate in elections?[19] The mobilization of a very large number of citizens to participate in the material organization of the
elections represents an essential element in this participation.
The electoral process is not the candidates' affair. Once they are
chosen, they appear as passive elements in the campaign. The
most active elements are the electoral commissions and the
agitators. The electoral commissions (nearly 10 million people)
exist in every district of more than one thousand voters and in
every polling place. The members of these commissions,
elected by social organizations following the model of elections
of deputies, have the function of preparing the elections, of
registering the voters, and then of supervising the progress of
electoral operations. The electoral agitators mobilize the population in agitation centers *(agitpunkty)* throughout the campaign. They organize all the meetings, from which the candidate is practically always absent, and inform the voters, listen
to them, and invite various personalities—war veterans, specialists in all areas—who, on the occasion of the elections, once
again provide political education for society. More than nine
million agitators work in this way in contact with the body of
voters. They are characterized by the fact that most of them are
Party members, their activity is orchestrated by the local organs
of the Party, and this electoral agitation is for the Party a means
of mobilizing society around the elections.[20] The agitators are
responsible as a group for an agitation point which serves from
a few dozen to two thousand people, and each agitator is in
addition individually responsible for a few dozen voters. Their
task is to transform the election campaign into direct contact
between the Party and each voter, to give life to campaign

slogans by the personal relations they carry on with the voters, and to note their reactions or even their collective or private requests. A final category of active participants in the elections is that of the candidates' representatives *(doverennoe litso)*, chosen by the collectivity that has selected the candidate to speak occasionally in his place.

Candidates, representatives of candidates, members of electoral commissions, agitators—altogether more than 20 million Soviet citizens play an active role in elections. In the face of this figure, which is substantial in relation to the total number of voters (approximately one participant for eight voters), one can understand what pressure these active figures can exercise on the society as a whole to bring it to the polls, and also what an effort and what a capacity for social mobilization is represented by this electoral organization.

Voting in the U.S.S.R. is an imperative moral duty from which it is very difficult to escape. Aside from this supervision, which operates so that direct social control weighs on the voter, the facilities placed at each person's disposal are such that abstention appears as a direct refusal to vote. Everything is foreseen in this organization. The agitators are in charge of verifying the conditions in which the voters under their jurisdiction will vote. Travelers have polling places on trains and boats, in stations and airports. The sick vote in polling places set up in hospitals and rest homes. In extreme cases, the bedridden being cared for at home vote at home.[21] For voting is a personal matter and proxy voting has no raison d'être, since the polls go to the voter throughout Soviet territory. It is up to the agitators to foresee particular needs and to call on electoral commissions to make certain that no material detail (transportation, watching a child or a sick person) may prevent a voter from voting.

It is also up to the agitators on election day to make certain that "their" voters go to the polls. That day, each agitator verifies that listed voters have voted and, if necessary, goes to get them at home.

For anyone who wants to abstain, the enterprise has to be

carefully prepared. There are two possibilities open to the recalcitrant. The first is to announce in advance to the agitator
that one will be absent, get crossed off the voting list, and
receive a certificate of absence with permission to vote anywhere—and the voter can thus appear nowhere. Sometimes,
when the number of voters missing at closing time exceeds the
accepted rate of abstention, the electoral commission itself
crosses off the names of a few voters and asserts that they have
received a "certificate." Thus the ratio between the number of
voters registered and those actually voting remains within acceptable bounds. The second method for abstaining consists
simply of disappearing for the day.

Until 1978, abstentionists almost always used the device of
the certificate of absence, which had the advantage of not drawing attention to them. For not voting means exposing oneself
to moral reprobation and even reprisals from the community to
which one belongs. Voting with enthusiasm is part of Soviet
political culture. As minimal as it may be, abstention is considered by the authorities as a manifestation of disagreement. This
is why the election procedures adopted in the last few years
have attempted to control the use made of certificates of absence, even though the election law of July 6, 1978, preserves
them in principle (article 23). But the agitators must carefully
note and transmit to the electoral commissions the identity of
those who ask for certificates of absence. Verification is now
made as to whether they vote elsewhere, and the behavior of
bearers of certificates is compared over several elections. The
detection of abstentionists by this method has without doubt
helped to reduce their number. But despite the efforts made by
the agitators, despite the dates chosen for elections (March for
the Supreme Soviet because the voters have few reasons for
being absent), a small fringe of Soviet society refuses to vote. It
is, moreover, very localized.[22] The highest rate of abstention in
1979 was registered in Latvia and especially in Estonia, where
there were four thousand abstentions (slightly more than 0.5
percent of the voters). Sometimes, also, abstentions fall to an

improbable level. In 1979, Uzbekistan admitted fourteen abstentions out of a total of more than 7 million voters. All the republics of the Caucasus also claimed a rate of participation of 99.99 percent. What the results of the 1979 elections suggest first of all is that pressure against abstentionists has increased, and that abstention is therefore easier to practice in a social or national milieu that has already accepted the principle. The Baltic republics, sovietized late, with a still-vivid memory of democratic life, are probably the most favorable milieu for this demonstration of discord. Another observation is that abstention is now clearly designated as a demonstration of discord by the authorities and by those who practice it.[23] The controls exercised over voters clearly emphasize this a social aspect of abstention, which cannot possibly be identified with a simple demonstration of political passivity. Finally, it is plausible that the rate of electoral participation, exceptionally high in 1979, is due—to a very small degree, no doubt—to some slightly irregular practices. Testimony provided by recent Soviet émigrés emphasizes this point. Sometimes an official in an apartment house collects the internal passports of his recalcitrant co-tenants or co-owners; sometimes the members of an abstentionist's family replace in the same way the one who intended to demonstrate discord. These procedures are accepted with understanding by the electoral commissions, whose first wish is to see their polling station beat the participation records and who therefore willingly close their eyes to the identity of the person who is voting.

Thus we see what explains the exceptional rate of electoral participation in the U.S.S.R. and the limits of the lessons that can be drawn from it. The political culture, the significant mobilization of voters to animate the election, the pressure that the whole society exercises, and the festive atmosphere all help to push the Soviet citizen toward the polls. We can even add a negative factor: the slight importance voters attach to their vote for a single candidate, whom they have not chosen, absent from the campaign, not presenting any program except for the collective slogans. "What's the good of being on the fringe" of a society that pays attention to all forms of behavior? That, too, is a supplementary reason for voting.

But does this exceptionally massive and unanimous vote remove all meaning from the small proportion of abstentions and names crossed out on ballots and the few voices that have been raised to organize collective demonstrations of electoral boycott?

Should this massive vote not be nuanced—even within the limits, already indicated, of a choice made in advance not by the voters and of a large-scale social mobilization—by the possible manipulations by electoral commissions able to adjust the real number of voters to the ideal size of those eligible, also capable, on occasion, of silencing a negative vote that would be too scandalous? Although election reports readily evoke the enthusiasm of the voters for the leaders and the warm remarks written on the ballots for Leonid Brezhnev,[24] they never mention that a leader may have received a negative vote. And yet it happens. In the elections of 1966, General Grigorenko crossed out Kosygin's name on his ballot.[25] If he had not said so, no one would ever have known.

Does the unanimity that comes out in elections have only the aim of simulating the role that Soviet citizens play in public life? Or is it to reassure the authorities about the docility of their citizens? In the U.S.S.R., elections play a much more important role than that of a mere screen for authoritarian power. They must above all contribute to the integration of Soviet society. No other collective manifestation allows the authorities periodically to gather society together in such a massive way around their slogans and projects. The solemnity with which the leaders consider the results of each election[26]—although they are known in advance—and the satisfaction they proclaim are indications of the importance the system attaches to this mode of socialization. What it concludes regularly is that the magnitude of the election campaigns, the quality of the candidates, and the unanimity of the voters "are a convincing demonstration of the monolithic cohesion of our society."[27]

This demonstration is unquestionably a means of social pressure, probably as powerful as coercion. How can one escape from this unanimity, from the feeling of belonging to a system supported by everyone?

Elections also help to transmit a social model embodied in the candidates. They have been chosen by the collectivities to which they belong because they are, in principle, the "best." The theoretical criteria for choice are clear. It is work, social activity, and adhesion to the system that single them out for choice by their peers, not individual virtues. The sense of the Soviet community and community virtues, the authorities think, ought to be strengthened by this model.

Moreover, it is significant that the real leaders of the U.S.S.R., the members of the Politburo, appear in this system as the "best of the best." In fact, broad publicity is given to the wish expressed by many districts to offer a deputy's seat to Brezhnev, Kosygin, and their peers. They are thus presented as though they were invested with the confidence of the whole society, as though they had been elected by the whole country, even though the election law forces them to choose a single district. And they leave this choice to the Party, as they explain to all the districts that offer them their votes.[28]

Finally, the authorities find in elections a source of legitimacy. What counts in fact is not the representation of those elected but the demonstration of unanimity around the leaders and the Party program, for which elections are the pretext. Election speeches all emphasize this displacement of confidence from the candidate to the Party. Thus, candidate P. N. Demichev, deputy member of the Politburo and Minister of Culture of the U.S.S.R., said to his electors of February 13, 1979, "I consider my selection as an expression of your absolute support for the policies of our Party, for the Central Committee, for the Politburo led by Leonid Brezhnev."[29]

In the last analysis, we must conclude that the peculiarities of Soviet universal suffrage are indissolubly linked to a political culture that excludes the idea of diffusion of authority, or a competition of ideas and programs, and replaces it with unity of decision, authority, and thought and unanimity of behavior. It is this absolute match between Soviet political culture and electoral procedures that gives so much importance and meaning to elections in the Soviet system. In the present, they must help to mobilize society; in the long run, to shape a society in harmony with the Party program.

Participation in Legislative and Administrative Organs

The whole society votes, and 20 million Soviet citizens actively participate in the organization of elections. But the participation of citizens in public life takes on many other forms which the authorities present as so many indications of the existence of direct and real democracy in the U.S.S.R.

Society is theoretically asked to express its opinion on all important questions in the life of the state, on "decisions of national and local importance."[30] This participation by society in decision making was affirmed in 1961 and is contained in the Constitution of 1977 (article 5). It sometimes takes the form of a referendum.[31] A good example of this general discussion by society of important decisions is the one provided by the Constitution of 1977: "It was debated by 140 million people in meetings organized at every territorial and political level; it provoked considerable correspondence in the newspapers and gave rise to four hundred thousand suggested amendments; this process led to changes in 118 out of the 173 articles in the draft constitution."[32] A comparison of the original draft[33] with the final text of the constitution makes it very tempting to conclude that the mountain gave birth to a mouse, that popular consultation was primarily a pretext for a massive mobilization of society, like elections, and that it allowed social reactions on certain points to be tested. Besides, the Soviet regime has always been inclined to consult society massively. In 1936, Stalin organized a similar debate to gather the opinions of his citizens on his draft constitution; in a country where the terror was in full cry, he was easily able to draw the conclusion of popular unanimity. More than half the adult population attended constitutional rallies and 154,000 amendments were proposed, 43 of which were accepted. Khrushchev similarly called on society to express its opinion on the great reforms he proposed; the agricultural reform of 1957 (sale of the MTS) provoked 3 million meetings and for weeks mobilized the press, which published 126,000 articles and letters on the subject. The same thing happened with the education reform of 1958.

In certain cases, when the daily lives of individuals are really affected, participation in discussions is not a mere formality. The authorities then have to convince people of the usefulness of the measures proposed, while the participants attempt to make substantial changes in laws that seem unacceptable to them. This was the case for the educational reform and the laws on marriage and the family. Newspapers and the various institutions of state and Party were inundated with letters, and the press, despite careful filtering, gives us a sense of the depth of popular feeling.[34] The authorities, who encourage and orchestrate this type of participation, thus sometimes come up against the drawbacks of the system they have created. Society, which is ready to demonstrate formal support in general debates or elections because it knows that development of policy is not its affair, is less passive when its immediate interests are at stake, when one moves down from the level of general policy to that of everyday life. The authorities themselves have finally consented to this, because it is a means of obtaining social participation and of showing society that its intervention in public affairs can have visible results in which it is directly concerned.

This mixture of formal participation and real contributions to public life can also be found in the development of voluntary activities associated with the soviets or other organisms. At the top of the hierarchy of participation are the soviets, whose deputies, because of their status and because they are theoretically invested with the confidence of their electors, have a certain degree of authority in local affairs. In 1980, the U.S.S.R. had 2,274,699 deputies elected to local soviets[35] and 6,728 elected to the soviets of the republics.[36] If the soviets of the republics are a rather faithful reflection of the social and ethnic composition of the Supreme Soviet of the U.S.S.R., the local soviets are rather remarkable in their resemblance to the Soviet population. They give substantial space to women (49.5 percent), to workers (43.3 percent), to kolkhozniks (25.4 percent), and to those under thirty (33.3 percent).[37] There are even many more "non-Party" members than in other representative organs (25 percent to 30 percent in the Supreme Soviet of the U.S.S.R., around 33 percent in the soviets of the republics, 56.9 percent in the local soviets). Thus, the lower one goes on the scale of power, the closer the representatives are to the people. If this is the case, it is not—as the process of selecting candidates indicates—because the people choose candidates in their image, but because of the desire on the part of the central authorities to bring local power close to society, to give it representatives with whom it might better identify, and to integrate into management activities a fraction of the population that is outside the Party but still enjoys its confidence. Besides, it is clear that the "non-Party" elements elected to the soviets are not placed in the most responsible positions. The Supreme Soviet of the U.S.S.R. offers an enlightening example of the place of the Party in representative institutions. In each chamber of that assembly, there is a Council of Elders composed of about a hundred people who seem to hold their seats ex officio and who are therefore socially representative. At the same time, the Supreme Soviet has a Party Group, which plays an official role, although no document provides for this. Thus, when the assembly elected in 1979 was seated, the press announced that "the

Party Group and the Council of Elders proposed the reelection of the supreme procurator of the U.S.S.R., Rudenko."[38] That the Party Group, which has no statutory existence, actively participates in the choice of the supreme procurator of the U.S.S.R., who heads up the entire Soviet judicial hierarchy; that, in addition, this unofficial body is mentioned *before* the Council of Elders, whose existence is based on the statutes of the Supreme Soviet: all this shows clearly, if it were necessary, how Party organs overlap with and in fact are superior to elected institutions. In every type of soviet, the Party's authority is exercised within the elected organs, by its members forming a "Party Group" that is a majority in the executive committees of the soviets *(ispolkom)*, where their representation ranges from 65 to 95 percent, according to whether it is a village soviet or a regional soviet.[39]

However, the relative similarity between the structure of the Soviet population and the structure of the body of elected officials should not conceal the fact that here, too, education is an important factor in promotion. Already by 1970, 16 percent of the deputies had received higher education, 70 percent secondary education, and 22 percent only elementary education, which was distinctly superior to the general level of education of the Soviet population at the time.[40] This situation is due to three factors: the authorities' desire, at elections, to push forward examples of their success in the field of education; the desire also to bring competent officials (those who have some specialized training) into local management; and, finally, the proliferation of supplementary education and retraining programs offered the deputies by the Party or by associations like Znanie, which has already been mentioned.

The turnover in the body of deputies has led a significant number of citizens to participate, at some point in their lives, in the tasks of administration. In his dream of a society of total participation, Khrushchev had included in the Party program a provision that the soviets should have a minimum turnover of

one third at each election. For his successors, the current practice—deputies are generally reelected once—has the virtue of
guaranteeing continuity in the work of the soviets. The current
rate of turnover is thus 50 percent, and this means that the
system of participation admits nearly a million new deputies at
each election. If we consider them closely, we note that, as in
the Party, if the soviets have a regular turnover, their executive
organs are more durable; they are all the more so the higher one
goes on the territorial ladder.

The people's deputies are, in principle, intermediaries between the political and administrative system and society; at
the same time, within the political system, they are citizens who
are more active than the others. They have to fulfill three very
divergent functions, in which they appear sometimes as intermediaries between the authorities and society, sometimes as
the most aware citizens. First, they have to respond to the
needs and problems of their constituents, by helping to present
their requests to the administration and, as a way of facilitating
administrative work, by making certain of the seriousness and
validity of the requests. Their activity in this domain is essentially concentrated on problems of pensions and, in the cities,
of housing.[41] The "social" aspect of their area of activity is
further emphasized when we consider that deputies are sometimes involved in family problems, trying to resolve or smooth
over conflicts or reform the conduct of an unfaithful spouse.[42]
By giving them these tasks of personal assistance, the system has
tried to make them into substitutes for the traditional authorities—village elders, heads of great families, or even religious
leaders—on whom people relied in the past. Their second task,
more in harmony with what one expects from a people's representative, is to organize the political instruction of their constituents, particularly with respect to the activities and objectives of the local soviets. They are not alone in undertaking this
informational task, but they overlap with the work carried out
by the Party's agitators and propagandists. At best, they help to

create around every Soviet citizen a tight network of agents charged with permanently mobilizing that citizen. Finally, through the contacts they maintain with their constituents, the deputies have the mission of recruiting around them other active citizens whom they impress into their own groups of activists and who may constitute a future source of deputies.

Being a deputy is not simple, first of all because the Soviet system does not want to professionalize the function, and because ordinary deputies continue their professional activity[43] while having the simultaneous duty not only of fulfilling the functions already indicated but of participating in groups of deputies and in permanent commissions of the soviets alongside citizen volunteers, in which they organize participation by these volunteers in local administrative life. The society of participation promised by Khrushchev is in fact characterized by an extraordinary proliferation of institutions for social mobilization, the aim of which is to include the citizens in various activities while maintaining control over them. These various institutions cross, overlap, and often paralyze one another. As for the deputies, who are supposed to participate in everything, while working elsewhere and without any authority over the administrative organs, they often complain of being overworked. And no less frequently, they resolve the problems posed by this overload by spending little time on their duties. Is it surprising that exasperated voters sometimes use their right to recall their deputies?[44]

For the citizens who are not deputies, the contexts for participation are innumerable, but some are particularly important because of the mass of activists incorporated into them. First of all, there are the volunteers who make up for the deficiencies of the administration. In the early sixties, when it was believed that full communism was at hand, this voluntary work was considered a central element in the disappearance of the state and the replacement of officials by ordinary citizens.[45] The local soviets, which had been deprived of some of their employees by

Khrushchev's administrative reforms, thus used volunteers—
unpaid, of course—who contributed to the work of certain administrative departments and supplied the entire personnel for
some of them. Retirees in particular greatly swelled the ranks
of these volunteers, who were often competent and whose activity was supervised by the executive committees of the soviets. However, after Khrushchev's disappearance, when his conception of the state of the whole people was laid to rest, this
type of voluntary service was substantially reduced. His successors have reestablished the idea of a genuine, responsible administration, and, although they have kept on some volunteers,
they are used as unpaid assistants to the administrators and not
as a potential substitute for the administration. The "professional" concern that the Brezhnev group has demonstrated in
the organization of the Party is revealed here as well. The
administration has again become a reserved, specialized domain, where voluntary workers have only a marginal place.
Moreover, the tendency noted in the early sixties for this group
of volunteers to act also as an element of social control over the
administration has been firmly rejected by a group that is quite
willing to use available abilities to make up for the deficiencies
of the bureaucracy but will not accept this cooperation's leading to any control over the administration by active citizens.

Participation or Control?

Control is one of the goals of the participation of autonomous
social organization (obshchestvennoe samodiatel'nye or-
ganizatsii), but it is a matter of exercising control over the rest
of society, not the organs of authority. Aside from activism in a
permanent commission of the soviets, or voluntary cooperation
in an administrative department of the soviets, citizens have
various other opportunities to take an active part in public life.
For this purpose, there are various committees (neighborhood,
street, building) which, under the indirect authority of the so-

viet, supervise and mobilize the population at the level of the residential unit. They may also join the ranks of groups connected to work—councils of volunteers or repair teams—which, as the need arises, accomplish tasks that the local soviet cannot complete. Thus, road work and repairs of schools and apartments are finally taken in hand by teams of volunteers, who devote their time to improving their surroundings or those of their relatives and neighbors. Is this a manifestation of social conscience or simply a wish not to break one's leg on the way home? A good deal of evidence adds up to a strong case for the second hypothesis. Finally, they may take part in the tribunals of comrades or join the people's militia (Druzhiny).

This multiplicity of organizations designed to put the citizen in contact with civic life is a phenomenon whose social and political significance needs to be understood. It is very difficult for individuals to ignore or perennially to refuse to take part in the very diverse activities that solicit their participation. It is clear that, at one moment or another of their existence, all Soviet citizens are brought to go along with this participation. To reject it is to be asocial, and therefore to cut oneself off from any possibility of advancement in Soviet society. Although it is impossible to know in detail the present number of participants in all the autonomous social organizations, we know that in 1965 there were approximately 10 million of them. In 1975, there were 179,000 people's militias with more than 7 million members.[46] Thus, the proportion of the adult population of the U.S.S.R. that participates in these activities is not negligible. But at the same time, even if the figures were precise, they would be incapable of giving a true picture of popular enthusiasm for participation. In fact, many members of these organizations are Communists or Party activists. There are also many deputies who can be numbered among the leaders of voluntary organizations. It is impossible to sort out those who have already been counted as participants in the work of socialization from the ordinary citizens.

Rather than figures devoid of real meaning, it is the function of these participatory organizations that deserves attention. In theory, they emanate from society itself and not from the authorities; they are thereby a powerful means of control over individuals in every area of their existence. The individual at home is surrounded and helped by the voluntary committees in buildings, streets, and neighborhoods. These committees, bringing together neighbors who know one another, penetrate the lives of others and are also useful intermediaries between the authorities and the individual. By their very existence, they exercise psychological pressure on whoever is within their range of authority. Asocial behavior in all its dimensions, human, social, political, is taken in charge by these associations, whose task is precisely to embody and propagate Soviet culture in a particular environment.

Again at home, but especially at work, the individual is confronted with another, more constraining means of control, the tribunal of comrades.[47] This institution, which goes back to the earliest days of the revolution, was also given new strength in the Khrushchev period.[48] At the time, the justification for these tribunals, operating in workplaces or residences with a minimum of fifty people, was once again the utopian idea of the disappearance of the state and the transfer of its judicial functions to society. But the tribunals of comrades have survived utopia and represent a very dangerous element of social pressure. The idea that justifies their preservation is that society has an acute awareness of the values to which it adheres, that it is in a position itself to guarantee respect for its values, and that all citizens are accountable to the collectivity for their acts. No doubt the jurisdiction of the tribunals of comrades is not very extensive. They are above all to educate their neighbors and spare them from falling into evil ways. This implies the right to spy on others. These tribunals consider only minor infractions and can inflict only light penalties, essentially fines. What characterizes them—and they have grown particularly in workplaces—is the lack of judicial training of their members.[49] Because of this incompetence, and also because they represent a people's tribunal obeying an abstract popular conscience and not written laws, the tribunals of comrades frighten Soviet citizens, who generally express a strong preference for regular courts.[50]

This mistrust of society for institutions that fit badly with the socialist legality proclaimed since 1956 unfortunately goes against the currently prevailing tendency in the U.S.S.R. to increase the standing and the jurisdiction of these tribunals of the people. We can see two reasons for this tendency. The first is the one that helped to increase, for a time, voluntary administrative personnel: the congestion of the regular courts, which can thereby pass unimportant cases over to parallel jurisdictions. But another reason governs the growth of these tribunals, more in conformity with the spirit of the current Soviet leadership, which seeks to control society to the maximum extent without having that control imputed to it. The growth of asocial attitudes and activities—hooliganism, "parasitism," muffled protest—has led the authorities to strike ruthlessly. It is tempting to let society strike, in the name of "spontaneous indignation," against political attitudes that are transformed into infractions. This has been the case with "parasitism," which often includes an individual's inability to find work because the political or nationalist stands taken have made it impossible to be hired anywhere.

In the impulse to refer growing number of cases to the tribunals of comrades, there is thus a process that recalls Khrushchev's utopia, but in a distorted way. The state transfers what it finds embarrassing to society not so that society may replace the state but simply to enable it to avoid the responsibility of judging embarrassing cases. It is significant that the people's militias have the right to refer offenders to the people's tribunals, just as the regular courts and the procurator may.

The people's militias,[51] in fact, supplement the activity of

control of the voluntary organizations, first of all, by their field
of activities. We have seen that individuals are subject to social
control at home and at work. There remains only to supervise
people when they are on the street. For the street is the real
domain of this institution created in 1959. The popular militias
are charged in the first place with maintaining public order in
the streets and in every place of assembly. They are made up
of politically active elements—komsomols, students, members
of various voluntary organizations—who also make sure that
public behavior does not adversely affect the ideal image of the
Soviet citizen. Like most participatory institutions, after having
been for a while under the direct, official authority of the Party,
the popular militias in 1974 were moved under the control of
local soviets, and they elect their own leaders.[52] This with-
drawal of the Party corresponds to a general evolution en-
shrined in the Constitution. The Party has presented itself with
increasing frequency as an inspiration for social development,
instead of being riveted to tasks of supervision and command
at the lower levels. But this evolution has also gone along with
the growth of the Party. Since it has become a mass party with
its 16 million members, it is present through them in all social
organizations. This is the case for the popular militias, in which
the proportion of members of the Party and the Komsomol is
very high. Once organizations contain a hard core of Party
members, generally installed in the most responsible positions,
official control by the Party over the organization becomes un-
necessary. And here again the Party gains by effacing itself, in
the thankless tasks of maintaining public order, behind a people's organization, dependent by law on elected institutions and
therefore representing a manifestation of the general will.

Through all these forms of participation, society is ever increasingly called on to demonstrate its community feeling, to
integrate itself into the community, and to support the social
and moral values proposed to it. This system of participation,
which inserts the individual into a tightly knit fabric of obliga-

tions, tasks, and constraints, has continued to develop and accurately characterizes the social evolution of the U.S.S.R. under Brezhnev.[53]

We return now to the initial question. Where is participation, a reality that is present at every moment and at every level in the U.S.S.R., heading? Is it a royal road leading a community of subjects to the formation of a genuine civil society, a society in which will be exercised what political scientists call the "competence of the citizen"?[54] In order to answer this question, which is decisive for an understanding of the Soviet system, we must make several remarks.

The society of participation in the U.S.S.R. is dependent on two developments: the progress of local power and the progress of voluntary activities alongside power.

The development of local powers, or rather the insistence on their role, is a permanent characteristic of all of Soviet history. The revolution was made within the framework of local powers, representing the popular will. Stalin never underestimated their importance. He wrote, "Their function [that of the soviets] is to serve as a barometer, to detect every change, to warn of storms."[55]

Khrushchev, whose penchant for utopia shone forth on this point, hoped for a while to make local powers something entirely different from a tool used by power to make contact with society, something other than a controlled safety valve for social aspirations and frustrations. But his dream of participation gradually replacing the state was only an isolated and incongruous episode in the history of the U.S.S.R. The whole movement that revitalized the local soviets after Stalin's death,[56] and the recent provisions in their favor, are contained within a coherent conception of local power. It is above all the privileged point of contact between power and society. Society is excluded from decision-making power, and it cannot manifest itself or communicate with the supreme power except on the local level. It is there that the decisive break between real power and society is to some extent attenuated and concealed.

Local power is also the level at which the system can be rationalized and adapted to the demands of society. It is this desire to use local power more effectively to respond to the demands of society that has led to an extension of the areas of participation to many volunteers. The soviets—the assembly and the administration—are constantly overwhelmed by requests and complaints, since the slightest needs of citizens in everyday life depend on them. To all these demands that have to do with immediate needs—the condition of an apartment house, the neighboring restaurant's inability to serve customers, the lack of medicine at the clinic, the shortage of day-care spaces, or simply the lack of day care—the soviets are often incapable of answering, and they do not answer. Nor does the Supreme Soviet, which is also inundated with complaints. Newspapers sometimes reflect them, and it has happened that when exasperation has become widespread a few officials are dismissed.[57] But citizens' complaints generally have fewer effects than the reliance on substitute solutions. This is why the authorities have called on volunteer services of all kinds, since that displaces the solution of the problems from official institutions to the shoulders of the citizens.

This system possesses many advantages. First of all, it suggests that participation by citizens in public affairs is growing. In fact, what has been progressing is the help citizens provide to an administration incapable of responding to their needs. Participation in management can finally be reduced to the use of free manpower. A second advantage is that, thanks to this popular participation, the local authorities are able to respond to some citizen demands without burdening the public budget. Finally, and this point is far from negligible, the system moderates social demands. Knowing that they will have to pay for the satisfaction of their demands with a few days of unpaid work, Soviet citizens often prefer not to formulate demands. Thus, a certain self-censorship has developed which allows the superficial observer to conclude that the Soviet citizen is perfectly satisfied with living conditions and inadequate services, while this silence really expresses only the refusal to take on personally the State's tasks. Since Khrushchev was eliminated from power, the narrow utilitarian meaning of participation and voluntary service has imposed itself on Soviet citizens. If participation has progressed, this is less because people rush into it than because it sometimes allows them to satisfy their own needs, and especially because the authorities see it as an essential element in the political system.

It is participation in social organizations of all kinds, the activism of society—with political participation in the elections and in great debates and assistance to local power—that is allowing the authorities to complete their enterprise of socialization. This participation responds to several of the authorities' preoccupations.

In the first place, the disappearance of coercion as the principal mode of relations between power and society presupposes a reliance on other methods to supervise society, to prevent it from taking advantage of weakened coercion to organize itself against the authorities. Socialization, which is indispensable to obtain the voluntary and total adhesion of society to the system, is achieved through the many channels of participation.

The evolution of society has moreover forced the authorities constantly to advance further on the road of this social mobilization. In fact, Soviet society in the eighties has some new characteristics. It is educated. It is less ignorant of the external world than it used to be, because the U.S.S.R. is no longer totally enclosed within its borders and because foreign radio stations enable a considerable number of Soviet citizens to hear facts and ideas that contradict their news and their culture. Whatever the degree of internalization of specifically Soviet values, the mental universe of every citizen of the U.S.S.R. is in the process of changing simply because its monolithic character is

crumbling. If the older generations, educated in fear and rejecting the idea that their suffering and their sacrifices were futile,
sometimes hang on to the coherent universe of the past, the
young, who no longer know fear and who have witnessed the
questioning of many certainties, are more exposed to the movement of ideas. Moreover, Soviet society is rapidly urbanizing.[58]
The young live in cities. Urbanization has opened the way to
new behavior patterns. Many studies have shown that the
U.S.S.R. is now experiencing serious urban delinquency,[59] as
opposed to the stability of behavior in rural settings.[60] It has also
been shown that criminality is growing at a great rate in country areas in the process of being urbanized.

These changes in the mental universe of individuals and in
patterns of social behavior require, without any doubt, intervention from the authorities, who have experienced a rapid rise
in political criticism, or at least skepticism, and pure and simple
delinquency. But this evolution has coincided with the obvious
desire on the part of the leaders to avoid a return to pure and
simple coercion. How can these tendencies be contained and
controlled except by developing, through participation, social
control, pressure by society on all its elements that are gradually
slipping outside Soviet norms? We can understand that the
authorities have increasingly called on society to carry out—on
the surface, at least—the functions of control and constraint
they do not wish to assume. Social pressure, when it must take
the place of coercion, naturally devotes considerable attention
to methods of control, surveillance, and intimidation. The increased importance of the tribunals of comrades and the people's militias gives evidence of this use of participation for ends
that are not only educational and integrating but also as disguised constraint.

Urbanization in its two forms—rural exodus and urbanization
of the countryside—has also created another problem of adap-
tation for Soviet power. Soviet political culture glorifies above
all the community and its values; individual flowering takes
place in the community, and the community's interest is what

should guide society, while individual interests fade, blend with the common interest, of which the Party is the bearer and the guarantor. But urban civilization is destructive of the sense of community. It isolates individuals, pushes them into the sphere of personal interests, and encourages narrow solidarities—close family, friends—at the expense of collective values and broader solidarity. Soviet power is thus placed in a paradoxical situation. It wanted urbanization in order to destroy peasant society and its moral universe, because it was convinced that the "new man" could come into being only in cities, cut off from his roots and in schools where he would be shaped. The first part of the program has been perfectly realized. The "new man" lives in cities and is a stranger to the universe that once was his; the rural world itself, after a long series of tragedies, has lost its specificity and is in search of a new culture. But the product of this willed uprooting has not been a new community. By killing the sense of community so rooted in rural societies, so various but so real in the diverse societies of the Empire—*sobornost'* of the orthodox; tribal or class solidarities of the southern peoples —this work of spiritual transformation has given birth to fierce individualism. The authorities are seeking, through participation, to re-create this community sense. By including men in neighborhood, street, or factory committees, the authorities attempt to inspire them with a feeling of belonging to those groups. There is also an attempt to broaden the range of their solidarity from the family, which has resumed considerable importance, to the neighborhood or work group. For Soviet power, the family should be a link in the system of general solidarities, and in no case a refuge. But this is what it has more and more become.

The entire immense body of activities in the U.S.S.R. has as its function not only to draw others toward activity, to persuade and control them, but also to conquer the tendency toward a retreat into oneself and one's family and to create a new form of life and sense of community.

Finally, permanent participation is a dike the authorities

have constructed against the possibility of a social organization not dependent on them. For it is always afraid that this educated society, which has unlearned fear, will take the road toward an autonomous life. On this point, Soviet power has not changed since 1917, and even Khrushchev the iconoclast was faithful to the essential points. The authorities are perfectly willing to carry on dialogues with individuals. Everyone is free to send complaints or requests to the local soviet, to the Central Committee, or to Brezhnev. And many letters of this kind are written in the U.S.S.R. The authorities are also perfectly willing to allow aware individuals to come together in social organization. What they cannot accept is that associations be established outside their control. That would be to sanction an independent organization of society, the construction of a civil society, the end of the system that has only those interlocutors it chooses. The extraordinary effort of social mobilization is also in response to that anxiety. Soviet power, by organizing it, occupies the totality of social space in order to leave room for no possibility of mobilization or organization foreign to it. This enterprise of social mobilization—unique in extent and duration—is extremely coherent in its goals and in the results it has obtained.

In the U.S.S.R., social participation is a phenomenon that has continuously grown, but this progress has taken place in the framework of an unchanged sytem, fiercely attached to the defense of its ideological unity and the monopoly of power held by the Party. Besides, this participation does not at all develop the competence of the citizen; it provides no access to the sphere of decision making. Its goal is to obtain adhesion and support for the policies defined by the Party.

Far from fostering the creation of a civil society, extended participation is Soviet power's privileged method for preventing it from coming into being. The society integrated by this exceptional effort of socialization is a society of false citizens, for their area of competence is adhesion, not free choice.

CHAPTER 8
DISCORD AND
CIVIL SOCIETY

When the Soviet authorities draw up their accounts, they include among their assets—the assets of Brezhnevism—the progress in social participation. They should also claim, to be just, progress in another area which they did not seek, quite the contrary: the slow but unquestionable growth of manifestations of discord, which perhaps make up the embryo of a civil society.

Since its birth, the omnipotent Soviet state—sole entrepreneur, sole employer, sole decision maker—has been able to prevent the establishment of distinct groups conscious of their particular interests and their proper place in the social order, groups that might form a counterweight to the political authorities. Soviet political culture urges total social integration, with a hierarchically structured society based on the Party's criteria, and it opposes social differentiation.

However, in the last twenty years, differentiations have appeared and developed within society. Their point of departure has been an act of stepping back from political culture on the part of individuals and groups. This is dissidence, a phenomenon the Russians call *inakomysliashchii*, or "thinking differently." The term is very explicit, and it indicates a high degree of awareness as to the significance and seriousness of the phenomenon. Thinking differently, while the essence of Soviet political culture is unanimity and total adhesion, means placing oneself outside that political culture, hence outside the system. But thinking otherwise is only a first step. As soon as individuals are able to step outside the closed world of Soviet political culture, they know that there are only two possibilities for them: to be destroyed by the system that they are now looking at from the outside (destroyed physically or psychologically) or else to try to change it. Since suicide is not one of man's fundamental aspirations, this different thinking that has appeared in various forms in the U.S.S.R. in recent years has attempted to find ways of reaching the sphere of power in order to have an influence on it. To think differently, to be a dissident, implies in itself a new system of values, objectives still imprecise but which are gradually taking shape. These are values and objectives with which individuals identify, which serve as rallying symbols for groups. Out of a dependent society made up of subjects, people are slowly emerging who aspire to civic competence and who are trying to find the means of reaching that goal. Whether they like it or not, for the first time the Soviet authorities are confronted by forces they have not called forth and that they do not totally control.

When one speaks of dissidence, the term is immediately attached to a few names, to the protests of isolated intellectuals. That dissidence is too well known to be discussed here. But the term can be used in its broad sense; it covers all the center of different thinking and has developed in three areas of society: the intelligentsia, the churches and nationalities, and finally among the workers.

We can see how multifarious this nascent discord is, how it follows different lines whose points of convergence are difficult to detect. It also occurs within institutional frameworks that cannot be compared with one another. Sometimes it is a phenomenon on the fringes of the system that is almost acceptable to it, sometimes removed from it, sometimes openly hostile. If these differences in the signs and tendencies of discord make it still unthreatening to the system, it would be excessive to conclude that the scope of discord is small. Its very existence is a breach of extreme seriousness in a system that permanently invokes its citizens' unanimous adherence to its culture and objectives, a system whose legitimacy rests on the identification of the whole society with the authorities.

Demobilization and Mobilization of Minds

In the Soviet Union, intellectuals—writers, artists—are honored and privileged in proportion to the role assigned them. They are supposed to help transmit the political culture. Are the writers not called "engineers of souls"? The Soviet authorities have always been clear in their definition of the social role of the creative intelligentsia. It is an integral part of the system, and there is no autonomy of creation. Its nobility is its contribution to socialism. Artistic creation must reflect society, transmit its values, and shape it. This conception of the relations between "intelligence"[1] and the political project that welds society together comes out clearly in the state organization of creative activity. Like functionaries, intellectuals and creative artists recognized as such by the state are assigned a place in a professional hierarchy—in unions of creators (writers, painters, musicians), in academies of one's republic or of the U.S.S.R., as corresponding or full members—a place involving rights and privileges. There is the right to be published, if one is a writer, in a state where all publications are state publications; and there are clearly defined privileges: apartments, dachas, cars, travel, and so on. What is important in this system is its hierarchical structure. Here again we discover a veritable table of ranks.[2]

Outside the state's area of recognition, there is no creative work. To convince oneself of this, it is enough to refer to the testimony of intellectuals rejected by the system. Two recent examples are particularly enlightening. First there is Lydia Chukovskaya, author of a considerable body of work, notably an account of the years of the purges, remarkable because it was written at the time.[3] In a recent book, she relates her tribulations as a member excluded from the Writers' Union for having expressed her disagreements.[4] This exclusion resulted not only in the impossibility of being published but also the suppression of all her previously published works and the elimination of her name from all bibliographies and catalogs in which it had been included. When you lose the status of "Soviet writer," writes Lydia Chukovskaya, you cease to exist as a writer for the future, but also for the past.[5] The example of Efim Etkind is no less significant.[6] Excluded from the Writers' Union on April 25, 1974, he was not only deprived of the right to be published and dismissed from the Herzen Institute (thus deprived of his livelihood), he was even stripped of his university titles. In short, by thinking differently, an intellectual loses not only the means of survival but the qualifications acquired in the past—including university titles and previous work.

We can thus see the link between the intellectual's ideological behavior and status in society. Adherence to common values takes precedence over ability and is what gives meaning to university or professional titles.

To place oneself on the fringes of this system is an act of extraordinary courage, which is part of the long tradition of the Russian intelligentsia. This was the voice that spoke out against imperial power and its censorship. Under Stalin, a few intellectuals perpetuated this tradition of independence. Osip Mandelstam died because he had depicted Stalin as a "man-eater."[7] But what were in the Stalinist past totally isolated and silent manifestations (the poems of Mandelstam and Anna Akhmatova were circulated by word of mouth, and Chukovskaya wrote for her desk drawer and then concealed her manuscript in terror), has in post-Stalinist years taken the form of open and public manifestations of discord. Literature provides the most frequent and most significant testimony, for writing has always been the clearest and most effective translation of thought. It is also the form the authorities fear most. In the years 1956–62, the intellectuals' discordant views were sometimes accepted and sometimes supported by the authorities. It was part of the "restoration of order" of the period, and it was still considered as a contribution to the work of the Party.[8] This is why authors could at the time demand that literature serve the truth.[9]

Encouraged as they were to rediscover the path of sincerity, is it surprising that a number of Soviet intellectuals have continued on this path while the Party, for its part has turned its back on its past orientations? Official literature itself, the literature that has the right to be published, has expressed this evolution in its own way by giving up commitment. There are untold works in which socialist realism and ideological commitment no longer have a place. There are also many that transmit specifically Russian values, an idealized vision of a harmonious rural world in which modernity, the working class, and social change are unknown. And there are many writers who, forgetting that paradise is on earth, have turned anew toward religious values and raised the question of man's fate, as though the Russian Revolution had not answererd it.

After having tolerated, for a while, this literature that moved away from or ignored Soviet political culture, the authorities no longer accept it.[10] And, as it had done in 1946, in the late seventies, the Party mobilized all the cultural dignitaries to explain its position. Chakovski, editor in chief of *Literaturnaia gazeta,* clearly set forth, in a text which has perhaps the same normative force as Zhdanov's exhortations of 1946, what is now the writer's "duty": "Soviet literature is the mirror of a transformed and homogeneous society."[11] This is the source of the writer's responsibility. The work must be in harmony with society, must serve it, and an apolitical stance in literature is already a betrayal. Not only does Chakovski condemn demobilized literature, he vigorously denounces nostalgia for the past or for rural society and the glorification of pre-revolutionary history— that is, everything foreign to the Soviet world.

If "uncommitted" literature, despite Chakovski's alarmed tone, does not constitute a particularly threatening act of protest against the authorities, even though it evidences the growing weariness of the elite with a system whose intellectual criteria they challenge, what is new and threatening is the movement from autonomous individual thought to the formation of groups. The adventure of the writers who come together in the collection *Metropolis* is an example. In 1979, a group of well-known and recognized writers (Vasily Aksenov, Erofaev, Fazil Iskander, Bytov, E. Popov), enjoying all the rights attached to their status as writers, agreed to pool their aspirations to liberate literature from ideological constraints. They revived the old nineteenth-century Russian tradition of massive periodicals *(Tolstoyi Jurnaly)* and put together a large five-hundred-page volume of pieces in which they presented, essentially, subjects that the "Soviet writer"[12] is not supposed to treat— God, death, sex, and so on. Their action deserves close consideration. They did not present themselves as an opposition, and to emphasize this fact they addressed their work, *Metropolis,*[13] to the Writers' Union and then explained the meaning of their action in a letter to Brezhnev. But while not opposing the system, they claimed the right to choose their own themes and publish their writings. Even more, by joining together, they started down the path, so feared by the authorities, toward the establishment of social communities united by their own values and interests; communities identified with values, which thereby break the social homogeneity that the system prides itself on. The reaction of the authorities—who condemned the whole movement[14] and punished some of its members[15]—far from intimidating the intelligentsia, provoked another kind of manifestation, also new and very significant: self-exclusion from the Writers' Union. We have already pointed out what it implies for an intellectual to be a member of various organizations of professional and creative artists. It means recognition of status and the possibility of working. Since the mid-sixties, the Writers' Union had resumed the practice of exclusions, rejecting those of its members who deviated from ideological norms. What was new was that now writers themselves decided to leave their union, and they assumed the consequences of such an act. The first example was the resignation of the writer Vladimov, who coldly declared to the Writers' Union in October 1977, "I exclude you from my life."[16] In 1979, a whole group of writers—among them some great names of Soviet literature: Aksenov, Iskander, Akhmadulina—left the Union in turn to affirm their solidarity with the excluded authors of *Metropolis*.

This is far beyond the depoliticization of the intellectuals. From the desire for independence of mind they have moved on to form groups and, finally, to organize their own intellectual order. Soviet hierarchy, is inverted as soon as intellectuals proclaim not only their autonomy but their refusal to be identified with the Soviet writer.

A second form of identification is making its appearance. From heterodox ideas confined to desk drawers to this organized demonstration of discord, a long road has been traveled. A fraction of the Soviet intelligentsia now thinks that *samizdat* is not a second best, designed to replace official publication, but a veritable means of expression which should allow the shaping of opinion outside conformist channels. These publications are also a way of affirming, in the face of the state and its cultural organizations, that the intelligentsia is returning to an autonomous existence and intends to assume the critical role of protest that it has so often played in the course of Russian history. At least three journals attest to this new awareness on the part of the intelligentsia that, to testify, it must possess its own channels of expression. These journals, whose regular periodical appearance is often interrupted by the reactions of the authorities, are distinguished by their ability to be reborn and to persist. The oldest is the *Chronicle of Current Events,*[17] which, despite many interruptions because of repression, has since 1968 succeeded in keeping a diary of the awakening of minds in the

U.S.S.R.; it is closely connected to the Movement for the Defense of Human Rights. The newest is the journal *Poiski* ("Research") launched in August 1978,[18] which has brought together some very different political tendencies—democratic socialists, Christian socialists, non-socialists—in a debate about the Russian future.

Are these innocent dreams of intellectuals? The dreams now have greater scope thanks to techniques of the diffusion of thought. In the early sixties, *samizdat* still resembled the anonymous satires of the nineteenth century; the typewritten texts were difficult to reproduce because private citizens rarely had the necessary equipment, and their circulation remained limited. But *samizdat* has now been transformed into *magnitizdat*, tape recordings which allow rapid reproduction of an abundant clandestine literature. This literature has been developing in two distinct directions: the diffusion of strictly literary works prohibited in the U.S.S.R., or those by definition unpublishable; and a literature providing political information. In the second case, in recent years the information has become very elaborate, covering primarily five areas: limitation of national rights, persecution of religious believers, obstacles to emigration, political use of psychiatry and the general condition of prisoners, and social problems, notably working conditions. From these publications, which will be archives of inestimable value for later historians, there emerges a picture of the U.S.S.R. that bears no resemblance to the image transmitted by the "Soviet writers" and professional journalists in the U.S.S.R. The record for clandestine literature is held by Lithuania, which has twelve different publications. This activity by the intelligentsia explains the violence of the attacks against intellectuals "manipulated by imperialism" and the campaign of ideological mobilization, most strikingly evidenced in the decree of the Central Committee of May 6, 1979.[19]

Despite repeated calls for ideological rigor, pressures, and repression, the balance sheet for clandestine intellectual life in

Brezhnev's U.S.S.R. is impressive. On the fringe of state-controlled and state-serving creation, a whole world of creators has hidden itself from the state and, by its increasingly apolitical attitude, opened its public to *another* universe, far from the dominant political culture. Finally, intellectuals have committed themselves in order to give testimony, to restore to the Soviet people the memory that has been taken from it, to create the archives of a past and a present which have no place in Soviet thought and yet reflect reality. This memory which is being established, recorded, and hidden is also helping slowly to shape opinion.

Religious Loyalties: From Faith to Organization

The "new man" is supposed to have no convictions foreign to Soviet political culture. Religion is not a part of that culture. As for nationalist feeling, the authorities have carefully defined its limits and content. For sixty years, a society has been educated in this way, and the authorities can now measure the success of their enterprise.

To begin with, what has happened to religious faith? After engaging in open warfare against all religions—from 1921 to 1943, their institutions were systematically destroyed—the Soviet authorities granted them a limited right of existence, a status, hoping that the religious indifference of a society educated in Marxism would lead to their spontaneous disappearance. At the time, this optimism was justified by patterns of social behavior. Surveys made after the Second World War of Soviet citizens who had refused to return home in fact gave evidence that religious convictions were regressing rapidly.[20] But as soon as Stalin had died, when behavior was subject to less constraint, the authorities were worried by the religious "survivals" it observed in a part of the population. Liberalization did not affect the domain of religion, and in 1957, Khrushchev, attentive in other areas to social demands, once again launched an attack by the authorities against the church. It was a campaign of a new kind: no longer a question of destroying the churches but, through an intense effort of ideological mobilization, of isolating them from society and showing their uselessness. In the accelerated march toward communism on which Khrushchev engaged his country, there was no room for what he readily called superstition.[21]

At the dawn of a new decade, is the balance sheet of the ideological struggle more positive than it was under Stalinist violence? A preliminary answer can be derived from observation of places of worship. No doubt the number of "working" places of worship, following the Soviet expression, is very small, and this makes the fact that they are crowded much less significant. But the Soviet authorities themselves have been anxiously considering the religious activities of the "new man" and trying to specify what his attitude should be toward religion. A large number of books, opinion surveys, and official declarations have been published in the U.S.S.R. in the last few years, showing the unquestionable existence of a religious problem.[22] One observation comes out from all these materials. Religion, in various degrees, is present in the mind if not in the behavior of an appreciable fraction of the Soviet population. This fraction is not only appreciable because of the number of people who make some room for religion in their system of values but also because of their quality, their age, and their educational level. A recent work devoted to religion and the ideological struggle,[23] while challenging ideas expressed in the West about a "religious revival" in the U.S.S.R. and asserting that the number of believers declines every year,[24] concludes on the basis of surveys that religion has not disappeared in the U.S.S.R. and that, in some regions, from 25 to 30 percent of adults are subject to "religious influence."[25]

What troubles the authorities more than attendance at worship services, which remains a marginal phenomenon, is above all the weakening of anti-religious and a-religious attitudes. All

of Soviet education tends not only to keep individuals away
from religious observance but also to convince them that they
are atheists. But surveys show a distinct evolution of mental
attitudes, or at least of the way in which they are expressed. At
the end of the Stalinist years, a crushing majority if not the
totality of Soviet citizens questioned about their convictions
said they were atheists. Today, in a survey conducted in an
institution of higher education, only 29.4 percent of the students displayed the same certainty.[26] No doubt the number of
those who openly declared themselves to be believers was ridic-
ulously small: 2 percent. But, between these two extremes, 10
percent were in doubt or leaned toward religion, and the majority, though not believers, were neither hostile to nor unaware of the religious phenomenon. Polls conducted in universities and schools confirm this tendency of young people to
reject atheism, even though this rejection may not lead to
clearly expressed convictions. The religious uncertainties of
university and secondary-school students are in themselves surprising, if we consider the influence and psychological pressure
exerted on them by the pioneers' association and the Komsomol.

But the answers are entirely different as soon as we leave this
narrow milieu and turn toward other social strata or religions
other than Orthodoxy. In Georgia, where the Independent Orthodox Church stands as a symbol of national life, there are
often spectacular demonstrations of faith. The Georgian Party
organ gave a good example in reporting how a religious festival
transformed the village of Alaverdi into a veritable center of
pilgrimage, drawing a crowd: "They set up a city of multi-
colored tents to accommodate the crowd, there was a veritable
armada of cars of every description, and a throng of children
waiting to be baptized."[27] In the Ukraine, the secretary of the
Odessa Obkom noted that "although the number of Orthodox
believers seems to have stabilized, the ranks of religious sects
are constantly growing,"[28] and the head of the Ukrainian Party,

Vladimir Shcherbitski, has complained that the Soviet regulation of religions is widely ignored.[29] In Byelorussia, 16 percent
of the urban population and 39 percent of the rural population
openly display their religious convictions.[30] In Lithuania,
predominantly Catholic, three quarters of the population affirm
their faith and, what is more, practice their religion.[31] It is true
in this case that Catholicism and national history are closely
connected, as in Poland. It was Catholicism that enabled the
nation to assert itself and to survive. Similarly, in the peripheral
republics of the south the population generally declares itself to
be Moslem, although sociological surveys show that "being a
Moslem" covers both religious convictions and total indifference to religion, Islam being first of all a means of national
identification.

Behind what the Soviet authorities alternately call "religious
survivals" and "superstitions" there are thus several distinct
phenomena: a certain degree of religious observance, more
frequent in the country than in the city, among Catholics than
among the Orthodox or Moslems, more developed in the old
than in the young, among women than among men—this last
point is true for the Orthodox religion, but in Lithuania the
frequency of observance is about equal between men and
women—religious observance that does not always mean, incidentally, religious faith (in numerous surveys, a portion of the
people questioned have answered that religious observance is
the result of family influence); a certain degree of religious
conviction which is not necessarily accompanied by religious
observance; and, finally, a decline in total indifference to the
religious phenomenon. Moreover, convictions are not always
based on uniform motives. In the case of non-Christian religions, the link between religious identification and national
identification is often very strong. Even among the Orthodox,
religion is often linked with the existence of the nation
(Georgia) or else with the development of an archaizing nationalism infused with religious values (this is now the case for many
Russians).

Whatever the forms adopted by the religious phenomenon in the U.S.S.R., we can agree with the authorities that it is indeed a present tendency of Soviet society, and not a survival. It is significant that the first secretary of the Odessa Obkom referred to the "stabilization" of the number of Orthodox believers, a statement which runs counter to the usual thesis of a religion in the process of disappearing. The authorities are perhaps more troubled by the uncontrollable aspects of the religious phenomenon than by its persistence. The major religions have a well-established status which allows the authorities to follow their activities and to regulate their relationships with the faithful. But the controlled religions are not the only centers of attraction for believers. The innumerable sects,[32] which are beyond all control, have enjoyed very great popular success.[33]

Another particularly interesting aspect of these tendencies is the spread of religious chain letters. For several years, the Soviet authorities have been troubled by circuits of correspondence organized around what is called in the U.S.S.R. "holy letters" (sviatye pisma). These letters are very curious in content.[34] They start with a miracle: the appearance of a young man in white to a young child, ordering him never to forget God. On the basis of the miracle, the letters develop an apocalyptic vision of the imminent end of the world. Copied nine times by the recipients, who are promised eternal happiness for doing so or immediate earthly punishment if they break the chain, these letters are widely distributed in rural areas but also in large cities.[35] They go beyond the bounds of the Christian religions, since there are variants among the Turkomans[36] and the Uighurs.[37]

This phenomenon is interesting in three respects: first of all because, like the success of the sects, it is evidence of the mistrust felt by believers toward the churches accepted by the state. This is particularly true of the Orthodox hierarchy, which —with the authorities' agreement—enjoys a privileged position because of the traditional links between Orthodoxy and the Russian nation. This position was strikingly illustrated in 1978 in the pomp with which the patriarchate celebrated the sixtieth anniversary of its reestablishment.[38] It was indeed an event of national importance. The patriarch pointed out at the time what united the Orthodox Church and the Soviet state, to which he attributed the virtue of having allowed the Church an independent existence, thanks to the decree on the separation between church and state. For many believers, such declarations indicate not sovereignty but the Church's state of dependence on the authorities, and this drives them toward religious structures that are outside state control. Another remarkable aspect of the "holy letters" has to do with the ideas they transmit. The apparition (God himself, according to a Soviet newspaper),[39] the certainty of imminent apocalypse, everything helps to dramatize faith, to cut it off from everyday life, to assert the inanity of earthly agitation in view of the approaching end. If the official religions try to accommodate themselves to the authorities and their ideals, to coexist, the "holy letters" are a complete break with the authorities. Finally, these letters have created networks for the diffusion of ideas that are situated entirely outside the institutional framework. It is not an accident that some articles have referred to the Criminal Code provisions on the diffusion of unacceptable ideas.[40] In a system in which the propagation of ideas is strictly controlled, the letters are a way of getting around the law. For the religious problem lies precisely in its political extensions. The director of religious affairs on the Council of Ministers of the U.S.S.R. has often pointed out that the Soviet regime grants its citizens freedom of conscience, hence the freedom to believe what they are told by any religion at all, but that it recognizes a right to expression in this area only to antireligious propaganda. The chain letters are thus a clever means of getting around this discrimination.

The authorities have especially prohibited the mixture of politics and religion and the use of religion as a political instrument.[41] But this is precisely what is happening today in the

U.S.S.R. The believers have established groups to defend their collective interests or their political rights. In Lithuania, the Catholic Committee for the Defense of Believers, founded in November 1978, has developed the demands of believers (not only of Lithuanian Catholics) concerning religious freedom. These demands, contained in a document proposed for the signature of the Lithuanian clergy, constitutes a veritable charter for the rights of churches, the ministers of worship, and the believers.[42] It is above all a thoroughgoing condemnation of the Regulation on Religious Associations adopted in July 1976 by the Supreme Soviet, which deals with these problems. What the charter demands is that the state have no means, no channel, to intervene in or regulate the life of the churches; that it consider all ministers of worship and their assistants as full citizens (priests have no state pensions); that all children be allowed to receive religious education; and that minors be allowed to be members of religious associations. This program invokes both the Soviet Constitution and canon law because, for the authors of the charter, believers choose their system of reference as they please. This republic-wide group thinks of itself as a structure that is genuinely representative of the interests and demands of believers, and it has affirmed its willingness to cooperate and engage in dialogue with the state to achieve the development of a normal status for believers. This represents a shift from spiritual to organizational unity. This tendency to organize around specific subjects is also found in the Orthodox Committee of Christians for the Defense of Believers, which has declared itself to be nonpolitical and ready to cooperate with the state. But the aim of the cooperation it has offered to the state is to enlarge the place of the churches in the U.S.S.R. and to guarantee to believers total freedom and the means to worship: open churches, a sufficient number of priests, religious education.

The authorities are not mistaken when they detect in these committees real pressure groups[43] and when they denounce their ramifications—small study groups[44] and *samizdat* publications—as organizing tools and means of distributing religious ideas and materials. What is unacceptable to the Soviet authorities is the formation of a group to defend a cause, whatever it may be, and the diffusion through uncontrolled channels of ideas that do not form a part of the political culture of the Soviet citizen. What is unacceptable to them are the collective demands for emigration visas from the Pentecostals, who support their demands with their religious convictions and thus identify themselves as Pentecostals, not Soviets.[45] Also unacceptable are the attitudes of the Seventh-Day Adventists[46] and the Baptists, who have organized themselves into active communities to propagate their convictions, to defend their rights, and especially to assert that their religious choice takes precedence over Soviet norms and the Soviet way of life. In disregard of Soviet regulations, the Baptists give children religious education and keep them out of the pioneers organization so that they will not be exposed to an antireligious ideology. The True Orthodox—separated from the Orthodox Church since 1917, they have refused to accept Soviet principles in religious matters—still live on Soviet territory today totally outside the system. They do not work for the state, do not send their children to school, do not vote, do not go into the army, and refuse to communicate with the rest of Soviet society.[47] Moreover, they don't ask anything from the state either, neither economic aid nor pensions, and they are generally found in the camps. A reading of the Soviet press permits an indefinite extension of this catalog of manifestations of religious feeling in the U.S.S.R., orthodox or heterodox, and of activities of the churches. It indicates the authorities' hesitations about the attitude to adopt in the face of this phenomenon that they no longer deny. Periodically, they worry about the weakness of the educational and ideological system that they consider responsible for the failure of atheism, and at moments they repress the religious activists, as soon as their activity seems about to lead to political action.[48]

Are the vigilance of the authorities and the exasperation demonstrated by political leaders justified? Is religion a disturbing phenomenon in the U.S.S.R, and why? The rise of religious feeling—even if the feelings are confused, even if the phenomenon remains limited—expresses without any doubt the inadequacy of the political culture to answer all the questions people raise and its inability to occupy the entire ideological space. But can the Soviet system, which has accommodated itself to many survivals and persistent loyalties—to the individual plot of land, to patriotism—not accommodate itself as well to religious feeling? It can up to a certain point, no doubt, as is indicated by the coexistence between state and religions established in 1943. But there are aspects of the religious awakening that the Soviet system cannot accept. First of all, it cannot accept ideological competition. Religious feeling as a private matter is acceptable. But when religions, as systems of values, are spread throughout society, when society places Marxism and religion on the same plane and moves from one to the other, this is unacceptable because it means dispossessing Soviet political culture of its absolute value; relativized, it is called into question.

Added to the refusal of competition between ideas is the refusal to allow the formation in society of groups established around particular interests with which they identify themselves. And the various groups of Christians that have been established in the last decade have defined themselves by their religious affiliation and, in the name of that affiliation, have made themselves the defenders of particular rights—religious or political. If the state is particularly troubled by these groups, in themselves hardly dangerous since they do not bring together large crowds, this is because it is badly armed to struggle with the churches and their substitutes. In the tightly knit network of Soviet controls, the churches are, in fact, the only institutions—by virtue of the separation of church and state—that have a certain freedom of action. Places of worship are places where one can gather without prior authorization; ideas can be spread without control through sermons and religious publications. In other words, the only free places of assembly, the only less controlled vehicles for the spread of ideas, are available to the churches alone. They also have channels for access to the authorities and to the outside world. The Moscow patriarchate has substantial international involvement, which it puts at the service of the system,[49] but this is not true for members of the transnational religions—Catholics, Protestants, Jews, Moslems, Buddhists—who have ties and solidarities outside Soviet territory. In certain areas, the Soviet authorities have already taken the measure of the problems created for them by the believers, or those who proclaim themselves to be religious. If the Pentecostals who addressed President Carter were too few to be heard, the Soviet Jewish community owes the emigration visas that are, parsimoniously, granted to it to the support of the Jewish community of the United States. Soviet believers have gradually discovered that they possess exceptional structures to defend their ideas. In spite of the differences between one religion and another and between one church and another, they have in common a system of values that is foreign to the one at the basis of the Soviet regime, and the associations that have been established among Christians indicate that the solidarity of believers in the face of atheism has also made progress. It is these possibilities for organization, for the use of ecclesiastical structures, and the growing identification with an overall system of values based on faith that trouble the authorities, much more than the immediate activities of the religious groups or church attendance. For the present, the authorities see the religious manifestations as an ideological evasion, but they may become a lever for political action in the future. And, if they can in the end accommodate themselves to believers who are "escapees" or "internal émigrés," they cannot accept the hypothesis that the believers' organizations are means of constructing a civil society.

National Loyalties: The Defense of Diversity

Growing religions are not the only rallying points for Soviet society, which until now has been so well integrated by the Party. National loyalties are another path toward difference.[50] As in religious matters, here too the Soviet authorities are held back by the ambiguity of their own policies, a mixture of theoretical egalitarianism that recognizes differences and a practice based on rigorous control of those differences. The constant goal of this practice is to neutralize differences in the short term and abolish them in the long term. This compromise between theory and practice, between a well-defined internationalist program and the demands of reality, between the socialist "substance" and the national "forms" granted to all peoples of the U.S.S.R., had until now encouraged differences rather than the march to unity. In the course of the last ten years, the Soviet authorities have measured the nations' will to survive by considering various kinds of reactions (such as demography, cultural resistance, wish to emigrate, open opposition); they are now showing greater prudence in defining their political perspective and have launched an attack against the various nationalisms through a linguistic battle of unprecedented dimensions. The authorities have attempted to calm the troubled nations about the prospects for the future. The Constitution of 1977 maintained the federal principle which provides a juridical framework for the existence of the nations. And the authorities have kept silent about the plan to establish a "single Soviet nation"[51] while defending the idea of a Soviet *people (sovetskii narod* as opposed to *sovetskaia natsiia)*[52] which is defined in terms of social, not ethnic, unity.[53] The peoples of the U.S.S.R. thus should not dissolve artificially into a single entity which would absorb ethnic and cultural differences; they are called upon to form a community welded together by a shared social and historical development.[54]

But theoretical concessions are balanced by the struggle the

Soviet authorities are conducting in practice to establish Russian as the common language and thereby to weaken cultural differences among the peoples. The role assigned to the Russian language is precise. It is first of all the vehicle for the political ideas of the system. Vladimir Mayakovsky's 1927 poem, "Our Youth," is well remembered in the U.S.S.R. It says that, in all circumstances, "I would have learned Russian/because Russian was the language of Lenin."

The Russian language, because it shapes minds, is a decisive element in the integration of the Soviet people. It is also indispensable to its defense, since the Soviet army uses only that language. And here we touch on one very serious concern of the authorities. The damage caused to national defense by lack of knowledge of Russian has been thoroughly studied in the U.S.S.R. in recent years. How is it possible to use draftees who do not understand the most elementary orders and who, "having learned certain articles of the military regulations by heart, are unable to explain afterward what they have remembered in this way"?[55]

The consequences of the almost total ignorance of Russian among certain peoples are many. The recruits are unusable, so they tend to be shunted into auxiliary tasks, "which affects the morale of draftees . . . leads to repression, and sometimes toward a negative attitude toward military service."[56] The combat readiness of these draftees is affected, and therefore the quality of future combatants and the effectiveness of the army.[57] Moreover, lack of knowledge of Russian makes it impossible to recruit officers from nations wrapped up in their own language, which helps to give the Soviet army—the professional army—too European a coloration, in which certain peoples cannot be found.[58]

In the end, what comes out in many statements and publications on the current state of the Soviet army[59] is the fact that, at a point when the demographic balance is tilting in favor of the non-Russian peoples, when their relative strength in the army is growing, the authorities have realized that recruits who do not understand the common military language are a burden and not an asset to national defense; that, kept apart from military responsibilities, the non-Russians, far from being integrated by the army, develop nationalistic frustrations there; that, finally, non-Russian society can hardly identify with an army whose language is foreign to it and the majority of whose officers are Russian. The correctness of this analysis could be observed when Afghanistan was invaded in 1979. At first, the authorities used primarily non-Russian soldiers in the intervention force, but these soldiers from the republics of central Asia had to be quickly removed and replaced by Europeans, to put a stop to fraternization with the Afghan population.

This explains the campaign that has been undertaken since 1970 to rapidly spread knowledge of Russian to the entire school population. In 1975[60] and 1979,[61] two nationwide conferences brought together the heads of education from all the republics, Party leaders, and leaders of the Komsomol and various cultural establishments to define a general policy for the teaching of Russian to the non-Russian peoples. Between the two conferences, by a decree of October 13, 1978,[62] the Supreme Soviet of the U.S.S.R. set out the measures which were to permit the attainment of genuine bilingualism in the nation. The proliferation of meetings and decisions in the seventies allowed the authorities to give the Russian language a more important place at every level of education. It was to penetrate early education as soon as possible, often as early as kindergarten; intensive courses were established in secondary and technical schools at the expense of other subjects; and there was a proliferation of "Russian" events as a supplement to teaching, like the "Russian days" and the "Olympics of Russian" organized in the republics. Finally, Russian was substituted for foreign languages in higher education. These efforts were supplemented by a considerable effort to improve the pedagogical materials—publications, audiovisual techniques—available to teachers of Russian in non-Russian schools.[63]

The effects of such an intense and extended effort are certain. The census of 1979 and other scattered evidence indicates as much. In the 1979 census, the number of non-Russians who had adopted Russian as their maternal language increased from 13,000,000 (1970) to 16,300,000, and those who were bilingual and knew Russian well from 41,800,000 to 61,100,000.[64] This progress was very significant, greater than had been foreseen. No doubt we must add that linguistic assimilation (a complete shift from the maternal language to Russian) affected especially those peoples who were exposed to it because of the proximity of their language to Russian—Ukrainians and Byelorussians— the peoples who were steeped in a Russian environment—such as Tatars and Chuvashes—and, finally, those who had no national territory of their own. The progress of bilingualism—46 percent from 1970 to 1979—is much more impressive because it was widespread; it affected almost all the peoples of the U.S.S.R. but particularly the peoples of central Asia, unreceptive to Russian ten years earlier but who now, according to the statisticians, had very quickly become bilingual. No doubt we can question certain overly spectacular successes (the progress of bilingualism among the Uzbeks is supposed to have reached 361 percent);[65] nevertheless, it is evident that, in the linguistic field, the Soviet authorities registered results commensurate with the exceptional effort, to which the nationalities had to bow. Information has also come from the republics corroborating these results and emphasizing that bilingualism, naturally enough, is accompanied by an "extension" of the areas in which Russian is now used,[66] and it is also accompanied by a change in the linguistic balance of cultural establishments and the media. Thus, in the Kirghiz, 21 percent of the books published in 1940 were in Russian; that proportion has now reached 50 percent.[67] We can get a precise idea of this campaign to promote Russian in the rather extreme example of Byelorussia, whose minister of education asserted, at the 1979 conference, that "the Byelorussian people have always wanted to master Russian to accede to great Russian culture."[68] In this republic, 61 percent of the students go to schools where the language of instruction is Russian, and, in schools where the language is Byelorussian, the study of Russian—or, rather, studies conducted *in* Russian—occupy thirty-six and a half hours a week; that is, almost all teaching in Byelorussia is now in the Russian language.[69]

Even if the results of the census present a slightly "improved" reality—the *quality* of the knowledge of Russian is another side of the question—this linguistic battle is seen in the republics as a real threat to the survival of the nations. Language remains a privileged means, even if not the only means, for the transmission of national values and the identification with a common culture and a common fate. This explains the fact that the sharpest nationalist reactions have occurred in this area. In the Ukraine, the writer and academician Oles' Honchar publicly proclaimed before the entire Ukrainian Academy of Sciences that, if Russian was the language of friendship and international relations, "Ukrainian, which was forged in the course of centuries by the combined efforts of the masses and the intelligentsia, which was the language of resistance to czarist reaction, has a great future. The Ukrainian language allows us to grasp the fifty volumes of the immortal work of Lenin, to transmit through the ages the imperishable beauty of the works of Homer, and the totality of contemporary knowledge, for example, the encyclopedia of cybernetics."[70]

This declaration, despite the obligatory and brief salute to the Russian language, shows the magnitude of nationalist reactions. Honchar denies all usefulness to the Russian language and any justification for its penetration into the Ukraine, by asserting that the Ukrainian language can transmit everything, Marxist–Leninist thought, world culture, and modern technology. Deprived of its ideological, cultural, and modernizing function, the Russian language is no longer anything but one language among others. Finally, Honchar concluded by calling on his compatriots to protect their "spiritual environment"; he thus openly opposed the official positions and the constantly repeated idea that the use of the Russian language goes far beyond communication between nations and that it is the means "to master and accumulate the accomplishments of contemporary civilization."[71]

This is where the essential debate now lies: between those who advocate the expansion of Russian in the name of its superiority over other languages and who equate russification with modernization, and those who, on the contrary, think that a nation lives because it develops a civilization which is its own and who want to participate in the Soviet universe while preserving their own environment.

Georgia provides perhaps the best example of the current tendencies of the national debate in the U.S.S.R. In 1972, the Communist Party of the U.S.S.R. imposed a change of political personnel on this unruly republic, using as a pretext the generalized corruption that had been prevalent there for a long time. Since then, the new head of the Georgian Party, Eduard Shevarnadze, has carried out a subtle political program that makes him similar in many respects to Janos Kadar, brought to power in Hungary by the Russian invasion of 1956. Like Kadar, Shevarnadze has demonstrated unconditional loyalty to Moscow. He constantly proclaims that Russia has at all times played an emancipating role for his country and affirms the necessity for all Soviet citizens to master the Russian language.[72] Above all, he continues to struggle tirelessly against all forms of corruption by purging the Georgian bureaucracies, particularly the police[73] and judicial[74] apparatus, whose indulgence of or collusion[75] with non-socialist practices seems to be perpetuating itself in the republic. Through these purges, Shevarnadze is trying to replace the traditional image of a corrupt Georgia contemptuous of the rules of Soviet behavior with a new image, that of a model republic where an "absolute social order" reigns.[76]

But this adhesion to the intentions of the central authorities is not without its compensations, all of which have a national content. Armed with the support he gets in Moscow for his attitude, Shevarnadze argues there for developing Georgia's industrial potential.[77] One of the major demands of the various nationalities in fact concerns the economic division of labor within the U.S.S.R. and the specialization of the republics that places them in a situation of total dependence on the center. The Georgians do not want to be reduced to the rank of producers of tropical luxury products (tea, citrus fruits). In return for restoring order to his country, Shevarnadze has asked that they be given the means to engage in diversified economic activity. In Georgia itself, he has accepted the idea that the difficulty of the Georgian language requires an effort of education particularly in the area of teaching the language.[78] And he has assured the intelligentsia that the language will be fostered and will keep an unquestioned place in the development of society.[79] This nationalist attitude is no doubt in contrast with the Party's repeated warnings against "manifestations of nationalist exclusivism and all negative phenomena of the same kind."[80] But we are forced to note that Shevarnadze publicly worries about Georgian demographic decline[81] and has called upon his compatriots to have larger families, in keeping with the Georgian tradition.[82] In spite of the rhetorical precautions with which he surrounds his appeals, behind every proposal he makes can be seen the interest of the Georgian people and its future. In a similar vein, we should point out that Georgian literature published recently through official channels has an astonishingly nationalistic ring. It is dominated by interest in the historical and cultural legacy of the nation and the constantly repeated desire to preserve the society's traditional values. This example indicates that a policy imposed from the center to reduce national particularism can lead to an unexpected expression of what it sought to destroy. Whether or not Shevarnadze has consciously created this, it is clear that his policies have increased national feeling while simultaneously allowing it to express itself.

A final aspect of these manifestations of national feeling is linked to the strength which that feeling can draw, in certain cases, from the outside world. This is true for the Moslem peoples, whose links with Islam outside the country help to encourage particularism, especially since Islam has become an active political force on the Soviet borders. The first precise indications of external influences on Soviet Moslems are recent but extremely significant. They come from the head of the Agitation and Propaganda Department of Turkmenistan. In 1979, a few weeks before the fall of the Shah,[83] he declared that the Turkemenic population near Iran regularly listened to the religious programs broadcast by Radio Gorgan (the station broadcasts from the city of Gorgan, in the Iranian Khorasan). Surveys conducted in Turkmenistan have shown that these broadcasts have helped maintain Islamic convictions and practices. And their impact has been all the greater because they have been recorded and distributed to Moslem communities too distant from the border to listen directly to the broadcasts.[84] This distribution is all the more important because it is not carried out only by mullahs with official status but by religious figures without any status and by the members of the numerous brotherhoods in the U.S.S.R. who participate in this "Moslem news" of foreign origin. In the Islamic lands of the Soviet Union, there has been a growth of the religious propaganda through cassettes that played such a great role in Khomeini's rise to power in Iran. It is worth recalling that Ayatollah Khomeini has shown a definite interest in his Soviet brothers.[85]

It is difficult to be precise about the influence of these broadcasts, but we may be certain that they have had some effect on the minds of listeners. In June 1980, the first secretary of the Turkmen Communist Party, Gapurov, made a public speech in which he emphasized the point.[86] He expressly accused Radio Gorgan and Radio Meshed of indulging in propaganda that developed "nationalist" ideas in the neighboring republics. And he connected religious beliefs with national ideas, for, he said, "they feed one another." He clearly accepts the fact that there are devotees of Allah in the U.S.S.R.: "We have many believers in the republic. We must also keep in mind that our ideological enemies are now very strongly emphasizing the propagation of Islam . . . to enflame the nationalist struggle and to undermine the ideological and political unity of the Soviet people." If we are to believe the first secretary of the Turkmen Party, the problem is all the more serious because believers are not the only ones who are troubled; activists, agitators, propagandists, and other Party auxiliaries have confused unacceptable social values borrowed from religion and the past with the norms of Communist life in society. Is it possible to say more clearly that nationalism based on Islam, far from regressing, has gained ground and that believers are not the only ones concerned?[87] No doubt the different ways of defining attachment to the nation limit, for the moment, the scope of nationalist demands. The Soviet authorities are confronted with scattered national communities. But on two points they have frustrations—indeed, demands—that are identical. They all want a more balanced national life—that is, more autonomous. Isn't this the demand within the Socialist camp which drove Rumania to oppose the U.S.S.R.? All of them also refuse to be stripped of their culture. And here the consequences of the progress achieved by the Soviet authorities in bilingualism, or even linguistic assimilation, may be harmful either to the integrity of the nations or to the U.S.S.R. For the moment, the reactions in the Ukraine and Georgia seem to indicate that this progress stirs up nationalist feeling rather than eroding it.

The Workers: Tomorrow's Protestors?

The ideas and behavior of the working class—the most numerous element in Soviet society—are difficult to define because the data that would enable us to study them are lacking. However, there is no lack of evidence pointing to moments of agitation in the working class; and the activism of the Polish working class in 1970 and 1980 indicates that workers' discontent is a reality in the socialist countries.

The situation of the working class in the Soviet Union can be characterized by certain distinctive traits. First of all, there was a change in the statutes. The war decrees that chained workers to their jobs were abolished in 1956, and workers then acquired great freedom of movement. They could leave a job as they pleased and take work wherever they wished. The manpower needs in the developing regions—Siberia, the far north—and, beginning in the seventies, the general manpower shortage encouraged worker mobility, which had reached 20 percent by the end of the decade—that is, every year one worker out of five changed jobs.[88] Absenteeism, instability, resignations without warning were disorganizing factory life.

Inequality is another aspect of working-class life. A rigid barrier separates skilled from unskilled workers. Wages from one category to another, from one industrial sector to another, and finally from one region to another are very different. In addition, wages have been raised on several occasions, notably in 1979.[89] The average monthly wage of the industrial worker in 1979 was 176 rubles (in construction, 191 rubles), that of a laborer approximately 100 rubles, but on the Baikal–Amur railroad the average worker earned 360 to 370 rubles, and the highly skilled got as high as 500 rubles.[90]

Finally, the working class is difficult to define because it is constantly incorporating peasants, for whom the urban and industrial world is synonymous with better living conditions. Since 1974, peasants have had the right to hold an internal passport; they can leave the countryside and have thus escaped from the servile position they were in until then. Without skills, they accept the lowest-paid jobs in the cities, but this is nevertheless definite progress in their eyes, even though the authorities, through social measures and improvement of the rural environment, have been attempting to keep them in the country.

Despite the increase in status and the material progress of the last two decades, and despite a great weakening of discipline, Soviet workers demonstrate genuine and growing discontent when they are questioned. Thus, in a survey conducted in 1968, 54 percent of the workers complained about the inadequacy of their wages. In 1973, after several raises, the discontent in this respect had reached 66 percent. Moreover, 70 percent of the workers complained about working conditions, and 28 percent expressed a negative judgment on their entire existence.[91]

The measures taken by the government in 1979–80 to improve the functioning of the economy have every likelihood of distinctly increasing the more or less openly expressed frustrations. The authorities have in fact decided to reinforce controls over the workers, to put an end to absenteeism and especially to limit the mobility of manpower. The economic reform of July 1979[92] provides, among other things, for the organization of workers into brigades (the Zlobin method), which is a means of supervising and controlling them more effectively. A decree of January 1980 restored labor discipline by providing for a series of severe sanctions for lateness, idleness on the job, and unjustified absences.[93] This toughening of working conditions coincided with a toughening in the attitude of the leaders. In 1979, in order to improve production, Chernenko called for "very strict discipline in production,"[94] and he pointed out the working-class virtues necessary for economic success: Stakhanovism, producing more than the plan, workers' enthusiasm, discipline, ideological inspiration.[95] It is remarkable that he mentioned only moral, not material, stimulants.

To what degree can the working class be satisfied with these calls for order and work? To what extent can it accept a substantial reduction in the freedom it has enjoyed? A movement of workers' protest is still difficult to imagine, because the working

class has no cohesion but is dispersed into many groups separated by differences in education, skills, and wages. Moreover,
it has no experience of autonomous organization, for the unions
are primarily organs of production. Even though they are supposed to defend the interests of the working class, those interests are understood as "dependent on the progress of production."

The creation in February and October of 1978 of two workers' movements that presented themselves as free unions was
a significant demonstration of worker discontent. For these
were not initiatives of the intelligentsia but a movement that
genuinely originated in the working class. The first union, the
Association of Free Unions of Workers of the Soviet Union, was
founded by a miner named Klebanov, who brought together
unemployed workers and appealed simultaneously to international labor organizations and the Soviet public authorities to
manifest its existence and explain its aims. The founders of the
free union pointed out that every initiative on the part of the
workers to establish organizations that really defended their
interests—that is, outside the official unions—was immediately
punished in the U.S.S.R. and transformed those involved into
unemployed workers. This union was thus a grouping of those
who demanded an autonomous role for the workers and those
who had already paid for that demand with their jobs and even
their freedom.[96] Quickly neutralized by police action (Klebanov was sent to a psychiatric hospital), this first union was immediately replaced by the Free Interprofessional Association of
Workers (SMOT), which held a press conference in Moscow on
October 28, 1978. The essential difference between the Klebanov union and SMOT, which also originated with the workers,
was that the organizers of SMOT had more political experience
than their predecessors. Some founders of SMOT—like Vladimir Borisov—had already had political activities in the past, and
the movement could rely on the journal *Poiski,* thus gaining the
advantages of a means of expression and support from the intel-

ligentsia. The founders of SMOT were, above all, able to draw a lesson from the union experience of their precedessors and could thereby attempt to provide more effectiveness and security for their organization. Unlike its predecessor, which had published a list of candidates for a possible free union election, SMOT made public only the names of the eight members of its council, concealing the identity of other adherents and sympathizers. In order to protect them, it also adopted an organization of small groups, concentrated in Moscow and Leningrad. But, as in other cases, tape recordings have enabled SMOT to reach distant sympathizers, for whom the union has prepared a veritable syllabus of political and union education.

We must simultaneously avoid exaggerating the impact and underestimating the importance of these working-class initiatives. No doubt these are extremely limited steps: a few hundred people meeting in the largest industrial cities. These groups are, moreover, very vulnerable, because of the effectiveness of the KGB but also because of the mobilization of the working class by the authorities, which removes every immediate possibility that the workers will hear the protestors.

But with these reservations, we must take the full measure of the event. Despite the brutal halt produced by the arrest of the chief identified leaders of the two unions, it is remarkable that as soon as the first union was annihilated a replacement appeared. As limited as the number of workers interested in establishing free unions may be, it has now been proved that a desire for change on this point exists and that, to bring it about, men are capable of confronting the loss of work and especially the loss of freedom. Moreover, these unions, by their very existence, however ephemeral and threatened it may have been, raised the question of the state's right to identify itself with the workers. They showed that the unity of Soviet society was a myth, that the conflict between Party-State and workers still exists in the first of the socialist societies. The union leaders being called schizophrenics, and the Soviet press denouncing

free unions as an "imperialist and anti-Soviet maneuver fo-
mented in a foreign country,"[97] cannot conceal the fact that the
paternalist attitude of the Soviet state toward its workers has
now been called into question within the working class of the
U.S.S.R. The idea of union freedom, of free elections with candidates chosen by the working class and not imposed by the social
organizations, has penetrated, though weakly, into Soviet society.

Once the idea has moved on and reached other socialist countries, or even imposes itself, as in Poland, the repression of the
embryonic free unions in the U.S.S.R. counts less for the future
than do the seeds that have been planted and the echo of outside events. The attempts to create free unions in the U.S.S.R.
are first of all an indication of working-class frustrations and of
the existence among the workers of a small fringe of politically
conscious elements who are ready for action.

Beyond this evidence, there is the question of the extension
of the movement to the Soviet working class. Can it mobilize
and become an active force? Its great weakness is its lack of
unity, increased by the constant arrival of peasant elements in
its midst. This heterogeneity of the working class has engen-
dered a great degree of political indifference rather than conscious adhesion to the current system. Surveys conducted
among the workers give evidence of this and show what fraction of the working class would be permeable to agitation. What
comes out is the difference in attitude and curiosity between
the unskilled workers, whose educational level is low, and the
skilled workers, who have received a more extended education
(eight years of schooling or partial secondary education). The
former readily declare that they are not very interested in
sociopolitical activities and know very little of the economic
reforms that directly concern them. Thus 63 percent of the
workers questioned in Taganrog who had gone to school for
only four years answered that they hadn't the slightest idea
about the content of the reforms.[98] Moreover, they showed no

desire to be informed. On the other hand, the attitude of workers who had received at least some secondary education was entirely different. More than 90 percent of them were aware of the reforms that concerned them and ready, according to other surveys—in Kharkov, for example—to participate (around 80 percent) in sociopolitical activities.[99] The content of family libraries reveals the same imbalance. Almost all the skilled workers questioned in the Ukraine said that they had political works at home and that they subscribed to newspapers, while only a third of the unskilled workers had their own books, which were almost never political.[100] These surveys, and we could provide many more examples, point to two realities: the heterogeneity of the working class and a division based on education, which is generally linked to a division of generations. The extension of an eight-year program of secondary education suggests that the category of less-educated workers covers the older age groups. The younger workers are better educated and more politically interested. If a politicization of the working class takes place outside the official structures, it will happen in this part of the working class, because their political curiosity is greater and because these young, relatively well-educated workers are not satisfied with their social condition. Their education is often too advanced for the jobs they fill. Their feeling of being declassed in the world of work is real, all the more so because manual labor enjoys no prestige, even when the wages rewarding it are high. No doubt the extension of the Zlobin method to all of industry is designed, among other things, to interest workers directly in their work by giving particular responsibilities and a certain autonomy to each brigade.[101] But is is doubtful that this will be enough to calm the frustrations of young well-educated workers who confront a working world in which stratification is becoming more pronounced, chances of promotion are diminishing, and the restoration of discipline has imposed many constraints. We should finally remember that, if the older generations of workers can compare their present condition to the stifling universe of Stalinism, the generation of those under thirty compares the climate of discipline and moral order in the process of being restored to the laxity of recent years, and balances the current economic stagnation of the U.S.S.R. against the rapid growth of the seventies.[102] In this context, as well, the reasons for discontent are decisive. It is thus in this young segment of the working class, educated, only slightly or not at all marked by a tragic past, that there may arise a coherent set of demands, and we must not forget that advance signs of this have already appeared.

The apparent stability and unanimity of Soviet society should not totally deceive us. There is no doubt that the society is perfectly supervised, disciplined, and unanimous in its manifestations of support for the authorities. The newspapers give substantial space to this "voice" of society, which vigorously demands the condemnation and rejection of those who, by thinking differently, have excluded themselves from the Soviet universe. There were untold miners from Donets, kolkhozniks lost in the distant countryside, or modest workers from Leningrad or Rostov-on-Don who wrote to *Pravda* or *Izvestia* to express "popular anger against Pasternak's 'betrayal' " or, later, that of the academician Sakharov.[103] If we compile these innumerable manifestations, we might conclude that the unity of Party and people is total and that manifestations of discord are only signs of individual imbalance that deserve more pity than indignation.

However, this preliminary conclusion based on widespread patterns of social behavior must be corrected in the light of other patterns of the same magnitude. Soviet society is the victim of social evils condemned by the Party, the magnitude and growth of which are attested to not only by *samizdet* publications and the testimony of observers but also by the Soviet authorities themselves. Rising criminality is one aspect of this situation. However, we will not consider it here as an instance of behavior foreign to the "new man" because it is part of the urban landscape of all industrial societies, and the rapid industrialization of the U.S.S.R. has come at that price. Two mass phenomena are, on the other hand, characteristic of contemporary Soviet society and at odds with its norms: alcoholism and perpetual fraud.

Let us begin with alcoholism, whose ravages are impressive. Traditionally a masculine pattern, alcoholism has now spread among women. It has been responsible for untold work accidents and family dramas. The Soviet authorities have attempted to reduce it by constantly increasing the price of alcohol. The measures that increase work discipline provide for the repression of drunkenness at the workplace. But what gives a real measure of this social plague is the existence of specialized institutions, the drunk tanks, which take in the drunks picked up on public streets every day. Even more significant is the integration of the struggle against alcoholism into the governmental organs. It is remarkable that, in the government of the Russian Federated Republic, there is now a Committee to Combat Alcoholism[104] which is in the same institutional category as the Committee for Popular Control. This widespread alcoholism is a sign of flight from everyday life into another universe; even if it does not express social discord, it at least indicates widespread dissatisfaction. And the extension of the phenomenon, despite economic obstacles and the constant mobilization of propagandists and educators on the subject, clearly shows the limits of their influence.

Widespread fraud is another aspect of Soviet society. Soviet society, perpetually and at every level, cheats the state: on hours of work, on public resources—robbing the state is robbing no one—with statistics, with accomplishment of planning goals, and so on. Usually the state closes its eyes to ordinary fraud, for it is a means of survival. From time to time, it discovers major perpetrators of fraud and represses them, sometimes going as far as the death penalty. But it also sometimes integrates into its system elements that are halfway between resourcefulness and fraud and yet are indispensable to its functioning. Thus the *tolkach* [105]—an intermediary between factories and the administration, charged with obtaining for factories, in any way, through the most questionable methods, authorizations, capital goods, or spare parts allowing them to operate—long looked on with suspicion and considered in any case an unacceptable excrescence of the economic system, is being integrated into the system and acquiring respectability and status.[106] The oscillations and empirical approach of the authorities toward perpetual fraud limit neither its use nor its meaning. Every Soviet citizen knows that, to be safe, one must know the limits within which fraud is possible. And it can be said that fraud is as stratified as society, that every level of status has corresponding particular practices and frequency. Fraud also has a geography, and in certain republics, notably in the Caucasus, it is linked to a long tradition. This is why fraud and the wish to challenge the central authorities are readily confused, and repression of fraud is then seen as an attack on national rights. But from one republic to another or from one milieu to another, it remains true that a-socialist behavior is the rule in the U.S.S.R., which is another index of the distance that separates the "new man" from his living double. Soviet man is a double man,[107] and the unanimity we have been discussing has to do with only one side of these double men.

What alcoholism, cheating, the dualities of Soviet man, and even criminality show is the existence of deep flaws in the social consensus. But these flaws are often not seen as flaws by those concerned, nor are they articulated. Revealing as they are of the limits of social transformation, these human "defenses" lead to no organization of society; rather, they tend to calm it down. Alcohol and fraud are outlets for, just as much as they are signs of, frustration.

The case is entirely different for the more or less explicitly expressed manifestations of discord represented by the dissidence or indifference of intellectuals, the awakening of religious consciousness, the rallying to national symbols, and the first hesitant steps of an independent unionism. What all these manifestations have in common is that they set forth a system of values and signs of identification that are not those of Soviet political culture. All of them claim to separate two ideological spheres, that of power, which they do not necessarily call into question, and the domain of personal choices and loyalties. These manifestations have therefore introduced into the Soviet universe the seeds of ideological pluralism, which are unacceptable in a system whose raison d'être is monolithic control of ideas and a monopoly of authority. These signs of discord, as weak and scattered as they may be, take away the regime's legitimacy based on the unanimous adhesion of society which it is constantly attempting to organize, for they demonstrate that this adhesion is neither unanimous nor certain.

Finally, what is new in the disagreement are the attempts made to organize it. Those who "think differently," in every domain, have gradually moved from the stage of solitary, individual dissent to the desire to make this discontent explicit and to bring together, around the ideas thus brought out, other minds in search of change. Making things explicit and gathering together are first steps, but decisive ones, on the path of political action. As soon as individuals come together around interests and ideas with which they identify, a society is no longer entirely unformed or amorphous; we can glimpse in it the seeds of a civil society. The gathering in fact permits the expression of demands, the attraction of new sympathies, and eventual access, through pressure or dialogue, to the closed sphere of power. Soviet society is without doubt still far from being a civil society capable of standing up to the authorities, but we can detect in it elements that are favorable for such an evolution.

We need hardly recall that Russian history, more than that of any other country, has been characterized by an extraordinary social passivity but that, sporadically, storms have arisen from the depths of this immobile society, threatening each time to sweep away the government, and that in 1917, with the help of external circumstances, they definitively destroyed it. History does not repeat itself, no doubt, but every society has deeply rooted traditions, and the recent history of the U.S.S.R. shows that Soviet society is made up of "new men" who remain fiercely attached to old ways.

CONCLUSION

To the present-day historian who witnesses an event, the event seems decisive at first. But with time the event often loses meaning, so much so, on some occasions, that it fades from memory. The fall of Khrushchev in 1964 echoed throughout the world like a thunderclap, even though his departure seemed at the time more important than the rise to power of a group which was expected to be merely a transition. Nearly two decades later, the feeling of the moment has been confirmed by the facts. October 1964 was indeed a capital date in the political history of the Soviet Union. On that date an epoch began, characterized by exceptional domestic stability, the extreme personalization of power, and the international transformation of the U.S.S.R. from a regional power into a global superpower. If the tendencies defining the evolution of the U.S.S.R. after October 1964 are clear, if the importance of October 1964 is unquestionable, one question remains: What was the real meaning of that date and the following period? In other words, was 1964 a radical break in Soviet history, the opening of a new path, or was it simply the movement from one known policy to another within the framework of a cyclical history characterized by fundamental continuity?

Brezhnev's manifest authority, the pursuit of dissidents, and external expansion have all inspired judgments without nuances. After Khrushchev's "thaw," the Brezhnev era is thought of as a mere return to Stalinist "glaciation." Yet there is a great distance between Stalinism and the present Soviet system, and there is nothing in its operation or its evolution that appears to be leading again to Stalinism.

Stalin's power was characterized by personal dictatorship, voluntarism, total arbitrariness in his relations with the political elite as well as with society, and finally by the fact that everything was unpredictable. Soviet power is now, and has been for nearly two decades—education is very important here because it weighs in favor of stability—exercised by an oligarchy that speaks in the name of the only Party and, in many respects, really represents it. This oligarchic power is based on several elements.

First is the preservation at the top of the pyramid of a coherent group—the permanent core of the Politburo—installed since 1964 and held together by the desire to perpetuate its power by blocking any alternate solution. This coalition has been able to last because of its agreement on a few essential points that define the rules under which power functions at this supreme level. It has reserved the power of decision, but it exercises it collectively. A certain unanimity is necessary, even if there has been debate, at the moment when a decision is made and publicized. Moreover, Brezhnev has pointed out that the Politburo votes very rarely, that discussion lasts as long as necessary to reach a consensus.[1] Under Khrushchev, on the contrary, when the Presidium was divided, voting was a common practice.[2] The unanimity that reigns in the coalition has allowed it to put to the fore a leader who represents it, embodies its solidarities, but who threatens at no point to overwhelm it. In the period beginning in 1964, the personalization of power by the general secretary of the Party was evidence of the Party's general authority and the unity and harmony of those who were at the top. Brezhnev's power flows from the confidence of his peers, he is limited by them, and he is finally the embodiment of the coalition's consensus. Moreover, successes and failures are now associated with the whole system much more than with the man who embodies it. Brezhnev has emerged from the political elite as its representative, as the embodiment of the power of the U.S.S.R., but his personal prestige, with the passions that might excite, is far from reaching what Khrushchev enjoyed, not to mention Stalin.

This consensus around the leader and in decision making is based on the refusal to confront problems that create conflicts, where a compromise would be difficult to reach. In 1964, the coalition gave itself a first goal of preserving the collegial spirit that had united it and brought it to power; this implied the absence of fundamental debates and hence a systematic pragmatism instead of utopian projects that generate divisions; it also implied the recognition of the role and the interests of each member of the coalition.

The second basis for the oligarchic power established in the U.S.S.R. in 1964 was the link between the coalition and the major bureaucracies. The members of the supreme leadership of the U.S.S.R. and reached the summit because they represented bureaucracies, not because of their personal qualities. The Politburo was no longer a gathering of people struggling to increase their area of competence, or their influence, but the place where the various bureaucratic apparatuses were represented and their interests taken into account and balanced. Does this mean that Soviet power has evolved toward institutional pluralism—that is, toward equitable representation of the apparatuses? There is no doubt that this is not the case. In this system, the Party remains the integrating element. It is inside the Party, and first of all in the Politburo, that the different bureaucracies reach the sphere of power. The Politburo is the arbitrator among bureaucratic interests, but the Party exercises this arbitration. It is important to note that, when Brezhnev, general secretary of the Party, was absent from the Politburo, the sessions were presided over by Suslov or Kirilenko—that is, by the two men who followed Brezhnev in the hierarchy of the Party and not by the head of government or the head of state (before Brezhnev was appointed to this position). The preeminence of the Party hierarchy over all the apparatuses of the Soviet state is clearly demonstrated. The Party thus assumes its authority over the bureaucracies, which it associates with power through the *nomenklatura,* which gives it control over their leaders.

The third basis for this power was the recognition of the aspirations of the bureaucratic elites. In 1956, Khrushchev had started the system along this road, but because of the incoherences of his choices he had quickly lost the support of those elites. By calling for the constant circulation of elites, by alternately relying on different ones (the military, regional or national elites, and so on), by playing one against the other, he had quickly re-created among them a feeling of insecurity—insecurity about their jobs, no longer physical insecurity—which finally drove them to revolt against him.

The Brezhnev coalition, born of these frustrations and fears, has provided security for the elites. The absence of important conflict-laden decisions has considerably helped in this respect. The reforms carried out over the years have taken account of existing advantages while simultaneously allowing for the rise of newcomers. Two examples give evidence of this. The enlargement of the Central Committee, traditionally used to eliminate enemies, has been used since 1964 to promote cadres who were marking time, while keeping in place those who already belonged to the body. The program of investment in underdeveloped agricultural regions of the R.S.F.S.R. opened the doors of the Central Committee to the secretaries of the obkoms in the regions benefiting from the plan, and it thereby increased the representation of the group as a whole in the Party's parliament. Almost all decisions taken have thus stabilized existing situations and provided for a certain enlargement of the elites. In this respect, the Brezhnev group has served the privileged well. It has restored certain privileges abolished by its predecessor. Especially, it put an end to the utopian idea that it was necessary to return to a certain egalitarianism by limiting privileges and renewing those who had access to privileges by the rotation of cadres. Since October 1964, the elites have known that the jobs and the privileges connected to them are guaranteed. The consequences of such a choice are clear. The stability of the Brezhnev years has allowed the flourishing of powerful elites, sure of themselves and attached to their status, its advantages, and the possibility of reproducing themselves. These elites support the coalition in power because they owe it their own share in power and the stability of their positions. This is the basis for their loyalty to the leaders of the U.S.S.R. But this loyalty is conditional. The elites wish to be shielded from any initiative, any change that would threaten their positions and their ability to reproduce themselves. The power of the leaders runs up against its limits at that point. Their choices must coincide with the interests of the bureaucratic elites, and the surest means to accomplish this is to avoid great changes, radical decisions that necessarily call particular interests into question. This consensus within the ruling group and between the group and the elites assures it of great security, but it also condemns the group to immobilism. It can only manage what exists and is accepted by everyone.

If we consider the evolution of the Soviet political system for almost two decades, we can distinguish two periods that complement one another. The first runs from 1964 to 1976. It was marked by the institutionalization of collective power, of the representation of the bureaucracies underlying that power, and of its procedures. There was thus established a system that is difficult to define if we rely on the categories of Western political thought, a system that Alec Nove has baptized "centralized pluralism." Even though the term "pluralism" may produce misunderstandings, it has the virtue of expressing a tendency toward the representation of different bureaucratic groups with distinct interests on particular points. This tendency is especially clear on economic matters and questions of management. In the early seventies, a discussion developed in the U.S.S.R. that separated politics from economics and concluded that the rapidity of scientific and technical progress made it necessary to grant broad autonomy to those who had genuine competence to manage the economy or the administration. Was this the beginning of the age of managers? The creation of an Institute for the Administration of the National Economy in 1971 and the growing influence of Kosygin's son-in-law, Gvishiani, suggested as much. Certain writers went so far as to propose that managers be recruited by competition, on the basis of their competences, thus implicitly calling into question the principle of the *nomenklatura* and hence the Party's ability to maintain its control and its criteria in the choice of leaders. The Party itself seemed for a moment to encourage the promotion of competent professionals, to whom it opened its ranks.

But beginning in the middle of the decade—and the Twenty-fifth Congress showed its effects—the second stage opened in which the Party clearly showed *who* held power. Increased prominence of the general secretary (personalization of power developed during this phase) and the concentration in his hands of state functions and supreme military authority emphasized that power was a matter for the Party and that it dominated every apparatus. The Constitution of 1977 pointed in the same direction when it affirmed—and this is the first time that such a specification has been found in a fundamental state document —that the Party was the leading force of the U.S.S.R. The Party's authority was also asserted in the debate on political criteria and competence. Political criteria won out everywhere; Mikhail Suslov frequently pointed out that Party spirit—*partiinost'*—was the first element in determining the ability to assume responsibilities in whatever area. The Party's policy on cadres reflected this new insistence on its primacy. The Party expressed confidence above all in those who had behind them a long career in the apparatus. But this did not mean that they were incompetent bureaucrats, for the Party's recruits were the best educated, and it insisted on the technical training of its cadres, thereby having leaders at the decisive levels—especially regional—who were both apparatchiks and specialists well trained in the concrete problems they had to deal with.[3] The "professionalization" of the Party, which had been carried out at one stage by an opening to the world of the professionals, was continued, but from the inside.

The evolution of the Soviet political system since 1964 has not been anodyne. The system has progressed toward collegiality, the continued reduction of personal power (despite a parallel personalization of power), and guaranteed security for everyone participating in the system. No doubt, on one fundamental point, the Soviet system has not managed to grow beyond childhood: its inability to establish a normal, known, regular system of succession. Aside from this weakness, progress toward institutionalization has been definite. However, this progress—and this is an essential characteristic of the Soviet system—has taken place *within the sphere of power* and within Soviet political culture. It concerns only those who participate in power and has not changed the power relations with society.

Here, too, elements of change have appeared which have had different effects, depending on the time in question. After 1964, the Soviet authorities remained loyal to their refusal to resort again to terror. But this choice, which has profoundly changed social patterns of behavior—the disappearance of discipline in the area of work is one example—implied a new type of relationship with a society which, liberated from fear, had begun to express its material needs and sometimes its desire for greater freedom. The continuous development of social mobilization was one answer by the authorities to this problem. By multiplying organs of popular participation and calls to participate, the authorities attempted simultaneously to gain permanent knowledge of the aspirations and reactions of the rank and file, to include as many of these as possible in their decisions, and to restrain and control social movements. At no point in Soviet history has social participation been so extensive and multifarious, nor have the authorities ever so clearly explained its goals and limits. They have paid particular attention to popular demands having to do with the material needs of society. Austerity has long ceased to be a virtue that mobilizes Soviet citizens. Hence, this ruling group has made efforts to resolve the most urgent economic problems. The five-year plan adopted in 1966 had less grandiose objectives than those put forth by Khrushchev—"to catch up with and go beyond the United States"—but it indicated a recognition of the defects in the Soviet economic system and the fact that attention was being paid to the consumer. However, the desire to respond to social needs still remained within the confines of the requirement of safeguarding the system's essential principles: centralism, permanent priority accorded to heavy industry and military production, and, after 1964, a concern to protect the authority of political cadres. The Soviet authorities have thus oscillated between an inclination toward economic realism and the inertia of the system. All their reforms have attempted to combine these two preoccupations. The economic reform of 1965 associated local initiative of factories with the system of centralized and authoritarian planning. The reform of April 1973 on industrial associations was first of all a recognition of the failure of the 1965 reform, which had everywhere come up against bureaucratic inertia. The reform of 1979, which attempted once again to improve the functioning of the economy, was enclosed within the same dilemma: how to encourage initiative without removing any authority from the organs of central power. This perpetual debate between the priorities of the system and the interests of society has weakened the impact of a policy that was generally reasonable. The allocation of resources to the forgotten sectors of light industry permitted some slight increase and improvement in consumer-goods production. But these efforts were totally inadequate, because the authorities at the same time preserved the traditional priority granted to sector A. The improvements that resulted at first comforted society and then, because they were far below social needs, exasperated consumers' frustrations.

Agriculture, a perennial problem for Soviet leaders ever since the revolution, has been another field of action for the Brezhnev group, which has attempted both to make peace at last with the peasantry and to improve production. Many measures have been taken to establish peace between the authorities and the countryside.[4] There have been such substantial investments in agriculture that Alec Nove has written that "in contrast to the time when agriculture was exploited for the benefit of industry, it has now become a major burden on the rest of the economy."[5]

The material advantages and improvements in status conceded to the peasants are the central elements in this policy of reconciliation. Production turned over to the state is paid at a higher rate; the kolkhozes, whose contribution to the life of the consumer is essential (they still provide 60 percent of the potatoes, 30 percent of the vegetables and dairy products, 35 percent of the eggs),[6] have had their conditions of existence closely aligned with those of the sovkhozes. Kolkhozniks now have a guaranteed minimum wage and a system of insurance and pensions. The state has also recognized more and more directly that the private sector in agriculture has its place in the Soviet economy; the Constitution of 1977 refers to it, as does Leonid Brezhnev in the *Trilogy* that earned him the Lenin Prize for literature. In fact, he wrote that "a peasant who has no land is a tree without roots."[7]

In 1969, the authorities even created a particular structure of participation for peasants on cooperatives, the Council of Kolkhozes, which operates at various territorial levels—republic, region, district—and, in principle, allows the representatives of this sector of agriculture to communicate with and possibly to participate in the economic administration of the corresponding level.

Finally, the issuance of internal passports to the peasants has put an end to their serflike situation and made them full citizens.

However significant they may have been, these reforms were not enough to resolve the problems weighing on the U.S.S.R. The peasants' new rights did not reconcile them to life in a countryside that had lost its material and spiritual framework. Moreover, the authorities, in this case too, were unable to carry their decisions out to the full. They wanted to reassure the peasants, win them over, but at the same time integrate the countryside more fully into the Soviet way of life. The agricultural units—sovkhozes and kolkhozes—were afflicted with overexpansion;[8] urbanization of the countryside continued inexorably, transforming rural areas into pitiful substitutes for cities; the future lay in the agricultural city, the *agrogrod.* It is easy to understand why the peasants, once they were granted freedom of movement, fled the countryside, whose social landscape had been disfigured and in the long run condemned, to go to what was still the model, the real city. Agricultural production declined because of the desertion of young and active elements; at the end of the chain, the consumers became aware that the state was incapable of providing continuous economic progress. After a few years, every reform led to a dead end. And these dead ends were unavoidable, because the reforms were based on a desire to resolve the problems without touching on their essential sources: centralization, initiative in the hands of the bureaucracies alone, and the refusal to let society as a whole participate in the management of its interests. This choice on the part of the Soviet authorities has had inevitable consequences. All the reforms have awakened hopes; their mitigated success or their semi-failure has increased frustrations and social demands.

Two responses were possible. First, there might have been profound reforms in every area, loosening the grip of centralization and granting some degree of initiative and power to the entire social body. Such a reformism would have changed the system and attacked the rights and privileges of the ruling class. This is why the Soviet authorities, shaken by the timid steps taken in this direction between 1953 and 1964, have totally refused the reformist road. The logic of the coalition established in 1964, its bureaucratic foundation, and the support of the apparatuses are precisely this refusal to change the system. The other possibility was a pure and simple return to coercion, and the Brezhnev group could not consider that either. Coercion could not fit in with the growing institutionalization of power and the security that the ruling class had managed to guarantee for itself. Security of power was linked to a change in the means of relating to society. Refusing both reformism and constraint, the authorities have condemned themselves to absolute immobility. After having demonstrated a certain dynamism, the Soviet system has become totally blocked.

How can this blockage be justified, in the face of social demands that are expressed more or less clearly? The Brezhnev period is not only characterized by an evolution toward immobility, but also by the general progress of society and its awareness. Widespread education, fading fear, the many signs of hesitation on the part of the authorities, news from outside, all have helped to change social patterns of behavior. If the mass of Soviet citizens does no more than grumble, it is obvious that it has been doing so more and more strongly. The discontent aroused by their inability to respond to everyday needs is obvious in all statements. But popular grumbling is a phenomenon that has already been left behind because of the emergence from society of groups expressing these discontents who are seeking for means of organizing them in order to influence the political system. Society, passive as it may still remain, has noted the existence of these groups. It has noticed especially that

demands articulated by groups and not by individuals sometimes have positive results. The right to emigrate, even if it is
limited and paid for very dearly by those involved, has been
acquired by the Jewish community and even by Germans, because they met together, formulated common interests, and
looked for external support. The fact that the Pentecostals, so
disarmed in every other way, have understood this lesson so
well that they have formed a group and addressed the President of the United States indicates that the idea of autonomous
grouping as a method of action has made progress in the
U.S.S.R.

Soviet citizens have glimpsed the fact that the structures of
participation established by the authorities have as their goal
the transmission only of the social demands the authorities can
accept. This is why the idea of independent unions, capable of
presenting unsupervised demands and hence of mobilizing
working-class society in structures of participation in competition with the official structures has no place in the Soviet
scheme of things. The rapidity and harshness with which union
attempts of this kind have been repressed contrast with the
hesitation of the authorities when there is a question of breaking the activity of isolated dissidents.

How can this better-educated society still be made to accept
a system which is incapable of listening to its demands and
resolving its problems? The absurdity of this situation is striking.
When it confiscated power more than sixty years ago, the Party
invoked its historic mission—it was the bearer of social progress
—and the backwardness of society. In the decade of the eighties, the Party is incapable, in order to safeguard its power, of
accomplishing the slightest progress, while an advanced society
remains stripped of power which it would be able to use for its
benefit.

On what kind of legitimacy can the Soviet leaders now call?
Max Weber catalogued three types:[9] charismatic legitimacy,
based on the total authority of one man; rational-legal legiti-

macy, which appeals to the conviction that the established system and its rules are based on legality; and, finally, a legitimacy based on tradition. The Soviet system experienced a period of charismatic legitimacy at the beginning, under Lenin, father of the revolution and founder of the system. Stalinist legitimacy was more complex. It filled the mold of the charisma inherited from Lenin, because Stalin set himself up as Lenin's only true heir and killed all his possible competitors, because he based his authority on that of the Party, with which he fully identified, and finally because he laid claim to a historic mission as modernizer and founder of the first socialist state in the world. Stalin's successors wanted to rely on rational-legal legitimacy, by restoring the ideological authority of the Party, by returning to socialist legality, and by rationalizing the system in every area. Security and prosperity were to be the means by which society recognized this legitimacy and adhered to it. But this legitimation of the system failed on two planes. One fraction of society seized hold of socialist legality to demand the recognition of rights and of civic competence. Thus, the meaning given to socialist legality by the authorities and that given to it by the most politically active sectors of society are totally divergent. As for prosperity, the system's total immobilism has condemned it. The soviet authorities have no rational-legal legitimacy because society knows—at least in certain sectors—that legality is not what the Party designates by that word and that rationality stumbles over the imperative of preserving the system. What legitimates power now is simply the fact that it exists and perpetuates itself. This is a simple legitimacy of tradition in which the authorities invoke the historic mission of the Party and its knowledge.

Can a revolutionary power which is the bearer of social progress maintain itself in power through a simple legitimacy of tradition? The answer is unequivocally no. This is why, unable to find internal legitimacy, Soviet power has now taken refuge in a legitimacy of force, based on its foreign activities. This search for a new kind of legitimacy explains the paradoxical situation of the U.S.S.R. Domestically, the authorities have encountered nothing but increasing difficulties—a declining economy, a more conscious society, whole sectors of which have challenged the existing monolithic organization—to which they have opposed an inflexible attachment to the foundations of the system and total immobility. But in foreign affairs, the same authorities have demonstrated a flexibility and dynamism that have enabled them to raise the U.S.S.R. to the rank of the United States. Accumulated military power, newly acquired naval power—in 1964, the U.S.S.R. was practically absent from the sea—expansion in Africa and Asia, normalized relations with Europe and the United States, and recognition of the East European acquisitions of 1945 are all the work of Khruschev's successors. In foreign affairs, the prudent septuagenarians of the Kremlin have been audacious and innovative statesmen, taking all governments by surprise with their untold initiatives. Their international flexibility is no less remarkable than their enterprising spirit. With the Western world, they speak a language of peace and stability: "Détente is irreversible." At the same time, where détente does not apply, in the Third World, the U.S.S.R. has pursued a policy of destabilization, based either on support for the "national will" or on the exploitation of "revolutionary opportunities." For this dual policy—"détente" on the one side, destabilization on the other—all political and extrapolitical instruments are used, including diplomatic relations, Communist Parties or organizations of sympathizers, economic relations, arms supplies, and scientific and educational activities.

One thus has the impression that there are two juxtaposed Soviet Unions: a vulnerable country in which the system must take account of its failures; and a triumphant power, which is not always successful, to be sure, but which has shown its capacity to intervene effectively at any time at the other end of the globe. Just as Soviet man is double, Soviet power seems afflicted with a split personality.

We must call on Lenin to understand what is behind this apparent contradiction. The founder of the U.S.S.R. said, "It is false and dangerous to separate domestic politics and foreign policy." And his distant successor Brezhnev has echoed him by saying, "Our foreign policy is our great method for domestic politics."

This continuity between internal and world space is what remains in the U.S.S.R. of its original internationalism. And each leader has used it in his own way. Stalin justified his power by invoking the threat weighing on the U.S.S.R. because of capitalist encirclement. Khrushchev recognized the end of encirclement and tried to open the U.S.S.R. to the external world in order to resolve its problems. His successors retained from his openings the possibility of slowing the arms race and also of bringing the benefits of East-West exchange to a failing economy and backward technology. But the Brezhnev group has gone much further. It aims toward several goals through its dynamic foreign policy. One is to derive legitimacy from external successes. Is the progress of communism in the world not irrefutable evidence of the Party's historic mission? Doesn't it show that its mission is far from having been accomplished? International power is also a remarkable means of protecting the system from its internal difficulties. Soviet citizens know that the Soviet authorities do not want to use coercion against them but that they have the military means to crush any mass movement. They also know that Soviet power has forced the rest of the world to accept as definitive the Communist order in the U.S.S.R. and in Eastern Europe, and that no national or workers' uprising will benefit from external assistance. Through its international power, the Soviet system has thus defined the limits of its citizens' demands. The external power of the U.S.S.R. is designed both to protect the system and to give it a new dynamism, which the successes carried off in Africa and Asia since 1975 have confirmed. No doubt we can say that the weakening of the Western world, its divisions, and the destabilization of Africa, Asia, and Latin America are not always the direct result of Soviet policies, nor always for the benefit of the Soviet Union. But Soviet ideology has evolved in the Brezhnev period, abandoning the open vision of the world adumbrated by Khrushchev to return, if not to Stalinist Manichaeanism, at least to a more structured and dualist conception of world forces.

Détente is taking place within the framework of a long-term competition between the East and the West which presupposes victors and vanquished. And everything that weakens the Western world strengthens the Soviet world. Three questions must be considered in this connection. First, has this worldwide progress of the U.S.S.R. mobilized society in a patriotic transport and compensated in its eyes for internal difficulties? It is clear that the answer is negative. This is so first of all because society is sensitive to its immediate difficulties, and it easily evaluates the cost of power. Stalin used a logical argument to mobilize it. He said to his citizens, We are surrounded because we are weak. His successors assert simultaneously that the U.S.S.R. is all-powerful, that the West is weakened, ravaged by a serious crisis, *and* that the U.S.S.R. is threatened. Used to contemplating the military power of their country, soothed by its successes, Soviet citizens have difficulty in really experiencing a threat from the outside. The country that really frightens them is China, close and heavily populated, a country that is, according to Soviet leaders, in the process of disintegrating. This complex and contradictory argument has little mobilizing force. Patriotism, which holds a growing place in the Soviet system of values, in harmony with the growing role played by the army, also has a great weakness. For a long time, Soviet patriotism has been filled with Russian content: because the past referred to is Russian; because the language and traditions of the army, the great bearer of this patriotism, are Russian. And this russification of Soviet patriotism has helped to limit its role, to the extent that it concerns only a part—scarcely half—of the Soviet population. For all the others, this patriotism is a symbol of domination.

A second question concerns the manner in which this foreign

policy—the only active policy of the Soviet authorities—is decided. Who decides this policy? Is it the result of a consensus of
the political elite or the outcome of conflict? It is customary to
trace a demarcation line in the Soviet political elite between
those who are supposed to be the artisans of this dynamism, the
"hawks," and the "doves" who are supposed to be trying des-
perately to contain them. This division, which is an attempt to
put the Soviet system into traditional categories, does not
match the analysis of real facts. Certainly there are debates
about all these decisions, and there are disagreements. But the
evidence contradicts any notion that there are permanent divisions among persons and groups. In the face of each problem,
the Soviet leaders react in terms of a given situation and not on
the basis of a preestablished attitude. In order to understand
this, we must consider the narrow circle within which foreign
policy is developed. The fourteen men who have the authority
to speak (see Appendix V) are in the majority members of the
Politburo and the Secretariat—that is, they express above all
the interests of the Party. They are almost all interchangeable
in age and background. For the most part, they belong to the
generation born between 1900 and 1910; they come from a
modest social background; almost all of them were trained in
technical, industrial, or agricultural institutes in the period of
the first five-year plan, and they reached important positions in
the Party and state apparatus with the help of the purges and
the war. Since then they have worked side by side and survived
side by side through Stalinism and the pitfalls of de-Stalinization. Their common origin, generation, training, and experience have, without any doubt, created a common vision of
problems. Moreover, five members of the group, Suslov,
Ponomarev, Gromyko, Patolichev, and Skachkov, have been
involved in foreign policy problems, in the same position, for
more than two decades. The continuity of careers also helps to
create a common perception of the facts. This group has simultaneously made contradictory decisions. In 1968 it decided to

put an end to the Prague spring, and in 1969 it brutally "normalized" Czechoslovakia. But at the time it held out the olive branch to Western Europe and committed itself to the path of détente. Should we assume that the hawks spoke louder for Czechoslovakia and the doves louder for détente or that there was bargaining to satisfy both parties? Here again, what we know of the positions defended by certain leaders gives no support for the idea of such a division. Thus Suslov, who is unfailingly placed in the camp of the hawks because he speaks in the name of ideological rigor, argued against intervention in Czechoslovakia because he saw its negative ideological effects. The same logic led him to adopt a reserved attitude toward détente. Brezhnev, who is readily granted the label of dove and considered a determined partisan of détente, has continuously defended the interests of heavy industry and pushed to the fore a number of his former colleagues who now represent at the summit the military-industrial complex, which is considered the center of the hawks. Khrushchev himself, who is generally contrasted with his successors as an apostle of coexistence, went much further than they on the road to confrontation with the West (Berlin in 1961 and Cuba in 1962) and demonstrated in the Middle East an adventurism that frightened Molotov, Stalin's former Minister of Foreign Affairs, generally catalogued as a hawk. Circumstances inspire positions, and the Party, here as in domestic politics, decides on the basis of the stakes, the first of which is its authority.

The final questions concern the future of the U.S.S.R. and are tied to the displacement of governmental activity from the domestic to the international sphere. To what extent will the political succession which must take place, simply because of the laws of nature, be affected by foreign policy? Are the military and the KGB,[10] whose international role has been increasing, thereby now in a better position in the race for power? And, from the other direction, will the succession be of a character to change foreign policy?

The answers derive from a simple observation of Soviet practices and of historical precedents. What the system and the past show is that power has always fallen into the hands of those who controlled the Party machinery and who were therefore well placed to manipulate men and positions. These "strong men" have always presented themselves in the race for power as defenders of the system, of its ideology, and of order, and have relied on the corresponding apparatuses. Stalin leaned on the army, forcing rivals to place themselves outside the tradition and to call on dispersed and secondary forces. It is more than probable that the succession will come from within the system, relying on its values and on military and police forces. In other hands, foreign policy may differ on a number of points, but its logic will remain identical: It will have to confirm and perpetuate power.

In the end, what comes out of an analysis of the Soviet system is its anachronism and its contradictions. The improvements made in the system of government have transformed a bloody personal tyranny into the administrative dictatorship of an oligarchy. But this transformation has not changed the basis of the system; it has adjusted it. The Soviet system has remained identical to itself for sixty years. Power remains in the hands of a coherent ruling group, supported by bureaucratic apparatuses; it still has control over all national resources and is thereby the veritable owner of the state. From top to bottom of this pyramid of power, privileges are distributed according to the position held. The basis of power in this system is very specific. It is in fact not tied to possession of capital but derives from the simple fact that one is located within the sphere of power, and one of the fundamental privileges conferred by that position is the possibility of perpetuating it. The ruling class and its ramifications are self-recruiting, and they reproduce themselves. Their desire to preserve their positions and their privileges and their absolute capacity to control everything have considerably reduced social mobility in the course of the last two decades. But society has changed. Social consciousness, which the authorities have tried to mobilize completely, has discovered that it has been stripped of a power that belongs to it. It knows that it will obtain nothing through the intermediary of the structures of participation offered to it, and that it must look for its own structures of organization to finally accede to the sphere of power and change it.

The fact that this social consciousness is still weak, dispersed, and badly expressed is of little importance. The essential exists: the absurd and recognized gap between a petrified power that survives to survive, incapable of adapting itself to social reality, and a changed society. Extraordinary external power is of no use domestically, except as a force for intimidation and dissuasion. For Lenin, the history of human societies was a perpetual conflict: *Kto kogo?* "Who will win out over whom?" This is in fact the ultimate question: Between a petrified power determined to perpetuate itself and a living society determined to live, who will win out over whom?

"Brezhnevism," a product of the U.S.S.R. of the seventies, is now coming to a close. And the conditions under which it is ending are disconcertingly ambiguous. Domestically, the desire to rationalize the political and economic system that characterized the choices made by Khrushchev's successors has hardly produced conclusive results. In foreign affairs, the policy of détente, symbol of the Brezhnev era, has led to the invasion of Afghanistan and the suppression of the Polish experiment. Is this the logical conclusion of Brezhnevism? Have we already left the Brezhnev era? What light does this evolution at the beginning of the decade shed on the future of the Soviet system?

It is within the U.S.S.R., in the political system, that the limits and the cost of post-Stalin change can now be seen. Brezhnev and his group have consolidated the ruling class and the apparatus as a whole, assured their future by assuring them of the stability of the system and of the methods of power. The immediate consequence of this stabilizing choice has been the perpetuation of a group, and its aging. In the early eighties, the stability of the rulers, which was necessary for a while, has become intolerable. This is so because it leads to a politics of immobility, since age and habit incline the leaders more toward prudence and inactivity than toward new initiatives; but also because biological necessity demands replacement of the leaders. On this last point, we can now clearly recognize the drift of "Brezhnevism" toward absolute petrifaction of the system. There has been no lack of opportunities to prepare for replacement of the leaders. There have been the normal opportunities provided by plenums and Party congresses, when the organs of power could have accepted younger cadres who would later have been able to assume the duties of those who retired. There have also been special and imperative opportunities, when death itself has indicated that the Brezhnev leadership is nearing its end. In both cases, not only has renewal not taken place but everything indicates the leadership's desire not to recognize its necessity and to delay it still longer.

The only notable change in the ruling organs took place at the Central Committee plenum in October 1980, which witnessed the promotion to the Politburo of a young cadre who was given responsibilities generally reserved for septuagenarians. The new member, Mikhail Gorbachev, was forty-nine at the time of his appointment, and his arrival among the titular members of the Politburo reduced the average age of that body from seventy-one years and three months to sixty-nine years and ten months. Beyond this entirely relative rejuvenation of the Politburo, did the promotion of Gorbachev represent a step toward the arrival of a new generation? This was doubtful at the outset if one noted that this newcomer—member of the secretariat of the Central Committee since November 1978—although his age made his presence in a venerable political body striking, was also responsible for a particularly sensitive sector, agriculture, which had worn out a number of cadres before him, all of whom had therefore had unstable careers. Moreover, the Soviet authorities seem more willing to carry out changes in government positions than in the Party apparatus. The death of Kosygin was followed by a dozen retirements or displacements among the 110 members of the Council of Ministers of the

U.S.S.R. There was even the appointment as Minister of Fruits and Vegetables, a newly created position, of the very young (thirty-five) Nikolai Kozlov. Such changes have, without any doubt, reduced the average age of the Council of Ministers, and they suggest that a succession was in process. But to confirm this tendency, the Party, too, would have had to open itself to a new generation. The Twenty-sixth Congress of February 1981 clearly showed that this opening and political succession were not the order of the day. The ruling organs of the Party were reelected in their entirety, and the reelection of the eighty-two-year-old Arvid Pelshe as President of the Control Commission strikingly confirmed that the age of retirement did not exist at the heart of the Party.

However, this problem was bluntly posed by the death of two top leaders: Aleksei Kosygin in the winter of 1980, and Mikhail Suslov in January 1982. Confronted with the gaps that were thereby created, the authorities were forced to choose between gradual renewal and the perpetuation of a gerontocracy condemned to rapid extinction. The response to the dilemma was soon apparent. The ailing Kosygin was removed from power by his colleagues and replaced by a man of his age, his right-hand man, Nikolai Tikhonov, seventy-five at the time of his promotion, and his deputy appointed at the same time was only a year younger than Tikhonov himself. Thanks to this replacement carried out in extremis, Kosygin's death was relegated to the domain of private matters and the problem of renewal was not even raised. The death of Suslov, who was still in office, posed fewer urgent problems. The Party's *éminence grise*, Suslov, unlike Kosygin, held no government position that had immediately to be assigned to a successor. The role of Suslov—a simultaneously omnipresent and concealed actor on the stage of Soviet political life—was both too complex and too important to permit a successor to be improvised, nor was it indispensable to appoint one immediately. The designation of a new secretary, or a new titular member of the Politburo, does not imply that he will ever play the role played by Suslov. Thus, despite the disappearance of two historic figures of the Brezhnev leadership, the problem of the opening of the ruling organs to a new political generation was evaded.

This persistence in the refusal to undertake the process of succession is cruel evidence of the sclerosis of the system. The existence of a normal, open, regularly functioning means of succession is the true sign that a political system has reached maturity. The refusal of the Soviet ruling class to undertake the ineluctable process of the renewal of the groups in power is no doubt due to the desire to remain in place, but also to the fear of not being able to control an operation that has, until now, never taken place in the U.S.S.R. We must remember that the three preceding successions were exceptional, brought about by death or disgrace, but that the transmission of power in normal conditions remains in the realm of the unknown. This explains the leaders' concern to exclude from power all those who might lay claim to the succession and to patch the gaps that age opens up in their fragile group. But postponing the problem does not do away with it. And whoever has seen the photograph of Suslov's funeral in *Pravda,* with his exhausted companions grouped behind a coffin that they could not, as tradition requires, carry on their shoulders, knows that the Soviet political system must soon test its capacity to settle the problem of succession.

To the ruling class's inability to deal with this problem, we should add a final indication of the difficulties with which the system adapts itself to the problems of the moment. A Georgian healer has appeared in Leonid Brezhnev's entourage; she exercises her paramedical gifts in the hospital reserved for the personnel of the Gosplan. No doubt it is normal that an individual who has exhausted the capacities of medicine attempt to improve his condition by any means. But recourse to healers to extend the political longevity of a leader is surprising, and it carries a disturbing reminder that, at certain difficult moments of Russian history, thaumaturges, soothsayers, and healers have made regular appearances in the political landscape.

The economic situation of the U.S.S.R. is harshly affected by this immobility, and it demands quick solutions. For several years, Brezhnevism represented a desire to rationalize and modernize the economy. The death of Kosygin, advocate of great economic reforms and of a certain depoliticization of economic life, had been preceded by a decline in his authority. At the same time, economic orthodoxy and discipline gradually recovered their dominance at the expense of independent initiative and innovative research. By 1979, the fact that the economic system was marking time was obvious, and the balance sheet for the year 1980 confirmed Soviet difficulties, especially in the agricultural sector. In the course of the preceding five years, agricultural production had increased by only 9 percent, despite the program of state investments to develop an "agro-industrial" sector based on the example of Western policies of integrating agriculture and industry. Currently, the state provides massive subsidies for livestock breeding and has multiplied its grain purchases in the West. In spite of that, food shortages have become established in the U.S.S.R., making the usual lines still longer, emptying the stores still more, and requiring the occasional imposition of rationing in the provinces. Industry for its part has also fallen short of predictions, suffering above all from the low productivity of labor, the lack of a spirit of initiative and competition, but also from the enormous transportation difficulties in such a vast country (80 percent of the sources of raw materials and energy lie east of the Urals). Inflation, even though it is concealed, is already present in the U.S.S.R.

Confronted with these difficulties, which Leonid Brezhnev analyzed publicly at the Central Committee plenums of 1980 and 1981 and in his report to the Twenty-sixth Party Congress, the planners have had to adapt their ambitions to a gloomy reality, instead of continuing the solidly established tradition of concealing that reality behind grandiose objectives. The eleventh five-year plan (1981–85) is the least ambitious of all the plans proposed in the U.S.S.R. since the beginnings of planning. Drawing the lesson of the Polish crisis, the planners have above all tried to reassure consumers and to present the plan as though its first priority were their needs. However, a more attentive examination of the text reveals that military expenditure in the U.S.S.R.—12 to 15 percent of the gross national product at a minimum—will continue to weigh on the development of the country, affecting, as always, citizens and not the military forces.

The incontestable economic difficulties of the U.S.S.R.—the slowing down of growth is perceptible every day—have brought about far from negligible social consequences that express a variety of frustrations. Aware of these frustrations, the Soviet authorities have attempted both to take them into account and to explain them, although they have not been able to deal with them. The press has devoted increasing space to the discontent of the ordinary citizen, exasperated by the malfunctioning of the system, and it complacently recounts numerous examples of disorganization and incompetence. This appears to be a safety valve for complaints. But above all, the authorities have been considering with anxiety a particularly acute problem that is now visible in the U.S.S.R., a problem whose explosive force was revealed by the Polish example: the profound discontent of young workers and its consequences in the world of work. Numerous surveys have been undertaken in order to characterize the younger segment of the working class (those under thirty), very strongly differentiated from their elders in both their aspirations and their behavior. The Soviet press observes above all that most young workers wish to pursue higher education rather than to remain committed to the world of production. For Soviet youth, higher education is increasingly an end in itself, and to be deprived of it, to be forced into manual labor, represents social disgrace. For this frustrated

working-class youth, everything is a source of bitterness: the
vain dream of an interesting profession, the boredom of repeti-
tive manual labor that calls for no initiative, the gap between
their education and work for which they are overqualified, the
bad organization of Soviet enterprises. If these criticisms used
to be expressed rarely, they are now at the heart of the debate
about productivity. Can the Soviet authorities hope that this
disappointed generation, which until now has shown its frustrations by systematically violating work discipline, will agree to
participate in the indispensable effort to increase productivity?
Or must they see in this age group and this social class a possible
element of collective rebellion?

The Polish crisis, coming after the invasion of Afghanistan,
was another severe test for the Soviet collective leadership,
forcing it to consider the domestic dimension of Solidarity's
demands and the international consequences of a reaction in
Poland. The domestic dimension of the crisis was obvious to the
leaders of the U.S.S.R. by the time of the signing of the Gdansk
agreement in the summer of 1980. The organization of the
Polish working class around a free union represented a challenge to the political monopoly that had been held until then
by the Communist Party. And this monopoly is the basis of the
Soviet model that had been conceived by Lenin, preserved by
his successors through every crisis, and exported by them
throughout Eastern Europe. According to this model, power in
a Communist state is exercised by the Party-State; it represents
the interests of society as a whole and organizes those interests
through many channels, particularly through the unions. Solidarity, by establishing itself as a negotiating partner for the
political authorities, by claiming to represent the working class
and to defend its interests and demands before the Party,
opened an entirely new breach in the system.

From the outset, it was clear that the Soviet leaders could not
tolerate such a change at any point in the Communist system.
But, given that fact, they faced the concrete problem of what

attitude to adopt in order to check the evolution of Polish communism. Was it possible to intervene brutally in Poland, in the
name of the duty of socialist solidarity, as in Hungary in 1956
and in Czechoslovakia in 1968? The international environment
was hardly propitious for this in 1980. Détente, already badly
affected by the Afghanistan affair, might have totally collapsed.
And Poland was too populous, too accustomed to desperate
resistance, and too strategically important for such an operation
to be thinkable.

The rejection of direct intervention, which was very soon
made clear, forced the Soviet leaders to display in Poland the
kind of initiative and imagination lacking in their domestic
policies. Periodically brandishing the threat of intervention, the
U.S.S.R. at the same time encouraged the setting up of an internal system of repression—through the army and the police,
since the Party was incapable of doing it. The long delay in
reestablishing domestic order, the Soviet wait-and-see policy,
and countless provocations all encouraged Solidarity to abandon all prudence and to move toward a break with the system.
By proclaiming in November 1981 the necessity for a referendum to allow society to express its political will, Solidarity set
in motion a process of rejection of the Communist regime. By
challenging the system, the Polish union movement provoked
anxiety throughout the ruling strata of the Communist world
and helped to rally them around the U.S.S.R.

The emergence of military power on December 13, 1981,
explains the policy followed by the U.S.S.R. Because the Soviet
leadership had for a long time concentrated the attention of
Solidarity and of the international community on the possibility
of external military intervention (with the armies of the Warsaw
Pact nations) as a solution to the crisis, General Jaruzelski's coup
seemed to be a lesser evil. Solidarity was, without any doubt,
ready to mobilize the whole society against the tanks of the
Warsaw Pact, but it was caught short by the actions of the Polish
military and police forces. Soviet hesitation—seen as a sign of

weakness—had demobilized Polish suspicions, encouraged the idea that the workers' movement could develop without obstacles, and paralyzed its will to organize defensively. In the end, by allowing Solidarity to consolidate itself, the U.S.S.R. ran the unmistakable risk of a total collapse of the regime. But this collapse, which has taken place, was accompanied by economic collapse and a weakening of the suspicions and capacity for resistance of the Polish working class. At the same time, the Soviet leaders tested the solidity of the Polish military and police officer corps, and their predictable adhesion to law-and-order solutions as opposed to an evolution that they considered anarchical. A "lesser evil" in the eyes of a Polish society discouraged by the galloping economic crisis, the domestic restoration of order also sowed confusion in the Western camp, which was incapable of responding immediately and in concerted fashion. Here, too, the only possibility that had been seriously considered was a military intervention by the U.S.S.R.

The balance sheet of the Polish crisis must be drawn up from various perspectives. First of all, from the point of view of the Soviet ruling group, they have once again demonstrated that on the international scene—the Polish events were both internal to the Socialist camp and with an international dimension—they know how to react with coherence and prudence. At no point did the solution to the Polish crisis become a threat to international equilibrium. Moreover, in this crisis, Soviet power showed once again the limits of possible change within the Communist world. The preservation of the model of power is an absolute requirement, and this model depends upon the refusal to allow society to become a genuine partner in political life.

Having put an end to the Polish crisis by repression does not mean that the central elements of this crisis have been eliminated or that the crisis can be contained. The emergence of the working class, obvious in Poland, is also characteristic of the political evolution of all the other countries of the Socialist

camp, including the U.S.S.R. In Poland, the movement was able
to reach maturity; elsewhere, local conditions and the strength
of the authorities have kept it concealed. But this movement
exists everywhere, and it expresses the birth of a new society,
which challenges a repressive political system that is incapable
of justifying its existence by its effectiveness. The Polish crisis,
in this respect, is only the tip of an iceberg which is constantly
growing.

Indicative of the extent of the ills afflicting the Communist
world—economic and political difficulties, the inability of the
authorities to adapt to a society and a world that have been
transformed—the crisis has also revealed two other realities.
First of all, it showed that the Soviet government, despite its
internal weaknesses, is powerful enough, vis-à-vis its citizens
and the external world, to master such crises. The will to military and international power displayed by the U.S.S.R. finds its
justification in that fact. This will to power allows the political
system to survive, to impose itself on rebellious or skeptical
societies, and to force the entire world to recognize the certainty that the system cannot be called into question. The other
reality made evident by the Polish crisis is that, however powerful they may be, disturbances in the Communist world cannot
work themselves out to their natural conclusion as long as the
U.S.S.R. preserves itself and maintains its power.

Real change is possible only if it begins in the U.S.S.R. Simultaneously weak and powerful, the U.S.S.R. has based its power
above all on the impotence of the capitalist world, and it justifies
the continuation of a weakened and challenged system by invoking the weakness of and challenges to the alternative system. Is the future of the U.S.S.R., in the end, not contained in
the framework of East-West relations defined as a "competition
of decadence," which amounts once again to asking Lenin's
question, *Kto kogo?* Who will be the first, the U.S.S.R. or the
West, to be defeated by its own decline?

APPENDIXES

APPENDIX I

Dates of Plenums That Changed the Composition of the Politburo

POLITBURO
1952–1980

Composition
of the
Politburo
Since 1952

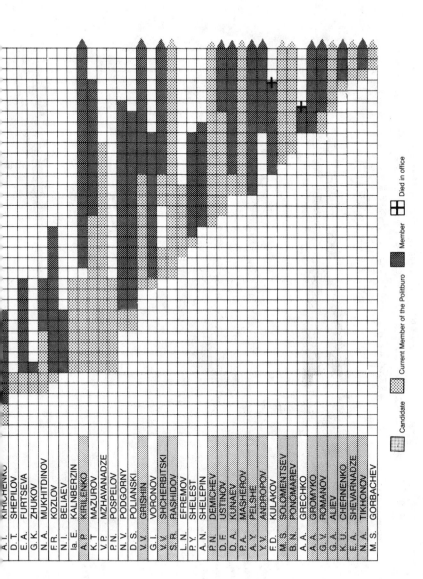

A. I.	KIRICHENKO
D. T.	SHEPILOV
E. A.	FURTSEVA
G. K.	ZHUKOV
N. A.	MUKHITDINOV
F. R.	KOZLOV
N. I.	BELIAEV
Ia. E.	KALNBERZIN
A. P.	KIRILENKO
K. T.	MAZUROV
V. P.	MZHAVANADZE
P. N.	POSPELOV
N. V.	PODGORNY
D. S.	POLIANSKI
V. V.	GRISHIN
G. I.	VORONOV
V. V.	SHCHERBITSKI
S. R.	RASHIDOV
L. N.	EFREMOV
P. Y.	SHELEST
A. N.	SHELEPIN
P. N.	DEMICHEV
D. F.	USTINOV
D. A.	KUNAEV
P. A.	MASHEROV
A. Y.	PELSHE
Y. V.	ANDROPOV
F. D.	KULAKOV
M. S.	SOLOMENTSEV
B. N.	PONOMAREV
A. A.	GRECHKO
A. A.	GROMYKO
G. V.	ROMANOV
G. A.	ALIEV
K. U.	CHERNENKO
E. A.	SHEVARNADZE
N. A.	TIKHONOV
M. S.	GORBACHEV

Candidate   Current Member of the Politburo   Member   Died in office

Dates of Plenums Affecting the Composition of the Secretariat

SECRETARIAT
OF THE C.C.
1952–1980

Composition

of the

Secretariat

Since 1952

K. U. CHERNENKO
M. V. ZAMIANIN
Y. I. RIABOV
K. U. RUSAKOV
M. S. GORBACHEV

Current Member of the Secretariat   Member of the Secretariat   1 Approximate Date   Died in Office

APPENDIX III

**Executive Apparatus of the Central Committee
after plenum of May 24, 1982**

POLITBURO

13 members: Andropov, Brezhnev, Chernenko, Gorbachev (Oct. 1980),
Grishin, Gromyko, Kirilenko, Kunaev, Ustinov, Pelshe, Romanov, Shcherbitski,
Tikhonov. (Gone: Kosygin [died 1980]; Suslov [died 1982])
9 candidates: Aliev, Demichev, Dolgikh (May 1982),
Kisselev (Oct. 1980), Kuznetsov, Ponomarev, Rashidov,
Shevarnadze, Solomentsev. (Gone: Masherov [died 1980])

SECRETARIAT*

General Secretary:
L. I. Brezhnev
Secretaries: Andropov (May 1982), Kirilenko, Chernenko, Gorbachev,
Ponomarev, Kapitonov, Dolgikh, Zimianin, Rusakov.
(Gone: Suslov [died 1982])

PARTY CONTROL COMMITTEE

A. Y. Pelshe

---

* The order of these names is from *Bol'shaia sovetskaia entsiklopedia ezhegodnik,*
1981, p. 15.

APPENDIX IV

Administration of the Central Committee

Departments of the Central Committee*		Date of Birth	Position
Administration	G.S. Pavlov	1910	C.C.
Agriculture	V.A. Karlov	1914	C.C.
Cadres—Foreign	N.M. Pegov	1905	C.C.
Commerce	I.I. Kabkov	?	Cand. C.C.
Construction	I.N. Dimitriev	1920	Cand. C.C.
Construction of Machinery	V.S. Frolov	?	Cand. C.C.
Culture	V.F. Shauro	?	Cand. C.C.
General Department	*K.U. Chernenko*	1911	P.
Defense Industry	I.D. Serbin	?	Cand. C.C.
—heavy industry	*V.I. Dolgikh*	1924	Cand .P.
—chemical industry	V.I. Listrov	—	—
—light industry & food production	F.I. Mochalin	1920	Cand. C.C.
International Department	*B.N. Ponomarev*	1905	P.
International Intelligence	L.M. Zamiatin	1922	C.C.
Liaison with Communist and Workers Parties of the Socialist Countries	*K.V. Rusakov*	1909	C.C.
Administrative Organs	N.I. Savinkin	?	C.C.
Planning & Finances	B.I. Gostev	?	Cand. C.C.
Propaganda	E.M. Tiazhel'nikov	1928	C.C.
Science and Education	S.P. Trapeznikov	1912	C.C.
Transportation and Communication	K.S. Simonov	1917	Cand. C.C.
Organizational Work of the Party	*I.V. Kapitonov*	1915	C.C.

† The italicized names are members of the Secretariat
* C.C.   = Member of the Central Committee (Candidates   = Cand. C.C.)
   C.C.C. = Member of the Central Control Commission
   P.   = Member of the Politburo (Candidates   = Cand. P.)

APPENDIX V

Decision-Making Group in Foreign Policy*

Name	Position	Date of Birth
L. I. Brezhnev	General Secretary of the Communist Party	1906
	President of the Presidium of the	
	of the Supreme Soviet	
	President of the Council of Defense	
	Member of the Politburo	
A. A. Gromyko	Minister of Foreign Affairs	1909
	Member of the Politburo	
Y. V. Andropov	Secretary of the Central Committee	1914
	Member of the Politburo	
D. F. Ustinov	Minister of Defense (in charge of	
	defense industries)	
	Member of the Politburo	1908
B. N. Ponomarev	Secretary of the Central Committee	1905
	Chief of the International Department	
	of the Central Committee	
K. V. Rusakov	Secretary of the Central Committee	1909
	Chief of Liaison with Communist and	
	Workers Parties of Socialist Countries	
	Member of the Council of Ministers	
I. V. Arkhipov	Vice-president of the Council of Ministers	1907
	and President of the Foreign Trade Com-	
	mission of the Council of Ministers	
	Member of the Central Committee	
V. V. Fedorchuk	President of the KGB	1918
N. S. Patolichev	Minister of Foreign Trade	1908
	Member of the Central Committee	
S. A. Skachkov	President of the State Committee on	1907
	Foreign Economic Relations	
	Member of the Central Committee	
N. M. Pegov	In charge of the Foreign Cadre Depart-	1905
	Department of the Central Committee	
	Member of the Central Committee	

Name	Position	Date of Birth
A. M. Alexandrov Agentov	Assistant to Brezhnev in the General Secretaryship Member of the Central Committee	?
V. F. Mal'tsev	First Deputy Minister of Foreign Affairs Member of the Central Committee	1917

*This table is based on the list given by Hough in *The Coming Generational Change in the Soviet Foreign Policy-making Elite,* paper, AAASS, 14 October 1977, pp. 1–3.

NOTES

Chapter 1: The Power of the People: Myth and Reality

1. John Plamenatz has a stimulating analysis on this point: *Man and Society* (London, 1963), vol. 2, ch. 6.
2. Marx, Engels, *Werke* (Berlin, 1961), XXI, p. 167.
3. Ibid., XXII, p. 198.
4. Berdyaev, *Origin of Russian Communism* (Ann Arbor, 1960).
5. On this point see the essay by I. Meiendorff in Auty and Obolensky, eds., *Companion to Russian Studies* (Cambridge, 1976), vol. 1, pp. 315ff.
6. Berdyaev, op. cit., pp. 40–42.
7. P. Pascal, *La Révolte de Pougatchev* (Paris, 1971). Stenka Razin's revolt took place in 1670, Pugachev's between 1773 and 1775.
8. Berdyaev, op. cit.
9. *Obshetvennoe dvizhenie v rosii 60–70 gody XIX veka* (Moscow, 1958). F. Venturi, *Les Intellectuels, le peuple et la révolution* (Paris, 1972), traces their itinerary. J. Baynac, *Les Socialistes révolutionnaires* (Paris, 1979).
10. Lenin, *Polnoe sobranie sochinenii*, 5th ed., vol. 33, pp. 1–120; cited hereafter as *Polnoe*.
11. This is the argument of N. Sukhanov, *Zapitski o revoliutsii* (Berlin, 1922–23). See the condensed version by J. Carmichael, *The Russian Revolution, 1917* (London, 1955), or the abridged French edition (Paris, 1965).
12. M. Ferro, *La Révolution de 1917 et la chute du tsarisme* (Paris, 1967), pp. 255ff.
13. *Sovety kak takticheskaia problema revoliutsii* (Moscow and Leningrad, 1928), pp. 99ff. cf. "The Interpretation of This Strategy by the Twentieth Congress," *Voprosy istorii* (1957), pp. 17–42.
14. "The Civil War in France," in Marx, *The First International and After* (Harmondsworth, 1974), pp. 206–7.

15. *Protokoly TSK RSDRP* (Moscow, 1958), p. 138.

16. *VII s'ezd RKP (b) mart 1919: Protokoly* (Moscow, 1959), pp. 428–29.

17. Lenin, *Polnoe*, vol. 28, pp. 277–78. On the reality of power at the time, see E. N. Gorodetsky, *Voprosy istorii*, 8 (1955), pp. 26–39.

18. Lenin, *Polnoe*, vol. 28, p. 279.

19. T. H. Rigby, "Politics in the Mono-Organizational Society," *Authoritarian Politics in Communist Europe* (Berkeley, 1976).

20. *VII s'ezd RKP (b)*, pp. 390–410.

21. *Polnoe*, vol. 33, p. 93.

22. Ibid., vol. 27, p. 315.

23. M. Matthews, *Privilege in the Soviet Union* (London, 1978), p. 67.

24. E. N. Danilova, *Deistvuiushchie zakonodatsel'stvo o trude SSSR* (Moscow, 1927), vol. 1, p. 358.

25. *Pravda*, December 18, 1927, defines the tasks of the Cheka.

26. See A. Rosenberg, *Histoire du bolchevisme* (Paris, 1967), for a useful discussion of this point.

27. *Literaturnaia gazeta*, 16 (August 5, 1929), editorial, which allows a comparison between the ideology of the lowly and that of the shift.

28. E. H. Carr, *The Bolshevik Revolution* (London, 1966), vol. 1, pp. 167–74.

29. Ibid., pp. 187ff.

30. Matthews, op. cit. note 23, p. 89; M. I. Parshin, *L'goty voenno-sluzhashchim i ih semiam* (Moscow, 1976).

31. N. I. Boldyrev, ed., *Direktivy VKP (b) i postanovlenie sovetskogo pravitel'stva o narodnom obrazovanii* (Moscow, 1947), 2 vols. The decrees of 1918–20 are in the first volume. Cf. Lenin, *O vospitanie i obrazovanie* (Moscow, 1963), pp. 337–49.

32. *Pravda*, March 7, 1929.

33. Ibid., December 21, 1929; Stalin's speech; *Sochinenya* (Moscow, 1951), vol. 13, pp. 55, 59–68.

34. Matthews, op. cit. note 23, p. 106.

35. Quoted by W. D. Connor, *Socialism, Politics, and Equality* (New York, 1979), p. 250.

36. On the first appearance of the device, see *Dekrety sovetskoi vlasti*, vol. 3, p. 552.

37. N. Murray, *I Spied for Stalin* (New York, 1951), p. 84.

38. T. D. Alexeyev, *Zhilishchnoe zakonodatel'stvo* (Moscow, 1947), p. 164, gives precise details on rents for the army and the NKVD.

39. Matthews, op. cit. note 23, p. 123.

40. *Gosudarstvennye universitety* (Moscow, 1934), pp. 12–44, and N. DeWitt, *Education and Professional Employment in the U.S.S.R.* (Washington, 1969), p. 655.

41. M. I. Movshovich and A. M. Khodzhaev, *Vyeshaia shkola* (Moscow, 1948), p. 65.

42. Quoted by S. Fitzpatrick, *The Commissariat of Enlightenment* (Cambridge, 1970), p. 220.

43. On the respective benefits, see *Bol'shaia sovetskaia entsiklopedia* (Moscow, 1939), vol. 43.
44. Matthews, op. cit. note 23, p. 121.
45. *Literaturnaia gazeta,* 60 (October 29, 1935) and 65 (November 24, 1935); A. Stakhanov, *Razkaz o moei zhizni* (Moscow, 1937).
46. *Literaturnaia gazeta,* 4 (January 20, 1939).
47. H. Carrère d'Encausse, *Staline, l'ordre par la terreur* (Paris, 1979), ch. 4.
48. Ibid., p. 66.
49. Ibid., p. 59.
50. E. Ginzburg, *Le Ciel de la Kolyma* (Paris, 1980), pp. 335–46.

Chapter 2: The Time of Hope

1. *Pravda,* July 10, 1953.
2. R. Kolkowicz, *The Soviet Army and the Communist Party,* p. 127; *New York Times,* December 24, 1953.
3. On this entire period, two works are enlightening about the changes that took place: M. Tatu, *Le Pouvoir en U.R.S.S.* (Paris, 1967), and C. Linden, *Khrushchev and the Soviet Leadership* (Baltimore, 1966).
4. *Pravda,* April 6, 1953.
5. H. Berman, *Justice in the U.S.S.R.* (Cambridge, 1963), pp. 66ff.
6. *Pravda,* March 4 and 5, 1951; *Bakinski rabochii,* May 26, 1951.
7. Milovan Djilas, *Conversations with Stalin* (New York, 1962), pp. 78ff.
8. *Izvestia,* February 9, 1954; *Sovetskoe gosudarstvo i pravo,* 3 (March 1956), pp. 6–7.
9. *Deputaty verkhovnogo soveta* (1958).
10. This was the first occasion on which a comparison was made, in the Central Committee, between Western successes and the malfunctions of the Soviet economy.
11. H. Dinerstein, *War and the Soviet Union* (New York, 1962), pp. 28ff.
12. *XX S'ezd kommunisticheskoi partii sovetsko soiuza, stenografecheskii ochet* (Moscow, 1956), 2 vols.
13. A. Nekritch, *Otreshis'ot straha* (London, 1979), pp. 119ff.
14. Ibid.
15. L. Chukovskaya, *Entretiens avec Anna Akhmatova* (Paris, 1980), p. 278.
16. Tatu, op. cit. note 3, pp. 117–25.
17. *Izvestia,* May 8 and 11, 1957.
18. *Izvestia,* March 28 and April 1, 1957.
19. *Pravda,* July 4, 1957.
20. *XXII S'ezd K.P.S.S.,* vol. 1, pp. 251ff.
21. Tatu, op. cit. note 3, pp. 274–75.
22. Ibid.
23. R. E. Blackwell, Jr., "Cadres Policy in the Brezhnev Era," *Problems of Communism,* March–April 1979, pp. 32–33.
24. M. Matthews, *Privilege in the Soviet Union* (London, 1978), p. 101.

25. *Izvestia,* December 24 and 25, 1958.
26. *Izvestia,* January 15 and 16, 1960; followed by contradictory decisions: *Pravda,* July 9, 1961, and December 5, 1963.
27. I. P. Pishugina, *Pravo na obrazovanie v. S.S.S.R.* (Moscow, 1957), p. 89.
28. Ibid., p. 83.
29. Ibid., p. 90.
30. M. N. Rutkevich and L. I. Sennikova, *Sotsial'nye razlichiia i ikh preodolenie* (Sverdlovsk, 1967), pp. 60ff., demonstrate the slight effect of the reform on the social composition of the student body.
31. Tatu, op. cit. note 3, p. 275.
32. *Pravda,* November 25, 1962; *Spravochnik partiinogo rabotnika* (Moscow, 1964), pp. 300ff.
33. See, for example, *Belorusskaia S.S.S.R., kratkaia entsiklopedia* (1979), vol. 1, pp. 101, 145, 186, 212, 388, 406, which gives the composition of the secretariat of obkoms from 1938 on.
34. *Spravochnik partiinogo rabotnika* (1964), p. 299.
35. *Plenum tsentral'nogo komiteta kommunisticheskoi partii sovetskogo soiuza* March 24–26, 1965 (Moscow, 1965), p. 89.
36. *Programma kommunisticheskoi partii sovetskogo soiuza, proekt* (Moscow, 1961; revised version, 1968).
37. *Pravda,* March 7, 1964; *Kommunist,* 15 (October, 1964), pp. 42–46.
38. P. M. Cocks, "The Purge of Marshal Zhukov," *Slavic Review,* XXII, 3 (September 1963), pp. 48–49; *Pravda,* November 3, 1957.
39. *Pravda,* May 12, 1963; on the history of its publication, see Solzhenitsyn, *The Oak and the Calf* (New York, 1980).
40. *Pravda,* December 22, 1962, launched the attack against the arts.
41. *Pravda,* October 16, 1964.

Chapter 3: Power in a Closed Circuit

1. Constitution of 1977, *Konstitusiia (osnovnoi zakon)* (Moscow, 1977), chap. I, art. 2, p. 6.
2. Ibid, art. 6.
3. J. F. Hough and M. Fainsod, *How the Soviet Union Is Governed* (Cambridge, Mass., 1979), p. 409.
4. J. S. Reshetar, *The Soviet Polity* (New York, 1978), p. 115.
5. *Partiinaia zhizn',* 10 (May 1976) pp. 13–22.
6. Compiled from Reshetar, op. cit. note 4, pp. 115–19.
7. *Voprosy istorii,* May 5, 1970, pp. 13–15, on the operation of the supreme institutions during the war.
8. The Central Committee was called into session six times between March 1953 and February 1956.
9. R. Medvedev, *Le Stalinisme* (Paris, 1972), pp. 241ff.
10. The lists of members of the Central Committee have been compiled from the Soviet press and from *Bol'shaia sovetskaia entsiklopedia ezhegodnik* (1979), cited hereafter as *B.S.E. Ezhegodnik.*

11. The obituaries published by *Pravda* allow us to follow the evolution of the Central Committee.
12. *Partiinaia zhizn',* 10 (May 1976), pp. 13–22.
13. Ibid.
14. N. Galay, "Military Representation in the Higher Party Echelons," *Bulletin of the Institute for the Study of the U.S.S.R.,* III, 4 (April 1956), pp. 6–7. List of members in the reports of congresses: *XXII S'ezd,* III, pp. 356–60; XXIII S'ezd, pp. 381ff; *XXIV S'ezd,* II, pp. 313–18; *Pravda,* March 6, 1976.
15. *BSE Ezhegodnik.*
16. Ibid.
17. Ibid.
18. Ibid.
19. *Pravda,* March 6 and 7, 1979.
20. Another criterion is the representation of workers: The majority was Russian, the minority Ukrainian. The other republics had no delegates from this group.
21. R. V. Daniels in Cocks et al., *The Dynamics of Soviet Politics* (Cambridge, Mass., 1976), p. 78.
22. Ivannikova, born in 1923 and elected for the first time in 1971, directly as a titular member of the Central Committee, is "representative" of the category of workers.
23. Daniels, op. cit. note 21, p. 80.
24. *Plenum tsentral'nogo komiteta—Stenograficheskii ochet* (Moscow, 1959–65).
25. *Pravda,* June 23, 1980.
26. In theory, the Central Committee meets twice a year. The dates of plenums have been compiled from *BSE Ezhegodnik.*
27. For the plenary session of November 27–30, 1979 (*Pravda,* November 28–30 and December 1–2, 1979). Presentation of the plan by N. K. Baibakov; of the budget by finance minister V. F. Garbuzov.
28. B. Levitsky, *The Soviet Political Elite* (Stanford, 1980), pp. 745–47.
29. The last reorganization dates from November 1979 (*Pravda,* November 13, 1979).
30. As in 1973, the Politburo of 1953 included the three ministers of Defense, Foreign Affairs, and Police (*Pravda,* July 7, 1953).
31. Representation of the republics consisted of only two deputies in 1953 (*Pravda,* July 7, 1953) and progressed from 1957 on (*Pravda,* December 19, 1957).
32. The police have not been represented since Beria's fall in 1953 (*Pravda,* July 7, 1953). The army was represented by Bulganin; then, after Zhukov's fall in 1957, had no representation until 1973, with the entry of Andropov and Grechko (*Pravda,* April 28, 1973).
33. See, for example, the Central Committee of November 1979 (*Pravda,* November 13, 1979).
34. Levitsky, op. cit. note 28, pp. 745–57.

35. On the operation of the Secretariat, see *Voprosy istorii K.P.S.S.*, December 12, 1976, p. 33.
36. M. Tatu, *Le Pouvoir en U.R.S.S.* (Paris, 1967), pp. 451–52.
37. G. E. Tsukanov, born in 1919, member of the Central Committee; A. I. Blatov, member of the Control Commission; A. M. Alexandrov-Agentov, candidate on the Central Committee. K. V. Rusakov had held this position before being named to the Secretariat in 1977.
38. The composition of this apparatus changes according to the needs of the Central Committee. *Pravda*, May 4, 1976, announced the creation of a "Correspondence" department.
39. *Pravda*, February 26, 1976.
40. *Pravda*, October 17, 1964.
41. *Spravochnik partiinogo rabotnika* (Moscow, 1957), p. 319.
42. A. Dallin and A. Westin, eds., *Politics in the Soviet Union: Seven Cases* (New York, 1966), pp. 113–64.
43. In this case Kosygin inherited naturally the functions of head of government which Khrushchev had obtained in 1958, for foreign policy reasons. P. A. Rodionov, *Kollektiv'nost-vyshyi printsip partiinogo rukovodstva* (Moscow, 1967), p. 219, says that the October 1964 plenum decided to separate Party and government.
44. J. Hough, "The Brezhnev Era: The Man and the System," *Problems of Communism*, March–April 1976, pp. 1–17; *Pravda*, April 5, 1965, and July 3 and 5, 1966, etc.
45. *Pravda*, July 11 and 12, 1965.
46. *Pravda*, December 10, 1965.
47. *Pravda*, April 1, 1966.
48. *Pravda*, April 4, 1966.
49. *Pravda*, April 1, 1966.
50. *Pravda*, October 15, 1976; *Bakinski rabochii*, October 25, 1976; *Zaria vostoka*, December 19, 1976; Suslov, *Partiinaia zhizn'*, 2 (1979), p. 4.
51. *Pravda*, October 15, 1976.
52. Ponomarev in *Kommunist*, 17 (1977), p. 26.
53. *Partiinaia zhizn'*, 1 (1979), p. 6.
54. Ibid., 2 (1979), p. 22.
55. *Pravda*, December 19, 1978. The decorations were accompanied by benefits and advantages established by a decree of September 6, 1967, and extended by a decree of April 30, 1975; *Pravda*, May 2, 1975.
56. *Pravda*, November 12, 1978; *Literaturnaia gazeta*, 17 (1979), p. 3.
57. *Actualités soviétiques*, 186 (January 4, 1980). We should point out that Brezhnev had previously received the International Lenin Prize in recognition of his struggle for peace.
58. *Pravda*, December 19, 1976.
59. Brezhnev's speech in *Pravda*, March 3, 1979, pp. 1 and 2; Kosygin's, *Pravda*, March 2, 1979, pp. 1 and 2; Suslov's, *Pravda*, March 1, 1979, p. 2; Kirilenko's, *Pravda*, February 28, 1979, p. 2. The other speeches were

published between February 15, and 27. The higher the leader's rank in the Politburo, the later the date on which his speech is published.

60. The candidates of the Politburo and the secretaries of the Central Committee spoke first, and their speeches were published between February 3 and 14, the space ranging between three and three and a half columns, always on page 2.

61. Azhubei joined the Central Committee at the Twenty-second Congress, worked as an editor on *Sovetskii soiuz;* he was dismissed on October 14, 1964, and expelled from the Central Committee at the November plenum.

62. *Pravda,* March 22, 1979. The decree appointing Yuri Brezhnev was published in *Sobranie postanovlenii pravitel'stva S.S.S.R.,* 9 (1979), p. 196. We should note that the promotion to deputy minister in 1976 received no publicity.

63. Yun Churbanov was elected to the Central Commission at the Twenty-fifth Congress.

64. *Izvestia,* February 28, 1980.

65. General Paputin was in Afghanistan in December 1979; his death was announced in *Pravda,* January 3, 1980.

66. Mikhail Suslov himself, the official guardian of party orthodoxy, used this title (*Partiinaia zhizn',* 2 [1979] op. 4).

67. This was the case for the Twenty-fifth Congress.

68. B. Harasymiw, "Nomenklatura: The Soviet Communist Party's Leadership Recruitment System," *Canadian Journal of Political Science,* 4 (1969), pp. 493–512.

69. See Khrushchev, *Khrushchev Remembers* (Boston; 1971).

70. *Pravda,* June 17 and 18, 1977.

71. *Pravda,* April 19, 1979.

72. *Pravda,* May 25, 1977.

73. *Pravda,* January 1, 1974.

74. *Pravda,* April 17, 1975.

75. Report on Radio Moscow, May 8, 1976. An article by Colonel General Sredin in *Voennyi vestnik,* 10 (1977), mentions that he is commander-in-chief of Soviet armed forces.

76. The composition of the Defense Council is not known, for this body is surrounded by the greatest discretion. It is known, however, that four members of the Politburo were on it in 1976: Brezhnev; Kosygin, the head of government; Podgorny, president of the Presidium of the Supreme Soviet; and Ustinov, Minister of Defense.

77. *Pravda,* December 14, 1976. This revision of Brezhnev's military past is contradicted by the testimony of General Grigorenko, *Mémoires* (Paris, 1980), pp. 327ff.

78. *Pravda,* February 21, 1978.

79. On the conditions for awarding this order, see *Sbornik zakonov S.S.S.R. i ukazov presidiuma verkhovnogo soveta S.S.S.R., 1938, 1958* (Moscow, 1959), p. 332.

80. *Pravda,* March 29 and 31 and April 1–10 and 15, 1978.
81. *Voenno istorisheskii jurnal,* 12 (1976), p. 5.
82. During the exchange of Party cards (1972–75), the card marked number 1 was attributed to Lenin and number 2 to Brezhnev. On the exchange of cards, see Brezhnev, *Ochet tsentral'nogo komiteta K.P.S.S. i osheredzne zadachi partii* (Moscow, 1976), p. 77; *Pravda,* June 24, 1976.
83. This was the inscription on the statue of Stalin erected on Mount Elbrus.
84. Shevarnadze's speech at the Twenty-fifth Congress, February 27, 1976.
85. *Pravda,* July 20, 1966.
86. *Pravda,* August 26, 1979.
87. Gerth and Mills, eds., *From Max Weber* (New York, 1958), pp. 246–47.
88. *Pravda,* April 18, 1979.
89. *Pravda,* April 19, 1979.
90. See *Pravda,* August 4, 1966; July 16, 1970; July 27, 1974.
91. *Pravda,* April 18, 1979.
92. See *Sovetskaia kultura,* September 10, 1976, and *Pravda,* October 15, 1976 (Kirilenko receives the Order of Lenin and his second Hammer and Sickle gold medal); *Pravda,* November 20, 1977 (Suslov receives the Order of the October Revolution); *Pravda,* May 10, 1973, July 18, 1977, August 24, 1979 (two successive awards of the Order of Lenin and a Hero of Socialist Labor to G. A. Aliev, member of the Politburo).

Chapter 4: The Political Reservoir

1. Constitution of 1977: *Konstitutsia-osnovnoi zakon* (Moscow, 1977), arts. 71, 84–88, pp. 26–33.
2. *BSE Ezhegodnik,* pp. 11 and 13.
3. In the Constitution of 1977, art. 3, loc. cit. note 1, p. 6.
4. J. Hough, *The Soviet Prefects* (Cambridge, Mass., 1969), p. 3.
5. *BSE Ezhegodnik,* p. 13: 16,721,323 members on January 1, 1979.
6. *Partiinaia zhizn',* 10 (1976), p. 7.
7. *Narodnoe khoziastvo S.S.S.R., 1973,* p. 33; *Partiinaia zhizn',* 14 (1973), p. 12.
8. Brezhnev, *Ochet tsentral'nomu komitetu K.P.S.S.: Ocherednye zadachi partii v oblasti vnutrenei i vnechnei politiki* (Moscow, 1976), p. 77.
9. Kerblay, op. cit. note 9, pp. 207–9.
10. Ibid., p. 209.
11. B. Kerblay, *La Société soviétique contemporaine* (Paris, 1978), p. 207; *Narodnoe khoziastvo S.S.S.R., 1973,* pp. 456 and 468.
12. "K.P.S.S. v tsiffrakh," in *Partiinaia zhizn',* 10 (1976).
13. *Partiinaia zhizn',* 10 (1976).
14. Ibid. and *Partiinaia zhizn',* 21 (1977), pp. 32–33. And for 1978, *BSE Ezhegodnik,* p. 13, says that 25.6 percent of party members are women.
15. *Partiinaia zhizn',* 10 (1976), and *BSE Ezhegodnik,* p. 17. The latter indicates that Komsomol membership had reached 38,459,000 in 1978.

16. *Vesesoiuznaia perepis' naselniia 1959 goda S.S.S.R.*, p. 75, and *Partiinaia zhizn'*, 14 (1973), p. 16.
17. *Narodnoe khoziastvo S.S.S.R.*, *1974*, pp. 33–42, and *1975*, p. 38; *Partiinaia zhizn'*, 10 (1976) and 21 (1977), p. 29.
18. *Partiinaia zhizn'*, 1 (1962), p. 44; 19 (1967), p. 14; 10 (1976), p. 16.
19. H. Carrère d'Encausse, *L'Empire éclaté* (Paris, 1978), pp. 34–45.
20. Ibid., pp. 56ff.
21. Non-Russians settled in the R.S.F.S.R. are more likely to enter the Party than their compatriots who have remained in their republic, and sometimes more likely than the Russians. *Partiinaia zhizn'*, 21 (1977), p. 22; *BSE Ezhegodnik*; *Narodnoe khosiastvo S.S.S.R.*, *1973*, pp. 35–38.
22. Compiled from tables in *Partiinaia zhizn'*, 10 (1976).
23. Ibid.
24. See, for example, *Partiinaia zhizn'*, 3 (1979), pp. 27–32, and 9 (1979), pp. 50–54.
25. Ibid., 10 (1976) and 21 (1977), pp. 39–40.
26. Kerblay, op. cit. note 9, p. 246.
27. *Survey*, 22 (Spring 1976), p. 64.
28. Hough and Fainsod, *How the Soviet Union Is Governed*, p. 495.
29. J. Hough, op. cit. note 4; J. C. Moses, *Regional Party Leadership and Policy Making in the U.S.S.R.* (New York, 1974).
30. Compiled from local newspapers.
31. Compiled from *BSE Ezhegodnik*, pp. 90ff.
32. H. Rigby, "The Soviet Regional Leadership: The Brezhnev Generation," *Soviet Studies*, March, 1978, pp. 1–25.
33. Moses, op. cit. note 29, pp. 213ff.
34. Hough, op. cit. note 4, pp. 62ff, particularly the table on p. 63.
35. F. Fleron, "Towards a Reconceptualization of Political Change in the Soviet Union," *Comparative Politics*, 2 (January 1969), pp. 228–44; *Pravda*, February 1, 1959, p. 4; *Kommunist*, 13 (September 1965), p. 88.
36. *Partiinaia zhizn'*, 20 (1964), pp. 3–7; *Zaria vostoka*, June 29, 1965.
37. Hough, op. cit. note 4, pp. 20–25.
38. Brezhnev, in *XXIV S'ezd K.P.S.S.*, vol. 1, pp. 118ff; *Partiinaia zhizn'*, 5 (March 1972), pp. 32ff.
39. *Plenum tsentral'nogo komiteta K.P.S.S., mart 1965*, p. 119, on reactions to this provision. The speech was given by M. S. Solomentsev, first secretary of the Obkom of Rostov.
40. *Kommunist*, 16 (1964), pp. 7–8.
41. *Pravda*, November 17, 1964.
42. *XXIII S'ezd*, vol. 1, p. 90.
43. T. K. Mal'bakhov, first secretary of the Kabardino-Balkar Autonomous Republic, appointed in November 1956; I. I. Senkin, first secretary of the Karelian Autonomous Republic, September 22, 1958.
44. For example, K. F. Katushev, appointed first secretary of the Gorky Obkom (*Pravda*, December 28, 1965), secretary of the Central Committee in 1968,

and now vice-president of the Committee of Ministers of the U.S.S.R., despite his exclusion from the Secretariat.

45. Brezhnev, *XXIV S'ezd*, vol. 1, p. 124; *Kommunist*, 3 (February 1972), p. 38.

46. The only women known to have held high posts in obkom bureaus are D. P. Komarova, president of the Ispolkom of Briansk from 1962 to 1966, and L. P. Likova, second secretary of the Smolensk region from 1955 to 1961 (*Deputaty verkhovnogo soveta*, 1966, and *BSE Ezhegodnik*, 1962 and 1979). All the other women (about fifteen) are propaganda specialists.

47. Elected on December 6, 1978, and June 15 and December 31, 1975 (both secretaries of the Checheno-Ingush Autonomous Republic were changed in 1975).

48. The regions are distributed as follows: Ukraine, 25; Kazakhstan, 19; Uzbekistan, 11; Byelorussia, 6; Turkmenistan, 5; Tadzhikistan and Kirghiz, 3 *(BSE Ezhegodnik)*.

49. Kiev has had an autonomous organization since 1975 *(Radyanska ukraina,* May 15, 1975).

50. Rashidov, elected in Uzbekistan in 1959; Usubaliev in Kirghiz in 1961; Bodiul in Moldavia in 1961.

51. *Pravda*, April 5, 1978; *Kazakhstanskaia pravda*, December 15, 1979, and March 26, 1980.

52. *Pravda,* July 8, 1979.

53. Ibid.

54. *Pravda vostoka,* December 19, 1979. On this subject, see I. Zemtsov, *La Corruption en union soviétique* (Paris, 1976), on Azerbaidzha.

55. *Pravda,* April 5, 1978.

56. *Kazakhstanskaia pravda,* December 13, 1979.

57. The two first secretaries of the Ukraine (Poltava and Odessa) and one Kazakh (North Kazakhstan).

58. B. Harasymiw, "Nomenklatura: The Soviet Communist Party's Leadership Recruitment System," *Canadian Journal of Political Science,* 4 (1969), pp. 493–511; Levin and Perfilev, *Kadry apparata upravleniia v S.S.S.R.* (Leningrad, 1970) H. H. Salisbury, *Sakharov Speaks* (London, 1974) pp. 145–46.

59. *Dvenatsaty s'ezd R.K.P. (b)* (Moscow, 1968), p. 64; P. Morozov, *Leninskie printsipy podbora rasstanovki i vospitania kadrov* (Moscow, 1959), p. 39.

60. *Partiinaia zhizn',* 5 (1975), pp. 68–73.

61. M. Morozov, *L'Establishment soviétique* (Paris, 1974), p. 40.

62. Kerblay, op. cit. note 9, p. 258.

63. Hough, op. cit. note 4, pp. 151–54.

64. "Kalinkin thought that he was not just anybody, but a man of the *Nomenklatura."* *Sovetskaia litva,* February 25, 1962, quoted by Hough, op. cit. note 4, p. 390.

65. *Partiinaia zhizn',* 20 (1975), p. 41.

66. *Kommunist,* 14 (September 1977), pp. 49–61.

67. *Partiinaia zhizn'*, 10 (1976) and 21 (1979), p. 40.
68. *Radio Vilnius*, August 20, 1978, a program answering questions from American listeners about life in the U.S.S.R.
69. For Alec Nove, "Y a-t-il une classe dirigeante en U.R.S.S.?" (*Revue des études comparatives est-ouest*, 4 (1975), pp. 5–44), the *nomenklatura* is a tool of political power.
70. The supervision completing this mechanism is a permanent preoccupation of the Party (*Partiinaia zhizn'*, 4 [1977], pp. 50–57; 23 [1979], pp. 49–54; 9 [1979], pp. 54–60).
71. T. B. Bottomore, *Elites and Society* (New York, 1964), p. 8.

Chapter 5: The Victory of the Managers

1. *Pravda*, October 17 and November 6, 1964.
2. Suslov has also been a member of the Review Commission since 1939, of the Central Committee since 1941, and of the Presidium since 1955; secretary of an obkom from 1937 to 1944; editor in chief of *Pravda*, 1949–50. G. Hodnett provides a portrait of Suslov in *Soviet Leaders*, pp. 108–15. For careers in general, see G. Hodnett and V. Ogarev, *Leaders of the Soviet Republics, 1952–1972* (Canberra, 1973).
3. Shvernik entered the Party in 1905, the Central Committee in 1925; he was a candidate on the Presidium 1939–52 and 1953–57 and titular member 1952–53 and 1957–66, President of the Presidium of the Supreme Soviet of the R.S.F.S.R. 1944–46, President of the Presidium of the Supreme Soviet of the U.S.S.R. 1946–53, then president of various unions and, from 1956 to 1966, president of the Party Control Committee. See *Deputaty verkhovnogo soveta* (1962).
4. On Podgorny's position see the analysis by M. Tatu, *Le Pouvoir en U.R.S.S.* (Paris, 1967), pp. 541–46.
5. See the portrait of Shelepin by R. M. Slusser in *Soviet Leaders*, pp. 95–103.
6. *XXII s'ezd K.P.S.S.*, vol. 2, pp. 405ff.
7. *Pravda*, November 17, 1964.
8. M. Heykal, *Le Sphynx et le commissaire* (Paris, 1980), p. 165.
9. See Tatu, op. cit. note 4, pp. 543 and 558.
10. V. N. Titov, secretary of the Central Committee in charge of organization, was dismissed in April 1965 and sent to Kazakhstan as second secretary. Hodnett and Ogarev, op. cit., pp. 150–51.
11. *Partiinaia zhizn'*, 15 (August 1965), pp. 23–25.
12. *International Herald Tribune*, January 30, 1979.
13. *Pravda*, December 7, 1965.
14. The article by Semichasny in *Pravda*, May 7, 1965, on police authority gives no indication of the coming fall.
15. See J. S. Reshetar, Jr., *The Soviet Polity* (New York, 1978), pp. 146–50.

16. Kirilenko's career between 1957 and 1964 followed a sinuous course absolutely identical to that of Brezhnev. See the appropriate issues of *Deputaty verkhovnogo soveta.*

17. Hough and Fainsod, *How the Soviet Union Is Governed* (Cambridge, Mass., 1979), p. 247.

18. Tatu, op. cit. note 4, p. 558.

19. *Pravda,* November 17, 1964.

20. *XXIII s'ezd,* vol. 2, p. 292.

21. According to *Politicheskii dnevnik,* p. 243, in the spring of 1967, Shelepin was once again in a strong position.

22. *New York Times,* June 20, 1967.

23. Heykal, op. cit. note 8, p. 244.

24. Ibid., p. 227.

25. The criticisms of Shelest were expressed on many occasions in *Pravda ukrainy* (November 15, 1969; May 19, September 22, and November 11, 1971; and May 2, 1972).

26. M. Tatu, "Kremlinology: The Mini Crisis of 1970," *Interplay,* October 1970, pp. 13–19; B. Meissner, "Die KPd.S.U. und der Sowjet Staat zwischen dem XXIII und XXIV Parteitag," *Europa Archiv,* 7, pp. 223–48.

27. Nixon, *Mémoires* (Paris, 1978), p. 419.

28. Ibid., pp. 379 and 387.

29. Ibid., pp. 433 and 441.

30. Ibid., pp. 450–51.

31. Ibid., p. 451.

32. Ibid., pp. 455 and 461.

33. See the speech delivered at the fifteenth congress of the unions (*Pravda,* March 21, 1972, and *Kommunist,* 18 (1972), p. 17; *Kommunist ukrainy,* 4 (1973), pp. 77–82.).

34. *Pravda,* May 25 and June 17 and 18, 1977.

35. B. Levitsky, *The Soviet Political Elite* (Stanford, 1970), pp. 745–47; *Pravda,* March 7, 1953 (for the period before the Twentieth Congress).

36. T. Rakowska Harmstone, in *The Dynamics of Soviet Politics* (Cambridge, Mass., 1976), pp. 62–65.

37. *Pravda,* March 6, 1976.

38. *Pravda,* March 3, 1972.

39. H. Carrère d'Encausse, *L'Empire éclaté* (Paris, 1978), pp. 220–21.

40. *Radio Moscow,* April 16, 1975, announced the plenum held the day before in these terms, "We have just been informed that a plenum of the Central Committee was held yesterday," and devoted the bulk of its report to the foreign policy speech by the minister, Gromyko.

41. *Turkmenskaia iskra,* December 16, 1978.

42. Reuter, November 12, 1977.

43. Edward L. Warner, III, *The Military in Contemporary Soviet Politics* (New York, 1978), pp. 16–65.

44. Ibid.

45. *Pravda,* December 10 and October 20, 1964.

46. *Pravda,* July 12, 1965.

47. See Brezhnev's speech for the forty-seventh anniversary of the revolution, *Pravda,* November 7, 1964.

48. *Pravda,* November 8, 1964; for the complete text, *New York Herald Tribune* (international edition), November 9, 1964.

49. On the expulsion of Zakharov, *Krasnaia zvezda,* March 28, 1963 (his return was due to the accidental death of his successor).

50. *Krasnaia zvezda,* February 4, 1965.

51. Kosygin, present in Hanoi at the time, issued declarations of Soviet solidarity (*Izvestia,* February 4, 1965).

52. Malinovski, in *Krasnaia zvezda,* September 24, 1965.

53. *Krasnaia zvezda,* September 22, 1965.

54. *Kommunist vooruzhonykh sil,* 8 (April 1965), p. 17.

55. Ibid., p. 18.

56. Ibid., 13 (July 1965), pp. 8–9.

57. *Voprosy istorii,* 2 (February 1963), pp. 7–11.

58. In *Pravda,* on December 10, 1964, Kosygin announced a reduction in military expenditures for 1965 below the already low projections of Khrushchev, *Planovoe khoziaistvo,* 4 (April 1965), p. 6.

59. *Pravda,* May 22, 1965.

60. *Pravda,* June 5, 1965.

61. Report from the Minister of Finance, V. F. Garbuzov, *Pravda,* December 8, 1965.

62. Brezhnev's report to the Twenty-third Congress, *XXIII s'ezd,* vol. 1, p. 93. See also Kosygin's report, ibid., vol. 2, p. 64.

63. H. Carrère d'Encausse, *La Politique soviétique au Moyen-Orient* (Paris, 1975), and *Pravda,* January 24, 1968.

64. Brezhnev's report, *XXIII s'ezd,* vol. 1, pp. 39–44.

65. Speech by Malinovski, *XXIII s'ezd,* vol. 1, pp. 411ff; speech by Ipichev, ibid., p. 548.

66. *Pravda,* October 30, 1961.

67. *XXIII s'ezd,* vol. 2, pp. 381ff.

68. *XXIII s'ezd,* vol. 1, p. 415.

69. *Krasnaia zvezda,* January 5, 1967.

70. *Krasnaia zvezda,* April 25, 1969.

71. *Krasnaia zvezda,* April 6, 1967.

72. *Krasnaia zvezda,* January 5, 1967.

73. *BSE,* third edition, VII, p. 319.

74. *KPSS v resoliutsiakh i resheniakh s'ezdov, konferentsii i plenumov TSK* (Moscow, 1972), vol. IX, p. 329.

75. "Considerable sums are spent on defense, and the Soviet people understand the necessity for this. The socialist revolution, as Marx and Lenin taught us, must be able to confront its class enemy with invincible military power." Brezhnev's jubilee speech, November 3–4, 1967, in *Leninskim kursom: rechi i statii* Moscow, 1970), vol. 2, p. 126.

76. *Krasnaia zvezda,* February 20, 1968.

77. D. W. Paul, "Soviet Foreign Policy and the Invasion of Czechoslovakia," *International Studies Quarterly,* XV, 2 (June 1971), pp. 194ff.

78. *Le Monde,* May 4, 1968.

79. *Krasnaia zvezda,* April 27, 1969. The communiqué announcing this measure explained that it was a joint decision of the Central Committee of the Party and of the Council of Ministers.

80. *Pravda,* April 28, 1973. See the discussion of Western criticism by General Ogarkov in *Krasnaia zvezda,* July 10, 1973.

81. *Kommunist,* 3 (February 1974), p. 23.

82. The only military man who spoke at the congress was Major-General Kochemasov, whose speech was without great impact (*Pravda,* February 29, 1976); *Izvestia,* February 25, 1976, published a photograph of Grechko during the congress; but in *Krasnaia zvezda,* on March 17, 1976, Grechko published an article on the Twenty-fifth Congress in which he pointed out that the army had more and more Party members and that they were in all the key positions.

83. *Pravda,* April 27, 1976.

84. *Krasnaia zvezda,* July 31, 1976.

85. *Izvestia,* May 9, 1976. The decree was published the same day in *Krasnaia zvezda.*

86. *Pravda,* May 11, 1976.

87. *Pravda,* February 21, 1978.

88. *Kommunist,* 7 (May 1962), p. 64; *Izvestia,* February 10, 1975.

89. *Krasnaia zvezda,* August 10, 1975, published declarations by Guilovani, Vice-Minister of Defense, on the economic role of the army, which had, in the early seventies, built 30 percent of the prefabricated industrial constructions and participated heavily in housing construction; according to Guilovani, the five-year plan for 1976–80 anticipated a similar role for the army.

90. *Pravda,* August 28, 1975, on the participation of troops from the central Asian military district in the harvest. (It is to be noted that soldiers earn seven rubles a month, and the army's contribution to the economy is thus very profitable.)

91. P. Gelard, *Les Systèmes politiques des états socialistes* (Paris, 1975), pp. 278–79.

92. Decree of the Presidium of the Supreme Soviet, December 13, 1978.

93. *Izvestia,* December 21, 1967.

94. On the MVD, *Pravda,* November 29, 1968, p. 1.

95. M. Feschbach and S. Rapaway, "Soviet Population and Manpower Trends and Policies," *U.S. Congress: Joint Economic Committee,* October 1976, p. 131.

96. *Pravda,* March 5, 1977.

97. *Voprosy istorii KPSS,* August 1978, p. 66.

98. S. Bialer, "Succession and Turnover of Soviet Elites," *Journal of International Affairs,* XXXII, 2 (Fall–Winter 1978), pp. 181–200.

99. Zverev, Minister of Defense Industries, died at sixty-six on December 12, 1978; Alexeeivski, Minister of Hydraulic Resources, died at seventy-two on January 1, 1979; Grishmanov, Minister for the Construction of Industrial Material, died at seventy-two on January 4, 1979.
100. H. Rigby, "The Soviet Government since Khrushchev," *Politics*, 12 (May 1979), pp. 5–22.
101. J. Hough, "The Brezhnev Era: The Man and the System," *Problems of Communism* (March–April 1976), pp. 1–17.
102. *Kommunist*, 5 (March 1972), p. 57.
103. *Pravda*, June 24, 1980.
104. No doubt the plenums of the Central Committee generally set in advance the agenda for the congress. This was true for the Twenty-fourth Congress; see *Pravda*, July 14, 1970. But on the other hand, for the Twenty-fifth Congress, the report of the plenum that set the date remained silent on the organization of the congress (*Pravda*, April 17, 1975), and it was only shortly before the congress that a final plenum set the agenda (*Pravda*, December 2, 1975).

Chapter 6: The Manufacture of Souls

1. On the concept of political culture, see A. Brown and J. Gray, eds., *Political Culture and Political Change in Communist States* (London, 1977), pp. 3–10 and 58.
2. On the use of the slogan, see A. Zinoviev, *The Radiant Future* (New York, 1980).
3. Marx, *Capital*, vol. 3.
4. *Programma kommunisticheskoi partii sovetskogo soiuza*, proekt (Moscow, 1961).
5. See ch. VII, articles 39–69, of the Constitution of 1977.
6. Articles 13–16 of the Constitution of 1977.
7. A decree of September 20, 1965 (*Vedomosti verkhovnogo soveta R.S.F. S.R.-no. 38, art. 932*, p. 737) defined parasitism. Since 1975, it is still not an offense but an antisocial attitude; see *Komsomolskaia pravda*, August 10, 1977.
8. *The Communist Manifesto*, in Marx, *The Revolutions of 1848* (Harmondsworth, 1973), p. 78.
9. *Literaturnaia gazeta*, January 22, 1934, p. 1.
10. Lenin, *Polnoe*, vol. 45, pp. 378–89, admits that the task of the revolution is to adapt itself to the inertia of attitudes of thought.
11. Article 52 of the Constitution of 1977, p. 22.
12. *Deti i religia* (Minsk, 1970); *Nauka i religia*, June 19, 1979, pp. 14–15.
13. Document 45 of the Moscow Group for Monitoring the Helsinki Accords, April 1978, *samizdat*.
14. B. Kerblay, *La Société soviétique contemporaine* (Paris, 1977), pp. 149–51.
15. Ibid., p. 156.

16. *Bol'shaia Sovetskaia Entsiklopedia,* vol. VIII, p. 1523, and Dimov, *Les Hommes doubles* (Paris, 1980), pp. 39–40.

17. Brezhnev, *Leninskim kursom,* vol. 5 (1976), p. 545.

18. The newspapers of the youth organizations are one of the privileged instruments for this. They are *Pionerskaia pravda* and *Komsomol'skaia pravda.*

19. Nenashev, *Ratsional'naia organizatsiia ideologicheskoi raboty* (Moscow, 1976).

20. *Partiinaia zhizn'* 10 (1976), p. 23.

21. *Spravochnik partiinogo rabotnika,* 16 (1976).

22. *Partiinaia zhizn',* 21 (1977), p. 41.

23. *Partiinaia zhizn',* 13 (1978), p. 305.

24. *Pravda,* April 4, 1978, and *Partiinaia zhizn',* 7 (1978), p. 3.

25. *Pravda,* September 2, 1978.

26. *Partiinaia zhizn',* 7 (1978), p. 3.

27. *Ob ideologicheskoi rabote KPSS, sbornik dokumentov* (Moscow, 1977), pp. 436ff.

28. *Partiinaia zhizn',* 10 (1976), p. 23; 21 (1977), p. 42.

29. Ibid.

30. *Partiinaia zhizn',* 21 (November 1977), p. 43, indicates 1,316,900 propagandists for 1975. They were distributed as follows: 93,500 functionaries of the Party, the government, the unions, and the Komsomol; 202,900 directors of industrial enterprises, construction projects, or rural enterprises; 662,300 professionals (engineers, economists, doctors, agronomists, etc.); and 257,000 teachers and researchers.

31. *Partiinaia zhizn',* 10 (1976).

32. *Pravda,* January 11, 1968; Petrovich, ed., *Partiinoe stroitel'stvo* (Moscow, 1976), pp. 307ff.

33. *Partiinoe stroitel'stvo,* p. 313.

34. *Partiinaia zhizn',* 10 (1976), p. 23.

35. On this policy, see Struve, *Les Chrétiens en U.R.S.S.* (Paris, 1963).

36. See the sixteen posters: *Razum protiv religii* (Moscow, 1977).

37. "Znanie," *BSE Ezhegodnik,* 1979.

38. The Party press is constantly concerned with this: *Partiinaia zhizn',* 23 (1979), pp. 59ff.; *Literaturnaia gazeta,* May 28, 1975.

39. Kerblay, op. cit. note 14, p. 140.

40. *Pravda,* February 21, 1978.

41. M. V. Frunze, *Izbrannye proizvedenia* (Moscow, 1934), pp. 180ff.

42. *Voennye akademii i uchilishchie* (Moscow, 1974), pp. 100ff.

43. The army nevertheless continues to proclaim that it must constantly improve the quality of its cadres and make them more open to the intellectual world (*Krasnaia zvezda,* March 11, 1972).

44. Ibid., November 29, 1972.

45. Law of October 12, 1967, published in *Pravda,* October 13, 1967.

46. Article 13 of the law of October 12, 1967, stipulates that service is two years for land forces, aeronaval forces, and border guards, three years for the

navy and naval border guards, but only one year for those with higher degrees.

47. Decree of February 25, 1977, *Vedomosti verkhovnogo soveta S.S.S.R.* (Moscow, no. 9 [1875]), March 2, 1977, which increased the length of service for those with higher degrees to a year and a half for land forces and two years for the navy.

48. *Krasnaia zvezda,* February 3, 1972, article by Sapunov; *Kommunist vooruzhonykh sil,* July 25, 1975, p. 20.

49. Article 17 of the law of October 12, 1967 (*Pravda,* October 13, 1967).

50. *Krasnaia zvezda,* February 3, 1972.

51. The resources of the DOSAAF come from five sources: members' dues, gifts from institutions, income from enterprises belonging to the DOSAAF, lotteries organized by the DOSAAF, and, finally, gifts from the state of military equipment.

52. *Sovetskii patriot,* December 3, 1972.

53. *Sovetskii patriot,* September 9, 1973.

54. The reorganization of 1961 set up a national system of civil defense with Marshall Zhukov officially placed in charge in 1964.

55. A. T. Altunin, born August 14, 1921, is a General of the Army and was appointed to civil defense in July 1972. He was elected a full member of the Central Committee at the Twenty-fifth Congress. His predecessor, Marshal Zhukov, had been a full member of the Central Committee since 1961.

56. On their organizations, see *Krasnaia zvezda,* October 4, 1972, and March 17 and November 24, 1973.

57. *Krasnaia zvezda,* July 8, 1973.

58. Article 62 of the Constitution of 1977. Article 63 stipulates that military service is a "duty of honor."

59. *Partiinaia zhizn',* 19 (1977), p. 8.

60. A. K. Uledov, *Obshchestvennoe mnenie sovetskogo obshchestva* (Moscow, 1963), p. 323.

61. *Komsomol'skaia pravda,* June 21 and July 22, 1961; B. A. Grushin and V. V. Sikin, *Ispovod pokoleniia* (Moscow, 1962).

62. Grushin, op. cit., pp. 90–93.

63. See Sakharov, "Letter from Three Scientists," *Saturday Review,* June 6, 1970, for the creation of an Institute for Sociological Research.

64. Surveys cited by S. White, *Political Culture and Soviet Politics* (London, 1979), p. 124.

65. Ibid.

66. *Usloviia povysheniia obshchestvennoi raboty* (Volgograd, 1973), p. 101.

67. Quoted by S. White, op. cit. note 63.

68. Ibid., p. 129.

69. Ibid.

70. *Pravda,* June 28, 1979, p. 2.

71. *Kommunist,* 4 (1977), p. 33.

72. *Pravda,* November 28, 1978, p. 2.

73. Quoted by Kerblay, op. cit. note 39, p. 220.
74. W. D. Connor, *Socialism, Politics, and Equality* (New York, 1979), table p. 270.
75. Ibid., pp. 269ff. See also V. Lepeshkin, in *Kommunist bielorussii,* 7 (1975), p. 35.
76. Ibid., p. 317. *Izvestia,* April 10, 1973, emphasized the necessity of changing the goals proposed by education to the young in order to increase the prestige of manual labor.
77. *Izvestia,* August 31, 1979.
78. Examples: *Kommunist:* from 995,000 to 945,000; *Partiinaia zhizn':* 1,127,500 to 1,060,000; *Agitator:* 1,646,000 to 1,600,000; *Molodoi kommunist:* 995,000 to 890,000; *Sovetskie profosozhuzy:* 664,145 to 599,630.
79. *Sotsiologicheskie issledovaniia,* 3 (1975), p. 59.
80. Quoted by G. Hollander, *Soviet Political Indoctrination,* pp. 168–83.
81. Kerblay, op. cit. note 14, p. 140, and M. T. Iovchuk and L. N. Kogan, eds., *Dukhovnyi mir sovetskogo rabochego* (Moscow, 1972), pp. 376ff.
82. Kerblay, op. cit. note 14, p. 140.

Chapter 7: Subject or Citizen?

1. Russian text, p. 4.
2. On these problems, see J. G. Collignon, *La Théorie de l'état du peuple tout entier en union soviétique* (Paris, 1967). V. V. Varshukh and V. I. Razin have provided a bibliography of Soviet work on this problem in *Voprosy filosofii,* 4 (April 1967).
3. See N. N. Sukhanov, *Zapiski o revoliutsii* (Berlin and Moscow), 1922–23, 7 vols. (condensed French edition: *La Révolution russe 1917* [Paris, 1965]).
4. Article 96 of the Constitution of 1977, p. 35; the electoral system is the subject of Chapter XIII of the Constitution, pp. 34–36.
5. Until 1977, terms were for four and two years. Article 90 provides for their extension. See Brezhnev's speech presenting the Constitution, *Kommunist,* 15 (October 1977), pp. 5–20.
6. Before 1977, the three elections were separate.
7. *Pravda* and *Izvestia* publish speeches by titular members of the Politburo, one per issue. Those of the others are published two per issue. Speeches by Brezhnev and Kosygin are on page one, the others on page two. See *Pravda* and *Izvestia,* from February 5 (Grishin) to February 23, 1980 (Brezhnev). It is interesting to compare Brezhnev's speech in 1980 with the one he made in 1979 (*Pravda,* March 8, 1979).
8. Radio Moscow, February 14, 1979, Ivan Kapitonov: "The makeup of the body of candidates for deputy indicates that the most eminent representatives of our people, the finest sons and daughters of our nation, have been selected."
9. Election speech by Brezhnev, February 22, 1980; see *Pravda,* February 23, 1980.

10. Electoral law of July 6, 1978, article 9 (*Pravda*, July 8, 1978).
11. V. F. Kotok, *Sovetskaia predstavitel'naia sistema* (Moscow, 1963), p. 36.
12. Grigoriev, *Vybory v mestnye sovety deputatov trudiashchikhsia* (Moscow, 1969), p. 37.
13. On the votes *against* candidates, see the election results of 1979, *Pravda*, March 6 and 7, 1979.
14. Ibid.
15. *Izvestia*, January 14, 1969.
16. *Pravda*, March 6, 1979.
17. *Verkhovnyi sovet, statisticheskii sbornik* (Moscow, 1970), p. 48.
18. *Pravda*, March 6, 1979.
19. *Izvestia*, March 16, 1979.
20. *Pravda*, January 24, 1979, on the composition of the electoral commissions of the Supreme Soviet, and *Pravda*, December 20, 1979, for the organization of the 1980 elections.
21. *Izvestia*, March 16, 1979.
22. *Pravda*, March 6 and 7, 1979, and the report by I. Kapitonov, Radio Moscow, March 6, 1979.
23. In 1972, the Jehovah's Witnesses, for example, called on their followers to boycott the elections (*Sovetskaia kirghizia*, January 12, 1972).
24. Report by Kapitonov quoted above (*Izvestia*, June 15, 1975).
25. "Open letter to voters to explain why I am not voting for Kosygin," a *samizdat* document.
26. *Pravda*, March 5, 1980.
27. Report by I. Kapitonov to the Central Electoral Commission, Radio Moscow, March 6, 1979.
28. "Open letter to the electoral commissions," Tass, January 26, 1979.
29. Radio Moscow, February 13, 1979.
30. *Programma kommunisticheskoi partii sovetskogo soiuza* (Moscow, 1968), p. 104.
31. *Sovetskoe gosudarstvo i pravo*, 6 (June 1963), p. 25.
32. *Pravda*, October 5, 1977.
33. *Pravda*, June 5, 1977.
34. P. H. Juviler and H. W. Morton, eds., *Soviet Policy Making*, pp. 29–60.
35. *Vedomosti verkhovnogo soveta S.S.S.R.*, 10 (Moscow, 1980).
36. *Izvestia*, February 28, 1980.
37. *Vedomosti verkhovnogo soveta S.S.S.R.*, 10 (Moscow, 1980).
38. *Pravda*, April 20, 1979.
39. *Itogi vyborov mestnykh sovetov deputatov trudiashchikhsia* (Moscow, 1971), pp. 90ff.
40. T. H. Friedgut, *Political Participation in the U.S.S.R.* (Princeton, 1979), p. 172.
41. *Izvestia*, January 13, 1967.
42. Vasiliev, *Rabota deputata sel'skogo poselkogo soveta* (Moscow, 1969), p. 40.
43. *Pravda*, April 20, 1979.

44. Podgorny provided figures to the Twenty-third Congress on the recall of deputies in 1965. *XXIII S'ezd KPSS* (Moscow, 1966), vol. 1., p. 242.
45. *Sovetskoe gosudarstvo i pravo,* October 1961, p. 33.
46. *Bol'shaia sovetskaia entsiklopedia,* vol. VIII, p. 1523, gives 5 million members for 1970. For 1975, see note 51 below.
47. On the system, see H. J. Berman, *Justice in the U.S.S.R.* (New York, 1963), pp. 288–89.
48. *Izvestia,* October 23, 1959.
49. Friedgut, op. cit. note 40, p. 250.
50. *Spravochnik partiinogo rabotnika,* 1961, pp. 577ff.
51. On their status, see *Izvestia,* June 4, 1974, and "Dobrvol'nye druzhiny v okhrane obshchestvennogo poriadka," *Znanie* (Moscow, 1975), pp. 42–54.
52. Ibid., p. 53.
53. J. Hough, *The Soviet Union and Social Science Theory* (Cambridge, Mass., 1977), pp. 123–24, makes a positive judgment on participation in the U.S.S.R.
54. G. Almond and S. Verba, *The Civic Culture* (Boston, 1965), p. 168.
55. Stalin, *Sochineniia,* vol. 5 (Moscow, 1953), p. 260.
56. See the Central Committee resolution of January 1957 on the revival of the soviets and the material means put at their disposal, *Spravochnik partiinogo rabotnika,* 1957, pp. 451–54; *Partiinaia zhizn',* 9 (1977), pp. 3–8.
57. In *Pravda,* April 16, 1974, Podgorny attacked the local soviets whose negligence had been reported by citizens to the Supreme Soviet. See also *Pravda,* July 7, 1974.
58. *Vestnik statistiki,* February, 1980.
59. *Sovetskaia kirghizia,* January 22, 1980; *Zaria vostoka,* October 13 and 28, 1979.
60. J. M. Antonian, in *Sovetskoe gosudarstvo i pravo,* 8 (August 1978), pp. 78–85, emphasizes that rural delinquency is essentially confined to theft (fowl, cattle, shops) and that these thefts represent only 15 percent of the thefts in the U.S.S.R.

Chapter 8: Discord and Civil Society

1. On the concept of the intellegentsia, see J. Markiewicz-Lagneau, "La Fin de l'intelligentsia? Formation et transformation de l'intelligentsia soviétique," *Revue d'études comparatives est-ouest,* VII, 4 (1976), pp. 7–73.
2. R. Pipes, *Russia Under the Old Regime* (London, 1974), pp. 90–91.
3. The Russian title of the work is *Sophie Petrovna,* published in *samizdat;* American edition is *The Deserted House* (New York, 1977).
4. Chukovskaya, *Les Chemins de l'exclusion* (Paris, 1980).
5. Ibid., pp. 105 and 133.
6. E. Etkind, *Notes of a Non-Conspirator* (New York, 1977).
7. See the text of the poem in N. Mandelstam, *Hope Against Hope* (New York, 1976).

8. Khrushchev, in *Pravda*, May 24, 1959.
9. Pomerantsev, in *Novy mir*, 12 (1953), pp. 218–45.
10. *Pravda*, August 1, 1946; *Partiinaia zhizn'*, 1 (1946), editorial.
11. *Pravda*, December 26, 1979.
12. Chukovskaia, *Les Chemins de l'exclusion*, p. 186.
13. French edition, *Métropole* (Paris, 1980).
14. *Literaturnaia gazeta*, May 16, 1979, and September 19, 1979.
15. The Writers Union in Moscow expelled Erofaev and Popov in May 1979.
16. Letter of resignation by G. Vladimov, in Chukovskaia, op. cit., pp. 207–8.
17. On recent repression, see Reuter, October 12, 1979.
18. See the article by General Tsvigun, first vice-president of the KGB, in *Kommunist*, 4 (1980).
19. Decree in *Pravda*, May 7, 1979. The ideological decrees of the last few years are those dated June 4, 1976, October 12, 1976, January 18, 1977, and August 15, 1977. See *Spravochnik partiinogo rabotnika*, 1977 and 1978 editions; *Pravda*, March 5, 1978; *Partiinaia zhizn'*, 7 (1978); and Brezhnev's speech to the Central Committee of November 27, 1978, in *Pravda*, November 28, 1978.
20. R. A. Bauer and A. Inkeles, *The Soviet Citizen* (Cambridge, Mass., 1959), pp. 254ff.
21. V. N. Cherdakov et al., eds., *Ateizm, religiia, sovremennost'* (Moscow, 1975), pp. 128ff.
22. *Skolotazhu avize*, April 7, 1976, p. 3. *Materialy mezhvuzovskoi nauchnoi konferentsii po probleme vozrastaniia aktivnosti obshchestvennovo soznaia v period stroitel'stva kommunizma* (Kursk, 1968), pp. 360ff.
23. E. I. Lisavets, *Religia v borbe idei* (Moscow, 1976).
24. Ibid., p. 60.
25. Ibid., p. 42.
26. *Nauka i religiia*, April 1976, p. 4.
27. *Zaria vostoka*, October 27, 1976.
28. *Radyanska osvita*, March 7, 1979.
29. *Radyanska ukraina*, June 8, 1979.
30. T. Beeson, *Discretion and Valour* (London, 1974), p. 78.
31. H. Carrère d'Encausse, *L'Empire éclaté* (Paris, 1978), pp. 226–33.
32. See N. Struve, *Les Chrétiens en U.R.S.S.* (Paris, 1963). For the problems of various sects, see *Religion in Communist Lands*, 2 (Summer 1977), p. 89.
33. *Nauka i religiia*, December 1976, pp. 31–35.
34. *Nauka i religiia*, April 1977, pp. 55–58.
35. *Pionerskaia pravda*, July 7, 1979, and September 7, 1979; *Selskaia zhizn'*, August 15, 1979; *Komsomol'skaia pravda*, August 23, 1979; *Sovetskaia rossiia*, June 25, 1980.
36. *Sovet turkmenistani*, January 27, 1980.
37. *Kommunizm tughi*, December 7, 1978.
38. The patriarchate was abolished by Peter the Great in 1721 and reestablished in 1918. On the ceremonies, see *Izvestia*, June 1, 1978.

39. *Sovetskaia rossiia,* June 25, 1980.
40. *Sovetskaia kirghizia,* September 12, 1979.
41. *Izvestia,* January 31, 1976.
42. *Chronicle of the Catholics of Lithuania,* 38 (November 1979).
43. *Literaturnaia gazeta,* April 13, 1977.
44. Alexander Ogorodnikov, arrested on September 21, 1978, was one of the pioneers of the Christian Seminars, established in Moscow but later spread to various cities. His journal, *Obshchina,* was fairly widely distributed.
45. Twenty thousand requests for exit visas have been presented by Pentecostals since 1960 (*Sovetskaia litva,* December 22, 1978).
46. On their activities, see *Pravda vostoka,* March 15, 1979.
47. W. C. Fletcher, *The Russian Orthodox Church Underground 1917–1970* (Oxford, 1971), pp. 200ff.
48. Take the case of Father Dudko, whose sermons and "questions and answers" have been an important element in the crisis of consciousness of active Christians. He was arrested in January 1980 and forced to give a public televised confession the following summer.
49. *Izvestia,* June 1, 1978, emphasizes this aspect. *Vestnik moskovskogo patriarkhata* gives a precise idea of these contacts. See especially the issues of this publication since 1976.
50. *L'Empire éclaté,* pp. 226–55.
51. A. A. Iusupov, *Natsional'nyi sostav naseleniia S.S.S.R.* (Moscow, 1964), p. 9.
52. On the difference between the two concepts, see Brezhnev, *Leninskim kursom rechi i stat'i,* vol. 6 (Moscow, 1978), p. 525.
53. See the article by P. M. Fedosseev, vice-president of the Academy of Sciences of the U.S.S.R., in *Kommunist ukrainy,* June 1980, pp. 26–36, and *Kommunist,* 1 (1980), pp. 57–70.
54. But this point of view is not unanimous. See M. I. Kulichenko in *Voprosy istorii,* April 1979, p. 323; he remains prudently halfway between the two concepts.
55. R. A. Abuziarov, in *Russkii iazyk v natsional'noi shkole,* 4 (1978), pp. 64–69.
56. Ibid.
57. Saubanova, in *Russkii iazyk v natsional'noi shkole,* 4 (1978), pp. 54–55.
58. On the under-representation of certain nationalities in the officer corps, see, for example, *Bakinskii rabochi,* January 29, 1976.
59. *Kommunist vooruzhennykh sil,* April 1973, p. 93, and *Krasnaia zvezda,* January 20, 1973.
60. *Uchitel'skaia gazeta,* October 23, 1975, and *Russkii iazyk v natsional'noi shkole,* January 1976, pp. 79–82, for the recommendations of the conference.
61. *Uchitel'skaia gazeta,* May 24, 26, and 29, 1979.
62. Russkii iazyk v natsional'noi shkole, 1 (1979), p. 2.
63. *Narodnoe obrazovanie,* March 1979, pp. 94–95, describes the application of the provisions in the Ukraine.

64. *Naseleniie S.S.S.R. po dannym vsesoiuznoi perepisinaseleniia 1979 goda* (Moscow, 1980) and *Ekonomicheskaia gazeta*, 7 (February 1980).
65. *Naselenie S.S.S.R.*
66. *Sovetskaia kirghizia*, August 11, 1979.
67. Ibid.
68. *Russkii iazyk v natsional'noi shkole*, 6 (1979), p. 8.
69. *Narodnoe obrazovanie*, 9 (1979), p. 41, and *Russkii iazyk v natsional'noi shkole*, 6 (1979), p. 9.
70. *Visnyk akademii nauk ukrainskoi S.S.R.*, 7 (1979), p. 30.
71. I. K. Bilodid, in *Radyanska ukraina*, February 10, 1980. Bilodid is the director of the Institute of Linguistics of the Ukrainian Academy of Sciences and a fervent partisan of the progression of Russian. He has russified his name to Beloded.
72. See, in *Pravda*, June 28, 1980, the declarations of the Aktiv of the Georgian Communist Party, which met on June 26, 1980, on "the friendship of the Russian and Georgian peoples"; on the Russian language, see Shevarnadze, speech to the association of the Georgian Writers Union, in *Zaria vostoka*, April 3, 1980.
73. *Zaria vostoka*, November 4, 1976; April 24, 1979; January 19, 1980.
74. *Zaria vostoka*, February 12, April 2, and July 19, 1980.
75. See *Zaria vostoka*, April 8, 1978, on the inability of the procurator of Georgia to bring the fraudulent practices of several large enterprises into court.
76. Speech by Shevarnadze to the Aktiv of the Georgian Communist Party, *Zaria vostoka*, July 9, 1980.
77. On the objectives of the Georgian economy, see ibid.
78. *Kommunist*, April 13, 1979.
79. *Zaria vostoka*, April 3, 1980.
80. *Pravda*, June 28, 1980.
81. *Zaria vostoka*, October 31, 1979.
82. *Zaria vostoka*, January 22, 1980.
83. Nursakhat Bairamsakhatov, *Novyi byt i islam* (Moscow, 1979) pp. 26–195.
84. Ibid., p. 38.
85. *Washington Post*, January 18, 1979.
86. *Turkmenskaia iskra*, June 15, 1980.
87. Gapurov had already proposed this idea in 1979, in *Turkmenskaia iskra*, July 21, 1979; *Partiinaia zhizn'*, 12 (1979), pp. 8–10, bluntly accused certain organizations of the Turkoman Communist Party of connivance with the clergy.
88. B. Kerblay, *La Société soviétique contemporaine* (Paris, 1977), p. 188.
89. *Literaturnaia gazeta*, March 1979, p. 10.
90. *Narodnoe khoziastvo S.S.S.R. v 1978*, pp. 371–73. See also the wages compiled in *Panorama de l'U.R.S.S.* (Paris: Documentation française, February–March 1979).
91. *Financial Times*, November 15, 1973.
92. M. Lavigne, in *Le Monde diplomatique*, September 1979, p. 3.

93. *Pravda,* January 12, 1980.
94. *Sovetskaia moldavia,* February 27, 1979.
95. These remarks are taken from an article by K. Chernenko in *Voprosy istorii K.P.S.S.,* 9 (1979), pp. 1–18, devoted to an explanation of the Leninist approach to workers' education.
96. "Open letter" of January 30, 1978, addressed to the Soviet authorities.
97. *Krasnaia zvezda,* September 8, 1978.
98. Quoted by S. White, *Political Culture and Soviet Politics* (London, 1979), p. 159.
99. T. Iaroshevski and N. S. Mansurov, eds., *Aktivnost' lichnosti v sotsialisticheskom obshchestve* (Moscow, 1976), p. 163.
100. N. M. Sapozhnikov, *Struktura polichicheskogo soznaniia* (Minsk, 1969), p. 136.
101. I would like to thank Marie Lavigne, professor of economic science at Paris-I, for drawing my attention to this aspect of the reform. On the Zlobin method, see Lavigne, *Les Économies socialiste soviétique et européenne* (Paris, 1979), p. 105.
102. *Pravda,* November 28, 29, and 30 and December 1, 1979.
103. See the examples cited by Chukovskaya, op. cit. note 12, pp. 217–18.
104. *Directory of Soviet Officials, vol. II, R.S.F.S.R. Organizations,* CIA (Washington, July 1980), p. 63.
105. From *tolkat',* to push; a *tolkach* is one who helps things along.
106. On the new respectability of the *tolkachi,* see *Ekonomicheskaia gazeta,* 10 (1979), p. 13, and *Pravda,* June 30, 1979, and June 20, 1980.
107. A. Dimov, *Les Hommes doubles* (Paris, 1980).

Conclusion

1. Interview given to Western journalists of June 15, 1973, UPI.
2. *Pravda,* May 14, 1957.
3. Speech by Riabov to the Twenty-fifth Congress (*Pravda,* February 27, 1976).
4. On the personal role of Brezhnev, see *Pravda,* February 28, 1976.
5. A. Nove, *The Soviet Economic System* (London, 1977), pp. 147–48.
6. *Ekonomika sel'skogo khoziaistva,* 1 (January 1980), pp. 62–69.
7. *Tselina,* quoted by *Sel'skaia zhizn',* February 18, 1979, p. 1.
8. Kerblay, *La Société soviétique contemporaine* (Paris, 1977), p. 98.
9. Weber, *The Theory of Social and Economic Organization* (New York, 1947), p. 328. Weber emphasized that these forms of legitimacy are never found in a pure state.
10. The KGB has a dual function. It is an organ of internal security and at the same time an organ in charge of problems of "external security." It is the equivalent of the FBI and the CIA. Its international ramifications and its activities should take a central place in any work dealing with the foreign policy of the U.S.S.R.

SELECTED BIBLIOGRAPHY

This bibliography does not include all the titles referred to in the notes but simply mentions a number of works which, for reasons of language, are accessible to the Western reader.

J. A. Armstrong, *The European Administrative Elite.* Princeton, 1973.
J. Barron, *K. G. B.: Le travail occulte des agents secrets soviétiques.* Paris and Brussels, 1975.
C. Bettelheim, *Les Luttes de classes en U.R.S.S.* Paris, 1974 and 1977.
C. Black, *The Modernization of Japan and Russia: A Comparative Study.* New York, 1975.
———, *The Transformation of Russian Society.* Cambridge, Mass., 1967.
M. Bourdeaux, *Livre blanc sur les restrictions religieuses en U.R.S.S.* Brussels, 1978.
A. Brown and J. Gray, eds., *Political Culture and Political Change in Communist States.* London, 1977.
A. Brown and M. Kaser, *The Soviet Union Since the Fall of Khrushchev.* London, 1978.
W. Brus, *Socialist Ownership and Political Systems.* London, 1975.
Z. K. Brzezinski, *The Permanent Purge: Politics in Soviet Totalitarianism.* Cambridge, Mass., 1956.
H. Chambre, *L'Evolution du marxisme soviétique.* Paris, 1974.
J. Chapman, *Real Wages in Soviet Russia Since 1928.* Cambridge, Mass., 1963.
L. G. Churchward, *Contemporary Soviet Government.* London, 1975.

P. M. Cocks, R. V. Daniels, and N. Whittier Heer, eds., *The Dynamics of Soviet Politics.* Cambridge, Mass., 1976.

J. G. Collignon, *La Théorie de l'Etat du peuple tout entier en Union soviétique.* Paris, 1967.

M. Fainsod, *Comment l'U.R.S.S. est gouvernée.* Paris, 1957.

A. Gerschenkron, *Economic Backwardness in Historical Perspective.* Cambridge, Mass., 1962.

J. F. Hough, *The Soviet Prefects: The Local Party Organs in Industrial Decision-Making.* Cambridge, Mass., 1969.

———, *The Soviet Union and Social Science Theory.* Cambridge, Mass., 1977.

——— and M. Fainsod, *How the Soviet Union Is Governed.* Cambridge, Mass., 1979.

G. Ionescu, *Comparative Communist Politics.* London, 1972.

B. Kerblay, *Les Marchés paysans en U.R.S.S.* Paris, 1968.

———, *La Société soviétique contemporaine.* Paris, 1977.

D. Lane, *Politics and Society in the U.S.S.R.* London, 1972.

M. Lavigne, *Les Économies socialiste soviétique et européenne.* Paris, 1979.

N. Leites, *The Operational Code of the Politburo.* New York, 1951.

M. Lesage, *Les Institutions soviétiques.* Paris, 1975.

———. *Les Régimes politiques de l'U.R.S.S. et de l'Europe de l'Est.* Paris, 1971.

C. Linden, *Khrushchev and the Soviet Leadership, 1957–1964.* Baltimore, 1966.

M. Matthews, *Class and Society in Soviet Russia.* London, 1972.

———, *Privilege in the Soviet Union.* London, 1978.

M. Morozov, *L'Establishment soviétique.* Paris, 1974.

J. C. Moses, *Regional Party Leadership and Policy-Making in the U.S.S.R.* New York, 1974.

A. Nove, *Stalinism and After.* London, 1975.

D. E. Powell, *Antireligious Propaganda in the Soviet Union: A Study of Mass Persuasion.* Cambridge, Mass., 1975.

T. H. Rigby, *Communist Party Membership in the U.S.S.R., 1917–1967.* Princeton, 1968.

———, "Soviet Communist Party Membership Under Brezhnev," *Soviet Studies,* 3 (July 1976), pp. 317–38.

O. Semyonova and V. Haynes, *Syndicalisme et libertés en Union soviétique.* Paris, 1979.

H. Seton-Watson, *The Imperialist Revolutionaries: Trends in World Communism in the 1960s and 1970s.* Stanford, 1978.

G. H. Skilling and F. Griffith, eds., *Interest Groups in Soviet Politics*. Princeton, 1971.

G. Sokoloff, *L'Economie obéissante, décisions politiques et vie économique en U.R.S.S.* Paris, 1976.

M. Tatu, *Le Pouvoir en U.R.S.S. de Khrouchtchev à la direction collective*. Paris, 1967.

P. Vanneman, *The Supreme Soviet: Politics and the Legislative Process in the Soviet Political System*. Durham, 1977.

S. White, *Political Culture and Soviet Politics*. London, 1979.

E. Zaleski, *Stalinist Planning for Economic Growth, 1933–1952*. Chapel Hill, 1980.

I. Zemtsov, *La Corruption en Union soviétique*. Paris, 1976.

INDEX

Academy of Social Sciences, 218
Adzhubei, Aleksei, 96, 102, 361*n*
Afghanistan, 82, 97, 299, 337,
   344
agitators, 221, 222, 256–257, 258
agricultural production:
   collectivization of, 30, 235–236
   industrial sector integrated with,
      341
   investments in, 325
   1928–1934 fall in, 30
   reforms in, 263, 326
   on state farms, 113
   subsidies for, 341
agrogrods, 326
agrovilles, 49
Aktiv, 118–122
   functions of, 121–122
   in *nomenklatura,* 119, 121, 122,
      143
   organizational levels in, 119–120
   volunteer work by, 118–119, 122
alcoholism, 313, 314
anarchism, 6–7, 9–10, 11, 12
Andropov, I. V., 169, 183, 185,
   191–192
apparatchiks, 122–124
   in army, 184, 189
   numbers of, 123
   in organizational shifts, 127, 128

as territorial leaders, 123–124
Arab-Israeli wars:
   of 1967, 82, 162–163, 181
   of 1973, 82
Aristov, A. B., 130
army, 169–190
   apparatchiks in, 184, 189
   in Arab-Israeli war of 1967, 181
   Brezhnev's role in, 99–101,
      106–107, 184–185, 186
   in Central Committee, 77, 78,
      171, 173, 177, 178, 185
   in civil defense system, 230–232
   civilian power vs. power of, 172,
      173–176, 185, 232
   as closed social body, 188
   consumerist policies vs. needs of,
      174–176
   in Czechoslovakian crisis of 1968,
      181–182
   defense industries linked to,
      186–188
   in Defense Minister appointments,
      179–180, 184–185
   détente linked to power of, 183
   in domestic projects, 189, 368
   engineers and scientists trained
      by, 226–227
   in foreign policy, 172–174, 177,
      181–182, 185–186, 188

About the Author

Hélène Carrère d'Encausse, professor at the Sorbonne and School of Political Sciences in Paris, is recognized as a world authority on the Soviet Union. Born in Paris of Georgian and Polish parentage, she is fluent in Russian—with the pure accent of Leningrad—which has enabled her to move with ease in the Soviet Union and have access to official sources of information not usually available. For her work on *Decline of an Empire,* she received the internationally coveted Prix d'Aujourd'hui in France in 1978. She is the first woman to be awarded this honor.